The Measurement and Appraisal

of ADULT INTELLIGENCE

The Measurement and Appraisal

OF

ADULT INTELLIGENCE

by DAVID WECHSLER

Chief Psychologist, Bellevue Psychiatric Hospital. Adjunct Professor of Psychology, Graduate School of Arts and Science, New York University. Clinical Professor of Clinical Psychology, New York University College of Medicine

Fourth Edition

THE WILLIAMS & WILKINS COMPANY

Baltimore   1958

Made in United States of America

First Edition, April, 1939
Second Edition, October, 1941
Reprinted, February, 1943
Third Edition, April, 1944
Reprinted, April, 1945
Reprinted, July, 1946
Reprinted, November, 1946
Reprinted, October, 1947
Reprinted, September, 1948
Reset and Reprinted, July, 1949
Reprinted, February, 1950
Reprinted, December, 1950
Reprinted, January, 1952
Reprinted, December, 1954
Reprinted, April, 1955
Reprinted, April, 1956
Reprinted, March, 1957
Reprinted, May, 1957
Fourth Edition, 1958

Library of Congress Catalog Card Number 58-8896

COMPOSED AND PRINTED AT THE
WAVERLY PRESS, INC.
Mt. Royal & Guilford Aves.
Baltimore 2, Md., U.S.A.

To my wife
Ruth

PREFACE TO FOURTH EDITION

The present, like the previous editions of the Measurement of Adult Intelligence, centers around the theory, findings and applications of the author's Adult Intelligence Scales, but its scope as well as its content has been considerably extended. To a large degree it is a new book. Whatever has been retained from the older editions has been extensively rewritten, and five new chapters have been added. At the same time certain parts have been entirely omitted. The additions include chapters on the Factorial Composition of the W-B I and the WAIS, Changes in Intellectual Ability with Age, Sex Differences in Intelligence, Changes in Intelligence Consequent to Brain Damage and the Use of the W-B I and WAIS in Counseling and Guidance. No longer included in the volume is the manual of directions for the W-B I which constituted Part III of the earlier editions, and the chapter on the Need for an Adult Intelligence Scale.

In evaluating the many published studies of the W-B I, I have naturally tried to take cognizance of the findings and criticisms of other investigators. I have, however, not attempted to summarize the voluminous literature on the Scale, since extensive reviews of this literature have appeared on a number of occasions. On the other hand, the reader will find amply discussed the specific changes that have been made in the revised Adult Intelligence Scale (now called the WAIS). I have also devoted some space in this volume to a comparative analysis of the 1939 and 1955 standardizations, and have included many data not previously published. I hope that these additional data on the WAIS which is rapidly replacing the W-B I, will be useful to the clinician as well as the researcher.

As the reader will note from an even casual perusal of the book, and in particular from a reading of Chapter I, my views on the nature of intelligence have not changed radically. I have, however, become increasingly convinced that intelligence is most usefully interpreted as an aspect of the total personality. I look upon intelligence as an effect rather than a cause, that is, as a resultant of interacting abilities—nonintellective included. The problem confronting psychologists today is how these abilities interact to give the resultant effect we call intelligence. At this writing it seems clear that factorial analysis alone is not the answer. Probably a new statistic involving field theory and non-linear differential equations will be required. In the meantime, I remain a reformed but unchastened Spearmanite.

The wide use of the Wechsler Bellevue Adult Scale testifies perhaps not only to its value as a psychometric tool but also, I hope, to the validity of its underlying concept of the nature of general intelligence. The Scale has been translated into a number of languages and now is used in many countries throughout the world. No systematic comparison of results obtained in the different countries has yet been made, but one of the things by which I have been most impressed is the relatively few changes that have been necessary in the subtests other than those depending upon language (Vocabulary) or availability of certain kinds of knowledge (Information, Arithmetic and Picture Arrangement). This does not, of course, mean that the W–B I and now the WAIS are culture-free, but it does lend support to the view that the basic elements of human intelligence are less conditioned by accidents of geography and local mores than one gathers from current literature. No test is or can be entirely culture-free, but the absence of a need for radical changes in the foreign translations of the Wechsler tests would indicate the ultimate feasibility of an international scale.

In closing, I should like to thank the many persons who in one way or another contributed to the book. They are too numerous to mention individually. I am indebted to the members of the Psychological Staff of Bellevue Psychiatric Hospital and to colleagues at VA Hospitals in the New York area who, through presentation of case material and frequent discussion, helped to clarify many points taken up in the book; and to the members of the Test Division of the Psychological Corporation for their cooperation and assistance in preparing certain of the data now published for the first time. I am especially grateful to Mrs. Eugenia Jaros and Mrs. Katherine Hopf Bohling for their help in the preparation of the manuscript and their assistance in getting it into final shape. Finally, I wish to thank the various authors cited in the text for permission to quote or reproduce material from their articles, and the editors of the Journals in which their cited material appeared.

January 1958   DAVID WECHSLER

Contents

PART I

The Nature, Classification and Appraisal of Intelligence

Chapter 1

The Nature of Intelligence

The word intelligence, in spite of its wide current usage and ancient roots, is a relatively recent term in psychological literature. It is met with rarely before the turn of the century, and in Baldwin's encyclopedic *Dictionary of Philosophy and Psychology,* published in 1901, it did not rate a separate entry but was merely given as an alternate to or synonym of *intellect.* Even the textbooks of psychology of a generation or two ago seldom used the term and, when they did, never discussed it as a separate topic.[1] We must not infer from this that these authors were not concerned with what we now think of as intelligence, but bound as they were to the old faculty psychology they still relegated the treatment of the subject under such terms as intellect, judgment and reason which they seemingly considered synonymous with it. Thus, Baldwin defines intellect (intelligence) as "the faculty or capacity of knowing." Our present day concepts of intelligence have expanded considerably. They are broader, more pragmatic, more concerned with learning and adaptive human behavior. The chief trouble with them is that few psychologists are willing to spell out what they mean by intelligence and, when they do, seldom agree.[2]

The great interest in intelligence as a basic subject matter of psychology began with the publication of Binet's *Le dévelopment de l'intelligence chez les enfants* (54). Although Binet himself on several occasions made attempts to delimit the term, his primary concern was not with the definition but with the measurement or appraisal of intelligence, and this has been the main approach of psychologists since. A tremendous amount of research has been carried on in the area, actually more than 40 years of continuous endeavor. We can now measure intelligence in many more ways than Binet did, that is with many more different kinds of tests, and what is more important we know much more about what it is we are measuring, namely,

[1] As late as 1927, C. Spearman complained, "Right up to the present day a large number, perhaps even the majority, of the best accredited books on psychology do not so much as bother to mention the word 'intelligence' from cover to cover" (466).

[2] On this point see article by R. B. Cattell (94).

the elements or factors that enter into our measures. Most important of all, two revolutionary discoveries have been made; the first is that these elements or factors of intelligence do not coincide with the historic attributes of intelligence and, second, that it is not possible to express them in a simple formulation. One of the results has been that some psychologists have come to doubt whether these laborious analyses have contributed anything fundamental to our understanding of intelligence while others have come to the equally disturbing conclusion that the term intelligence, as now employed, is so ambiguous that it ought to be discarded altogether. Psychology now seems to find itself in the paradoxical position of devising and advocating tests for measuring intelligence and then disclaiming responsibility for them by asserting that "nobody knows what the word really means."[3]

The view that we do not know what we are talking about when we speak of intelligence is unfortunate not only because it is not true by any comparative standards—actually we now know more about intelligence than we do about any other mental function—but because it has nurtured a confusing pessimism and a profitless kind of account taking which almost completely misses the issue at hand. The issue is not, as is commonly supposed, the lack of agreement by psychologists on a standard definition of intelligence. If this were so, the problem might conceivably be resolved by an international convention, as has been done by physicists in defining various units of measurement. Unfortunately, the problem with which psychologists are concerned in defining intelligence is quite different from that which the physicist deals with when he defines amperes, farads and watts, or the biologist when he classifies living things as plants and animals. The difficulty involved is similar to what the physicist encounters when asked to state what he means by time or energy, or the biologist what he means by life. The fact is that energy and life are not tangible entities but limiting constructs. You cannot touch them or see them under a microscope even though you are able to describe them. We know them by their effects or properties. The same is true of general intelligence. It is not a material fact but an abstract construct. What we can reasonably expect of any attempt at definition is only a sufficiently clear and broad connotation as to what it comprehends. Mind you, not what it is but what it involves and eventually, what it distinguishes. Now that is precisely what the more effective definitions of intelligence have sought to do, though sometimes too tersely and sometimes with too special emphasis. Thus, intelligence has been defined as the ability to learn, the capacity to adapt to new situations, the ability to educe correlates, and so on. All these attempts to define intelligence as some broad function comprehend varieties

[3] C. Spearman and L. Jones (466a), p. 2.

of behavior which might reasonably be called "intelligent," although each from particular points of reference. The first might be more useful to the educator, the second to the biologist and the third to the psychologist. The pertinent question, however, is not whether intelligence is the ability to learn rather than the ability to adapt or to educe relationships. It is all these and, as we shall see later, much more. Learning, adapting, reasoning and other forms of goal directed behavior are only different ways in which intelligence manifests itself. But while intelligence may manifest itself in a variety of ways, one must assume there is some communality or basic similarity between those forms of behavior which one identifies as intelligent. For example, we must assume there is something common to learning to count, avoiding danger and playing chess which makes it possible for us to say that they are evidence of intelligent behavior as against learning to walk, being accident prone and playing bingo, which seemingly have little if anything to do with it.

Much of the productive work done on the measurement of intelligence during the past decades has been devoted to the problem of identifying the basic elements or common factors of intelligence, and we shall presently consider how fruitful that has been. But three points need to be made at once. The first is that discovery and isolation of the "vectors of the mind" is only part of the problem involved in the definition of general intelligence; the second, that it is not possible to identify general intelligence with sheer intellectual ability; and the third, that general intelligence cannot be treated as an entity apart, but must be envisaged as an aspect of a greater whole, namely, the total personality structure with which it shares common elements and with which it is integrally related.

One of the important aspects of intelligent behavior is that it is goal directed, that is to say, purposive with respect to some intermediate or ulterior end. Purposiveness, however, is only a necessary condition for and not an exclusive condition of, intelligent behavior. When the decerebrated frog scratches its leg in response to an irritating stimulus, when the newborn babe starts suckling at its mother's breast and when a worker at an automatic stamping machine presses a lever, each may be said to be performing some goal directed act, but none of these, though purposeful, could be taken as examples of intelligent behavior. They are what the physiologist would designate as reflex or automatic acts. But the situation is not so clear in instances involving complex reflex action, and ultimately a large segment of both human and animal behavior is commonly summed up by the term instinct.

Instincts are usually differentiated from learned acts as inherited rather than acquired patterns of behavior, but whether they also involve "intelligence" has been a matter of dispute. The side one espouses will largely depend on how one defines instinct and what one wishes to comprehend under the term of intelligence. Clearly, goal direction (purposiveness) and complexity of behavior alone are insufficient differentiae; otherwise the social behavior of the ants and bees, the nesting and homing habits of birds and a great many of the activities of the higher animals, and we might also add of human beings, would *ipso facto* be considered as evidence of intelligence. Some are. But biologists and psychologists have usually insisted that intelligent behavior meet two other conditions, namely, that it should involve insight and ratiocination. Whether the most complex behavior of higher animals meets these criteria is still a matter of opinion. Writers in the last quarter of the 19th century believed that they did, and expressed this opinion by saying that animals were able to think. Beginning with the turn of the century, particularly following the studies of Loeb, Jennings, Pavlou and the experimental biologist, this view gave way to the opinion that even the most complex of animal behavior was explicable in terms of stimulus response reactions (tropisms, conditioned reflexes, etc.). The term instinct itself fell into much disfavor and the question whether animals could think became a question which scientific investigators systematically avoided. The stimulus response psychology, however, received some severe knocks from the *Gestalt School*, especially from the studies of Köhler (297), who demonstrated that monkeys at least can show insight when they are confronted with novel situations. The question that now confronts psychology is whether the terms insight, learning and reasoning when used to describe behavior of animals are identical with or similar to processes so designated when they are applied to the behavior of human beings. Our view of this matter is that the higher mental processes in man and animals are on a psychological continuum. This does not mean that "mental" processes in the higher animals are identical in all respects to those of human beings, but that, so far as one can see, they are distinguishable primarily in terms of degree of complexity, communicability and level of awareness. When a chimpanzee solves a problem he cannot tell us how he does it, and we can only infer how he arrived at a solution. By our standards there is a limit to the kind of problem he can solve. There is also reason to believe that a chimpanzee is not aware (conscious) of what he is doing as he works at his problem, but that is a matter of speculation. In any event, his behavior is both rational and intelligent.

The question of whether animals are able to reason and think is of interest not only in and of itself, but because of the influence it has had on the definition of intelligence. Historically, the so-called higher mental processes, and abstract reasoning in particular, have been assumed to be phenomena *sui generis* to man, and accordingly have often been posited as the sole criteria of intelligent behavior. More important, however, than whether animals can reason is whether this ability is all that is needed to account for intelligence. The view adopted in this book is that it is not. Reasoning, to be sure, is often required for intelligent behavior but frequently only to a minimal degree and sometimes, alas (or perhaps fortunately), not at all. Intelligence embraces many other abilities.

[Intelligence, operationally defined, is the aggregate or global capacity of the individual to act purposefully, to think rationally and to deal effectively with his environment.]It is aggregate or global because it is composed of elements or abilities which, though not entirely independent, are qualitatively differentiable. By measurement of these abilities, we ultimately evaluate intelligence. But intelligence is not identical with the mere sum of these abilities, however inclusive. There are three important reasons for this: 1) The ultimate products of intelligent behavior are a function not only of the number of abilities or their quality but also of the way in which they are combined, that is, their configuration. 2) Factors other than intellectual ability, for example, those of drive and incentive, are involved in intelligent behavior. 3) Finally, while different orders of intelligent behavior may require varying degrees of intellectual ability, an excess of any given ability may add relatively little to the effectiveness of the behavior as a whole. It would seem that, so far as general intelligence is concerned, intellectual ability, *per se*, merely enters as a necessary minimum. Thus, to act intelligently one must be able to recall numerous items, *i.e.*, have a retentive memory. But beyond a certain point this ability will not help much in coping with life situations successfully. This is true of even more important capacities, such as the ability to reason, particularly when specialized. The unusual reasoning abilities of the mathematician are more highly correlated with the thing that we ultimately measure as intelligence than sheer memory is, but possession of this ability is no guarantee that behavior as a whole will be very intelligent in the sense defined above. Every reader will be able to recall persons of high intellectual ability in some particular field whom they would unhesitatingly characterize as below average in general intelligence.

Although intelligence is not a mere sum of intellectual abilities, the only way we can evaluate it quantitatively is by the measurement of the various aspects of these abilities. There is no contradiction here unless we insist upon the identity of general intelligence and intellectual ability. We do not, for example, identify electricity with our modes of measuring it. Our measurements of electricity consist of quantitative records of its chemical, thermal and magnetic effects. But these effects are not identical with the "stuff" which produced them. We do not know what the ultimate nature of the "stuff" is which constitutes intelligence but, as in the case of electricity, we know it by the "things" it enables us to do—such as making appropriate associations between events, drawing correct inferences from propositions, understanding the meaning of words, solving mathematical problems or building bridges. These are the effects of intelligence in the same sense that chemical dissociation, heat and magnetic fields are the effects of electricity;[4] but psychologists prefer the term mental products. We know intelligence by what it enables us to do.

E. L. Thorndike was the first to develop clearly the idea that the *measurement* of intelligence consists essentially of a quantitative evaluation of mental productions in terms of number, and the excellence and speed with which they are effected. Abilities are merely mental products arranged in different classes or types of operation. Thus, the class of operations which consists of effectually associating one fact with another and recalling either or both at an appropriate time is called learning; that of drawing inferences or educing relations between them, reasoning ability; that of merely retaining them, memory. The older psychologists were inclined to use a relatively small number of such classes based primarily on the kind of mental process supposedly involved. More recently, psychologists have altered their classifications to include subdivisions based on material content or factorial analyses. They speak not only of memory but of auditory memory, not only of reasoning but of abstract, verbal or arithmetical reasoning. In a like manner some psychologists have begun to distinguish various kinds of intelligence. Thorndike, for example, suggested subdividing intelligence into three main types: 1) abstract or verbal intelligence, involving facility in the use of symbols; 2) practical intelligence, involving facility in manipulating objects; 3) social intelligence, involving facility in dealing with human beings. The significant thing about this classification is that it emphasizes *what* a person can do, as well as *how* he can do it. This distinction between function and content is fully justified by experimental evidence. The rating which an individual attains on an intelligence examination depends to a considerable degree on the type of test used. His score on a test made up largely of verbal items may differ significantly from that obtained on a test involving questions of social comprehension and still more from another test made up of items involving predominantly psychomotor reactions and the perception of spatial relationships.

Though test results show that the rating which an individual attains will frequently depend upon the type of intelligence test used, they also show a contrary tendency. When large numbers of individuals are examined with a variety of intelligence tests, those who make high scores on any one of them tend to make high scores on the remaining ones, and the same

---

[4] The analogy to electricity must not be carried too far. Also, in contrast to the views expressed in the earlier editions, we no longer think it correct or even useful to look upon intelligence as a kind of energy.

holds true for those who make low and intermediate scores. This dual characteristic of human abilities—their specificity on the one hand and interdependence on the other—has been a long standing problem in psychology but is now approaching solution thanks to the contribution of factor analysis. The first and most important of these contributions was made by the great English psychologist Spearman some 50 years ago. It consisted of two parts: 1) He introduced a method for accounting for the variance between paired sets of correlated measures, and 2) he showed, or at least sought to show by this method,[5] that all intellectual abilities could be expressed as functions of two factors, one a general or intellectual factor (g) common to every ability, and another a specific factor (s), specific to any particular ability and "in every case different from that of all others." Both parts have been the subject of a great deal of discussion criticism and investigation. Spearman's original methods of factoring a correlational table has now given way to broader and more refined techniques, and his concept of one central or unifactor theory has been largely abandoned by psychologists. The evidence is now quite clear that other factors besides g are required to account for intercorrelations between tests of intelligence, and the famous tetrad equation was shown by Thurstone (493), to be only a special case of a more general factor theorem. Nevertheless, Spearman's demonstration of the existence of at least one pervasive factor in all performances requiring intellectual ability remains one of the great discoveries of psychology.

As has often been the case in the history of science, the proof of the two factor theory, in addition to being a discovery, was also an explicit formulation of an hypothesis which workers in the field had unknowingly been assuming for some time. The fact is, that from the day psychologists began to use a series of tests for measuring intelligence, they necessarily assumed the existence of a general or common factor. This becomes immediately apparent if one recalls what the actual contents of intelligence tests are. They consist of various intellectual tasks which we call tests that require the subject to do such things as define words, reproduce facts from memory, solve problems in arithmetic and recognize likenesses and differences. The variety of tasks used, their difficulty and the manner of presentation vary with the type of scale employed. But so far as measuring intelligence is concerned, these specific tasks are only means to an end. Their object is not to test a person's memory, judgment or reasoning ability, but to measure something which it is hoped will emerge from the sum total of the subject's performance, namely, his general intelligence. One of the greatest contributions of Binet was his intuitive assumption that in the selection of tests, it made little difference what sort of task you used,

[5] The method of tetrad differences.

provided that in some way it was a measure of the child's general intelligence. This explains in part the large variety of tasks employed in the original Binet scale. It also accounts for the fact that certain types of items which were found useful at one age level were not necessarily employed at other age levels. More important than either of these details is the fact that for all practical purposes, the combining of a variety of tests into a single measure of intelligence, *ipso facto*, presupposes a certain functional unity or equivalence between them.

The functional equivalence of the test items, an assumption implicit not only in the Binet Scale but in any scale which is composed of a variety or pool of intellectual tasks, is absolutely necessary for the validation of the arithmetic employed in arriving at a final measure of intelligence. This arithmetic consists, first, of assigning some numerical value to every correct response; secondly, of adding the partial credits so obtained into a simple sum; and, thirdly, of treating equal sums as equivalent, regardless of the nature of the test items which contribute to the total. For example, every test passed on the Stanford-Binet (between ages 3 and 10) contributes two months to the mental age (M.A.) score of the subject, irrespective of whether the test passed calls for the repetition of a series of digits, the copying of a square, the definition of a word or the correct reply to a commonsense question. To all intents and purposes, therefore, the simple addition of these groups necessarily assumes an arithmetical equivalence of the test elements so combined. If the different tests were taken to represent generically different entities, one could no more add the values assigned to them in order to obtain an M.A. total than one could add 2 dogs, 3 cats and 4 elephants and expect the unqualified answer of 9. That, of course, does not mean that their addition is impossible. If, instead of being concerned with the characteristics of the dog, the cat and the elephant that differentiate them one from another, we restrict our interest to those which they all have in common, we can say that 2 dogs, 3 cats and 4 elephants make 9 animals. The reason we can get an answer of 9 here is because dogs, cats and elephants are in fact all animals. The addition would no longer be possible if for cats we were to substitute turnips.

The same principle is involved when we attempt to add up the number of tests correctly passed on an intelligence scale into a simple sum. The reason we can add together scores obtained from tests requiring such seemingly different abilities as those involved in solving arithmetic problems, repeating digits and defining words is because they are alike in certain ways. They are similar in that they are all measures of general intelligence. This means that all must have a common characteristic, or to use the current psychological term *a common factor*, or factors. We might assume this *a priori*, and indeed such an hypothesis has been implicit in all tests of general intelligence whether acknowledged or not. But the assumption needed empirical validation—a validation which was eventually furnished by factor analysis.

Factor analysis is a statistical technique for separating common sources of variance between intercorrelated measures when these measures are arranged in certain ways. Its aims are to determine the smallest number of variables that must be posited in order to account for the observed variance and to calculate the degree to which they enter into the measures used. The independent variables or "reference" abilities thus defined are what the innovators of factor analysis have variously called central, common, primary and group factors. Their importance to psychology is that they testify to the probable existence of what are seemingly basic mental abilities capable of accounting for the way the mind operates. Similar intellectual entities are implied in the old concept of mental faculties, but the historic faculties were at best descriptive classifications with little proof of their uniqueness and no implication that they were functional unities. It is, of course, true that the modern factors may also be interpreted or even primarily construed as principles of classification (87). But factors are facts not just theoretical categories. Nor are they merely mathematical quantities intended to explain the correlations that exist between the most diverse sources of intellectual performance, as Spearman initially interpreted g (466). If mental factors were only mathematical quantities they would have no great importance for psychology. Mental factors, if they exist, are descriptive of actual modes of mental operation. The great contribution of factor analysis has been to show that they do exist.

Factors of the mind are most readily construed as native[6] tendencies and, in the field of cognition, as basic kinds of ability. More fundamentally, they are modalities of mental functioning which define these abilities—in the sense, as Thurstone (492) has pointed out, that vision, touch, hearing, etc. are modalities of sensation, but with no parallel assumption as regards cortical localization. It is probable that they are to some extent physiologically and anatomically determined but this is not a necessary condition for their acceptance. By hypothesis, primary abilities are generally conceived as independent variables, and are presumably identified as such only when they meet this criterion statistically. Nevertheless, in practice the posited independent factors almost invariably show some degree of positive correlation. This is due in part to a concomitant variance produced by the heterogeneity of any tested population,[7] and in part to the broader

[6] This is the author's opinion. Factor theory does not require that factors be innate.

[7] For a discussion of the ways in which population heterogeneity affects inter-test correlation, see T. L. Kelley (284a).

compass of the interaction principle which implies that no two forces (in our case, abilities) can exist side by side without in some way interacting to produce a resultant effect.[8]

Apart from the problems already considered, the most important question which confronts the application of factor theory to the concept of general intelligence is the definition of the nature of the factors, both as to number and identity, and as determinants of intellectual functioning. According to Spearman, only one general or central factor g was needed to account for basic intellectual ability: This factor he defined originally as a mathematical quantity "intended to explain the correlations that exist between most diverse sorts of cognitive performance." But, in the light of subsequent evaluation and application, it soon became clear that g stood for something more important. g is not only a mathematical but a psychological quantity; it is a measure of the mind's capacity to do intellectual work.

It is universally agreed that the capacity to do intellectual work is a necessary and important sign of general intelligence. The question is whether it is the only important or paramount factor. In this writer's opinion it is not. Spearman seemingly thought it was, although on this point he failed to declare himself unequivocally. On the one hand, he wrote, "Such a factor as this (g) can scarcely be given the title of intelligence at all." But after having said this, he devoted several chapters (466) to an attempt to prove that the best tests of intelligence are precisely those which contain the largest amounts of g. If this is so, then for all practical purposes, g and general intelligence may be said to be equivalent. This equivalence, indeed, is implied by the mathematical relationship of the g and s factors in the two factor theory. According to this relationship an intelligence scale made up of a large number of tests especially rich in g would in the end be a measure of g exclusively.[9] In the writer's opinion, such a scale would not be a very good measure of general intelligence because it would eliminate a number of abilities essential for effective behavior.

The view that other salient factors besides g enter into measures of intelligence is based on several sources of evidence. The first is clinical. We know from experience that individuals attaining identical scores on intelligence tests cannot always be classified in the same way. This is perhaps most obvious in cases where test results call for practical action, as for example when they are used as a basis for deciding whether or not a subject should be committed to an institution for mental defectives. In

---

[8] Thus, verbal and spatial ability will be concomitantly involved in abstract reasoning in the same way that hearing and vision combine in the perception of depth, even though both are conceived as independent functions.

[9] For, by pooling such tests, the g factor (being common) becomes cumulative, whereas the specific factors (being incidental) tend to cancel each other.

such cases, the test results, *e.g.*, a Binet IQ, cannot be used as the sole criterion. One child with an IQ of 75 may be definitely defective while another with an identical IQ, or indeed one 5 or 10 points lower, may be far from so classifiable. Of course, the objection may be made that the classification of mental deficiency is in part a social diagnosis. But is not the capacity for social adaptation also a sign of intelligence? Should not the capacity to avoid mischief and the ability to persevere at a task enter into one's definition of general intelligence, just as much as the ability to define words and perceive analogies? The clinician's answer has always been "yes." With this affirmation he implicitly assumes that there are other factors besides the intellective ones which enter into intelligent behavior. Hitherto he was unable to demonstrate their existence experimentally. In recent years, however, because of new correlational techniques, especially the methods of factorial analysis, a beginning has been made. Among the first and of particular significance is the study of W. P. Alexander, whose monograph on *Intelligence, Concrete and Abstract* (7) is in many ways basic.

Alexander set himself the problem of testing experimentally the evidence for and against the main theories until lately favored in psychological circles. The first of these is Professor Spearman's two factor theory to which we have already referred. The other is the unique traits theory, according to which intelligence involves several abilities or factors, each independent of one another. More specifically, his investigation took the form of an experimental study to determine whether test results supported the view that "practical" intelligence and "verbal" intelligence were each distinct and independent capacities, or the view of Spearman that both were essentially the same in that they were not independent capacities but only differed with respect to their non-intellective or specific factors.

Alexander's findings were extremely interesting. They confirmed Spearman's main contention that there was one and only one common factor in *all* measures of intelligence and, at the same time, showed that this factor alone is not sufficient to explain the total correlational variance which existed between the tests used to measure intelligence. In addition to the common factor there are seemingly other broad factors which, while not showing the same generality, are nonetheless recurrent in a significant number of abilities which form subgroups or "communal clusters." The individual tests by which these abilities are measured contain a common factor of their own with respect to which they function in much the same way. Alexander has termed abilities involved in tests showing such similarity of function *functional unities*. Thus, verbal ability is one functional unity, practical ability another, and so on. But while each of these functional unities requires a separate factor to take care of its respective contribution to any global measure of intelligence, they are nevertheless "definitely related," that is, correlated with one another.[10] This means that they cannot be unitary traits in the sense implied by the unique traits theory. On the other hand, neither can they be considered as specific factors in the sense required by Spearman's two factor theory. For, these factors, unlike the *s* factors, actually contribute a considerable amount to the correlation variance of the test composites of which they form a part.

Another important conclusion suggested by Alexander's investigation was that in order to account for the complete intercorrelation variance found in any large battery of intelligence tests, one has to posit other factors in addition to purely intellectual ones. After eliminating the general factor (*g*), and such other factors[11] as were contributed by the "functional unities" described above, Alexander found that a considerable amount of his total intercorrelational variance was still unaccounted for. In addition to these factors there were apparently certain other supplementary global ones which, though not directly measurable, nevertheless contributed significant amounts to the total variance of the observed data. These factors he has provisionally labeled *X* and *Z*. They cover such items as the subject's interest in doing the tasks set, his persistence in attacking them and his zest and desire to succeed—items which might more familiarly be described as temperamental or personality factors, but which nevertheless must be recognized as important in all actual measures of intelligence. For this reason, one might appropriately refer to them as the non-intellective factors or, more specifically, as the *non-intellective factors* in general intelligence.[12]

It appears, therefore, that the entity or quantity which we are able to measure by intelligence tests is not a simple quantity. Certainly, it is not something which can be expressed by one single factor alone, for example, the ability to educe relations or the level of mental energy. Intelligence is all this and something more. It is the ability to utilize this energy or to exercise this ability in contextual situations, situations that have content and purpose as well as form and meaning. To concede as much is to admit that any practical definition of intelligence must be fundamentally a biological one in the widest sense of the term. That has been the hypothesis assumed in the construction of the author's intelligence scales. We think that they measure general intelligence in the context defined above. We shall not, however, claim that they measure all that goes to make up general

[10] Thus verbal ability correlates with practical ability to the extent of 0.50.

[11] These were primarily the factors *v*, common to tests involving verbal ability, and *f*, common to tests purporting to measure practical ability.

[12] For further evidence as to the existence of these factors, see D. Wechsler: *The non-intellective factors in general intelligence* (519).

intelligence, because no tests at present are capable of doing this. The only thing we can ask of an intelligence scale is that it measure sufficient portions of intelligence to enable us to use it as a fairly reliable index of the individual's global capacity.

The Relation of Ability to Intelligence

All measures of intelligence eventually are derived from measures of ability, that is to say, from tests of specific types of performance. In practice, an individual is given a battery of such tests and on the basis of his scores is rated as showing such and such a level of intelligence. We begin with a series of aptitude measures but somehow end up with an IQ. How is this possible? The suggested answer is that in the process we are using measures of ability primarily as a tool, that is, not as an end in itself but as a means for discovering something more fundamental. Thus, when one employs an arithmetic or a vocabulary test as part of an intelligence scale, the object of the examiner is not to discover the subject's aptitude for arithmetic or extent of his word knowledge, although these are inevitably involved, but his capacity to function in over-all areas which are assumed to require intelligence. The term ability is here used in its most general sense, namely, that of "the power to perform responsive acts" (Warren) or as the manifestation of a human trait or attribute "in terms of what an individual can do" (Thurstone).

The tentative answer we are suggesting is that intelligence can be measured by way of abilities because what we are concerned with eventually is not the abilities themselves but what enters into or emerges from them. This hypothesis implies several postulates. 1) Intelligence, however defined, is not a simple entity but a complex function. 2) Intelligence is of the nature of a resultant effect. 3) The resultant effect depends upon the interaction of a theoretically infinite but practically limited number of qualitatively different but additive components or factors. These factors manifest themselves objectively in different forms of behavior. A factorially defined segment of behavior constitutes an ability. Such segments of behavior may be descriptively grouped into such broad classifications as verbal, spatial, numerical and other kinds of abilities, in the sense that they describe overlapping or similar modes of function.

A test is a device for evaluating a fragment of behavior; an intelligence test is one in which one seeks to appraise this bit of behavior insofar as it may be called intelligent. The abilities measured are of consequence only insofar as they permit the examiner to identify the behavior as intelligent. For this purpose some abilities are more generally or more readily available and, therefore, can be more profitably utilized in test construction. This is generally the case with verbal ability, which accordingly is oftener and more effectively made use of for measuring intelligence than other abilities, such as speed of motor response. But Vocabulary is a better test of intelligence than a Form Board, primarily because people can express themselves more meaningfully in verbal than in geometric symbols. This, of course, would not hold in the case of deaf-mutes or individuals who are in the habit of thinking spatially, manipulatively or in any other way. Hence, as a general principle, an effective test of intelligence should be made up of tasks calling upon as many "abilities" as possible. This was intuitively perceived by Binet, who was the first to devise an effective test of *general* intelligence.

The great merit of Binet's Scale is that it permits individuals to manifest their intelligence in many ways. Of course, some of his tests are better suited for some levels of functioning than others, but (contrary to Binet's belief) this fact involves no hierarchical concept of mental abilities. In the Binet Scale, copying a diamond is equally as "good" a test of intelligence at age 7 as detecting absurdities at age 10 or defining abstract words at age 15. The same may be said, *pari passu*, of the different subtests of the Wechsler Adult Intelligence Scales (WAIS) and the Wechsler-Bellevue (W–B) Scales. Of course, bases of selection other than age criteria can be employed to equate difficulty or level of task, but the specific abilities utilized are only of secondary importance, not only for the reasons already indicated but also because they are influenced to varying degrees by such things as culture and training as well as by differences in special endowment. What makes it possible to utilize them at all in appraising intelligence is that they do in fact permit the individual to evidence his capacity for directed, purposeful and adaptive behavior.

To sum up, human abilities are utilizable for measuring intelligence because when applied to goal directed activity they depend for their effectiveness on certain connate attributes or factors which constitute the basic components of intelligent behavior. These basic attributes are what contemporary psychologists, in searching for the "vectors of the mind," have described as general factors. The thing we seek to measure when we measure intelligence is the net result of the complex interaction between the various factors entering into intelligent behavior. In practice we measure this resultant fact by means of tests of ability. An intelligence scale is an assembled battery of such tests; the intelligence rating obtained from them is a numerical expression of their combined contribution. Although the amounts contributed by each test may be, and usually are, expressed as a simple sum, the factors which determine the scores ought not, strictly speaking, to be so combined, since the result is not a linear function of these factors. More likely it is what mathematicians call a complex functional, but the exact form of this function is yet to be determined.

Intelligence and Brain Function

In dealing with the brain as an "organ of the mind," its investigators have been concerned chiefly with two questions: 1) the manner and the degree to which brain structure is related to mental activity, and 2) assuming that mental activity is dependent upon brain structure, which parts of the brain are associated with which mental functions. More progress has been made on the latter, but no satisfactory answers can be given to either of these questions. Particularly vague is our knowledge as to where and how intelligence is mediated.

Like all mental functions, general intelligence may be said to depend upon the condition and structure of the brain, in the broad sense that no intelligent behavior is possible without at least partially intact cerebral hemispheres. But in this broad sense, the statement does not explain very much. In particular, it does not distinguish the possible role of the brain in the mediation of intelligence from the part it plays in sensory, motor, perceptual and other processes, since injury or removal of various parts of the cortex can involve one without the other. Especially challenging is the fact that except in cases of injuries involving the speech areas, human beings can apparently continue to function intellectually after considerable loss of brain substance, whereas much less damage areawise is sufficient to impair severely or destroy entirely specific sensory functions. In general, measures of global intelligence are less affected by local injuries than are measures of specific ability. A missile injury may severely impair visual, auditory or tactile discrimination without noticeably affecting the subject's IQ.

Findings of this kind and more especially observations of sequelae of cerebral lesions in animals (306) and man (392) have led to a distinction between at least two kinds of effect that may result from brain injury: (1) specific dysfunctions associated with circumscribed and generally small brain areas; (2) general intellectual impairment unassociated with any particular locus, and usually involving larger cortical areas. This distinction oversimplifies what actually happens in most cases. But it has been convincingly shown that disabilities, like scotomas, generally result from very circumscribed lesions, while other dysfunctions, such as loss of ability to discern hidden figures may ensue "irrespective of localization of lesions and presence or absence of other symptoms" (490).

Thus, the question of whether the locus of brain injury is or is not "a differential factor in performance increment" cannot be answered exclusively one way or the other. Some disabilities, namely those principally involving sensory, motor and simple perceptual functions, are established with delimited cortical areas; others involving more complex discrimination functions appear tied to such areas to only a limited degree; still more complex abilities, such as the capacity to profit from past experiences, are only negligibly or not at all established. This does not mean that levels of intellectual ability or of global intelligence are impaired by only certain kinds of brain lesion or are independent of either the size or locus of the lesion. On the contrary, subjects with severe brain lesions anywhere, when compared with normal controls, nearly always show significantly lower levels of performance (287). Nevertheless, there exist large portions of the cortex the suppression or removal of which, whether by trauma or excision, seems to have little effect on the function of the brain as a whole. These are the so-called "silent areas" of the cortex. Whether they are really silent or merely functioning in ways which we have not yet discovered still remains to be answered. It is possible that the limited changes observed after removal of these areas may be due to the fact that investigators are appraising functions historically imputed to them, but seldom, if at all, on the basis of actual proof. According to Penfield and Evans (392), the negligible role of the silent areas may be due not only to the fact that "there is bilateral representation of the function involved" but also to the fact that (in some cases) "the function is only weakly encephalized while the essential mechanism remains in the diencephalon."[13]

The points just discussed pose the problem of whether intelligence in any sense may be conceived of as being mediated by any localized area of the brain. Historically it has been asserted not only that "different parts of the brain are specialized for different functions" but also that "in the course of this development certain portions of the brain and especially the frontal cortex take on or are concerned with all the highest and latest acquired functions" (222a). This led to the view not only that the frontal cortex and oftener that the prefrontal lobes were primarily involved, but also that they constituted the centers of or seat of intelligence. Unfortunately for this point of view, neither direct experiment nor clinical observation gives support to the superior role of the frontal cortex. Most striking, as already pointed out, has been the finding that elimination of substantial portions of the frontal lobes or even complete removal of them, produces little effect on specific intellectual performance or on global intelligence ratings as measured by tests. Equally damaging to the claim of pre-eminence for the frontal lobes is the fact that comparative studies of the sequelae from

---

[13] The effect, however, is not so negligible as sometimes reported. See, for example, studies of Gardner, Karnash et al. (181). Also the discussion of the general problem on p. 217.

injuries to various parts of the cortex have shown that resultant decrements
in intellectual performance, if there are any at all, far from being greatest,
are actually least for injuries in the frontal lobes (489). These findings have
been repeatedly confirmed, but in spite of the negated findings (39, 366,
370a) several authors have sought to maintain the dominance of the
frontal lobes as centers of intelligence by distinguishing between different
kinds of intelligence. W. C. Halstead (230), for example, makes a differentiation between what he terms "psychometric and biologic intelligence,"[14]
the former merely representing intellectual ability as measured by tests
and the latter a basic capacity for nervous and mental organization by
which "the nervous system contributes to man's survival." Halstead
assigns the mediation of this "biologic intelligence" to the frontal lobes.
Apart from the fact, however, that the definition of "biologic intelligence"
is derived by its author from the performance of subjects in psychometric
tests, one must note that the capacity to survive, and in general to adapt,
even if equated with intelligence is a function oftener described as being
mediated by various other parts of the nervous system, for example, the
thalamus or even the brain stem. And so far as co-ordination and organization of conscious behavior are concerned, the frontal lobes seemingly play
an even more minor role. For, whereas the entire frontal area of the cortex
may be removed without any loss of consciousness, any considerable damage
in either the diencephalon or the midbrain produces immediate uncon-
sciousness. In the opinion of Penfield and Rasmussen (394) the most
important means of co-ordinating the functions of the cortical areas are
not the association mechanisms within the cortex. Such co-ordination,
they state, is produced largely by the integrating action of the subcortical
centers which lie in the mesoencephalon and the diencephalon.[15]

Not only does the bulk of contemporaneous experimental and clinical
evidence dispose of the role of the frontal lobes as unique centers of intelligence, it also counter-indicates the possibility of its exclusive localization
in any other part of the brain. The effort to locate centers of intelligence,
like the search for seats of consciousness, as I. S. Wechsler has clearly
shown (529), must inevitably end in disappointment, and for the same
reasons, namely, that intelligence like consciousness "is not a single entity . . . (but) the result of numerous integrations of simple and complex
neural activities." In this connection, the recent investigations of Magoun
(346a and c) on the arousal and activating function of the reticular system
in the brain stem further testify to the complex interrelationships of the

---

[14] Also two other kinds, namely, clinical and neurological intelligence. According
to Halstead these are associated with and dependent upon different primary factors
which are "differentially represented in the cerebral cortex" (230), p. 204.

[15] p. 235.

various parts of the brain in the mediation and production of higher mental processes. According to Magoun, "its cephalic influences upon the cerebral hemispheres provide the substrate of the state of wakefulness upon which most higher functions of the nervous system depend." (346b). In brief, neither electroencephalographic nor neurological evidence substantiates the existence of loci in the cerebral hemispheres that serve as centers for either consciousness or any specifically defined mental processes. But apart from neurological considerations, one cannot expect anything like fixed centers of intelligence for purely logical reasons. Intelligence deals not with mental representations but with relations that may exist between them, and relations cannot be localized. A man is bigger than a mouse and a five dollar bill is 'bigger' than a one dollar bill. One might conceivably posit the percept man, mouse and dollar bill as having some sort of cortical representation, for example as engrams, but where or how could one locate the logical relationship *bigger than* which has no spatial or substantiative existence. As a cognitive process, intelligence involves primarily the perception of relations, or to use Spearman's more precise phrase, *the eduction of correlates*, and this process is independent of the specific modality in which the terms are perceived. For effective functioning intelligence may depend more upon the intactness of some rather than other portions of the brain, but in no sense can it be said to be mediated by any single part of it. Intelligence has no locus.

Intelligence as a Physical Construct

Psychologists, like philosophers, have sought from time to time to account for the workings of the mind in terms of physical processes. The efforts[16] have concerned themselves primarily either with the general (and metaphysical) problem of the relation of the mind to matter or with the attempt, as in more recent years, from the cues of neurology and physiology, to account for the correlates of the specific actions of the nervous system.

---

[16] The earlier efforts usually ended with a *deus ex machina*; Leibnitz' monad and Descartes' cybernetic soul housed in the pineal gland are perhaps the most famous examples. Subsequent to the publication of Newton's *Principia*, and up to the middle of the 19th century, the models of brain function for the most part consisted of vague mechanical analogies supplemented later by hypotheses derived from the newly developed chemistry and the laws of thermodynamics. The mind in terms of these formulations operated as a complicated clockwork or self-regulating chemical engine. With the dramatic discoveries in electricity, and particularly its practical applications to communication and recording devices, the models became primarily electric. By the beginning of the present century the brain and its operation were most often compared to a telephone switchboard. This comparison can still be found in the textbooks of physiology of a generation ago. The telephone switchboard has now given way to more complex electrical relay systems involving built-in controls, feedback circuits, and black box properties.

These have resulted in some theories as regards the possible physical basis of sensation, perception and association but, so far as we have been able to discover, there has been no comparable attempt to explain intelligence. Spearman's interpretation of *g* as a kind of mental "energy" may perhaps be considered an exception, but he did not carry the physical analogy very far. More recently still, the remarkable performances of the automaton computer have suggested analogies between the physics of its operations and human thinking and by implication of the human intellect itself. It should be noted at this point that the achievements of the automaton computer, apart from furnishing physical models for the nervous system, present types of performances which, psychologically speaking, are most nearly identifiable as abilities.[17] These mental abilities can be directly explained in terms of the physics of the computer. Accounting for mental abilities, however, presents quite a different problem from that of general intelligence. The first seeks to explain the nature and manner in which mental operations are carried out; the second, the relevance and relation of these operations to certain ends and goals. But the achievements of the analogue and digital computers[18] are in many ways so similar to those of the human intellect that it will be useful to discuss in what way they are alike and in what way they are different.

The analogue and digital computers are remarkable machines. They can perform complex calculations, solve differential equations, compute trajectories and unravel codes. They can store information of a complex nature and give it back at a moment's notice. As already perfected, the digital computer can do many things which have hitherto been considered purely mental or restricted to human capability. For example, it can be made to exhibit retention and recall, make alternative choices, check its own mistakes (which it seldom makes), translate Russian into English, and if put to it, play a game of chess (454). But for all these remarkable "abilities" it lacks certain basic potentials of which only man and certain animals seem capable. The computer cannot initiate action, or learn from experience. It can only do what it is told to do, that is, what has been built into it. In short, it can only follow instructions.[19] Perhaps the most important thing to be said about the computing automaton is that while it can do things, it cannot understand them. It has abilities but these abilities do not go beyond performance.

[17] Such as performing arithmetical computations, storing and reproducing information, etc.

[18] The principles upon which these computers are built are too complex to be considered here. For an exposition of them the reader is referred to the masterful article by von Neumann in the Hixon Symposium on the cerebral mechanisms in behavior (501).

[19] But in this respect it does not really differ much from the average human being.

The distinction between intelligence and abilities emphasized in earlier pages is the crux of the matter. There is no doubt that machines can now be designed and have already been constructed that manifest mental abilities of various sorts, *i.e.*, perform many intellectual tasks including that of logical reasoning. But for the same reasons that abilities cannot be equated with intelligence, the electronic automaton cannot serve as a model for it. What is needed is a conceptual scheme that would yield some insight into the functioning of the brain, not only in terms of its individual components but also collectively, as a unit, as well. Here the idea of complementarity borrowed from quantum mechanics, rather than concepts derived from the mathematics of electric circuits, may shed some light. Such an explanation has recently been made available in a remarkable article by A. W. Stern (478), that should greatly modify our thinking regarding the nature of intelligence.

Stern begins by distinguishing between human abilities, mental factors and the interacting process by which the latter are integrated into intellective behavior; he correctly concludes that they cannot be consistently treated in any mathematical statistical scheme if they are posited to exist as purely isolated factors. Primary mental abilities, like the elementary particles of physics, exhibit a collective as well as an independent behavior; they have group as well as individual properties. Because of their group character the primary intellective factors, according to Stern, possess the basically important property of *connectivity*. This property is manifested psychologically as a *coupling* among the separate intellective factors. Furthermore, "the two modes of behavior form a fundamental *complementarity* suggestive of the complementarity exhibited by the well known wave-particle duality of quantum theory."[20] In terms of quantum mechanics, the wave-particle duality arises because "it is impossible to separate the behavior of the elementary particle from its interaction with the system representing the apparatus." In the case of mental functioning involving intellective behavior, the dual properties of the primary factors arise from the fact that the mind (brain) is an interacting system, "and the environmental situation of the mind plays a role similar to that of the experimental situation in physics under which the phenomena occur." Postulating the above, Stern concludes that "intelligence is the resultant collective behavior among the intellective factors," and *g* "the measure of the strength of the resonance evoked by the coupling process."

The foregoing is an epitome of the major points in Stern's paper on *g* and the nature of intelligence, which in turn is a summary of his mathematical analysis of the problem. The important implication of Stern's paper for psychology is that it presents a mathematical logical model which

[20] *Loc. cit.*; the other quotations are from the same article (478).

not only is consistent with current physical theory, but explains the existing inconsistency of psychologists' trying to measure global intelligence through the summation of intellective abilities. The point here is that while intellective abilities can be shown to contain several independent factors, intelligence cannot be so broken up. Hence, no amount of refinement of tests or addition of factors will account for the total variance of an intelligence test battery, because the variance in intelligence test performance is due not only to the direct contributions of the factors themselves but also to their collective behavior or integration. In order completely to measure intelligence, it is insufficient to extend the range of abilities measured, though this is needed too; we must also find tests which manifest both greater coupling potential and greater resonance characteristics.

Chapter 2

The Concept of Mental Age, IQ
and Deviation Scores

The term mental age, as now used in psychology, was first coined by Binet, who offered it as a way of defining different degrees or levels of intelligence. The novel point was that he proposed to define these levels in terms of the measured abilities of children at different ages. This presupposed that intellectual ability could be measured and that it increased progressively with age. Both of these assumptions have proved correct. Binet's great contributions, however, were more specific. (1) He devised a series of graded intellectual tasks whereby intelligence could in fact be effectively measured; (2) he described a mode of evaluating the results in terms of age units such that the average child of 6 might be said to have a mental age of 6, the average child of 9 a mental age of 9 years, and so on. The technique of scoring tests in terms of age units has come to be known as the mental age method, and the scores obtained by this method as mental ages (M.A.'s).

The method by which an age-intelligence-scale is devised is briefly as follows: A series of intellectual tasks of varying difficulty is assembled and administered to subjects of different age groups. The responses are scored and collated, and, on the basis of the percentage of individuals passing and failing the various tasks at different ages, certain of them are selected as suitable tests. The tests selected are then graded according to difficulty and combined into groups usually of six or eight to form various year levels. The number of tests per year level determines how many credits are assigned to each test. For example, if there are six tests per year, each test passed counts two months. The final score or M.A. which an individual gets on the tests is the sum of the partial credits he obtained for the tests passed at different year levels, expressed in months and years, plus a certain bonus for tests which it is assumed he could have passed if the tests had been given him.[1] The sum of both, expressed in months and years, is

[1] The bonus consists of the M.A. score automatically credited for items below the

24

the individual's mental age score. Thus if a child passes 6 tests at year IX, 4 tests at year X and 3 tests at year XII, his M.A. score is 12 + 8 + 6 + 96 (bonus), or 122 months. All this is, of course, quite familiar; the actual procedure for obtaining a mental age is here summarized in order to throw into focus a number of fundamental facts which even psychologists sometimes overlook.

The first of these facts is that a mental age, however obtained, is just a score. Basically it differs in no way from any other type of score given in terms of the number of items passed, out of a possible total. Thus when a child gets a mental age score of 122 months on the Binet Scale, the important fact is that he is credited with having passed 61 test items.[2] The fact that we multiply each item by 2 so as to be able to express the score in terms of months and years is primarily a matter of convenience. An intelligence rating expressed as a score of 61 points is as real and can be made as comprehensible as a mental age score of 122 months. It has the same arithmetical properties and the same possibilities of evaluation, including that of calculating intelligence quotients. Of course, it also has the same limitations.

The second point of importance about the M.A. method of evaluating intelligence is that it inevitably limits the range of possible scores. Beyond certain points M.A. equivalents are impossible. These limits are reached, for any given test, whenever the mean scores made on the test cease to increase with advancing chronological age. The limiting mental age varies from test to test. Thus on the Manikin Test the mean scores cease to increase above age 8; on the Ship Test, above 12; in the case of Memory Span for Digits, they stop increasing at 14; and in the case of the Vocabulary Test, at about age 22.

The point at which mean scores cease to increase with advancing age is in part dependent upon the difficulty of the test used and in part upon a function of the general maturation process. Thus, in the case of the Manikin and Ship Tests the mean scores fail to increase with advancing age because the tests are too easy. In the cases of the Memory Span for Digits and the Vocabulary Test the differences between the mean scores at higher ages disappear because the abilities measured by these tests no longer increase with age. Thus the ability to repeat digits stops improving at age 14, not because it is impossible to attain a higher score than those generally at-

---

year level on which the subject has passed all tests. For example, if a child passes all tests at year IX (known as the basal year) he is given full credit (96 months) for all tests through year VIII, even though he has not actually taken the tests of the lower year levels.

[2] Actually he will have been tested with considerably fewer items. This number 61 includes both the items actually passed as well as those for which he received automatic credit. See above footnote.

tained by the average 14 year old, but because the mean scores for the average 16, 18, and 20 year old are no higher.

What is true of the various abilities considered individually is equally true of measures of these abilities when they are combined into "batteries" of tests to yield measures of general intelligence. Beyond the age of 15 or 16, mean scores on most intelligence scales cease to increase *significantly* with age. Psychologists used to interpret this fact to mean that intellectual ability stops growing at about that age. Although we think this inference is essentially correct, this view no longer is so generally held, primarily because a number of scales, including our own, show that mean test scores tend to increase up to the age of 20 and even up to 25. Our own view is that this increase, and it is generally small, is largely due to the rise in the educational level and certain other factors rather than to a real increment in sheer ability.

Whether the peak of intelligence test score performance occurs at 15 or at 20, however, is here of secondary importance. Of more immediate concern to us now is the possible significance of the fact that all intelligence scales eventually reach a point beyond which test scores no longer increase with chronological age. The first implication is obvious: the mental age concept has a natural limit of applicability. When a test reaches a point beyond which mean scores cease to increase with age, then any higher scores for which the test allows can no longer be expressed in terms of mental age.

The fact that every intelligence scale attains a point beyond which mean scores for successive age groups no longer increase with age does not mean, of course, that scores higher than those calculated at the limiting age levels cannot be attained. On the contrary, the fact that the mental age scores are average scores shows that there must be a large percentage of individuals who attain higher scores than the mean. The only question is how to interpret, or at least make use of these. One way is to assign hypothetical values or IQ equivalents to them, based on the relative frequency of their occurrence; another is to accept them at their face value and to assume that if there were higher mental age scores they would increase with chronological age precisely in the manner in which the scale provides for it. In either case, we get what are obviously extrapolated values, that is, M.A.'s which are only hypothetically related to the actual data, and their maximal values are limited only by the range of the test scores. Thus, in the case of the Stanford Revision of the Binet it is possible to obtain an M.A. of 19 years and 6 months, on the Otis Tests of Mental Ability an M.A. of 18 years and 6 months, and on the Terman-Merrill Revision of the Binet an M.A. of 22 years and 10 months. With these limits, we are not particularly concerned. But it is very important to appraise their possible psychological significance.

A mental age score above an age beyond which mean scores increase with age, *e.g.*, an M.A. of 20 years, can have one of two meanings. The first and most important one is that which it could have had, if it signified the same thing as that which is implied when we say that a child has a mental age of 7 or 8 or 10, namely, that it represents the average mentality of the average individual of that age, expressed in months and years. Such an interpretation for a mental age of 20 years is clearly incorrect. The average mental age of the average 20 year old is not 20 but 15 years. The second possible meaning of mental age of 20 is that it represents a measurable level of intelligence that is above the average, the precise amount of which for the sake of convenience is expressed in the year-month notation. In that case, however, the above notation acquires an altered connotation and can only add confusion to the original concept.

What we have said thus far does not, of course, deny the value of the mental age concept altogether, but only points to its inevitable limitations. The most important of these limitations, as we have just seen, is that the M.A. method of defining intelligence cannot logically be used to define levels of intelligence higher than that obtained by that age group beyond which M.A. scores cease to increase with chronological age. The precise age at which this occurs is still in dispute. It cannot, in fact, be definitely fixed because the mental age limit attained is a function of the actual tests used, and there can be no possible agreement so long as different intelligence scales are composed of different batteries of tests. But whether the mean adult M.A. as the peak test age score is generally referred to as 16 or 18 or 25,[3] the fact is that the M.A. method of measuring intelligence breaks down even earlier. Actually, the method begins to fail at about age 12. For though the means of the actual test scores continue to increase with age above that age, they do so by progressively diminishing and ultimately negligible amounts.[4] This fact becomes an important source of error if not corrected for when indices of brightness or intelligence quotients are calculated.

The most universally used of all indices of intelligence is the intelligence quotient (IQ). In the Binet type of scale it is calculated by dividing a subject's mental age (M.A.) by his chronological age (C.A.). Thus, if a child of 10 attains an M.A. of 12, his IQ is 120. Calculated in this manner, an IQ is seemingly straightforward and easy enough to comprehend. But its full

[3] In the W–B standardization, the pooled mean of the 11 subtests used fell at approximately age 22; in the WAIS, more nearly at age 28 (see p. 140).

[4] For evidence in support of this view, see Wechsler, D. (521a).

meaning actually depends upon what we understand by the terms M.A. and C.A. The meaning of an M.A. has already been discussed at length. It is a test score expressed in a month-year notation. But what is a C.A.? We do not, of course, refer to its literal definition, namely the life or chronological age of an individual at the time he is examined, but its meaning as a part of the IQ formula.

As used in calculating IQ's, a C.A. like the M.A. is merely a score. It is a score which the examiner assumes an individual of a given age would attain if his ability were exactly equivalent to that of the average individual of his own (the subject's) life age. Thus, if a given individual's age is 8 years, his C.A. score, if he were an average 8 year old, would also be 8 years. If his life age were 12 years and 9 months, his C.A. score, assuming him to be an average individual, ought likewise to be 12 years and 9 months, and so on. A well standardized scale is one in which the tests are so arranged as to make this assumption warrantable and at least approximately correct.[5] But in any case, the important fact is that the C.A. is merely a converted score, just as the M.A. That which makes them alike, however, is not the fact that they have the word age in common, but that they are both test scores measured in identical units.

Bearing these facts in mind one may define an intelligence quotient as the ratio between a particular score which an individual attains (on a given intelligence test) and the score which an average individual of his life age may be assumed to attain on the same test, when both scores are expressed in the same notation. The usual formula,

$$IQ = \frac{M.A.}{C.A.}$$

should really be stated as follows:

$$IQ = \frac{\text{attained or actual score}}{\text{expected mean score for age}}$$

The great value of the IQ is that it furnishes us with a method of defining relative intelligence. It tells us in the first instance how bright an individual is as compared with someone of his own age. But it tells us, or at least is intended to tell us, even more than that. The IQ is offered as an index which is independent not only of the particular score which an individual makes

---

[5] Actually this has been shown to be the case for the midyear points only, for example, that the average 9½ year old child attains a mental age of 9½ and hence an IQ of 100. But it has not been shown for the average child of 9 years and 2 months, the average child of 9 years and 9 months, etc. It is probable, however, that within the limits of ages 5 to 12 years the deviations from the mean at any given intermediate age would not be very great, and the correspondence of the C.A. and M.A. values may for practical purposes be assumed to hold.

on a particular scale, but also of the particular age at which he happens to make it. It is thus a measure which presumably defines the relative brightness or intellectual possibilities of an individual, more or less permanently. Under ordinary conditions an individual's IQ is supposed to remain the same throughout life, or at least throughout the age limits covered by the scale. Psychologists refer to this property as the *constancy of the IQ*.

The constancy of the IQ is the basic assumption of all scales in which relative degrees of intelligence are defined in terms of it. It is not only basic, but absolutely necessary that IQ's be independent of the age at which they are calculated, because unless the assumption holds, no permanent scheme of intelligence classification is possible. If an individual at one age attained a certain IQ and a few years later another IQ, or if a particular IQ meant one thing at one age and quite a different thing at another, the IQ would obviously have no practical significance. It is, therefore, extremely important to ascertain whether IQ's, as now calculated, do in fact remain constant.

The facts regarding the constancy of the IQ are essentially of two kinds. The first pertains to the mean values of the IQ at successive chronological ages. In the case of most of the better standardized tests, it can readily be shown that, at least for the standardizing samples of population, the mean IQ's over the middle portions of the scale are regularly found to be about 100. The fact that they generally do not deviate more than 2 or 3 points from this value is interpreted to show that the IQ remains constant from age to age. This interpretation, however, goes beyond the fact. The only legitimate conclusion that can be drawn from them is that the IQ's not far from the average will remain constant. It does not necessarily imply that IQ's at any considerable distance from the mean, let us say 1 or 2 standard deviations from it (for example, IQ's of 85 or 70), will also remain constant. That will depend not only on the average values of the IQ at different ages, but also on their respective variabilities at these ages. Hitherto, it has been assumed that these variabilities were the same or differed by no greater amounts than might be expected from sampling errors. Actually, little evidence has been produced to test this assumption which remains distinctly controversial.

The early standardizations of the Binet Scale contained little data which would enable one to evaluate the comparative variability of the IQ at different ages. It was not until Burt's (86) revision appeared that such data became available. Burt himself did not actually take up the problem of the variability of the IQ (or mental ratio, as he termed it), but he did furnish data from which this variability might be calculated. One is able to do this because he gives for each life age not only the mean M.A. score, but also its standard deviation (S.D.). Using these figures one may calculate what IQ may be expected for an individual at any given age whose position is any given S.D. distance from the mean. If all IQ's were constant, not only at the mean, but any distance from it, all individuals deviating by the same fractional standard deviation from the mean would have the same IQ's. Actual calculation, however, shows that this is generally not the case.

Analysis of Burt's figures reveals that except between ages 6 and 10 the difference in variability of the IQ is so great as to alter its value significantly. For example, at the distance of 2 standard deviations from the mean an individual at age 6 attaining that rank would get an IQ of 76; at age 10, he would get an IQ of 81; at age 14, an IQ of 84.

More direct evidence of variability of IQ with age is furnished by the statistics of Terman and Merrill (488) in their new revision of the Stanford-Binet. Their tables merit detailed examination. They contain some interesting surprises. In the first place, even the mean IQ's show considerable variability, differing by as much as 9 per cent at different ages, for example, from a mean IQ of 109.9 at age 2½ to a mean IQ of 100.9 at age 14. But even more significant are the differences between the standard deviation of the means at different age levels. These differ by as much as 7.5 units, and in consequence give rise to significant deviations from the IQ expectancy. Thus, the standard deviation for the mean IQ at age 12 on the Revised Stanford-Binet (Form L) is 20.0, and at age 6, only 12.5. Accordingly, depending upon the age at which an individual is being tested, he may obtain different IQ's even though his relative brightness remains unchanged. Thus, on the supposition that he is an individual whose position is 2 standard deviations from the mean, he would get at age 6 an IQ of 75 and at age 12 an IQ of 60. This would imply that an IQ of 60 at age 12 means the same as an IQ of 75 at year 6.[6]

The fact is thus clear that IQ's calculated by the M.A. over the C.A. method do not remain constant for individuals whose ratings are any considerable distance above or below the average of their age group. It also appears that the method does not furnish constant values even for mean IQ's except at certain ages. This becomes apparent if instead of comparing the mean IQ's at different ages one compares the original test scores from which they were derived. The most effective way of doing this is by plotting original test scores directly against chronological age, without any further manipulation of the data than a prior transmutation of the scores into units of equal amount. We have done this with the Wechsler Bellevue

___

[6] Terman and Merrill are inclined to account for the large fluctuations in variability at certain ages as being primarily due to sampling errors or to the influence of pubescent changes. But though it is true that such differences are not obtained at all ages, they are by no means exceptional.

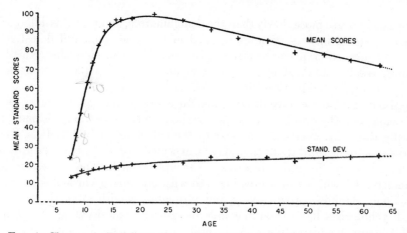

FIG. 1. Changes in Full Scale Scores of the Wechsler-Bellevue Form I. Ages 7–65.

Intelligence Scale (W–B I) data. The resulting growth curve is shown in Figure 1. The curve is a logistic growth curve. It shows that intellectual growth is not linear, that is, that it does not proceed by equal amounts throughout its development.

The assumption of the linear relationship between M.A. and C.A. leads to certain inevitable consequences. The first of these is that for the average individual the mean value of the IQ will change from age to age. At early age levels or at other periods when the mental growth is rapid, the IQ will tend to be above the mean of the entire population; at the upper ages, when mental growth is slower, it will be below the mean. Thus, on the Stanford-Binet (original 1916 standardization), the mean IQ for ages 3 to 5 is approximately 102; for ages 15 and 16 it is more nearly 98. On the 1937 (Terman-Merrill) revision of the Scale, the mean IQ's are systematically above 100 for all ages; those between ages 2½ to 5 average about 105; those at ages 14 and 15, about 101.5.[7]

A second result that might be expected from a study of the mental growth curve is that a child's IQ would tend to fall off as he grew older, and that this falling off would be more marked in the case of the mentally retarded than in the case of the normal or superior child. The explanation of these phenomena inheres in the particular logarithmic relationship that connects mental with chronological age. In a gross way this may be expressed by saying that the numerators used in calculating IQ's by the M.A./C.A.

---

[7] It should be added that the discrepancies would be much larger if the scaling methods employed did not compensate for them by using different criteria in selecting the tests at different age levels. At the lower ages, authors of tests usually require 60 to 70 per cent of "passes" for locating a test at a particular age level, whereas at the upper ages only from 50 to 60 per cent is required.

method increase more slowly than the denominators, and that this difference in the rate of increase is most marked in the case of mental defectives. Here again observation confirms what may be expected theoretically. Thus, results obtained by re-testing mental defectives (303) show that IQ's of such individuals decline systematically with age.[8]

Much of what we have discussed so far concerns the calculation of IQ's for children. The problem becomes more acute when an attempt is made to apply the M.A. over C.A. method to the calculation of adult IQ's. This brings us to the third result that may be expected from a study of the growth curve, namely the ultimate arrest of mental growth. The successive increments by which test scores increase with advancing chronological age, not only diminish progressively, but ultimately vanish altogether.

Psychologists have from the first recognized that dividing an adult's M.A. score by his actual C.A. in order to obtain his IQ would lead to absurd results. To avoid these absurdities, they generally adopted the plan of using as denominator the highest C.A. beyond which the observed M.A. scores cease to increase. This age was set by different authors at some point from 14 to 18 years. The actual age chosen has depended in part on the experiences of the author and in part on the particular scale employed. But apart from the fact that the assumed age has varied from test to test, the fixing of it at any particular point has introduced an assumption which has served to destroy the meaning of the IQ altogether. This assumption is that M.A. scores remain constant throughout adult life or, at least, up to the point where senility begins. If this were true, the curve of mental growth from age 16 on would be a straight line parallel to the C.A. axis. Actually, this does not happen; instead, after reaching a maximum, it flexes downward progressively.

We have already discussed the characteristics of the curve in Figure 1, up to the age of puberty. We shall now consider the changes in mental ability from 16 years on. We might add that the W–B I curve is very similar to the ones derived from other studies, and in particular those of Miles (364) and those of Jones and Conrad (281). These curves all show that scores on tests of mental ability after a certain point decline with age. The point at which they begin to fall off and the rate at which they do so vary from test to test. In most intelligence scales the differences in test scores between ages 18 and 30 are for most practical purposes negligible, but beyond that age the decline becomes appreciable. After 40, test scores may decrease so rapidly that the use of a single denominator for calculating

[8] Incidentally, the fact that the IQ's of individuals of low intelligence tend to decrease markedly with age entails some paradoxical consequences. One of them is that after being sent to a special school for several years, a mentally retarded child might well come out with a lower IQ than when he entered.

adult IQ's introduces serious errors; nor does it matter whether the equivalent M.A. is taken as 14, 15 or 16 years. All tests are equally fallacious in the sense that they assume that mental ability (as measured by tests) remains constant after any one of these ages. Use of a single denominator is tantamount to comparing subjects not with their peers, *i.e.*, individuals of their own age, but with those of some particular, usually optimally functioning, age group. When one does this, the resulting comparison furnishes not an intelligence but an efficiency quotient.

Our investigations into the nature and meaning of the IQ have led us to some very disturbing conclusions. First, we found that even if IQ's as hitherto calculated were constant about the mean, this could in no way imply that they were also constant at all other points. Next, we found that the M.A. over the C.A. method could not possibly give constant IQ's for all ages, because the assumed linear relation between C.A.'s and M.A.'s does not in fact obtain. Finally, we were forced to the uncomfortable conclusion that adult IQ's as customarily calculated were not IQ's at all, but some sort of efficiency quotients.

For these and other reasons,[9] many psychologists have felt that the IQ ought to be abandoned altogether as a measure of general intelligence. But this is hardly a legitimate conclusion, since the noted shortcomings are not due to any intrinsic defect in the IQ concept, but are only a result of certain correctable errors in the way the IQ has been calculated.

Actually, the IQ remains a basic concept in the measurement of intelligence and, indeed, as unequivocal a definition of it as is possible. It merely states that a person's intelligence at any given time is defined by his relative standing among his age peers. This assumes that though an individual's absolute capacity may change, his relative standing will not, under ordinary circumstances. The assumption requires that the level so established be independent of the subject's age, the type of test used and the variability of the population sample. Several statistical procedures by which this result may be attained are now available and we shall presently describe the one employed in the standardization of the W–B I and the WAIS scales. Preliminarily, there still remains one important problem that needs probing, namely, the definition of "zero ability" which is inevitably involved in any meaningful measure of intelligence.

The zero point in a scale of mental measurements, like that of any physical scale, may have one of two meanings. It may signify "just not anything" of whatever it is we are seeking to measure, as in the case of the zero of the absolute temperature scale, or it may merely represent some defined point of reference from which we find it convenient to start our measurements, as the freezing point of water in the centigrade scale. In

---

[9] In particular, its libaility to gross misinterpretation by the laity.

either case, its explicit definition is imperative, in order to express scalar amounts as multiples or fractions. All IQ's, of course, are precisely such multiples or fractions. Their magnitude obviously depends upon the points of reference from which they are being calculated. In the case of the M.A. over C.A. method of calculating the IQ's, the zero point for both the numerator and denominator is the assumed age of the child at birth. Actually, this assumption is incorrect. A child at birth has neither zero intelligence nor, for that matter, zero chronological age. When a child is born it is already 9 months old and manifests a certain amount of intelligence. Whatever the situation, however, it could not be used as a point of reference for a scale like ours. Accordingly we are forced to look for another point of reference for our zero that would be related in some quantitative way to actual test scores.

A number of suggestions have been made by various writers as to how zero intelligence might be defined in terms of scores. The most cogent one is perhaps that of Thurstone (491), who defined it "as the amount of test performance at which variability vanishes." Such an amount, it might appear, ought not to be difficult to determine for any given scale. All that is seemingly necessary is that we find a point below which no test score of any kind is possible. But the situation is not so simple. The reason is that what we are seeking is not a point on our scales beyond which there are no lower scores but really a point corresponding to a degree of intelligence below which intellectual ability may, to all intents and purposes, be said to be non-existent. That, of course, is quite a different matter. An individual failing to make any score on a given test might still make some sort of score on a much easier test. For example, a zero score on the Army Alpha is equal to a score of about 12 on the Army Beta;[10] and there are other tests even easier than the Army Beta on which individuals can obtain some sort of score, even when unable to do anything on the Beta. We therefore cannot take the lowest score attainable on any particular scale as the true zero point of intelligence. Some other method of arriving at it is necessary.

One way out of the difficulty is to turn to the normal curve for guidance. The technique consists of normalizing the data and assuming a zero point so far from the mean of the obtained distribution that the slight amount

[10] Conversely, a score of zero on the Army Beta would be equal to a score of about −71 on the Army Alpha. The reader who is puzzled by these numbers should recall that mathematically 0 is an indeterminate quantity. In psychology it means so small an amount of ability as to be just insufficient to enable its possessor to obtain the lowest possible score on a given test. Each test will therefore have a different zero point. Realization of this fact will show why scores on different tests forming a single battery cannot be added together unless they have been previously equated against one another.

of ability this assumed point represented would make it highly improbable that any individual could be so ill endowed. In terms of units of deviation, custom has tended to set this point at −5 S.D. from the mean, and our first IQ tables were calculated on this basis.

IQ tables calculated by setting a zero point at −5 S.D. from the mean gave us fairly satisfactory intelligent quotients. The method of obtaining them, however, seemed altogether arbitrary. We really had no rationale for the particular limits which we had chosen. It is true that when calculated with the zero limit set at −5 S.D. we obtained IQ's that were not very much different from those we could obtain by the M.A. over C.A. method, after transmuting the sigma scores into the equivalent M.A.'s, and indeed not very much different from those we eventually obtained by the method we finally adopted. But we could offer no justification for our procedure, other than that of matter-of-fact empiricism. Moreover, when we set the point at −5 sigma, we discovered considerable irregularity in the IQ limits for our various age groups. For all these reasons, we decided to abandon the idea of defining zero intelligence and to seek instead a base that was at once more logical and less difficult to manipulate.

The base which we finally chose to define was that amount of intelligence which was represented by the individual who was one probable error (P.E.) away from the mean. We chose that distance because, by convention, the deviation −1 P.E. is used as the dividing line between individuals who are referred to as average (normal) and subaverage (below normal). According to this view, an average individual is a person who falls within the middle 50 per cent of the group, a range which on the normal probability curve is defined by the value +1 to −1 P.E. from the mean.

After setting −1 P.E. as the definable point from which our IQ's were to be calculated, one had to decide next upon the value of the IQ which should be assigned to it. We say "decide" because the absolute numerical value of the IQ, as the reader will recall, is altogether a matter of convenience. An individual's IQ, to repeat, merely defines his relative position among the group with which he has been compared. The important fact about it is this relative standing and not the numerical rating which one may happen to assign to it. The numerical value of an IQ has no more fixed meaning than a passing mark on a scholastic examination. One can set a passing mark at 60, 70 or 90 without altering its implication, if by passing one means the attainment of relative excellence or level of efficiency. In this sense, the meaning which any mark has is derived from its relative position among the set of marks that are being evaluated. For example, a mark of 90 may mean very superior or barely passing, depending upon the total range of the marking scale. It is the same with IQ's. In the

final analysis, the level of intelligence which any IQ represents will depend
not on its absolute, but on its relative magnitude.

While the numerical rating that can be assigned to an individual's
attaining any distance from the mean (in our case −1 P.E.) is altogether
a question of convenience, certain practical considerations limit the particular values which we may employ. The most important of these is the
value of the mean IQ. Here, unchallenged custom has set it definitively at
100. For all other IQ's there is no such historical or statistical cogency.
The only limitation imposed upon us is that IQ's of individuals below the
mean must be less than 100. But in choosing a base from which all IQ's
were to be calculated, it was obviously a matter of common sense to select
such a value for it as would be in line with the order of numerical values
of IQ's now in general use. In the case of most intelligence scales, an IQ of
90 has come to be interpreted as the lowest limit of what is generally called
average intelligence. Since the distance −1 P.E. from the mean designated
the lower limiting value of the category "average" in our own classification,
we decided to use 90 as the IQ against which the distance of −1 P.E. might
conveniently be equated.

By equating the distance −1 P.E. against the IQ of 90 we at once defined not only this particular IQ but all other IQ's as well, because the
equation by which this is done automatically defines the zero point. This
zero point is obviously that S.D. distance from the mean which gives us an
IQ of 90 for any individual who attains the position of −1 P.E. from the
mean. Having obtained this zero point, it is then a matter of simple arithmetic to draw up one's IQ tables. All that is necessary is to determine the
mean and standard deviation of one's distribution, prepare a table of z
scores, and by the formula

$$\frac{X - z}{X}$$

obtain for each actual score the corresponding IQ. This is the method we
used for establishing the IQ tables of the W-B I.

In constructing the WAIS tables, essentially the same method was used,
except that this time instead of equating a score distance of minus 1 P.E.
against an IQ of 90, the same result was obtained by equating the test
scores against a set mean IQ of 100, with an S.D. of 15. The equation by
which this was done is given in Appendix 1B. IQ's calculated by either
equation have become known as *deviation quotients* since they are calculated
in terms of deviation from the mean rather than in terms of absolute
criteria. It should be noted, however, that while the equations used for
the W–B I and the WAIS give identical results, the rationale for the two
are not necessarily the same.

IQ's derived in the manner just described have several advantages. In the first place, they define levels of intelligence strictly in terms of standard deviation units and hence can be interpreted unequivocally. Second, they dispense with the necessity of making any assumptions with regard to the precise relation between mental and chronological rate of growth, and in particular to the linearity of the relation. Third, they dispense with the need of committing oneself to any fixed point beyond which scores are assumed unaffected by age, that is, to a fixed average adult mental age. Finally, all IQ's so calculated, if numerically equal, may be assumed to be identically equivalent irrespective of the age at which they have been determined.

In concluding this chapter, it may be well to remind the reader that, though the purpose of an IQ, however calculated, is to furnish a measure of relative brightness, the IQ in and of itself does not particularly define any level of particular brightness. The meaning attached to the numerical value of an IQ is a matter of convention, making use to be sure of certain criteria, but still arbitrarily arrived at. Thus, it is by convention that an IQ of 100 is set to represent an average, an IQ of 120 superior and an IQ of 60 mentally defective intelligence. One could, if one wished, use other numerical values to define these levels of intelligence. What is important is not the number but what the number defines, that is, the meaning one legitimately attaches to it.

So much for the meaning, implication and method of calculating a true IQ. All of this, however, is only a means to an end—the classification of intelligence itself. The purposes of an IQ are to enable us to tell how bright or how stupid a person is and on the basis of test scores to classify him scientifically with respect to what we are pleased to call his native intellectual endowment. This is a large order, and we shall need a more extended discussion to see how it may be done.

Chapter 3

The Classification of Intelligence

When psychologists speak of classifying intelligence, they use the term in a somewhat specialized sense. The purpose of a mental classification is not, as in most other scientific classification, "the detection of the laws of nature." It does not correspond, for example, to the chemist's arrangement of the elements into a periodic table or even the zoologist's subdivision of animals into vertebrates and non-vertebrates and then again into their various orders. The psychologist's effort at classifying intelligence is more what the layman does when he tries to distinguish colors of the rainbow. The analogy is more than a superficial one. General intelligence is a non-interrupted continuum like that of a rainbow spectrum. One level of intelligence merges into the next as colors seen through a refracting prism. Levels of behavior which present certain patterns (or hues, to return to the color analogy) are called defectives, others a little farther up the scale are called borderline, still others, dull-normal and so on until we reach the other end of the scale where they are labeled very superior, precocious or near-genius. The borderline runs into the dull-normal and the high average into the superior just as the orange-yellow runs into the yellow, and the deep violet into the indigo. In both cases it is convention or custom which has assigned them their respective names.

The earliest classifications of intelligence were very rough ones. To a large extent they were practical attempts to define various patterns of behavior in medical-legal terms. These terms, like idiot, imbecile and moron, coined by the early writers on the subject, still form part of our present day terminology. The contribution of modern psychology has been not so much in the matter of defining new configurations of intelligent behavior as in giving precision to the already available concepts, through the introduction of quantitative methods. A mental defective is now defined not only as a person who "through congenital arrest or imperfect mental development is incapable . . . of managing himself or his affairs with ordinary prudence," but as one who on standardized tests fails to

38

attain an IQ or an M.A. of a particular level. In brief, psychologists have attempted to classify intelligence by means of quantitative measurements. This has been a great step forward. The progress to be realized is like that achieved by physicists in designating colors by their wave-lengths instead of their hues.

While the theoretical advantages of classifying intelligence quantitatively are obvious, the practical gain of such classifications is not always so apparent. The reason for this is that the merit of any quantitative classification depends not only on the reliability of the data employed but on the validity of the interpretations assigned to them. Quantitative data on which mental classifications are based usually consist of measures of brightness derived from one or another intelligence test and defined as IQ's. But the calculation of a correct and reliable IQ is only the first prerequisite for its use as a base for classification. We still have to decide the meanings we can attach to the IQ, however obtained. In practice the procedure has consisted of matching IQ levels to historically defined clinical groups. Thus in Terman's classification, individuals attaining IQ's below 70 are designated as mentally defective, those between 80 and 90 as dull-normal, those between 90 and 110 as average, and so on. According to Kuhlmann, the IQ limit for the corresponding categories are: mental defectives below 75, borderline 75 to 84, dull 85 to 94, average 95 to 104. Other writers have used still other delimitations.

Such simple matching unless justified by an explicit rationale presents certain problems. One, for example, is why different authors have had different IQ cut-off points or class limits for the same clinical groups. These are, of course, a function both of the tests used and of the standardizing procedures employed. A more important stricture is the absence of reasons as to why the designated IQ intervals rather than other possible ones were used to limit particular clinical categories—for example, why the borderline group in the Terman classification was defined by IQ intervals 70 to 80 and not 73 to 82 or 69 to 75. In the past, this was seemingly done because the class interval chosen was sufficiently proximate to include most of the individuals functionally designated by the defined class appellations, and perhaps also because the numbers selected were easy to remember. These are not very satisfactory reasons. But the most serious objection to the earlier procedure was that IQ's were matched to *already defined* clinical groups rather than used to re-define these groups on the basis of attained IQ's. If IQ's are to contribute to a basic definition of intelligence, their utilization must have an objective justification. It is not the precise numerical value of the IQ that is important but whether it does or does not represent a definable measure of intelligence. The actual numbers that emerge are, in a sense, accidents of the system of notation used and, as already indicated, can be manipulated to suit practical needs. A free exercise of this privilege would, however, lead to confusion, because one would not be in a position to interpret the IQ's of any given scale without detailed knowledge of the author's standardizing technique. Some agreement, both as to system of notation and interpretation of results, is obviously necessary. Such agreement could best be achieved through conventions established by an international meeting of psychologists and psychiatrists. Unfortunately, authors of tests are far from ready for such agreement. One is, therefore, left in a position of either having to adopt schemes of classification already in vogue or risking further complication by the addition of others. In this situation, the *laissez faire* policy seems to prevail. New test scales, however contrived, seem to have gone along with already established IQ classifications irrespective of whether new data justified it or not. Thus, Terman's original classification has been used not only for IQ's for the revised Stanford-Binet but for IQ's derived from a host of other tests for which, at best, they could only roughly apply and which often led to egregious misapplication. Even the IQ distributions of the 1937 revision of the Stanford-Binet do not sufficiently overlap with those of the 1916 version to make the original IQ classification table valid for the revised scale. Actually, several tables have been found necessary, but these have been generally disregarded, and the original classification scheme has been continued without much regard to the revealed discrepancies.

To avoid the inevitable confusion resulting from the indiscriminate equation of IQ's derived from different tests, it seemed reasonable to attempt a re-definition of the basic categories of intelligence in terms of explicit statistical criteria. The classification proposed is that each intelligence level have a class interval embracing a range of IQ's falling at a measured distance from the mean, these distances being expressed as multiples of standard deviations (actually, P.E.'s). Thus, a mental defective is a person whose IQ falls three or more P.E.'s below the mean. In terms of percentile ranking he falls approximately among the lowest 2.2 per cent of the total population. Similarly, a person of *borderline* defective intelligence is an individual who attains an IQ that falls between a deviation of −3 P.E. and −2 P.E. from the mean or, in terms of percentile rank, a position anywhere from *circa* the lowest 3rd to *circa* the lowest 10th percentile. And so with the other categories. The choice of limiting points is only in part arbitrary. In the case of mental defectives, for example, there are available various estimates of the probable incidence of mental deficiency in this country based on different modes of evaluation. These estimates, though varying greatly among themselves, give a mean figure which is not far from about 2.5 per cent of the total population. It therefore seemed reasonable to define the mental defective groups as those individuals who attain IQ's falling at a distance of −3 or more P.E.'s from the mean. This distance, as already noted, is equivalent to about 2.2 per cent of the total area of the normal curve. For the intermediate categories, such as borderline and dull-normal intelligence, as well as those of average, high-average, superior and very superior, it was decided to use the intervening integral multiples of the probable error.

The scheme of classification is symmetrical, comprising as many classes above the mean as there are below it. In the case of categories described by IQ's below the mean, it was easy to take over the terms now in general use. In the case of categories above the mean, there were some for which no ready terms were available, in particular the one to describe the group falling in the interval +1 P.E. to +2 P.E. above the mean. Since the individuals composing this category form a group of subjects who are as much above average as the dull-normal are below the average, a logical term that suggested itself was that of *bright-normal.* The term is rather clumsy but better than most that come to mind. As a second choice there is the somewhat long but descriptive term *high-average to superior.* It should be noted that this phrase does not have the same denotation it has in the Terman classification.

The final classification of intelligence at which we have arrived, together with the percentage included in each category are given in Tables 1, 2 and 3. The specified percentages and limits, though justified by a rational statistic, are of course in nowise definitive. If, for some reason, future experience should show that the present limits are not the best, they can be altered in the light of that experience. Indeed, if anyone has reason to disagree with the percentage limits as set, he is free to substitute others and still use our basic data. A table of equivalent percentiles for the W–B I and WAIS Full Scale scores is given in Table 4.

The classifications offered above, as heretofore noted, are based essentially on a statistical concept of intelligence. They differ from other

TABLE 1
Statistical basis of intelligence classification (theoretical)

Classification	Limits in Terms of P.E.	Percentage Included
Defective	−3 P.E. and below	2.15
Borderline	−2 P.E. to −3 P.E.	6.72
Dull-normal	−1 P.E. to −2 P.E.	16.13
Average	−1 P.E. to +1 P.E.	50.00
Bright-normal	+1 P.E. to +2 P.E.	16.13
Superior	+2 P.E. to +3 P.E.	6.72
Very superior	+3 P.E. and over	2.15

TABLE 2

Intelligence classification of W–B I IQ's—ages 10 to 60 (actual)

Classification	IQ Limits	Percentage Included
Defective....................	65 and below	2.2
Borderline....................	66–79	6.7
Dull-normal..................	80–90	16.1
Average......................	91–110	50.0
Bright-normal................	111–119	16.1
Superior.....................	120–127	6.7
Very superior................	128 and over	2.2

TABLE 3

Intelligence classification of WAIS IQ's—ages 16 to 75 (actual)

Classification	IQ	Percentage Included
Defective.....................	69 and below	2.2
Borderline....................	70–79	6.7
Dull-normal..................	80–89	16.1
Average......................	90–109	50.0
Bright-normal................	110–119	16.1
Superior.....................	120–129	6.7
Very superior................	130 and above	2.2

classifications of this kind by the fact that they clearly abandon any attempt at an absolute definition of intelligence. An IQ now merely tells one how much better or worse, or how much above or below the average an individual falls when compared with persons of his own age.[1] What that average represents we really do not know. In a point scale it is some numerical score; in a mental age scale, an M.A. equivalent. Most people can readily see that a point score has no absolute significance, because among other things its numerical value is so obviously dependent upon the number of items that happen to comprise the scale. In the case of the mental age scores, even psychologists are often under the impression that we are dealing with some absolute quantity, and the impression is even more common among psychiatrists. There is a rather widespread view that in defining intelligence in terms of mental age we are doing so in terms of some basic unit of amount. That, as we have seen, is a mistake. A mental age is just a test score and differs from other arithmetical summaries only by the fact that it happens to be in a year-month notation. The mental

---

[1] Also, if one wished, when compared to a person of his own sex, socio-economic status, etc. For reasons later indicated, only the age factor has been allowed for in the construction of our tables.

TABLE 4

Equivalent percentile ranks for W–B I* and WAIS† full scale scores

Percentile Rank	IQ's	
	W–B I*	WAIS†
99	130	135
97	125	128
95	123	125
90	118	119
80	112	113
75	110	110
70	108	108
60	105	104
50	101	100
40	98	96
30	94	92
25	91	90
20	89	87
10	81	81
5	73	75
3	68	72
1	59	65

* Ages 10 to 60.
† Ages 16 to 60.

age notation has a number of advantages, but among these is not the magical one of being able to transmute a relative into an absolute quantity. In brief, mental age is no more an absolute measure of intelligence than any other test score.

We have at this point returned again to the question as to what a mental age really is, because a number of authors, and no less an authority than Doll (141), have suggested and indeed urged that intelligence be classified on the basis of mental age ratings rather than on IQ's. Their arguments in favor of this change may be said to be of two kinds. The main argument against the use of the IQ for the classification of intelligence is the fact that the IQ does not remain constant. This criticism, as we have seen, is justified to a degree. But, as we have further noted, this is not the fault of the IQ but of the particular method by which it has been calculated.[2] The second important argument in favor of the M.A. over the IQ as a

[2] This limitation is largely obviated by the method of calculating the IQ that is outlined in this book.

basis for classifying intelligence is that the M.A. does so in terms of fixed levels and hence definitely known amounts of intelligence. There is a further implication, though not stated in so many words, that an M.A. level can be looked upon as a sort of absolute measure. We have already shown that this cannot be so. But, in any case, it would be a mistake to set up the M.A. as a competitive base for the classification of intelligence. To do so would be tantamount to abandoning almost entirely the statistical concept of intelligence for which psychologists have so long worked.

One cannot emphasize too strongly the importance of the statistical concept of intelligence for the science of mental classification. It was first introduced in psychology by Galton when he defined genius. A genius, according to Galton, was a man "who (because of his eminent work) achieved the position of one in each million." Of course the genius' rarity or uniqueness is not the only characteristic which distinguishes him from the average man.[3] Genius is also determined by *what* a man does as well as the expertness with which he does it; the thing done must be esteemed by those capable of judging its merits. From this point of view, men of genius, according to Galton, are those "whom the whole intelligent part of the nation mourn when they die, who deserve a public funeral, and whom future ages rank as historical characters." But with his own intuitive genius Galton realized that it is not possible to define various degrees of ability, however great and however measured, in terms other than those of relative position. To Galton, a genius was one who with regard to estimated ability attained a position of one in a million, just as "an eminent man was one who reached the position attained by one person in 4000." Not being concerned in his studies of *Hereditary Genius* with other levels of intelligence he had no interest in defining dull, average, or even superior. But if he had, it is clear that he would have defined them in a very similar way. We have, in a sense, continued Galton's task of defining these remaining groups as regards intelligence. Like geniuses, the average, dull and defective individuals are persons who, on a particular intelligence scale, reach a position attained by one person in such and such total number. Our statistical notation is somewhat different from Galton's, but it can be readily translated into his. Thus, our average individual is one who attains a position of plus 1 to minus 1 P.E. from the mean, which is the same thing as the position attained by 1 in every 2 persons. A superior person is one who attains a position of plus 2 to plus 3 P.E. above the mean, which is the equivalent of saying that he is 1 person in 15, and so on with our other categories. Our scales do not pretend to measure genius. The highest rating we have is that of very superior intelligence, that is, a person who attains a position of 3 or more P.E.'s from the mean. This is a position attained by

---

[3] For other concepts of genius, see this author's *Range of human capacities* (521).

1 person in every 50. It is possible for individuals to obtain scores on our scales which would give them higher ranking, but we are rather reluctant about calling a person a genius on the basis of a single intelligence test score.

The statistical concept of intelligence and its logical implications are extremely difficult for some people to accept because at times it apparently leads to impractical if not absurd consequences. Such conclusions do not devolve from the concept itself but may result from an incomplete understanding of it. This is perhaps best illustrated by the reactions of certain psychologists to the question of the need for special norms for special groups. Clearly, the statistical definition of intelligence implies that norms obtained on any particular sample are valid only for such groups as the sampled population represents. It does not limit the *size* of the subsequent groups to which the norms can be applied; these may be as large as the representativeness of the tested sample provides for; but it does put a restriction on the type of individual who may be included for classificatory purposes. Thus, test norms obtained on Englishmen cannot be used for classifying Fiji Islanders.[4] This is obvious to everybody. The principle involved, however, becomes less obvious when applied to less divergent groups, for example, the use of identical test norms for Negroes which are identical to tests originally standardized on white populations; it becomes still less so when the differentiae which might distinguish the groups, such as nationality, economic condition and social status, are themselves hypothetical. Nevertheless, the limitations still hold. If, for example, social status *were* a factor that significantly influenced these scores, norms obtained on any particular social group could not be used on any other which differed significantly from it with respect to this factor. If they were used, the terms average, defective and superior would lose their statistical meaning.

Failure to understand this fundamental implication of the statistical concept of intelligence inevitably leads to confusion. You cannot on the one hand agree to define intelligence in terms of relative position and then disregard the rules by which such a classification is governed. When you do, incongruous and absurd consequences are inevitable. Thus, L. S. Holling-

---

[4] It might be argued that this limitation holds only for Fiji Islanders in the Fijis and does not apply to a Fiji Islander in London. Here he has to match his wits with the average Englishman and could therefore be legitimately tested by the same tests which we used on any other Londoner. The rejoinder is valid if by intelligence we mean intelligence as the Englishman conceives it. With this definition the Fiji Islander might well disagree. As scientists, we should at least allow him the opportunity of offering his own. It is possible that an Englishman tested with a Fiji Islander's test might not do very well either. The problem is obviously more complicated than this simplified statement of the case indicates. But we cannot dilate upon it without entering into a discussion which would carry us far beyond the scope of this book.

worth (256), rejecting the idea of separate norms for separate social classes, writes: "If carried out to its logical conclusion this would mean that by measuring the inmates of schools for the feeble-minded, we might obtain a norm which would be applicable to such inmates, on the basis of which they could be classified as 'normal'." This statement seems a conclusive argument, but it actually shows only how imperfectly its author has grasped the statistical connotation of intelligence. She is quite correct in inferring that on the basis of norms obtained from an institution for the feeble-minded, the average defective would rate as an individual of "normal" intelligence. Indeed, it is even conceivable that when classified on the basis of norms obtained from Fiji Islanders, many of the individuals of such an institution[5] might have to be classified as of superior intelligence. But what Dr. Hollingworth failed to see is that norms obtained on the feeble-minded inmates of a certain institution would be valid only for that institution, and that alone. The answer to Dr. Hollingworth's quandary is that the subjects of her illustrative institution are not a separate but a selected population. Her subjects are the tail end of our larger population which, for classification purposes, have been set apart. They are not mental defectives because they happen to be in an institution for the feeble-minded; they are in an institution for the feeble-minded because they are mental defectives.

The great advantage of using the IQ's as a basis for mental classification is that it does not permit us to lose sight of the fact that all measures of intelligence are necessarily relative. Nevertheless, for certain practical purposes, it is sometimes necessary to use test results *as if* they did represent absolute quantities. This is the situation when we use aptitude tests as measures of mental efficiency. In testing aptitudes, we may set up a minimal passing mark and then use this minimum as a standard for calculating indices of efficiency. The same sort of application may be made of intelligence tests. We may say, for example, that in order to be a good teacher or a good mechanic, a subject must have a minimal intelligence test score of such and such an amount. If now the IQ is used as a measure of the subject's intelligence, it is clear that the denominator used in calculating it assumes the role of the minimum score in the case of the aptitude test; and, if this denominator is constant, it will partake of all the properties of an absolute measure. Such application of the IQ is permissible, but when it is used in this way it is important to recognize that the IQ has been transformed into an E.Q. (efficiency quotient).

We have already referred to the difference between intelligence quotients and efficiency quotients. An intelligence quotient measures a person's ability relative to those of individuals of his own age group. For this com-

[5] Particularly if it were one "specializing" in high-grade defectives.

parison the entire group is assumed to be statistically homogeneous. In the case of an efficiency quotient we are not interested either in the person's age or any other factors which influence the IQ but only as to how his abilities compare with those of a fixed standard. Our point of view would be similar to one we would take in buying a machine. Our main interest would be to ascertain whether the machine could perform the required task economically and efficiently. Provided the machine met our specifications, the kind of material used or the mode of manufacture would, in most instances, be of little consequence. We can, if we wish, treat intelligence ratings in much the same fashion, but then it is only fair that we distinguish intellectual ability as a measure of intelligence from intellectual ability as a measure of mental efficiency.[6]

Although the IQ is the best single measure of intelligence, it is neither the only nor a complete measure of it. Intelligence, like personality, is too complicated an entity to be defined by a single number. It is a function of other factors besides sheer intellectual ability. We know that this must be so, because individuals having the same IQ's may differ considerably in either their actual or potential capacity for intelligent behavior. These other factors—drive, emotional balance, persistence—are not always measurable or even easily discernible but have to be taken into account in concrete situations. In the practical classification of subjects, one often has to go beyond the point of merely obtaining an accurate IQ. Sometimes it is necessary to weigh not only the subject's obvious and measurable responses during the examination, but also the record of his behavior prior to his examination.

Our last remarks suggest that in the definitive classification of a person's intelligence we also assess the subject's past history, that is, his social, emotional and, in the case of adults, his vocational and economic adjustments.[7] The kind of life one lives is itself a pretty good test of a person's intelligence. When a life history (assuming it to be accurate) is in disagreement with the "psychometric," it is well to pause before attempting a classification on the basis of tests alone. Generally it will be found that the former is a more reliable criterion of the individual's intelligence. Inexperienced examiners are likely to neglect this fact, just as psychiatrists tend to over-emphasize it. Similar disregard of this fact is often found in individuals who engage in what we may call *apersonal* psychometrics— teachers who give group tests, school psychologists who are restricted to getting IQ's, and college professors who merely write about them. Un-

---

[6] To meet the need of those who wish to use intelligence tests as measures of mental efficiency, we have calculated what we term Efficiency Quotients for Full Scale Scores on both the W–B I and WAIS. These are given and explained in Appendix 2.

[7] Doll's Social Maturity Scale is an attempt to do this in a systematic way. See Doll: *A genetic scale of social maturity* (142).

fortunately, the medical profession, until recently, has been inclined to restrict the psychologist to just such apersonal psychometrics.[8] Even more enlightened psychiatrists often look upon an intelligence examination as they do a Wassermann test; when an IQ does not come up to expectations, they feel privileged to disregard it. Apart from the fact that an analogy between a psychometric and a Wassermann test is at best a superficial one, our experience has shown that the average psychiatrist, without special training, is no more expert in the field of intelligence diagnosis than he is in any other specialty in which he has had no training. The role of a competent psychologist is not that of a laboratory technician. His techniques are not an end in themselves, but a means of diagnosis. More important than his ability to obtain an accurate IQ is his ability to interpret it correctly.[9]

Non-measurable factors enter into the classification of all levels of intelligence, but the evaluation of them is particularly important in defining the feeble-minded group. To call a person a mental defective is a serious diagnosis. At its mildest, the result is to stigmatize the person so labeled; at its worst, it may determine whether he be institutionalized for the greater part of his life instead of being permitted to work out his salvation in the community. In the case of the child, mental deficiency involves not only the general question of educability, but the specific problem of training and treatment. In the case of an adult it may also involve the question of legal responsibility. Mental deficiency is thus a medical and legal as well as a psychological and social concept. This fact complicates the problem of classification. Each science of necessity has its own points of view, and this gives rise to the question of whether any single system of classifying mental defectives can include them all. Our next chapter will be concerned with this problem.

[8] This is generally no longer the case. Most psychiatrists now appreciate that the psychological test is a diagnostic instrument.

[9] The interpretation of psychometric results, in our opinion, is or should be the job of the psychologist who administers them. Even the familiar IQ, as we have seen, is a rather complicated quantity. It is not reasonable to throw the onus of interpretation upon the average doctor, teacher, judge and social worker to whom reports containing IQ's eventually go. Unfortunately, the common practice of sending numerical data to schools, social agencies and courts has in many instances served to deprive the psychologist of that function. The net result has been that the doctor, teacher, judge and social worker frequently take it upon themselves to do the interpretation. This is in part due to the fact that persons in administrative positions in time acquire a belief in their own expertness on a great many different subjects. In part, however, it is due to the fact that psychologists themselves have too often been remiss in the way that they present their results. A psychological report which contains two or three different IQ's accompanied by a mass of technical analysis is hardly what the lay person wants or can digest. What he wants to know is what that IQ means in terms of general or specific ability for adjustment.

Chapter 4

Concepts of Mental Deficiency

The concept of mental deficiency has, like many other concepts in psychology, undergone considerable modification since the turn of the century. This change has involved two separate though not unrelated alterations in point of view. The first pertains to the abstract definition of the term; the second, to its practical application. Psychologists have not only sought to give a more definite answer to the question "Who are the mental defectives?" but also sought to furnish quantitative methods for differentiating them. The shift in point of view has been from the older moral, medicolegal essays at abstract definition of mental deficiency to the current quantitative, statistical, practical methods of measuring it. Accordingly, a mental defective is no longer defined merely as one who because of arrested mental development is unable to handle himself or his affairs with ordinary prudence, etc., but in addition as an individual whose lack of intellectual endowment is such as to render him incapable of attaining a minimum score or rating (M.A. or IQ) on certain standardized intelligence tests.

The definition of mental deficiency in terms of attained mental age or IQ represented a marked step forward but did not completely solve the problem of practical determination. In the first place, different intelligence tests sometimes gave discrepant results, as when for example an individual examined with two different scales might attain an IQ of 64 on one and an IQ of 76 on another. Such discrepancies do not occur as often as critics of the IQ claim, but are sufficiently frequent to permit questioning of test results in any given case. Second, there is the fact that IQ's derived from different instruments may not have the same meaning, either because of differences in abilities tapped (e.g., Verbal vs. Performance) or because they define different degrees of deviancy from the mean reference base, that is to say, because the tests compared have significantly different standard deviations. These strictures also apply to IQ's used to define all other levels of intelligence. But in the case of mental deficiency the clinician

49

is more concerned about them because of the serious consequence which the label "feeble-minded" has for the individual so diagnosed.

The danger of depending upon the IQ as the sole criterion in the diagnosis of mental deficiency has often been expounded and perhaps over- rather than under-emphasized. The limitation of the IQ is not due, however, as sometimes stated, to its unreliability as a measure, but to the fact that mental deficiency is not only a psychological but also a social concept. The latter concept takes into consideration, as Doll (143) so aptly put it, "not only what the person can but also what he does do"; and what a person does or is enabled to do depends to a considerable degree upon the stimulation which he gets from his social environment. This does not imply that social deprivation is the main cause of mental deficiency but only that behavior whether appraised through tests or level of social competency may be expected to be affected by the learning experiences of the individual.

Mental deficiency, unlike typhoid fever or general paresis, is not a disease. A mental defective is not a person who suffers from a specific disease process but one who by reason of intellectual arrest or impairment is unable to cope with his environment, to the extent that he needs special care, education and institutionalization.

A mental defective is characterized not only by a lack of ability to care for himself but also by an incapacity to use effectively the abilities he does have. His actions are often not only senseless and inadequate but perverse and antisocial as well. He may be not only stupid but vicious, and the question arises why he is sometimes one and not the other. Is it due merely to the fact that he is unable to comprehend the significance of his acts or is his perverse behavior due to other deficiencies? What we are asking, of course, by these questions is whether mental deficiency is exclusively a matter of lack of intellectual ability or whether it also includes inadequacies in other aspects of the individual's endowment.

The answer is that except in the case of individuals of very low intelligence (imbeciles and idiots) it is generally necessary in making a diagnosis of mental deficiency to take into account factors other than sheer lack of intellectual ability. This is particularly true of individuals who fall psychometrically into the moron, high-grade moron and borderline defective groups. Here an IQ alone, however accurately determined, is often insufficient for a definitive classification. This is evidenced by the fact that there are many individuals with IQ's above 70 whose behavior is definitely defective, and others whose manifest adjustment is such that they cannot be so classified, in spite of a much lower IQ.

The following case is illustrative of an individual with a relatively high IQ who must nevertheless be considered a mental defective.

J. M., 26 years old, native, white, was arrested on a charge of impairing the morals of a minor (a girl of 10 years). He is reported to have made similar attempts on several previous occasions and had, for some years, been a persistent problem on this account. The family states: "We have always kept an eye on him because we felt he would get into trouble."

Physical examination: Unattractive-looking youth who appears to be younger than he is. General physical and neurological examination as well as blood, Wassermann, negative.

Psychiatric examination: Appears dull and indifferent and childish. General reactions, immature. Careless about his person, but able to take care of himself. Diagnosis: Mental defective—moron.

Psychological examination: Stanford-Binet, 13 years 8 months, IQ (15 years) 91. Scatter IX–XVI, inclusive. Except for designs (patient had bad vision), no failures below XII year level.

Work history: Patient was never able to find work for himself but his father obtained several jobs for him. These he was unable to hold for any length of time.

The case just cited, while not very common, is typical of a sizable group of subjects who while frequently seen at clinics generally manage to escape commitment. Often the subjects are sex delinquents and, more often than not, individuals who have got into trouble with the law or otherwise proved themselves incapable of meeting the ordinary exigencies of social adjustment. On psychometric examinations they may rate dull-normal, or even average. Judged by social criteria they are mentally defective.

That such a group exists has long been recognized by those dealing at first hand with delinquent and socially inadequate individuals. They are patients whom Tredgold (495) has called "individuals lacking both in prudence and moral sense" although suffering from no scholastic or educational disability. An individual falling into this group "far from being illiterate, may have quite a good range of educational requirements. He may be nimble-witted, a good conversationalist, plausible in argument and be able to give a good account of himself." In spite of this he is antisocial and requires supervision for his own welfare as well as for the protection of others. What he lacks essentially is an ordinary adaptiveness of "wisdom in the moral sense," and it is important to realize, as Tredgold insists, that such a person "is mentally defective in the usual and necessary sense of the term."

In contrast to the above, there is another group of individuals who systematically rate as mental defectives on mental tests, but who can in no way be classified in this group when diagnosed on the basis of concrete social standards, i.e., in terms of capacity to adjust to the normal demands of their social and economic environment. They are frequently illiterate and, commonly, individuals coming from social strata where opportunity for education is small, and stultifying labor the general rule. However, the first case of this type that came to our attention was a native, white

Oklahoman of 28, who had come up for individual psychological examinations because he had failed to pass the Army Alpha and Army Beta intelligence tests. On the Stanford-Binet and other scales he obtained a mental age rating of less than 8 years. Nevertheless, before entering the Army he had got along very well, was supporting a family, had been working as a skilled oil-driller for several years and, at the time of draft, was earning from $60 to $75 per week. Incidentally, he was making the grade as a soldier and would not have come to the attention of the authorities had he not failed on the psychological tests.

Cases illustrative of both types of situations just cited can be multiplied, and indeed have been reported over and over again in the literature, but they are not typical in the sense that they present any considerable proportion of individuals designated as mentally defective whether in or out of institutions.

Most mental defectives who have low IQ's, are socially incompetent, emotionally immature, show a large incidence of sensory and motor defects, and give frequent histories of organic brain pathology at birth or early childhood. On the other hand, it is equally true that there are different kinds of mental defectives, different as to the etiology or type of behavior they manifest. The reason for it is that the concept of mental deficiency is far from a single entity. It includes not only individuals with intellectual arrest obvious at birth or soon after, but many others who develop or acquire it for any one of a number of causes. It includes not only individuals who manifest their inadequacy primarily on the basis of intellectual defect, but many on the basis of continued social incompetency, and still others because of an inveterate moral obtuseness refractory to the ordinary educative processes. There is usually a certain degree of correlation between the various defects, but this correlation is not sufficiently high to make any one an unfailing diagnostic indicator of the other.

Apart from the fact that mental defectives as individuals differ widely from one another, the classification of the feeble-minded has been made especially difficult by attempts to distinguish different types of deficiency on the basis of probable etiology. Perhaps the simplest classification on this basis is that of Tredgold (495), who divided the amentias into those due to inheritance as against those due to environment. The difficulty here is that, except for a small percentage of cases, it is not always possible to make such clear-cut distinction; nor is it very useful after it has been made. A similar type of classification which, however, does not commit itself to any implied genetic relationship, and which is adopted by many American writers, is the dichotomy of congenital *vs.* acquired. A third is the classification of endogenous *vs.* exogenous, with the usual connotation implied by these terms. Still another is the classification of mental deficiency by the distinction of developmental *vs.* pathological, where developmental refers to retardation due to mental arrest not referable to any assignable cause, and pathological to those instances ascribable to trauma, infection or disease. Finally, E. O. Lewis (322), representing the more recent thinking in England, has suggested the dichotomy of subcultural *vs.* pathological, where subcultural would define a degree of mental retardation sufficient to prevent the individual from meeting the social and economic demands of his local culture, and pathological, cases identifiable as consequent to brain damage, physiological imbalance, disease, etc. In practice, the group termed subcultural overlaps the categories designated in the United States as the familial or "garden variety" of mental deficiency (443). The term subcultural is unfortunate because there is implication that culture in some way determines mental deficiency, whereas in point of fact it merely defines what level or degree of retardation a particular community uses as a criterion for it. In any case, as Penrose (395) has pointed out, the broad sense in which this term has been defined makes it applicable to most subjects now classified as feeble-minded, with the possible exception of a small percentage of imbeciles and idiots.

In contrast to the above broad dichotomies, there are the more specific and historic medical classifications in which mental deficiency is classified in terms of disease process or associated physical symptomatology. Among the more common entities so classified are cretinism, mongolism, amaurotic idiocy, phenylpyruvic oligophrenia and the mental defect associated with cerebral palsies. Similarly classified is an increasing number of defective states due to such specific infections as encephalitis, German measles (Rh factor), and others. While this base of classification is useful for medical nosology, it spans too large a range of overlapping bands or degrees of mental retardation to be psychologically discriminating. Mongolian idiots, for example, are for the most part not individuals functioning at the idiot level of intelligence but include primarily imbeciles and midgrade morons. In any event, the medical classifications comprehend only a small fraction of those diagnosable as feeble-minded, and even when there is a close association between organic symptomatology and mental defect, it is generally more useful to evaluate this defect on the basis of level of intellectual functioning than on the basis of the associated physical stigmata. This would seem to be particularly true in one large group of intellectually arrested individuals, namely, that broadly encompassed by the term *cerebral palsy*.

Cerebral palsy (in children) is a disorder of the central nervous system caused by brain damage and most often associated with prenatal or birth trauma. Although the disorder is usually described as congenital there is apparently no hereditary or familial factor.[1] Its most general physical symptoms (530) are cerebral spasticity (infantile spastic diplegia), paraplegic rigidity, unilateral or bilateral hemiplegia, and chorioathetosis; psychologically, it is characterized by disturbances in perceptual and intellectual areas accompanied by varying degrees of mental retardation. Estimates of the incidence of mental deficiency in children with cerebral palsy have varied from 20 to 80 per cent. The lower figure probably reflects the tendency of many physicians to withhold making the diagnosis of mental deficiency in cerebral palsies because of a fairly considerable number of cases in which there is no accompanying mental retardation [20 per cent of subjects with cerebral palsy testing at average or above average intelligence (254)]. The presence of disabling motor symptoms and the consequent difficulty of administering standard tests to patients with cerebral palsy have also led to the view that accurate appraisal of the individual's intelligence by these means may be unreliable, with a consequent tendency to disregard findings that result in unfavorable intelligence ratings. Hill (254) has pointed out that most parents and some physicians seem to find it more satisfying to have a child diagnosed as having suffered a brain injury, rather than as a mental defective. "In the description of their child's handicap there appears to be an implicit faith on the part of parents that possession of brain damage increases the chances of eventual normal behavior." This hope is unjustified. Even if one takes the conservative figure of 50 per cent as the proportion of children with cerebral palsy who are seriously retarded mentally, the chances of normal development of such children is still discouragingly small.[2]

Efforts to differentiate mental defect exclusively in terms of causes lead, as we have just seen, to misevaluation and sometimes even to bypassing of the incident defect. An individual is no less (or more) defective if his mental arrest or impairment is due to prenatal rather than postnatal causes, to congenital lack rather than as a consequence of infectious disease in later life or to a developmental arrest of unknown origin. What is important is the determination of the amount of mental retardation and the degree to which the affected individual is thereby incapacitated. For appraisal of the latter, due consideration must be given to the environmental demands to which the individual needs to adjust and to the level of social acceptability of the individual's behavior (performance). In-

---

[1] The neurological view is that "there is some intrauterine influence which prevents or inhibits subsequent development" (530).

[2] Moreover, the training of cerebral palsy patients is much more difficult than that of the "garden variety," and the chances of returning to the community considerably less (443).

dividuals with equal degree of retardation, for example, have a better chance to adjust in a rural than in an urban community, but this does not mean that their defects were socially or culturally determined. A distinction must be made between cause and convenience. In World War II, about four times as many men were rejected for military service by U. S. Army draft boards as were rejected by comparable agencies in Australia. Could one infer from this fact that there were four times as many more inadequate individuals in the respective male populations of the two countries? Hardly so. The reason why the draft boards in the United States rejected many more than the Australian Selective Service was that they had a much greater man power to choose from and therefore could afford to be more discriminating. Much the same considerations enter into the definition of mental deficiency. Arbitrary and callous as it may seem, the definition of mental deficiency in terms of social criteria is a function of the number of individuals which a given community can afford to call so, that is, is able to institutionalize, or believes ought to be institutionalized if it had the resources to do so.

After our insistence, as in the early part of this chapter, upon the importance of social factors in mental deficiency, our last conclusion may strike the reader as a disturbing, if not a damaging, admission. It is. Practically, mental deficiency is a social and economic as well as a psychological diagnosis. But in a basic sense the causes of mental deficiency are neither social nor economic. They are primarily biological, physiological and to some extent genetic, although demonstrably influenced by a variety of other factors. Physiological and biological factors are obviously operative in cases of mental deficiency involving cretinism, phenylpyruvic oligophrenia, cerebral palsy and Mongolian idiocy, but they are also in evidence, though not so clearly, in the predominant familial or "garden variety" types of feeble-mindedness. This does not mean that social deprivation and cultural impact or lack of it may not affect a child's performance on tests of intelligence, but recent studies (559) attesting to this fact have been quite misleading. They have sought to show that emotional and social deprivation can impair the maturation and development of an individual to a point at which he will appear to be mentally defective—which is true— but they have further implied that these factors can account for most cases of mental deficiency—which is false. For even if the data presented are left unchallenged, the fact remains that these data are representative of only a very small proportion of individuals currently diagnosed as feeble-minded.

It is important to distinguish between educability, trainability and cure as a diagnostic criterion. On the one hand, there is much evidence that mental defectives can be educated and trained to a much greater extent than has been hitherto achieved. It is also true that many more severely mentally retarded individuals could be returned as useful members to the community. But the matter of "cure" is quite another question. To the best of evidence available, mental deficiency, if established, cannot be cured in the sense that a mental defective can be given more intellect or made normal by known therapeutic agents. And on this matter advocates of chemo- and endocrine therapies have by their implications, if not by by expressed claims, been even more misleading than the all-out environmentalists. What has been shown, as for example in recent studies with glutamic acid (552), is that by the use of certain drugs it is possible to raise a subject's IQ by some 10 to 15 points in a significant number of cases and for a defined period of time. But whether this is due primarily to the drug or other concomitant factors has not been demonstrated. What was found in the early glutamic acid studies, as in the case of other drugs, was that glutamic acid improved the behavioral pattern of the subjects, including their ability to respond to test situations. In this respect its action has been similar to the effect of thyroid extract in cases of cretinism or of some of the tranquilizing drugs in emotionally disturbed children. But in neither case has it been shown that these drugs have been able to transform a mental defective into an individual of normal or near normal intelligence.

The fact that mental deficiency is not curable does not, of course, imply that it is due to a specific genetic defect, any more than the fact that it is influenced by environment proves it is an acquired disability. Both environment and heredity obviously play important roles in the etiology of mental deficiency. Environment may be said to be a cause of mental deficiency in the sense that trauma and disease can produce mental arrest or retardation; heredity, in the sense that the incidence of mental deficiency in parents, siblings and blood relatives of diagnosed defectives has been found systematically greater than in the corresponding collaterals of the general population. Where ascribable to heredity, the "inherited" feeble-mindedness must be regarded as a sort of general mental inadequacy and not as a specific defect. This follows from the fact that general intelligence is not a simple genetic trait like hemophilia or albinism, and therefore cannot be expected to follow the Mendelian law. From a genetic point of view, intelligence is not a discrete entity but "represents the combined effect of a great number of genes" (Penrose, 395).

Irrespective of the posited causes of mental deficiency, one of the most important problems that still remains is how to diagnose and evaluate it. We have already discussed possible approaches to this problem, but whatever one's orientation, one must inevitably face the question as to how to define mental arrest and retardation operationally. The important contribution of psychometrics has been that this can best be done in terms of

TABLE 5

Classification of mental defectives according to IQ's (WAIS)

Classification	IQ Range	Percentage Included	Probable Error
Moron.................	69–50	1.9	−3 to −5
Imbecile..............	49–30	9.32	−5 to −7
Idiot...................	29 and below	0.002	−7 and below

TABLE 6

Actual and theoretical proportions of defectives in a state institution, testing at Different IQ levels

Classification	IQ Range	Actual	Theoretical
		%	%
Moron.................	69–50	36.4	85.5
Imbecile..............	49–30	33.5	14.4
Idiot.................	29 and below	29.4	0.1
Total...............		99.3	100.0

* Adapted and converted from data given by Dayton (131a). The IQ's are Stanford-Binet IQ's, but range limits are those used in the classification of the Wechsler Scales.

defined levels and amount of intellectual ability. In practice, this means reliance on objective tests of intelligence. Intelligence tests, to be sure, have limitations, but to date offer the most effective basis for the classification of mental defectives. Much will depend on what tests one uses, much more on one's concept or definition of the abnormal. So far as measured intelligence is concerned, an abnormal individual is one who falls at the extremes; in the case of mental deficiency, at the low end of the normal curve of distribution. Which norms and which deviations should be used to define levels of mental deficiency will vary from time to time and from place to place. At present, a definition which includes approximately the lowest 2 per cent of the population would seem to be a reasonable definition of that segment of the population which could be justifiably described as mentally defective. The recommended cut-off of the lowest 2 per cent to define the mentally defective group, minimal as it may seem, still adds up to a great number of people[3] when the population of an entire country is envisaged. A further breakdown into different grades of feeble-mindedness is therefore sometimes desirable. Such a breakdown in terms of WAIS IQ levels is given in Table 5. For some purposes, finer subdivisions may be

[3] In the case of the United States this total would amount to somewhat over 3 million defectives.

required and these can be obtained by using intermediate, statistically defined limits, but the suggested dichotomies should generally be sufficient for most diagnostic needs.

One additional remark needs to be made with regard to the utilization of psychometric classifications of intelligence, namely, that they are only one of the bases for the commitment of individuals to institutions. In general, it will be found that most communities will have resources for committing only the lower grades of defectives. Accordingly, the percentage of mental defectives given for each of the specified categories in Table 5 will not necessarily, and indeed not generally, correspond to the incidence of those in institutions for the feeble-minded. Imbeciles and idiots regularly constitute a disproportionate number of institutionalized defectives. For example, in the 1939 census of the institutionalized defectives in the State of Massachusetts, approximately two-thirds of all the inmates were imbeciles and idiots, and only one-third morons or higher. The actual distribution of defectives in the Massachusetts State institutions classified according to IQ is shown in Table 6.

PART II

The Wechsler Bellevue and The Wechsler

Adult Intelligence Scales

Chapter 5

Selection and Description
of Tests

In this chapter we propose to discuss some general questions relating to the selection of tests of intelligence, the nature and character of tests finally used in the construction of the author's Adult Scales and the implied abilities measured by the tests selected. Omitted for the most part will be questions pertaining to the populations tested and the techniques of standardization, since these are now treated separately in the manuals designed for the administration of the Scales.[1]

The first problem that confronts any one attempting to devise an intelligence scale is that of deciding upon the tests that should be included in the battery. This task is not a simple one, for, in addition to the necessity for fulfilling certain statistical criteria, there are a number of general considerations which, independent of all other factors, restrict one's choice to a greater or lesser degree. One of these is the author's defined or implied view as to the nature of intelligence. Thus, if he believes that intelligence involves primarily the ability to perceive logical relations and to use symbols, he is very likely to favor tests calling for verbal, arithmetical and, in general, abstract reasoning abilities. If he believes intelligence also involves abilities to handle "practical situations," he is very likely to include some tests calling for performance and manipulative abilities.

The choice of tests is further restricted by the special requirements of the various types of scales themselves. Certain tests, for example, which are suitable for age scales cannot be used satisfactorily for point scales, and vice versa. Thus items involving psychomotor ability, such as tying a bow knot or copying a diamond, are found excellent for age scales, but are almost useless for continuous point scales, not only because of their limited range but also because of the fact that by increasing their complexity one alters the type of ability measured by the tests. For example,

---

[1] *Wechsler Adult Intelligence Scale Manual* (524). *Measurement of Adult Intelligence*, 3rd Ed. (517).

at age 7, ability to copy a diamond is a very good indication of the child's intelligence, but if we increase the complexity of this task, say by demanding the reproduction of a bisected rhomboid, we succeed in making the test more difficult but add little to its discriminative value as a test of intelligence. If we make the task still more difficult, we are likely to wind up with a test that measures primarily some specialized or even "new" ability. In this connection, it may be noted that the same difficulty inheres in all tests to a greater or lesser degree. Beyond certain points, every test ceases to be an effective measure of the capacity which it was originally designed to measure, either because other factors begin to enter into the relationship or because the curve of its measured function tends to reach an asymptotic level. Thus memory span for digits correlates rather well with (global measures of) intelligence, roughly up to the ability to repeat six or seven digits forward, but beyond this point it becomes more and more a test of sheer rote memory.

What is true for tests taken individually is true of them when combined into scales. All mental scales eventually reach a point or level beyond which increasing scores show relatively little correlation with intelligence, as originally defined. That is inevitable. But, of course, different scales may, and do, differ considerably as regards the location of the point where they cease to be effective measures of intelligence. Naturally, every author of a scale seeks to extend this limit as far as possible, but if the range of the scale is at all wide, this desire to extend its limits entails serious restrictions in the choice of material. For example, certain tests cannot be used because of limited "ceiling"; others, because they fail to discriminate at lower levels; still others, because beyond certain points they cease to measure what they originally purported to measure.[2]

Apart from the matter of age, suitability, interest of appeal and power to discriminate at different levels of ability, the most important fact about any test is its over-all merit as a good measure of intelligence. Here, *a priori*, assumptions can be very misleading. Thus, simple tests of sensory discrimination often prove to be very good, while items demanding abstract reasoning are sometimes very poor measures. In general, tasks of a puzzle nature and items calling for esoteric knowledge or special ability are of uncertain value. Nor are statistical criteria alone sufficient. Two items may be of equal difficulty in terms of the frequency with which they are passed or failed, yet differ significantly as measures of intelligence. Statistical reliability must be supplemented by clinical validity. Items selected for tests of intelligence, especially those designed for adults, in addition to

---

[2] This limitation may be circumvented in part by age scales, such as the Binet, but such a test battery does not really constitute a single continuous scale; it emerges rather as a series of separate scales tied together by overlapping limits.

meeting statistical and empirical criteria, must have common sense appeal, that is, must not be tricky or appear foolish or unfair to the examinee. Inclusions of items in tests which do not meet this requirement have often aroused skepticism toward intelligence tests as a whole. This skepticism is in general unwarranted, but the strictures call attention to the multiplicity of factors that may impair the usefulness of a test. As a rule, tests that discriminate well at low levels of intelligence are not likely to do so at upper levels, and vice versa.

Before a final choice was made about the tests to be included in the initial standardization of the Wechsler Bellevue Scale, four procedures were followed: (1) A careful analysis was made of the various standardized tests of intelligence already in use. These were studied with special attention to authors' comments with reference to the type of functions measured, the character of the population on which the scales were originally standardized and the evidence of the test's reliability. (2) An attempt was made to evaluate each test's claim to validity on the basis of correlations with (a) other recognized tests and (b) empirical ratings of intelligence. The latter included teachers' estimates, ratings by army officers (as in the case of the Army Alpha and Beta) and estimates of business executives (in the case of various tests which had been tried out in industry). (3) An attempt was made to rate the tests on the basis both of our own clinical experience and of others. (4) Some two years were devoted to the preliminary experimental work of trying out various likely tests on several groups of known intelligence level.

On the basis of the data obtained with the above procedures, 12 tests were selected, 11 presently to be described and the Cube Analysis.[3] These were given to the various populations to be described in the next chapter, and they form the basis of our several scales. The Cube Analysis test was discarded after being given to over 1000 subjects because it showed large sex differences, proved difficult to get across to subjects of inferior intelligence and because it tapered off abruptly at the upper levels.[4] On the other hand, the Vocabulary Test was not added until a substantial proportion of our subjects had already been examined, and for this reason was originally designated as an alternate test on Form I of the W–B Scale. In the case of the WAIS, a vocabulary test was administered from the start to all subjects, and it is incorporated as a regular subtest in the Verbal battery.

The final battery of tests included in the original Wechsler Bellevue

[3] Test 3 of the Army Beta.

[4] Apparently others have had less discouraging results with the Cube Analysis test; it was included in the Army GCT (World War II). We still think that the test has serious shortcomings.

Scale and maintained in its present revision consists of six Verbal and five non-verbal or Performance tests as follows: (1) an information test, (2) a general comprehension test, (3) a memory span test (digits forward and backward), (4) an arithmetical reasoning test, (5) a similarities test, (6) a vocabulary test, (7) a picture arrangement test, (8) a picture completion test, (9) a block design test, (10) an object assembly test and (11) a digit symbol test. The grouping of the subtests into Verbal (1–6) and Performance (7–11), while intending to emphasize a dichotomy as regards possible types of ability called for by the individual tests, does not imply that these are the only abilities involved in the tests. Nor does it presume that there are different kinds of intelligence, *e.g.*, verbal, manipulative, etc. It merely implies that these are different ways in which intelligence may manifest itself. The subtests are different measures of intelligence, not measures of different kinds of intelligence, and the dichotomy into Verbal and Performance areas[5] is only one of several ways in which the tests could be grouped.

Apart from technical considerations (suitability for age level, ease of scoring, administration, etc.), final selection of tests was based primarily on 3 considerations: (1) that previous studies should have shown that the tests correlated reasonably well with composite measures of intelligence, (2) that the tests as a group encompassed sufficient diversity of function so as not to favor or penalize subjects with special abilities or disabilities and (3) that the nature and character of subjects' failures on the tests have some diagnostic implications.

The last criterion seeks to take into account the fact that, though subjects may obtain identical scores, they may arrive at them in quite different ways, and that this difference may be important. Two answers to a given question may be equally correct (or incorrect) but differ much as regards what they tell us about the background, attitudes, orientation of the subject and the extent to which these may influence the response.

If test performance is multi-determined, as it seems to be, it is extremely useful to have indication of the presence of these non-measurable factors that affect the subject's functioning level. All other things being equal, a test was considered more useful if it seemed sensitive to impacts influencing performance.

With the foregoing considerations in mind, we shall now briefly discuss the historical background and main characteristics of the tests listed.

[5] These areas presumptively, but not necessarily, coincide with the so-called primary factors of mental ability. Actually most of the Verbal tests show heavy loadings on a "V" and 4 of the 5 Performance tests on a "P" factor. For a discussion of the factorial composition of the subtests of the Scale see pp. 129–134.

Information Test

Questions formulated to tap the subject's range of information have, for a long time, been the stock in trade of mental examinations, and prior to the introduction of standardized intelligence tests they were widely used by psychiatrists in estimating the intellectual level of patients. Psychologists, however, were inclined for a long time to exclude rather than to make use of information items when devising intelligence scales. It was not until the development of the group test that such items found their way into the standardized intelligence examinations. It is probable, too, that their use here was largely inspired by practical considerations, such as the relative ease with which they lend themselves to scoring, rather than by any strong faith which psychologists may have had in the information tests as good measures of intelligence. One had always to meet the obvious objection that the amount of knowledge which a person possesses depends in no small degree upon his education and cultural opportunities. The objection is a valid one, but experience with the test has shown that it need not necessarily be a fatal or even a serious one. Much depends upon the kind of knowledge demanded of the subject and the type of question used in eliciting it.

The first strong support for range-of-information as a good measure of intelligence was furnished by the data obtained from the Army Alpha Examination. When the individual tests of the Army Alpha battery were analyzed with regard to their correlation with various estimates of intelligence, the information test, to the great surprise of many, turned out to be one of the best of the entire series. It correlated, for example, much better with the total score than did the Arithmetical Reasoning, the test of Disarranged Sentences, and even the Analogies Test, all of which had generally been considered much better tests of intelligence. Compared with the other tests on Alpha, the Information Test gave a much better distribution curve, showed a relatively smaller percentage of zero scores and showed little tendency toward piling up maximal scores at the upper end. All this could not have been an accident, particularly in view of the fact that the individual items on the Alpha Information Test left much to be desired. The fact is, all objections considered, the range of a man's knowledge is generally a very good indication of his intellectual capacity.

In practice, the value of an information test will depend in a large measure on the actual items which are included in it. There are no universal principles which can serve as unfailing guides to "good" questions. In general, the items should call for the sort of knowledge that an average individual with average opportunity may be able to acquire for himself. Thus, "What is the height of the average American woman?" is a much better question than "What state produces the most gold?"; "How far is it from New York to Paris?" much better than "What is the distance from the earth to the sun?". In general, specialized and academic knowledge is best avoided. "What is a tetrahedron?" and "What is the difference between an epic and a sonnet?" are poor questions, even for upper levels of intelligence. So are historical dates, names of famous people, whether of statesmen or movie actresses. But there are many exceptions to the rule, and in the long run each item must be tried out separately.

The W–B I Information Test contains 25 questions, the WAIS Information Test 29, each representing a selection from a much larger list. The method employed in choosing the items was to present the questions, generally in sets of 25 to 30, to groups of individuals of known intelligence level.[6] Selection of the items was then made on the basis of the incidence of successes and failures among the various groups. A question was held to be a "good" one if it showed increasing frequency of success with higher intellectual level. Of course, not all questions were equally discriminative at all levels. Thus, the question "Weeks in a year?" discriminates well between mental defectives and the borderline group and not at all between the average and superior. On the other hand, "What is the Koran?" does not discriminate at all the lower levels (since practically every individual there failed it), but showed quite significant differences between the respective percentage of average and superior individuals who passed it. In the restandardization of the WAIS a number of test items showed up as more difficult, e.g., Capital of Italy, population of the United States, and others less effective, e.g., function of the heart, discoverer of the North Pole, than others that were tried out. Altogether 7 of the original items were omitted from and 13 new ones added to the WAIS.[7]

The order in which the questions are listed approximates roughly their order of difficulty for the sample population at the time of standardization. No doubt, in different localities, the order will be somewhat different; it will also be affected to some extent by the national origin of subjects tested. Thus, "What is the capital of Italy?" is passed almost universally by persons of Italian origin irrespective of their intellectual ability. More interesting than such sources of expected variation are some findings not so easily accounted for on item difficulty. The question "What is the population of the United States?" turns out to be inexplicably hard. It is surprising how many native Americans do not know even the approximate number of inhabitants of their own country. Estimates by college graduates have ranged from 10 to 300 million. On the other hand, more people can tell

---

[6] Individuals for whom we had IQ's or other intelligence ratings.

[7] For description of changes in test items in the 1955 standardization, see *WAIS Manual* (524), p. 4.

what a thermometer is than state how many weeks there are in a year; more can give the name of the inventor of the aeroplane than of the author of *Hamlet*.

We shall now quote some comments about the test made by examiners in the field which will indicate some of the test's advantages and some of its limitations. "The test is of value because it gives the subject's general range of information." "It often indicates the alertness of the person towards the world about him." "It may reflect the social circle a person comes from; children from educated and intellectual families more often give the correct answer to the question 'Who wrote *Hamlet*?'" "It presupposes a normal or average opportunity to receive verbal information." "It is a poor test for those deprived of such opportunity as well as for those who have a foreign language handicap."

Altogether the Information Test proved one of the most satisfactory in the battery. It declines negligibly with age and correlates second highest with total score on both W–B I and WAIS.[8] Interestingly enough, it does not correlate as highly with rote memory (Digit Span) as it does with some of the purely performance tests, like Picture Arrangement or Block Design.

Comprehension Test

Tests of general comprehension have long been favorites with authors of scales, and our results justify this popularity. General comprehension questions are to be found in the original Binet as well as in all of its revisions. They occur also in many group examinations, such as the Army Alpha and the National Intelligence Tests. The test as it appears on the individual and group examinations, however, cannot be said to be equivalent. One important difference is that on the group test the subject is merely asked to select one of a number of possible answers furnished him by the examiner. On the test given individually, the subject must furnish his own answer to the questions. This way of giving the test not only reduces chance successes, but also enables the examiner to evaluate the subject's response even when it is incorrect. Indeed, one of the most gratifying things about the general comprehension test, when given orally, is the rich clinical data which it furnishes about the subject. It is frequently of value in diagnosing psychopathic personalities, sometimes suggests the presence of schizophrenic trends (as revealed by perverse and bizarre responses) and almost always tells us something about the subject's social and cultural background. The variety of replies one gets to such a question as "What would you do if you found a letter that was already sealed, stamped and addressed?", or "Why does the state require people to get a marriage license?"

[8] Inter-test correlations for all tests are given in the test manuals (517, 524).

is far greater than one would suspect, certainly far greater than an examiner could include in a multiple choice questionnaire. The following are sample replies to the first question: "Bring it to the man's house." "Leave it there." "Open it and see if there is any money in it."[9] And here are some answers to the marriage question: "To prevent bigamy." "For census purposes." "To protect the morals of the community." "To protect the honor of womanhood." "So people will know they are married."

The 12 questions which constituted the W–B I list were selected from some 30 in a manner similar to that employed for reducing the number of items on the Information Test. A few of the questions will be recognized as coming either directly from the Army Alpha or, in modified form, from those scattered among various tests discussed in the Army Memoirs. One or two turn out to be identical to some now appearing in the Terman and Merrill Revision of the Stanford—probably because they were borrowed from the same source. This duplication, however, will not seriously affect the usability of the items. Our experience has shown that the comprehension items are among those which suffer least from practice effect. It is curious how frequently subjects persist in their original responses, even after other replies are suggested to them.

In the 1955 WAIS revision, 2 of the original 10 questions were eliminated and 5 new ones were added, thus giving the WAIS Comprehension Test a total of 13 items. Of the 5 added, 3 were proverbs.[10] Proverbs were included in the comprehension series because of their reported effectiveness in eliciting paralogical and concretistic thinking. This finding was confirmed in the case of mentally disturbed subjects, but "poor" answers were also common in normal subjects; often even superior subjects found the proverbs difficult. A possible reason for this is that proverbs generally express ideas so concisely that any attempt to explain them further is more likely to subtract than add to their clarity. Most subjects when asked to give the meaning of a proverb tended to respond with specific instances rather than with equivalent abstract generalizations.

Precisely what function the Comprehension Test involves is difficult to say.[11] Off hand it might be termed a test of common sense, and it is so called on the Army Alpha. Success on the test seemingly depends on the possession of a certain amount of practical information and a general ability to evaluate past experience. The questions included are of a sort that the

---

[9] The first of these answers was given by a simple defective; the second, by a delinquent; the third, by a psychopath.

[10] The other new comprehension items are two "easy" questions introduced at the beginning of the series and designed to extend the range of the test at the lower end, and to eliminate the piling up of "O" scores for subjects at the mental defective level.

[11] Interpretation of the possible significance of the individual tests will be further discussed in the chapter on the factorial content of the Scales (Chapter 8) and the chapter on clinical diagnosis (Chapter 11).

average adult may have had occasion to answer for himself at some time, or heard discussed in one form or another. They are for the most part stereotypes with a broad common base. In this connection, it is of interest to note that in the foreign adaptations of the Scale the translators have not found it necessary to make any important changes either in the form or in the content of the questions. The questions involve no unusual words, so that individuals of even limited education generally have little difficulty in understanding their content. Nevertheless, poor verbalizers often make low scores on the test.

The Comprehension Test holds up well with age and when it begins to fall off, drops less than most of the other tests. It correlates best with Information and Vocabulary and least well with Digit Span and Object Assembly. Correlations with Full Scale are as follows. W–B I: ages 20–34 = 0.66, ages 35–49 = 0.68; WAIS: ages 25–34 = 0.77, ages 45–54 = 0.82.

Arithmetical Reasoning Test

The ability to solve arithmetical problems has long been recognized as a sign of mental alertness. Even before the introduction of psychometrics, it was used as a rough and ready measure of intelligence. Now most intelligence scales include items calling for arithmetical reasoning in some form. The inclusion of such items is fully justified; arithmetical reasoning tests correlate highly[12] with global measures of intelligence.

In addition to being a good measure of general intelligence the Arithmetical Reasoning Test enjoys the advantage of being easily devised and standardized. But its merits are lessened by the fact that it is influenced by education and occupational pursuit. Clerks, engineers and businessmen usually do well on arithmetic tests, while housewives, day laborers and illiterates are often penalized by them. Another shortcoming of the test is that individual scores may be affected by fluctuations of attention and transient emotional reactions.

The general appeal and interest which the Arithmetical Test has for most adults should be mentioned. Most adults regard arithmetic questions as a task worthy of a grownup. They may be embarrassed by their inability to do certain problems, but they almost never look upon the questions as unfair or inconsequential. Perhaps our choice of problems has something to do with this attitude. All the problems touch upon commonplace situations or involve practical calculations. Moreover, they have been so devised as to avoid verbalization or reading difficulties.[13] The computation skills required to solve most of our problems are not beyond those taught in the

---

[12] They do so, however, to a lesser degree than certain other tests that enjoy less popularity, e.g., the Information and Similarities Tests.

[13] The last two questions on the W–B I are read by the subject; on the WAIS, all arithmetic items are presented orally by the examiner.

grade school or what the average adult could acquire by himself in the course of day-to-day transactions.

A practical consideration in drawing up an arithmetic test as part of an intelligence battery, as indeed in other tests so used, has to do with the number of items that need to be used. The number of items included must be sufficient to make the test reliable, but not so numerous as required for an aptitude examination. The 1939 W–B standardization contains 10 graded items. These on the whole proved adequate but seemed to need reinforcement at the lower end at some intermediate points. Items at these levels were accordingly added to the 1955 WAIS standardization, thus increasing both the range and reliability of the test.[14]

Although the influence of education on the individual's ability to answer arithmetical problems lessens the value of the test as a measure of adult intelligence, the effect of the interrelation between the two factors is not entirely negative. It appears that children who do poorly in arithmetical reasoning often have difficulty with other subjects. A number of examiners reported they were sometimes able to diagnose educational abilities on the basis of scores obtained on this test, especially when supplemented by scores obtained on the general Information Test. The combined scores of these two tests frequently furnished an accurate estimate of the subject's scholastic achievement.

The correlations between the Arithmetical Reasoning Test and Total Scale scores are neither among the highest nor the lowest obtained. They vary with the age at which they are calculated, being generally higher at the upper than lower ages. The correlations of Arithmetic with Full Scale Score are the following: For the W–B I: ages 20–24 = 0.63, ages 35–49 = 0.67; for the WAIS: ages 25–34 = 0.73, ages 45–54 = 0.81.

Memory Span for Digits

Perhaps no test has been so widely used in scales of intelligence as that of Memory Span for Digits. It forms part of the original Binet Scale and all the revisions of it. It has been used for a long time by psychiatrists as a test of retentiveness and by psychologists in all sorts of psychological studies. Its popularity is based primarily on the fact that it is easy to administer, easy to score, and specific as to the type of ability it measures. Nevertheless, as a test of general intelligence it is among the poorest. Memory span, whether for digits forward or backward, generally correlates poorly with other tests of intelligence. The ability involved contains

---

[14] Another change introduced was the addition of a time bonus to two of the more difficult items. However, though the number of items receiving time credit was increased from two to four, the proportion of time to accuracy credits was actually decreased by some 15 per cent.

little of g and, as Spearman has shown, is more or less independent of this general factor. Our own results confirm these observations. For a long time we considered the desirability of eliminating the test from our battery altogether, but finally decided to retain it for the following reasons: (1) Although Memory Span for Digits backward and forward is on the whole a poor measure of intelligence, it is nevertheless an extremely good test at the lower levels. Except in cases of special defects or organic disease, adults who *cannot* retain 5 digits forward and 3 backward will be found, in 9 cases out of 10, to be feeble-minded or mentally disturbed.[15] (2) Special difficulty with the repetition of digits forward or backward is often of diagnostic significance. Obvious examples are the memory defects which constitute clinical symptoms in certain organic diseases and other types of cases. A marked falling off in memory span is often one of the earliest indications of mental impairmet.[16]

Low scores on the Memory Span Test when not associated with organic defect can be due to anxiety[17] or inattention. In either case, difficulty in the reproduction of digits correlates with lack of ability to perform tasks requiring concentrated effort. Individuals with these defects seem to have a special difficulty repeating digits backward. This deficiency is sometimes referred to as lack of mental control. The term is rather unfortunate because it implies, and is often interpreted as meaning, not only an inability to hold things before the mind, but also a lack of self-control, in the broader sense. Both are over-generalizations. Nevertheless, the failure to repeat digits backward does often correlate with difficulties of attention and lack of ability to perform tasks which require concentrated effort. Knowledge of this fact is frequently an aid to clinical diagnosis. The question, however, still remains whether the digit-span test might not better be used as a supplementary test rather than be included in the general intelligence test battery.

It should be noted that, as included in the W–B and WAIS batteries, Memory Span for Digits Forward and Memory Span for Digits Backward

---

[15] Rote memory more than any other capacity seems to be one of those abilities of which a certain absolute minimum is required, but excesses of which seemingly contribute relatively little to the capacities of the individual as a whole. The Memory Span for Digits Test has the great merit of quickly indicating whether an individual has that relative minimum.

[16] Wells (535) has pointed out that the relation between the number of digits that an individual can repeat forward and those he repeats backward is often of diagnostic value in certain organic cases. Alcoholics with Korsakoff syndrome, for example, do much better on digits forward than on digits backward. Where the discrepancy is great, it often indicates mental deterioration.

[17] For further discussion of the effect of anxiety on this and other tests see Siegman (456).

have been combined into a single test. The reasons for doing this were twofold. The first concerns the limited range of each series when taken separately. On digits forward, a score range of only 4 points (repeating 5, 6, 7, or 8 digits) includes about 90 per cent of the adult population, and about the same percentage is included by the ability to repeat 4 to 6 digits backward. Such a range is obviously too small for a point scale. By combining the scores obtainable on both into one test measure, we succeeded not only in extending the test's range, but also in closing up wide gaps that obtain between successive scores when the tests are used singly. The second reason for combining digits forward and backward into a single test was to limit the contribution of the memory factor to the total scale. If incorporated as separate tests, they would have contributed $\frac{1}{6}$ instead of $\frac{1}{11}$ of the total score.

Although Memory Span for Digits is a familiar test, it is of interest to include comments made by various examiners regarding it. "The effectiveness of this test depends upon calmness and strict attention to the material presented. Care must be taken not to give the test when the individual is fatigued." "The test is sometimes influenced by the auditory factor. People with defective hearing sometimes fail on it because they do not hear the numbers distinctly." "It is really best for picking out mental defectives." The last comment corroborates the point previously stressed, namely, that many abilities enter into intellectual functioning only as necessary minima.

Ordinarily, an adult who cannot repeat at least 4 or 5 digits forward is either organically impaired or mentally defective. Nevertheless, mental defectives sometimes do well on the Memory Span Test. On the whole, a good rote memory is of practical value in many situations, but beyond a certain point has little relation to global intelligence. This is shown by the fact that the Memory Test correlates least not only with Full Scale Score but also with most of the other tests of the Scale. It also shows greater decline with age than most other abilities.

Correlations of memory span with Full Scale Score are as follows. W–B I ages 20–24 = 0.51, ages 35–49 = 0.52; WAIS: ages 25–34 = 0.64, ages 45–54 = 0.68.

Similarities Test

Although encountered as occasional items on tests of intelligence, similarities questions have been used very sparingly in the construction of previous scales. It is hard to account for this neglect, as all correlational studies show that a well constructed similarities test is one of the most reliable measures of intellectual ability. A possible reason for the bypassing of the test may be that, at first glance, it impresses one as a kind of task that would be greatly influenced by language and word knowledge. Practical experience, however, has shown that while a certain degree of verbal comprehension is necessary for even minimal performance, sheer word knowledge need only be a minor factor. More important is the individual's ability to perceive the common elements of the terms he is asked to compare and, at higher levels, his ability to bring them under a single concept. It is possible to increase the difficulty of test items without restorting to esoteric or unfamiliar words.

The list of similarities used in W–B I contained 12 paired words. In the 1955 WAIS standardization, 2 of the original 12 similarities were dropped and 3 new ones added, making for a net increase of 1 in the list administered. Some changes were also made in the placement of the items in order to comply with the newly established order of difficulty. The words used in each of the standardizations and their order of presentation are given below.

W–B I		*WAIS*	
Orange	Banana	Orange	Banana
Coat	Dress	Coat	Dress
Dog	Lion	Axe	Saw
Wagon	Bicycle	Dog	Lion
Daily paper	Radio	North	West
Air	Water	Eye	Ear
Eye	Ear	Air	Water
Egg	Seed	Table	Chair
Wood	Alcohol	Egg	Seed
Poem	Statue	Poem	Statue
Praise	Punishment	Wood	Alcohol
Fly	Tree	Praise	Punishment
		Fly	Tree

The Similarities Test has several merits. It is easy to give and appears to have an interest appeal for the average adult. It is the kind of test which has been recognized by all investigators as containing a great amount of g. Over and above this, the test has certain qualitative features, the most important of which is the light that the type of response sheds upon the logical character of the subject's thinking processes. There is an obvious difference both as to maturity and as to level of thinking between the individual who says that a banana and an orange are alike because they both have a skin, and the individual who says that they are both fruit. As already noted by Terman and others, it is not until the individual approaches adult mentality that he is able to discriminate between essential and superficial likenesses. But it is remarkable how large a percentage of adults never get beyond the superficial type of response. It is for this reason that, unlike previous methods of scoring, the one employed in our scale distinguishes between superior and inferior responses by allowing different credits for each. Thus, when the subject says an orange and banana are alike because "you can eat them," and a bicycle and wagon "because they have wheels," he receives a credit of 1, whereas the responses "both are fruit" and "means of conveyance" are scored 2. This qualitative difference in response is of value not only because it furnishes a more discriminating scoring method, but also because it is often suggestive of the evenness and level of the subject's intellectual functioning. Some subjects' total scores, even when relatively good, are largely made up of 1 credits, whereas the scores of others are of an unpredictable proportion of 0, 1 and 2 credits. The former are likely to bespeak individuals of consistent ability, but of a type from which no high grade of intellectual work may be expected; the latter, while erratic, have many more possibilities.

Correlations for Similarities with Full Scale Score are among the highest. For the W–B I: ages 20–34,[18] $r = 0.73$; for the WAIS: ages 25–34, $r = 0.79$, ages 45–54, $r = 0.80$. The decline of Similarities Test Score with age occupies an intermediate position among verbal tests. It is interesting to note that although, like the Vocabulary, the Similarities Test deals with word meaning, it does not hold up nearly as well (but on this point see subsequent discussion).

Picture Arrangement Test

The Picture Arrangement Test consists of a series of pictures which, when placed in the right sequence, tell a little story. The picture series is not unlike the short comic strips found in the daily papers. The pictures are presented to the subject in a disarranged order and he is asked to put them together in the right order so that they make a sensible story. The correct order is the one originally given to the pictures by the artist.

A test of this type was first used by DeCroly (132). In 1917, several Picture Arrangement series were tried out by the Army psychologists, as subtests on a group examination, and found inadequate, but another set (the Foxy Grandpa series) ultimately found its way into the Army Performance Scale (27). It was, however, not used to any great extent. Nor have other tests of this kind had great vogue in this country, possibly because of the difficulties in scoring as well as in getting up good sequences. But recently Cornell and Coxe (116) again experimented with some picture series and included them in their scale.

The picture series of the W–B consist of 7 sets, 3 adapted from the Army Group Examinations and 4 entirely new ones selected from Soglow's

---

[18] The correlation for ages 35–49 on the W–B I is not available for the reason indicated above.

well known "King" series which appeared in *The New Yorker* magazine some years ago. Those adapted from the Army Group Tests were completely redrawn and in some instances slightly altered as to content. In the WAIS series, 1 of the W–B I items (No. 3) was eliminated and 2 new ones added. One of the new items is by the well known cartoonist Hanan; the other is a reproduction of a cartoon in a Brazilian adaptation of the tests.

The set of pictures included in our battery represents the final choice from among more than twice that number originally tried out. They were selected on the basis of interest of content, probable appeal to subjects, ease of scoring and discriminating value. Any attempt to satisfy all these conditions was bound to occasion difficulties, and in spite of the considerable labor spent before definitive choices were made, the final selection leaves much to be desired. The fault, however, is not so much with our particular selection as with the limitations inherent in all picture arrangement tests, namely their dependence upon actual content. It is of some importance whether the story told by the pictures is that of a bird building a nest or a policeman pursuing a thief in a radio car. The former is a situation a country boy may grasp at once; the latter may puzzle him a good deal. And what is true for such simple situations plays an even greater role when the story told by the pictures is more complicated. The Picture Arrangement items in both W–B and WAIS represent essentially American situations and sense of humor, and their appreciation may be expected to be influenced by cultural background. That certainly may often be the case. Nevertheless, taken as a whole, it was rather surprising to discover how few changes were introduced in foreign adaptations and translations of the test. These will be considered in our later discussions of the subtests. Cartoons appear to have an international language of their own.

In spite of certain definite limitations, the Picture Arrangement test has some very worthwhile merits. In the first place, it is the type of test which effectively measures a subject's ability to comprehend and size up a total situation. The subject must understand the whole, must get the "idea" of the story, before he is able to set himself effectively to the task. There is, of course, some trial and error experimentation, but the subject is also called upon to attempt appraisal of the total situation more than in most other tests. Secondly, the subject matter of the test nearly always involves some human or practical situation. The understanding of these situations more nearly corresponds to what other writers have referred to as "social intelligence."[19] The author, as already indicated, does not believe in such an entity. His point of view is that social intelligence is just general intelligence applied to social situations. Individuals who do fairly well on the

---

[19] Alas, both delinquents and psychopaths often do very well on this test.

Picture Arrangement seldom turn out to be mental defectives, even when they do badly on other tests.

A word as to the method of scoring. In a test of this kind the question always arises whether one should allow part credit for possible but incorrect combinations. The answer depends upon how much the test gains, that is, improves its correlations with total score when such allowance is made. In the short series the gain was practically nil; accordingly these were given either full or no credit depending upon whether they were or were not arranged in the exact way called for. For the longer series there seemed to be some advantage in allowing credit for arrangements other than those envisaged by the cartoons, and certain credits were allowed for them if they seemed to make sense. What makes sense was determined by a group of four judges who had inspected arrangements obtained from some 200 subjects. In general, the number of credits assigned to imperfect arrangements was roughly proportioned to the frequency with which the several arrangements occurred. The final credit system, nevertheless, turned out to be more or less arbitrary.

This finding was reinforced by additional studies made during the standardization of the WAIS, with the result that partial credit was abandoned in most of the Picture Arrangement series. Only the last two items are now given partial credit, and the number of alternate responses has been substantially reduced. The basis for these part-credit arrangements was their relative correlation with total test scores. On the other hand, time credits are now allowed on more of the picture series, thus increasing the test score range.

The arrangements given in the manuals cover pretty well most of the rational orders which the individual series permits. Occasionally, however, a subject does produce a different one for which he is able to give a convincing explanation, but for which no credit is allowed in the manual. In most instances, it will be found that disallowing the subject's response does not materially influence his total score on the test, but provision is made for the examiner to credit the subject with a reasonable additional score in special cases. More interesting than the question of credits allowed, in such cases, is the explanation which the subject may give for his unusual arrangement. Consistently bizarre explanations are suggestive of some peculiar mental orientation or even psychotic trend. Even after correct arrangement is made by a subject, it is often useful to ask him to explain the sequence. This procedure is not an integral part of the test but is highly recommended whenever time allows. Some examiners have found it useful to ask the subject to make up a story. With either procedure much dynamic and characterological material is often obtained, particularly if the stories are treated in the fashion of a Thematic Apperception Test (TAT) protocol.

Correlations of Picture Arrangement with Full Score are as follows. W–B I: ages 20–34 = 0.51, ages 35–49 = 0.62; WAIS: ages 25–34 = 0.77, ages 45–54 = 0.76. The test correlates unevenly and sometimes unpredictably with other subtests of the Scale, but on the whole the correlation is higher with the Performance than with the Verbal tests of the Scale.

Picture Completion Test

The name "Picture Completion" is usually associated with a test similar to the Healy Picture Completion II, in which the subject is required to complete the sense of a picture by selecting a fitting piece from among several possible choices. The Picture Completion of the W–B and WAIS tests merely require the subject to discover and name the missing part of an incompletely drawn picture. He is shown a picture, e.g., a steamship minus its funnel or a watch with its second hand missing, and asked to indicate the missing part. In its present form the test is very much like that of the Mutilated Pictures of the Binet Scale.

Tests such as the Picture Completion form a part of many group examinations.[20] Its popularity is fully deserved[21] even though the procedures used in adapting it for group testing generally limit its possibilities. One of these limitations is that the subject is required to draw in the missing part; another, that the number of items used have generally been too few and often far from satisfactory. Preliminary experiments with pictures previously used on group examinations showed that, for the most part, they were haphazardly chosen. Many of the items were much too easy and some, unusually difficult.

Suitable items for a Picture Completion Test are hard to find and present a number of difficulties. If one chooses familiar subjects, the test becomes much too easy; if one turns to unfamiliar ones, the test ceases to be a good test of intelligence because one unavoidably calls upon specialized knowledge. The 15 pictures included in the W–B I were selected from some 30 to 35 that were tried out over a period of six months with various groups of subjects of known intelligence levels. Each picture was tried out separately and admitted or rejected on the basis of its discriminating[22] value. While a few were included which did not meet all criteria, the final set of pictures chosen on the whole proved satisfactory. The tests' most serious limitation turned out to be a relatively restricted range. This limitation

[20] Among the more familiar are the Army Beta, the Pintner Non-Language, the Haggerty Delta, the Detroit Kindergarten and Kellogg-Morton Revised Beta.

[21] On the Army Beta the test correlates 0.74 with total score and 0.72 with the Stanford-Binet Mental Age.

[22] The method by which this was done was similar to that employed in selecting the General Information items.

was corrected in the WAIS standardization. The test now consists of 21 instead of 15 pictures and extends through the full weighted score range of the Performance part of the Scale. The WAIS Picture Completion retains 11 of the original W–B pictures and adds 10 new ones; 2 or 3 of the retained pictures have also been partially redrawn.

From a purely psychometric point of view the Picture Completion has several assets worth noting. It takes relatively little time to administer, is given *in toto* and may be repeated after short intervals without risk of significant practice effect. The test is particularly good in testing intelligence at the lower levels. Ostensibly it measures the individual's basic perceptual and conceptual abilities in so far as these are involved in the visual recognition and identification of familiar objects and forms. To be able to see what is missing from any particular picture, the subject must first know what that picture represents. But, in addition, he must be able to appreciate that the missing part is in some way essential either to the form or to the function of the object or picture. In a broad sense the test measures the ability of the individual to differentiate essential from non-essential details. But one must note, again, that the ability of an individual to do this depends in a large measure upon his relative familiarity with the object with which he is presented, that is to say, upon the actual content of the picture. A person who has never seen or read about a steamship cannot be expected to know that all such boats have funnels and that these are generally to be found at the center of the ship. Unfamiliar, specialized and esoteric subject matter must therefore be sedulously avoided when pictures are chosen for this test. However, this cannot be done altogether. If nothing else, there is always the factor of sex differences to be considered. For example, in examining the incidence of correct responses to series, we found that more men than women failed to detect the missing eyebrow in the picture of a girl's profile, and more women the missing thread in the drawing of the electric bulb.

Picture Completion generally correlates higher with Performance than with Verbal tests and usually shows highest loading under the visual motor factor. Nevertheless, Cohen (112) in his factorial analysis of the WAIS found it to have a specificity of its own, extractable as a separate factor, which, however, he was unable to interpret. Correlations of the Picture Completion with Full Scale Scores are: W–B I: ages 20–34 = 0.61, ages 35–49 = 0.60; WAIS: ages 25–34 = 0.78, ages 45–54 = 0.80. Interestingly enough, the test holds up with age better than any of the Performance tests, and for this reason is included as one of the "hold" tests in calculating deterioration ratios.

Block Design

The Block Design Test was originated by Kohs, who offered it as a comprehensive measure of non-verbal intelligence. The initial enthusiasm for its originator seems fully justified. Adaptations of Kohs Test now appear in a number of intelligence scales, and our own experience shows that it conforms to all criteria of a "good" test. It correlates well with a variety of criterion measures, with total scale score and with most of the subtests of the scale. It also correlates better with Comprehension, Information and Vocabulary than some of the verbal tests themselves. Oddly enough, individuals who do best on the test are not necessarily those who see, or at least follow, the pattern as a whole, but more often those who are able to break it up into small portions. In this connection, an early study by Nadel (375) on intellectual disturbances following certain (frontal lobe) brain lesions is of interest. As between "following the figure" and breaking up the design into its component parts, patients with frontal lobe lesions in contrast to the control group used the former method almost exclusively.

The Block Design Test, as adapted for the W–B I and WAIS Scales, is basically similar to that employed by Kohs in his original standardization, but its content has been modified to a considerable degree. The most important of the changes introduced pertain to the reduction in the number of test cards used and the alteration in the figure patterns which the subject is asked to reproduce. The reduced number of designs was for the obvious purpose of cutting down the time allowed for any one test on the scale. The W–B Block Design Test consists of 7 instead of 17 figures, with a consequent reduction in the time required for completing the test, from about 35 to somewhat less than 10 minutes. A change in pattern was effected, both to avoid reproduction of items used on other scales[23] and to eliminate the possible factor of color confusion. The original Kohs included figures made up of red, yellow, blue and white; the W–B I makes use of only red and white. In the WAIS standardization, the test was further modified by having all the sides painted red or white, or a one-half white and one-half red. This was done to eliminate the possible influence of the color factor, and to equate more nearly the amount of turning required by subjects for finding the faces of the blocks appropriate to the designs.

The Block Design is not only an excellent test of general intelligence, but one that lends itself admirably to qualitative analysis. One can learn much about the subject by watching "how" he takes to the task set him. Already mentioned is the matter of method that may be employed in assembling the designs, by following the figure *versus* breaking it up into

[23] The Kohs cards form part of the Grace Arthur Scale.

its component parts. There is also the difference of attitude and emotional reaction on the part of the subject. One can often distinguish the hasty and impulsive individual from the deliberate and careful type, a subject who gives up easily or becomes disgusted, from the one who persists and keeps on working even after his time is up, and so on. A number of other temperamental traits manifest themselves not infrequently in the course of a subject's performance.

The diagnostic value of the test is particularly worth mentioning. Patients with mental deterioration and seniles have particular difficulty in managing the test and often cannot complete the simplest design, however much they try. This is also true of most cases of brain disease. The difficulty here seems to be due to a lack of synthesizing ability, or loss of the "abstract approach," in K. Goldstein's sense of the term. Nadel found that in many cases of frontal lobe lesions, the patient's inability to reproduce the design could be explained on the basis of a loss of ability to "shift." Some patients seemingly did not know when they had finished, others had difficulty in attending simultaneously to color and pattern. Still others would get stuck at certain portions of the design, apparently from an inability to integrate the rest of the pattern with it. On the other hand, Eisenson has observed[24] that in many patients with aphasia there is relatively little impairment in Block Design performance. Our own view is that the role of the abstract approach has been greatly overestimated. It is, of course, reflected in certain types of cases, but in most, low scores on Block Design are due to difficulty in visual-motor organization.

Examiners' comments on the test are as follows. "The test involves the ability to perceive forms and to analyze these forms." "It involves the ability to perceive pattern." "In the Block Design, speed and success (of reproduction) is largely dependent upon the individual's ability to analyze the whole into its component parts." "Older adults do not do so well on it." "It is very good for picking out low grade people." "Artists and artisans do much better on the test than others." "The Object Assembly and Block Design Tests seem to get at some sort of creative ability." "Some subjects are penalized by the time score and by the fact that they 'haven't played with blocks for a long time.'" "This test and the Object Assembly are perceptibly influenced by a person's occupation."

Correlations of the Block Design with Full Scale Score are as follows. W–B I: ages 20–34 = 0.71, ages 35–49 = 0.73; WAIS: ages 25–34 = 0.76, ages 45–54 = 0.72, ages 65–69 = 0.74. Considering the fact that the test correlates highly with all measures of general intelligence, and yet falls off consistently with increasing age, we are inclined to interpret the finding as supporting the view that over-all intellectual ability does in fact decline

---

[24] Personal communication to author.

with age. For the same reason it may be regarded as an excellent measure of deterioration, a conclusion which is confirmed by a number of studies (267).

Digit Symbol Test

The Digit Symbol or Substitution Test is one of the oldest and best established of all psychological tests. It is to be found in a large variety of intelligence scales, and its wide popularity is fully merited. The subject is required to associate certain symbols with certain other symbols, and the speed and accuracy with which he does it serve as a measure of his intellectual ability. The one concern that presents itself in the use of the Digit Symbol Test for measuring adult intelligence is the possible role which visual acuity, motor co-ordination and speed may play in the performance of the task. Experience with the test shows that, except in cases of individuals with visual defects and specific motor disabilities, the first two are not of significant importance; but the case for motor speed cannot be discounted. We know from general observation and from some experimental studies that older persons do not write or handle objects as fast as younger persons, and what is perhaps equally important, they are not as easily motivated to do so. The problem, however, from the point of view of global functioning, is not merely whether the older persons are slower, but whether or not they are also "slowed up." In trying to resolve this point we are confronted with the following somewhat paradoxical situation. When the Digit Symbol is administered over a wide adult age range, scores on the test begin to decline earlier and to drop off more rapidly with age than other tests of intelligence. At the same time, however, the test's correlation with Full Scale scores at different ages remains consistently high. This suggests that the older persons may be penalized by speed, the penalty being "deserved" since resulting reduction in test performance is on the whole proportional to the subject's over-all capacity at the time he is tested. There is strong evidence that the older person is not only slower but also "slowed" up mentally. The question that remains is whether speed as well as power should be given weight in the evaluation of intelligence. The author's point of view is that it should, and for this reason the Digit Symbol Test has been systematically included in his intelligence scales.

Neurotic and unstable individuals also tend to do rather poorly on the Digit Symbol (as indeed on all other substitution tests). The inferiority of neurotic subjects on tests of this kind was noted as long ago as 1923, by Tendler (486). Tendler suggested that this was due to some sort of associative inflexibility in the subject, and a tendency toward mental confusion. More obviously neurotic subjects do badly on this test because they have difficulty in concentrating and applying themselves for any length of time and because of their emotional reactivity to any task requiring persistent effort. The poor performance of the neurotic represents a lessened mental efficiency rather than an impairment of intellectual ability.

The Digit Symbol Test incorporated in the W–B Scale was taken from the Army Beta.[25] This particular form of Substitution Test (originally devised by Otis) has several advantages over many of the others commonly used. One is that it comprises a sample demonstration which permits the examiner to make certain that the subject understands the task. Another is that the subject is required to reproduce the unfamiliar symbols and not the associated numerals. This fact lessens the advantage which individuals having facility with numbers would otherwise have. The only change made from the way the test is administered is in the matter of time allowance. The two minutes allowed on the Army Beta was found to be too long. There was a tendency for scores to pile up at the upper end. Reducing the time not only eliminated this shortcoming, but also improved the distribution of test scores when these were converted into standard deviation equivalents. Several different time allowances were tried out, and a period of 1½ minutes was found to give best results. Correlations of the Digit Symbol with Full Scale Scores are as follows. W–B I: ages 20–34 = 0.67, ages 35–49 = 0.69; WAIS: ages 25–34 = 0.63, 45–54 = 0.69.

Object Assembly

The Object Assembly Test consists of three or four figure form-boards (3 on the W–B, 4 on the WAIS). The W–B I "objects" comprise a *Manikin*, a *Feature Profile* and a *Hand*. The Manikin is essentially the same as that devised by Pintner and first used on the Pintner-Paterson scale (399), except that the features have been redrawn to make them more human in appearance. Our Profile resembles that used by the Pintner-Paterson test but differs from the original in several respects. It is a profile of a woman's head instead of a man's, the ear is divided into two instead of four parts, and a piece has been cut out at the base of the skull. The Hand is entirely new and was devised by the author. As presented to the subject, it consists of a mutilated hand from which the fingers and a large section of the palm have been cut away. The *Elephant* has been added to the WAIS series and was also devised by the author. It consists of a side view of a smallish pachyderm which has been cut up asymmetrically into six pieces which the subject is required to put together. Details as to method of presentation and scoring will be found in the Scale manuals.

The Object Assembly was included in our test battery after much hesitation. We wanted at least one test which required putting things together into a

[25] It likewise forms part of the original Army Performance Tests; the test has also been included in the Cornell-Coxe Performance Scale.

familiar configuration. Our experience over a long period with the commonly used form-boards had convinced us that whatever their merit when administered to children, they were often ill-adapted for testing adults. Most of the standardized form-boards are much too easy for the average adult, and at the high levels have very little discriminative value. The distribution tables[26] for these form-boards, moreover, have unusually large scatter. Taken singly, most of them have low reliability and predictive value. The Manikin and Feature Profile seemed better in this respect than most of the form-boards, but not much. Like all form-boards, they also show great practice effects.

In spite of the foregoing limitations, the Object Assembly Test has a number of compensating features, and it is primarily because of these that it was kept in the Scales. The first point to be noted is that while the test correlates poorly with most of the subtests, it does contribute something to the total score. Secondly, examination of the Object Assembly scatter diagrams shows that the low correlations it has with the other tests, are due primarily to the large deviations of a relatively small and seemingly special group of individuals. This means, perhaps, that the Object Assembly is a poor test only for certain types of individuals. If the test is appraised on the basis of criteria which are not influenced in a marked degree by the atypical individual, its rating is considerably enhanced. For example, if one considers mean scores alone, the Object Assembly shows a rather good rise with age up to about 16 years, and remains relatively stable up to age 40.

The best features of the Object Assembly, however, are its qualitative merits. Various examiners have praised the test repeatedly, because "it tells you something about the thinking and working habits of the subjects." The subjects' approach to the task may in fact be one of several kinds. The first is an immediate perception of the whole, accompanied by a critical understanding of the relation of the individual parts. This is particularly true of responses to the Manikin test, from which one can distinguish between the individual who recognizes from the start that he has a human figure to put together, and another, usually a mental defective, who has no idea what he is assembling but merely fits the pieces together by the trial and error method. A second type of response is that of rapid recognition of the whole but with imperfect understanding of the relations between the parts. This is best evidenced by the manner in which many subjects handle the Feature Profile. Still a third type of response is one which may begin with complete failure to take in the total situation, but which after a certain amount of trial and error manifestation leads to a sudden though often belated appreciation of the figure. Such performances

---

[26] For distribution tables, see Pintner-Paterson (399), pp. 97–137.

are most frequently met with in the case of the Hand. Altogether, the Object Assembly Test has a particular clinical value because it often reveals the subject's mode of perception, the degree to which he relies on trial and error methods and his manner of reaction to mistakes.

Among the comments made on the test are the following. "The Object Assembly, like the Block Design Test, seems to get at some sort of creative ability, especially if the performance is done rapidly." "Successful reproduction of the Object Assembly items depends upon the subjects' familiarity with figures and their ability to deal with the part-whole relationship." "People with artistic and mechanical ability seem to do very well on this test." "It sometimes reveals the ability to work for an unknown goal." "Some subjects continue working at putting together the Hand although they seem to have not the slightest notion as to what it is they are putting together." To this extent the tests are of value in revealing the capacity to persist at a task. Some subjects tend to give up very quickly and are discouraged by the slightest evidence of lack of success. Correlations on the Object Assembly with Full Scale Score are as follows. W–B I: ages 20–34 = 0.41, ages 45–59 = 0.51; WAIS: ages 25–34 = 0.58, ages 45–54 = 0.65.

Vocabulary Test

Contrary to lay opinion, the size of a man's vocabulary is not only an index of his schooling, but also an excellent measure of his general intelligence. Its excellence as a test of intelligence may stem from the fact that the number of words a man knows is at once a measure of his learning ability, his fund of verbal information and of the general range of his ideas. The one serious objection that could be raised against it was that a man's vocabulary is necessarily influenced by his educational and cultural opportunities. In deference to this objection, the Vocabulary Test was employed, in the early stages of the W–B I standardization, only as an alternate test,[27] but its general merits soon became so apparent that in the 1941 edition of the *Measurement of Adult Intelligence* its use as a "regular" test was strongly recommended. In the case of the WAIS, the Vocabulary Test has formed an integral part of the Scale from the start.

The WAIS vocabulary is a new word list of about the same difficulty as the W–B I, but consisting of 40 instead of 42 items. Another difference (not intended) is that the WAIS list contains a larger percentage of action words (verbs). The only thing that can be said so far about this difference is that

---

[27] Actually, the main reason for its provisional omission was the fact that it might be unfair to illiterates and persons of foreign languages, but this factor proved less serious than first thought, and the omission of the Vocabulary or any other subtest which, for diverse reasons, may be considered unfair to particular subjects is now left to the judgment of the examing psychologist.

while responses given to verbs are easier to score, those elicited by substantives are frequently more significant diagnostically.

A test calling for definition of words is often of value because of its qualitative aspects. There is an obvious difference in the reasoning ability[28] between two adults, one of whom defines a "donkey" as "an animal" and the other who defines it in such terms as "it has four legs" or that "it looks like a jackass." Sometimes the quality of a subject's definition tells us something about his cultural milieu. The type of word on which a subject passes or fails is always of some significance. Dull subjects from educated homes often get uncommon words like "vesper" and "encumber" but fail on "gamble" and "slice;" the pedant will get "espionage" but fail on "spangle," get "travesty" but fail on "matchless," etc. Perhaps more important from a clinical point of view, is the semantic character of a definition which gives us insight into an individual's thought processes. This is particularly true in the case of schizophrenics, the formal aspects of whose language disturbance is frequently diagnostic.[29]

In estimating the size of a person's vocabulary, items of the kind just discussed do not enter into the quantitative evaluation. What counts is the number of words that he knows. Any recognized meaning is acceptable, and there is no penalty for inelegance of language. So long as the subject shows that he knows what a word means, he is credited with a passing score. The general rule, when in doubt, is to match the subject's responses against the acceptable definitions and to score accordingly.

The Vocabulary Test holds up better with age than any other test of the Scale. The number of words correctly defined by successive age groups between 25 and 50 remains fairly constant, but the words "passed" by the groups are not of the same order of difficulty. In general, the more difficult words are passed by the older groups with greater frequency than by the younger groups. Table 66 (Appendix 3) compares the percentage of words passed and failed on the WAIS vocabulary in the age groups 16–19, 25–34 and 55–64. Correlations of Vocabulary with total score as well as with most of the Verbal tests are systematically high between 0.7 and 0.9 and remain consistently so across the age range. WAIS Vocabulary with total score at ages 25–34 correlates 0.82; ages 45–54, 0.83.[30]

[28] We entertained for a long time the possibility of using preciseness and accuracy of definition as a basis for scoring, but actual attempts to do so proved impractical.
[29] See Chapter 11.
[30] The correlations of W–B I Vocabulary with Full Scale Score were not done in the original standardization, but have been supplied by later studies. They are of about the same order as those of the WAIS.

Chapter 6

Populations Used in 1939 and 1955 Standardizations

The W–B I Scale was standardized on 1750 subjects of both sexes, ages 7–69; the WAIS on 1700 subjects, both sexes, ages 16–64, plus an additional 475 subjects of both sexes, ages 60–75 and over. Description of the sources and demographic characteristics of the subjects examined have been analyzed elsewhere.[1] In this chapter we shall touch upon the major population factors or variables that may affect the validity and applicability of the norms obtained. These factors need special consideration because the diagnostic value of a test depends, to a large measure, upon the degree to which the characteristics of the originally tested groups approximate those of the general population to which the test will be subsequently administered.

The first of these factors is that of age. In the case of children, its bearing on test scores is so obvious that separate norms for different ages have been the rule almost from the time that intelligence scales were introduced. But in adult testing this was not always the case. In evaluating intelligence test performance of adults, the practice for a long time was to treat all individuals over 16 years as constituting a single age group. This assumption was unwarranted and, as we have seen, led to serious error in the interpretation of test findings. One cannot use the norms for a boy of 16 in evaluating the performance of a man of 60 any more than one can use the norms of a child of 6 in evaluating that of a boy of 16. The age factor has to be taken into account at every age.[2] This was done on the W–B I and the WAIS by establishing separate age norms for different ages and age groups. The age distribution of subjects used in the W–B I and WAIS standardizing samples are given in Tables 7 and 8.

The second important factor in the standardization of any intelligence

---

[1] Wechsler, D. (519, 525); Doppelt & Wallace (147).

[2] Changes of ability with age and the problems they present in the evaluation of adult intelligence will be discussed in some detail in Chapter 9.

TABLE 7
Distribution of subjects used in WB–I standardizing samples (by age)

Children		Adults	
Age group	No. of cases	Age group	No. of cases
7	50	17–19	100
8	50	20–24	160
9	50	25–29	195
10	60	30–24	140
11	60	35–39	135
12	60	40–44	91
13	70	45–49	70
14	70	50–54	55
15	100	55–59	50
16	100	60–70	85
Total............	670		1071

TABLE 8
Distribution of subjects used in WAIS standardization sample (by age and sex)

Age Group	Male	Female	Total
16–17	100	100	200
18–19	100	100	200
20–24	100	100	200
25–34	150	150	300
35–44	150	150	300
45–54	150	150	300
55–64	100	100	200
Total...............	850	850	1700
Old age sample used in Kansas City study			
60–64	52	64	116
65–69	51	59	110
70–74	51	55	106
75 and over	58	85	143
Total...............	212	263	475

test is education. Practically all studies show that educational attainment (as measured by test scores) correlates to a high degree with scores on tests of intelligence. The correlations range from about 0.60 to 0.80. The r's between the last grade reached and Full Scale scores on the W–B I and WAIS are respectively 0.64 and 0.68. A correlation of this order suggests that the ability to do well on intelligence tests may be largely dependent upon formal education, and has so been interpreted by a number of authors (326). This conclusion, without considerable qualification, is misleading as well as unjustified, and will be further discussed in Chapter 9. In this chapter we shall deal with the problem of education primarily as a variable that needs to be considered in test standardization.

Dealing with the educational factor in the standardization of an adult test presents a number of problems. It might seem that the simplest way of dealing with it would be to establish separate norms according to amount of schooling. This would be an ideal procedure but to do so, even for a limited number of categories, would require considerable increase in the number of individuals needed for the standardization. For example, if only five educational levels were taken into account, one would have to increase the standardizing population fivefold, if eight categories, eightfold, and so on. The procedure would not be so extensive in the case of school children, because at this level there is a fairly close correlation between school age and chronological age. But in the case of adults one runs into all sorts of difficulties, not only because of the unevenness in scholastic attainment in different segments of the population, but also because the educational distribution of the American adult population is constantly changing. Added to these problems is the fact that other criteria or differentiae, for example that of occupational status, must be simultaneously considered. In the 1939 standardization, this seemed to offer a much more satisfactory basis of selection with the facilities available, and was the one primarily used for the W–B I sampling. In the case of the 1955 (WAIS) standardization, occupation and education, as well as sex and age,[3] were simultaneously considered. Thus, the demand upon an examiner might be to obtain a male semi-skilled laborer, age 30–34, grades completed eight years or less; or a housewife, age 25–29, a college graduate. Comparison of the educational level of the population of the country as a whole at the time of standardization is shown in Tables 9 and 10. As will be noted, the tables present the data in somewhat different form but furnish essentially similar information.

A third factor which might be thought of as possibly important in the standardization of an intelligence test is that of sex differences. With respect to this factor most of the available data, until recently, related to differences observed in test performance of boys and girls. Briefly summarized, the data showed occasional significant, though generally small, differences on certain individual tests. For example, boys tend to do better on arithmetical reasoning, and the girls better on vocabulary tests (539).

[3] Also, geography, urban *vs.* rural, and color.

TABLE 9

W–B I adult sample by education (male and female, ages 17–65)

Educational Level	U. S. Population*	W–B I Sample
	%	%
College graduates........................	2.93	5.10
Some college work.......................	4.08	3.77
High school graduates...................	6.85	10.81
Some high school work..................	18.99	18.76
Elementary school graduate..............	18.68	28.85
Some elementary school.................	43.58	30.17
Illiterates...............................	4.69	2.55
Total (1081 subjects).................	99.80	100.01

* Estimated level of education of United States adult population derived from data (1934) furnished by Dr. David Segal, Educational Consultant, Education Office, Department of Interior.

TABLE 10

WAIS standardization sample by education (male and female, ages 16–64)*

Educational Level	U. S. Population†	WAIS Sample
yrs.	%	%
16 or more‡...................	4.28	4.86
13–15........................	7.57	8.57
12...........................	22.71	23.28
9–11.........................	28.06	27.78
8 or less.....................	33.35	35.49
Total (1700 subjects).......	99.97	99.98

* For a more complete breakdown by age and sex, see Table 5 in WAIS manual (524).

† Based on 1950 United States census reports; for complete reference, see WAIS manual (524), p. 10.

‡ Schooling completed.

But when the total score is taken into consideration, that is to say, when the individual tests are combined into batteries, these differences tend to cancel each other. It is not clear, however, whether this nullification of sex differences is due to a real average or to an artifact resulting from a special selection of tests. For example, in the 1937 Stanford Revision, Terman and Merrill (488) eliminated items which were significantly in favor of one sex or the other. In the original W–B I selection of tests the same procedure was generally followed. Thus, the Cube Analysis Test was dropped from the W–B I battery when it was discovered that the mean scores for men and women showed systematically large differences in favor of the former.

On the W–B I, women tended to obtain higher mean total scores at almost every age. The differences were small, but the author, unduly impressed by the trend rather than the magnitude of the differences, interpreted the findings as indicating female superiority. Unfortunately for this interpretation, subsequent studies with the W–B I (73, 263) did not confirm the conclusion. Moreover, the 1955 WAIS restandardization showed the very opposite trend; this time the male subjects tested systematically higher.[4] If one averages the two sets of data, the difference becomes negligible, but this conclusion applies only to the *Full Scale Scores*; the individual subtests of both Scales continue to show clear-cut sex differences, with women doing better on some of the tests and men on others. These findings and their broader implications will be considered in Chapter 10.

Finally, we come to a group of factors which on both theoretical and practical grounds can be assumed to influence intelligence test results, but whose specific impact is difficult to evaluate because of the complexity of their interaction. We refer to the factors of race, social milieu and economic status. Here again, our view is that in an ideal standardization there ought to be separate norms for each of these categories, to make allowance for their respective influences. We do not think, however, that it is possible to do this at present, particularly when those to whom we might look for the facts are at such great odds among themselves as to what the facts are. In the original W–B standardization we circumvented the "white *vs.* non-white" problem by not including non-white subjects in the standardization norms. Non-white subjects were omitted because it was felt at the time that norms derived from a mixed population could not be interpreted without special provisos and reservations. This appears now to have been an unnecessary concern, first because the admission of non-white subjects into the standardization would, in view of their number, have only negligibly altered the norms, and second, because certain other groups whose inclusion might have similarly been questioned were nevertheless used. In the 1955 WAIS standardization some 10 per cent of the total sample were non-white subjects. This percentage roughly represents the proportion of non-white to white population in the United States at the time (1950 census). "Practical" handling of the problem does not, of course, imply an answer to the question of whether or not there are ethnic and cultural differences in intelligence. That such differences exist appear open to little doubt. How significant they are or to what degree they need to be taken into account in a national standardization such as ours is a matter that still is to be answered. In any event, no attempt was

---

[4] Both findings could, of course, be the result of sampling errors; in the case of the WAIS, they do not appear to be so (see p. 101, 103).

made to establish separate norms for different racial (or national) groups in either the W–B I or the WAIS. The norms as they stand, particularly on the WAIS, seem to be reasonably representative of the country as a whole, and to this extent may be said to represent a fair cross-section of

TABLE 11

WAIS means and standard deviations (on Verbal, Performance and Full Scale Scores of national sample) by age and urban vs. rural residence*

Age Group	Urban or Rural	No. of Subjects	Verbal		Performance		Full Scale	
			Mean	S.D.	Mean	S.D.	Mean	S.D.
16–17	U	113	57.75	13.91	51.57	10.79	109.32	23.18
16–17	R	85	51.18	11.84	45.55	10.57	96.73	20.79
18–19	U	122	60.79	12.88	51.70	10.13	112.48	21.25
18–19	R	76	52.74	15.41	46.30	13.23	99.04	27.19
20–24	U	131	62.45	14.55	53.17	11.37	115.62	24.40
20–24	R	67	54.72	14.03	46.15	11.61	100.87	24.08
25–29	U	105	64.33	13.85	52.61	10.21	116.94	22.19
25–29	R	46	58.26	15.06	48.78	13.60	107.04	27.98
30–34	U	98	60.65	13.94	48.63	11.29	109.29	23.53
30–34	R	49	57.14	14.80	46.53	11.56	103.67	24.64
35–39	U	106	62.58	15.36	48.27	11.62	110.85	25.73
35–39	R	62	58.40	13.71	46.81	10.93	105.21	23.44
40–44	U	89	62.71	13.47	46.51	10.33	109.21	22.21
40–44	R	41	53.71	12.76	39.51	9.34	93.22	20.03
45–49	U	109	61.88	16.98	44.39	10.87	106.27	26.68
45–49	R	56	55.25	15.47	38.84	10.53	94.09	24.60
50–54	U	91	57.58	15.95	39.78	11.25	97.36	25.89
50–54	R	42	54.02	12.70	39.00	10.85	93.02	21.72
55–59	U	80	57.96	16.14	37.91	11.78	95.88	26.51
55–59	R	39	53.18	15.18	36.00	8.53	89.18	22.73
60–64	U	54	59.52	16.09	39.39	10.36	98.91	24.80
60–64	R	25	47.36	13.29	32.88	8.02	80.24	20.12

* These age groupings do not correspond to groupings used in the WAIS Manual, n which 10 year age groupings were used starting with age 25.

TABLE 12

Means and standard deviations on Verbal, Performance, and WAIS Full Scale Scores of total national sample by urban-rural residence*

	No. of Subjects	Verbal		Performance		Full Scale	
		Mean	S.D.	Mean	S.D.	Mean	S.D.
Urban.......	1098	60.90	14.94	47.60	12.05	108.50	25.04
Rural........	588	54.33	14.32	43.48	12.03	97.82	25.46

* This table does not include the institutionalized feeble-minded.

what may be called "American intelligence" as of the time of standardization.

The subjects tested in the W–B standardization, though matched against the total population of the United States, were mostly urban from the City and State of New York. This, in the absence of other resources, seemed a reasonable procedure since the mean intelligence level of the white population of the State of New York had been shown by previous studies to be not far from the average for the nation as a whole. In the case of the WAIS no such assumption was necessary. Subjects from all parts of the country in rough proportion to the population of the different sections covered were tested. The actual proportions allotted to the different parts of the country are given in detail in the WAIS Manual (524).

In addition to age, sex and education (and race in the limited way described above), the following other factors were considered in the standardization of the WAIS: occupation, geographic distribution, urban *vs.* rural residence. That these factors can and do influence test performance to some degree is a necessary assumption, but no effort was made to determine to what extent each may have affected the norms. What was done was to match subjects so far as possible in terms of over-all national distribution (524). In general we were guided by and, wherever possible, we followed the categories employed in the United States census. The WAIS matching for geographic regions and urban residence is given in Tables 2 and 3 of the WAIS Manual.

The separation of our sample into urban *vs.* rural subjects was important not only because it gave proportional representation to the various parts of the country but also because it revealed what might have been expected on the basis of previous studies (498a), that populations so dichotomized attained different score levels on tests of intelligence. On the WAIS standardization, urban populations attained scores on the Full Scale approximately ½ sigma greater than rural subjects, and this difference seems to hold for Verbal and Performance at most age levels (Tables 11 and 12). The differences observed may be variously interpreted, but are perhaps best accounted for by the selective operation of associated occupation and education. Another explanation sometimes given is that, in the past half century, migration to larger cities has tended to drain off the more enterprising (?) segments of our rural population. But this has to be verified.

As regards the population sampling as a whole, it should be noted that all individuals examined were voluntary subjects. No known hospital or mentally disturbed subjects were included. On the other hand, the total sample includes roughly 2 per cent of known mental defectives examined in the State institutions.

Chapter 7

Basic Data and Test Results

The intelligence examinations presented in this book are point scales. This means that an individual's intelligence rating is obtained ultimately from a summation of the credits (or points) which he is given for passing various test items. The first problem which confronts one in such a scale is to decide what portion of the total number of credits should be assigned to each of the tests. This is the statistical problem of "weighting." One way of meeting it is to let the test weights take care of themselves by simply allowing one point for each item correctly passed. Such, for example, was the procedure employed on the Army Alpha, where the number of items on the several tests determined the final amount that each test contributed to the scale. A second way is to use some predetermined scoring system that will fix in advance the proportion which each test contributes to this total score, irrespective of the number of items it may happen to contain. The latter method was the one employed in the standardization of the WAIS and W–B I Scales.

An assumption made in the standardization of both scales was that once a test was admitted as a suitable measure of intelligence, it was to be accorded the same weight as any of the others so admitted. This is based on the theory that intelligence is "assortative" rather than "hierarchical." The theory does not imply that the tests are equally "good" or effective measures of intelligence, but only that each test is necessary for the comprehension measurement of general intelligence. It is for this reason that the author has rejected suggestions to drop such tests as the Object Assembly and Digit Span. Despite their limited reliability and relatively low correlation with the rest of the scale, they nevertheless contribute measures which need to be taken into account in appraising the effective intellectual ability of the individual. In any event, it may be noted that when a scale consists of a considerable number of tests, the weight allocated to any single subtest does not ordinarily affect the total score to any significant degree. This approach also has the advantage of not penalizing individuals who may have limited aptitude (and of not favoring others who may have special aptitude) for the type of performance called for by a given test.

The methods used by the author in equating the individual subtests of the WAIS and W–B I are described in detail in previous publications (517, 524). In general, scaled scores for each test were derived from basic reference groups from the standardization samples, comprised of 500 subjects between the ages of 20 and 34 in the case of the WAIS and 350 subjects in the case of the W–B I. The raw scores attained by the subjects in these reference groups on each of the subtests were individually distributed, and then converted to scales with a mean *scaled* score of 10 and a standard deviation of 3.[1] The object of this conversion was, of course, to equate each of the subtests of the scales with one another. It enabled us to establish tables of equivalent scores in which the original raw scores on each test were now expressed in terms of multiples or fractions of their converted S.D.'s. It is these scores that are used in calculating IQ's and in obtaining all norms that define a subject's final IQ[2] rating on each of the scales.

Principal Results

Detailed results of the W–B I and WAIS standardizations will be found respectively in the earlier editions of the *Measurement of Adult Intelligence* and in the WAIS manual. In the following section we propose to bring together the major findings of both standardizations, and add some new data which for one reason or another were not available at the initial publication. We shall not, however, attempt to review the extensive literature dealing with the W–B I and shall refer to only such of the findings in these studies as may be relevant to our argument. The basic data for both standardizations are given in Tables 13 and 14. These present in running form the mean scores (and standard deviations) by age of the entire populations tested in the 1939 and 1955 standardizations of our scales.

The first fact revealed by the tables is that age, as anticipated, is an important factor in intelligence test performance. The age curve for the W–B I has already been given and discussed (p. 31). A comparable curve for the corresponding WAIS data is now presented in Figure 2. The WAIS and W–B I curves are essentially alike except for two possibly important points: 1) The age of maximal performance on the WAIS is advanced some 5 years, *i.e.*, is now located in the interval 25 to 29 years instead of the

---

[1] Details of the statistical methods employed are given in Appendix 1.

[2] The concept of the IQ has already been discussed in Chapter 2. The statistical method by which W–B I and WAIS IQ's were derived is given in Appendix 1.

TABLE 13

Wechsler Bellevue Intelligence Scale—Form I
Means and standard deviations of sums of scaled scores on 5 Verbal, 5 Performance and Full Scale of 10 tests

Age Group	No. of Subjects	Verbal		Performance		Full Scale	
		Mean	S.D.	Mean	S.D.	Mean	S.D.
10.5	60	30.0	9.4	31.6	9.7	62.3	16.8
11.5	60	36.4	9.9	37.1	9.9	73.2	17.4
12.5	60	40.9	10.1	42.4	9.9	82.6	17.8
13.5	70	43.5	10.2	46.2	10.0	89.8	18.0
14.5	70	45.0	10.4	48.3	10.0	93.4	18.3
15.5	100	45.5	11.0	49.5	10.1	95.0	18.8
16.5	100	46.2	11.2	50.7	10.4	96.2	19.0
17–19	100	46.8	11.5	51.5	10.5	97.8	19.6
20–24	160	47.0	11.9	50.8	10.9	97.9	20.8
25–29	195	47.0	12.4	48.3	11.2	95.0	21.9
30–34	140	46.5	12.5	45.5	11.6	91.6	22.5
35–39	135	45.5	13.0	42.6	12.0	88.0	23.4
40–44	91	44.5	13.4	39.8	12.5	84.8	23.9
45–49	70	43.5	13.6	36.8	12.8	81.3	24.0
50–54	55	42.2	14.0			78.0	24.2
55–59	50	41.0	14.5			74.8	24.5

TABLE 14

Wechsler Adult Intelligence Scale (WAIS)
Means and standard deviations of sums of scaled scores on 6 Verbal, 5 Performance and Full Scale of 11 tests

Age Group	No. of Subjects	Verbal		Performance		Full Scale	
		Mean	S.D.	Mean	S.D.	Mean	S.D.
16–17	200	54.59	13.85	48.78	11.25	103.37	23.61
18–19	200	57.31	14.88	49.43	11.83	106.74	25.16
20–24	200	59.47	15.21	50.64	11.97	110.10	25.69
25–29	152	62.30	14.64	51.25	11.69	113.55	24.98
30–34	148	59.31	14.43	47.78	11.54	107.09	24.30
35–39	168	61.04	14.91	47.73	11.39	108.77	25.06
40–44	132	59.23	14.72	43.93	10.89	103.17	24.04
45–49	167	59.28	16.99	42.25	11.24	101.53	27.04
50–54	133	56.46	15.09	39.53	11.13	95.99	24.73
55–59	121	55.86	16.43	36.97	11.12	92.83	26.27
60–64	79	55.67	16.27	37.33	10.14	93.00	24.97
Kansas City old age sample							
60–64	101	55.24	14.51	34.97	10.94	90.21	24.15
65–69	86	53.73	14.51	34.40	10.05	88.13	22.92
70–74	80	47.66	13.73	29.53	9.45	77.19	21.42
75 and over	85	44.02	14.16	24.68	9.54	68.71	21.56

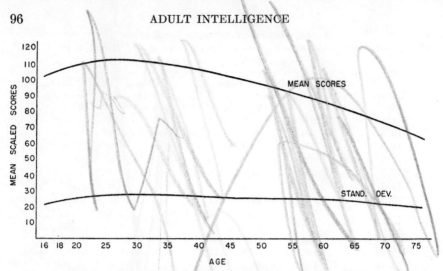

FIG. 2. Changes with age in Full Scale Scores of the Wechsler Adult Intelligence Scale. Ages 16–75 and over.

interval 20 to 25 years. 2) Beginning with age 30 and continuing at least up to age 65, the mean test scores of the WAIS show a consistently smaller falling off with age than do the W–B I scores.

A second important fact revealed by the data in Tables 13 and 14 is the change in relative variability of the test scores with age. This change observable in both WAIS and W–B test scores is more clearly seen if one

TABLE 15

Coefficients of variation—WB–I weighted scores, ages 10–60

Age Group	No. of Subjects	Verbal Scale	Performance Scale	Full Scale
10.5	60	31.33	30.70	26.97
11.5	60	27.20	26.68	23.77
12.5	60	24.69	23.35	21.55
13.5	70	23.45	21.64	20.04
14.5	70	23.11	20.70	19.59
15.5	100	24.18	20.40	19.79
16.5	100	24.22	20.51	19.75
17–19	100	24.57	20.39	20.04
20–24	160	25.32	21.46	21.25
25–29	195	26.38	23.19	23.05
30–34	140	26.88	25.49	24.56
35–39	135	28.57	28.17	26.59
40–44	91	30.11	31.41	28.18
45–49	70	31.26	34.78	29.52
50–54	55	33.18		31.03
55–59	50	35.37		32.75

TABLE 16

Coefficients of variation—WAIS Scaled Scores, ages 16-75 and over

Age Group	No. of Subjects	Verbal Scale	Performance Scale	Full Scale
16–17	200	25.37	23.06	22.84
18–19	200	25.98	23.93	23.57
20–24	200	25.57	23.63	23.33
25–29	152	23.49	22.80	21.91
30–34	148	24.32	24.15	22.69
35–39	168	24.42	23.86	23.04
40–44	132	24.86	24.78	23.30
45–49	167	28.66	26.60	26.63
50–54	133	28.49	28.71	25.76
55–59	121	29.41	30.07	28.30
60–64	79	29.38	27.16	26.84
Kansas City old age sample				
60–64	101	26.26	31.28	26.77
65–69	86	27.01	29.21	26.01
70–74	80	28.80	32.00	27.75
75 and over	85	32.16	38.65	38.38

divides the successive S.D.'s by their corresponding means. Tables 15 and 16 give the coefficients ($\sigma/M \times 100$) so obtained. The coefficients of variation show systematic decline until about age 17; then, reversing their trend, they increase in magnitude, slowly at first, and more rapidly after age 40. The increasing variability of intellectual ability in later adulthood (as well as higher variability in children) is in line with similar observations made of many other biometric functions (435).[3]

It should be noted that the changes of variability with age which we have been discussing have to do with variance in absolute test score and not in IQ level. IQ's by definition, that is, the way we calculate them, are independent of age, and so no differences may be expected other than those due to sampling. This makes for the so-called constancy of the IQ, a problem which can be discussed from several points of view. Actually, the problem of the constancy of the IQ involves two questions: 1) the reliability of the IQ test as a measuring instrument, and 2) the stability of the measures obtained with it. The two are closely related, but it is

[3] The decrease of variability in the intelligence test score with age in the early years may be due in part to the unevenness in the rate of maturation of children and in part to the hidden role of education. The effects of education, contrary to hopes of educators, are to make us more, rather than less, alike (511). A comparable factor serving to increase variability among adults is the selective effect of professional and vocational pursuits. What we do in daily life changes us more than what we have learned in school.

TABLE 17

Comparisons between intercorrelations of subtests of W–B I and WAIS with Full Scale Scores, ages 20–34 and 25–34, respectively

	WB–I*	WAIS†
Information........................	0.67	0.84
Comprehension.....................	0.66	0.71
Arithmetic........................	0.63	0.66
Similarities.......................	0.73	0.74
Digit Span........................	0.51	0.56
Vocabulary........................	(0.75)‡	0.84
Digit Symbol......................	0.67	0.63
Picture Completion................	0.61	0.72
Block Design......................	0.71	0.79
Picture Arrangement...............	0.57	0.69
Object Assembly...................	0.48	0.58

* Each test *vs.* total minus test. Number of subjects, 355.

† Each test *vs.* total corrected for contamination. Number of subjects, 300.

‡ Vocabulary *r* of W–B I estimated.

primarily with the latter that the problem of the constancy of the IQ is associated, that is, with the question of whether an individual retested with the same or equivalent instrument at varying intervals may be expected to attain the same or roughly equivalent IQ. The answer to this question is much more difficult. Much depends on how we define the terms same or roughly equivalent, that is, the range of admissible differences between test and retest IQ. Nevertheless, if the IQ is to have any practical (predictive and diagnostic) value, one must assume and, of course, eventually demonstrate that it remains invariant over a considerable period of time. The extent to which the W–B I meets this criterion has been attested by clinical experience over the years and verified by at least one controlled study (477). Both sources indicate that the W–B I (and WAIS) IQ remain reasonably constant.[4]

Test and Inter-test Variability

In selecting tests for a composite scale, common practice posits that the subtests should correlate highly with the total score (as criterion) and only modestly with each other. This is on the theory that a high correlation with total score indicates that the tests measure essentially the same thing while the lower inter-test correlations imply that the tests measure different aspects of the criterion. The subtests of both the W–B I and the WAIS are for the most part in accord with this expectation. Table 17

[4] For further discussion of constancy of IQ, see Chapter 11, p. 157.

TABLE 18

*Correlations of the individual subtests of the WAIS with Full Scale Score
at different age levels**

	Age Levels						
	18–19	25–34	45–54	60–64	65–69	70–74	75+
Information..........................	0.84	0.84	0.84	0.81	0.83	0.76	0.78
Comprehension......................	0.72	0.71	0.77	0.70	0.66	0.66	0.70
Arithmetic..........................	0.70	0.66	0.75	0.75	0.77	0.73	0.73
Similarities.........................	0.80	0.74	0.75	0.70	0.68	0.71	0.66
Digit Span..........................	0.61	0.56	0.62	0.55	0.53	0.63	0.57
Vocabulary..........................	0.83	0.82	0.83	0.79	0.83	0.82	0.73
Digit Symbol.......................	0.68	0.63	0.69	0.74	0.73	0.72	0.70
Picture Completion.................	0.74	0.72	0.76	0.70	0.66	0.73	0.59
Block Design.......................	0.72	0.69	0.67	0.77	0.68	0.56	0.65
Picture Arrangement...............	0.68	0.72	0.71	0.70	0.74	0.60	0.46
Object Assembly...................	0.65	0.58	0.65	0.63	0.55	0.50	0.58

* Abstracted from Tables 16 and 17 of WAIS manual (524).

gives the inter-test correlation of the subtests of the W–B I and the WAIS
with Full Scale Score for the age groups 20–34 and 25–34, respectively.
Table 18 gives the correlation of the individual subtests of the WAIS
with Full Scale Score at different age levels for the entire standardization
span. Tables 19 and 20 give the individual subtest intercorrelations for
the W–B I and the WAIS for ages 20–34 and 25–34, respectively.

A question of recurrent interest is the possible influence of sampling,
sex and age on the order of the correlations obtained. *A priori*, we should

TABLE 19

*Intercorrelation of the tests—W–B I, ages 20–34, 355 subjects, male and female**

Test	Information	Comprehension	Arithmetic	Similarities	Digit Span	Digit Symbol	Picture Completion	Block Design	Picture Arrangement	Object Assembly
Comprehension...........	0.67	—								
Arithmetic..............	0.60	0.52	—							
Similarities..............	0.68	0.72	0.60	—						
Digit Span..............	0.48	0.44	0.44	0.38	—					
Digit Symbol............	0.56	0.48	0.43	0.51	0.54	—				
Picture Completion.......	0.47	0.46	0.40	0.46	0.30	0.40	—			
Block Design............	0.49	0.47	0.51	0.54	0.40	0.54	0.57	—		
Picture Arrangement.....	0.38	0.39	0.37	0.49	0.26	0.44	0.39	0.48	—	
Object Assembly........	0.22	0.29	0.23	0.31	0.16	0.32	0.44	0.54	0.27	—

* From *Measurement of Adult Intelligence* (517), p. 223.

TABLE 20

Intercorrelation of the tests—WAIS ages 25–34, 150 male and 150 female subjects*

Test	Information	Comprehension	Arithmetic	Similarities	Digit Span	Vocabulary	Digit Symbol	Picture Completion	Block Design	Picture Arrangement
Comprehension..........	0.70									
Arithmetic..............	0.66	0.49								
Similarities.............	0.70	0.62	0.55							
Digit Span.............	0.53	0.40	0.49	0.46						
Vocabulary.............	0.81	0.73	0.59	0.74	0.51					
Digit Symbol...........	0.57	0.44	0.43	0.53	0.41	0.60				
Picture Completion......	0.67	0.56	0.50	0.56	0.39	0.61	0.48			
Block Design...........	0.58	0.49	0.51	0.52	0.39	0.53	0.47	0.62		
Picture Arrangement.....	0.62	0.57	0.49	0.52	0.47	0.62	0.51	0.57	0.58	
Object Assembly........	0.45	0.43	0.37	0.39	0.30	0.43	0.44	0.54	0.61	0.52

* From *Wechsler Adult Intelligence Scale Manual* (524), p. 16.

expect that all would have some relevance. Sampling clearly does (284a). As regards the influence of sex, the number of cases included has been generally too small to warrant definitive conclusions. In the case of age, the documentation is considerably better. In both the WAIS and the W–B I inter-test correlations as well as subtest correlations with total score are fairly even throughout the adult ages (18 and over), although in the case of the W–B I there is a slight tendency for correlations to increase with age. There is some variation in the individual subtests but this, as a

TABLE 21

WAIS range and median of inter-test correlation coefficients for each of seven age groups*

Age	Verbal Tests		Performance Tests		Verbal vs. Performance		All Tests	
	Range	Median	Range	Median	Range	Median	Range	Median
18–19	0.48–0.81	0.64	0.45–0.69	0.59	0.37–0.65	0.52	0.37–0.81	0.55
25–34	0.40–0.81	0.59	0.44–0.62	0.53	0.30–0.67	0.50	0.30–0.81	0.52
45–54	0.45–0.85	0.66	0.48–0.64	0.56	0.42–0.65	0.54	0.42–0.85	0.57
60–64	0.32–0.76	0.61	0.48–0.68	0.57	0.35–0.67	0.53	0.32–0.76	0.54
65–69	0.38–0.82	0.59	0.37–0.71	0.54	0.22–0.67	0.48	0.22–0.82	0.51
70–74	0.41–0.71	0.61	0.28–0.66	0.54	0.26–0.66	0.44	0.26–0.71	0.51
75 and over	0.28–0.77	0.61	0.31–0.68	0.50	0.08–0.63	0.41	0.08–0.77	0.46
r's for each age group........	15		10		30		55	

* From Doppelt and Wallace (147).

rule, is not significant. The range and median of the intercorrelations for each of the seven age groups of the WAIS are given in Table 21. The relatively similar order of correlations obtained is perhaps related to the like factorial composition[5] at different ages.

Reliability of W–B I and WAIS

Reliability coefficients for the W–B I and the WAIS Full Scale Scores and IQ's vary from 0.90 to 0.97 and for the Performance and Verbal parts from 0.84 to 0.96. In the initial W–B I standardization, a 4 × 4 test correlation (Information, Digit Span, Picture Completion and Block Design × Comprehension, Arithmetic, Picture Arrangement and Digit Symbol) gave a reliability coefficient of 0.90. Unfortunately, the SE_m was not obtained at the time. This omission was remedied by other investigators (135) through subsequent test-retest studies. Results of one such study is given in Table 22. In the case of the WAIS, split-half reliabilities were done on the main standardization population for all subtests as well as the principal parts of the Scale, and these are shown in Table 23. The W–B I reliabilities for Full, Verbal and Performance parts of the Scale are somewhat lower than those of the WAIS, but still generally satisfactory.

Equally as important as the values of the reliability coefficients obtained on the W–B I are the data regarding changes in IQ that may be expected on retest. The average change in IQ has been found to vary (214) from 5 to 8 points for the Full Scale, with the change in Verbal IQ approximately half that of the Performance. In general the amount of increase is unrelated to the interval between retests for intervals from 2 weeks to 3 months (477). The larger increase in the Performance IQ as compared to the Verbal is due primarily to the practice effect to which performance tests are liable. Similar findings have been reported in comparisons made between pre- and postlobotomy test scores, although in these instances the changes in Full Scale IQ's are either negligible or in a negative direction (288).

While the reliability of the WAIS and the W–B I Scales as a whole (Full, Verbal and Performance) is quite satisfactory, that of the individual subtests, with some exceptions, leaves much to be desired. The low reliability of some of the W–B I and WAIS tests is primarily due to the fact that most of these subtests contain too few items, particularly as regards the number of items available for any given level of performance—an inevitable consequence of the time limit set for the Scales as a whole. The low reliabilities of the subtests nevertheless bring up the question of the legitimacy of using individual test scores for establishing clinical

[5] This was found to be the case in the factor analysis of the WAIS; it was not, however, always true, in the case of factorial studies of the W–B I. On this point, see Balinsky (34).

TABLE 22

*Reliability coefficients and standard errors of measurement for W–B I subtests and Scales**

Subtests†	Average Correlation	SE_m
Information..........................	0.86	0.68
Comprehension.....................	0.74	1.21
Digit Span.........................	0.67	1.68
Arithmetic.........................	0.62	2.06
Similarities........................	0.71	1.22
Vocabulary........................	0.88	0.73
Picture Arrangement...............	0.64	1.82
Picture Completion................	0.83	0.95
Block Design......................	0.84	1.10
Object Assembly...................	0.69	1.31
Digit Symbol......................	0.80	1.06
Verbal IQ.........................	0.84	3.96
Performance IQ...................	0.86	4.49
Full IQ...........................	0.90	3.29

* From Derner *et al.* (135).

† Standard errors are in terms of weighted score points for the subtests, and IQ points for the Scales.

diagnoses. The compelling answer to this question is that tests of low reliability cannot be so used with any degree of confidence. But it must also be borne in mind that diagnostic patterning does not depend entirely upon the reliability of the subtests employed. Equally important are the validity of the individual subtests and the number of other tests brought into the configurational relationships which one is seeking to establish. This matter will be discussed in the chapter on clinical diagnoses (Chapter 11).

Differences Between Verbal and Performance Parts of the W–B I and the WAIS

The correlations between the Verbal and Performance parts of both the W–B I and the WAIS vary from 0.55 to 0.80 (median 0.65) depending upon the sample of population investigated. For the age group 20–25 (original W–B I Standardization) the correlation was 0.71. For the principal age groups of the WAIS the correlations were as follows: ages 18–19, 0.77; 25–34, 0.77; 45–54, 0.81. These correlations are fairly high but not sufficiently high that substantial differences in the separate IQ's obtained by any individual may not occur.

TABLE 23

*Reliability coefficients and standard errors of measurement for WAIS
subtests and Scales*

Test	Age 18–19 (200 subjects)		Age 25–34 (300 subjects)		Age 45–54 (300 subjects)	
	r_{11}	SE_m*	r_{11}	SE_m	r_{11}	SE_m
Information...............	0.91	0.88	0.91	0.86	0.92	0.87
Comprehension.............	0.79	1.36	0.77	1.45	0.79	1.47
Arithmetic.................	0.79	1.38	0.81	1.35	0.86	1.23
Similarities................	0.87	1.11	0.85	1.15	0.85	1.32
Digit Span.................	0.71	1.63	0.66	1.75	0.66	1.74
Vocabulary.................	0.94	0.69	0.95	0.67	0.96	0.67
Verbal IQ.................	0.96	3.00	0.96	3.00	.96	3.00
Digit Symbol..............	0.92	0.85	—	—	—	—
Picture Completion..........	0.82	1.18	0.85	1.14	0.83	1.15
Block Design...............	0.86	1.16	0.83	1.29	0.82	1.15
Picture Arrangement.........	0.66	1.71	0.60	1.73	0.74	1.39
Object Assembly............	0.65	1.65	0.68	1.66	0.71	1.59
Performance IQ.............	0.93	3.97	0.93	3.97	0.94	3.76
Full Scale IQ..............	0.97	2.60	0.97	2.60	0.97	2.60

* The SE_m is in Scaled Score units for the tests and in IQ units for the Verbal,
Performance and Full Scale IQ's.

The mean difference between Verbal and Performance IQ's on the
standardizing populations (WAIS) was, as expected, approximately zero.
This, of course, only means that the positive and negative differences were
on the whole equal and symmetrically distributed. To ascertain the chance
of a subject's attaining a Verbal minus Performance difference of stated
magnitude, one needs to note the degree of dispersion of the individual
measures about the mean. This information is furnished in Table 24.

TABLE 24

*Mean differences between WAIS Verbal and Performance IQ's (V–P)
for 3 age groups (unclassified)*

Ages	No. of Subjects	Mean	S.D.
18–19	200	0.10	10.17
25–34	300	−0.11	10.21
45–54	300	0.01	9.72
Total...............	800	−0.02	10.02

TABLE 25

Mean differences between WAIS Verbal and Performance IQ's (V–P) for 3 combined*
age groups (18–54) when classified according to Full Scale IQ's

IQ Range	No. of Subjects	Mean	S.D.
79 and below...........	72	1.54	7.44
90–110................	431	−0.73	10.24
120 and over..........	77	1.58	10.24

* The "Ns" for IQ's of 79 and below and 110 and above were too low to be treated separately.

The means and standard deviations of the WAIS Verbal *minus* Performance differences calculated for about half of the standardization population are given separately for three age groups. From the figures in Table 24 it is clear that the chances are about 1 in 3 that an individual tested with the WAIS will show a difference of 10 points or more between the Verbal and Performance IQ's which he attains on the Scales. This difference is of about the same order as that found for the W–B I, which was estimated, however, in a somewhat different way (517).

A question of practical interest is whether an obtained Verbal minus Performance difference is related to IQ level. *A priori*, one might expect that individuals of high IQ's, because of their ostensibly superior word fluency and abstract ability, would do better on the non-verbal part of the Scale and hence tend to show systematic positive Verbal minus Performance differences, and, on the other hand, that persons of low IQ, because they do better on manipulative tests, would show correspondingly negative Verbal minus Performance differences. This expectation was supported by earlier analysis of the W–B I findings (517) but was not confirmed by the more systematic analysis of the WAIS data. An analysis of the Verbal minus Performance differences of the WAIS according to IQ level is given in Table 25.

Correlation of the W–B I and the WAIS with Other Scales

There are now a considerable number of studies comparing test scores of the Wechsler Scales, mostly with the W–B I, with performance and ratings on other tests of intelligence. The correlations vary, as may be expected, with the type of test used, the character of the population studied and the range of intelligence level of subjects compared. The average correlation between the W–B I and some 15 different tests reported is about 0.75, with a range from 0.50 to 0.90. Correlations with the Verbal part are about of the same order as with the Full Scale; those with the Performance part alone average some 10–15 points less. At the time of this writing, we were acquainted with only two correlational studies between the WAIS and other scales. The first of these (524) was between the WAIS and the Revised Stanford-Binet (Form L) on 52 reformatory inmates, ages 16–26, with the following results: S–B × WAIS Full Scale IQ 0.85, S–B × Verbal 0.80, S–B × WAIS Performance 0.69. The second was a correlation with a modified form of Raven's Progressive Matrices (223). For an N of 82 the correlations were as follows: Matrices × Full Scale 0.72, Matrices × Verbal 0.58, Matrices × Performance 0.70. The correlations cited are roughly of the order of those found between the W–B I and other scales (Table 26).

The substantial correlations found between the W–B I and other tests of intelligence, including some of very different composition, testify to the solidity of the Scale as a measure of adult intelligence (408, 409). It should be borne in mind, however, that correlations of the order of

TABLE 26

Illustrative correlations of Wechsler Adult Scales (W–B I) with other intelligence scales

Test	Subjects	No.	r	Source
Stanford-Binet, 1937 Rev.	College freshmen, female	112	0.62	Anderson *et al.* (22)
Stanford-Binet, 1937 Rev.	Mental patients, male and female, ages 10–69	227	0.89	Mitchell (368)
Stanford-Binet, 1937 Rev.*	Reformatory inmates, male, ages 16–26	52	0.85	Wechlser (524)
AGCT†	Soldiers, ages 21–30	400	0.86	Wechsler (517)
AGCT	Veterans, ages 20–33	100	0.83	Tamminen (482)
Army Alpha	Adult female nurses	92	0.74	Rabin (408)
ACE	College freshmen, female	112	0.53	Anderson *et al.* (22)
CAVD	Male adults, ages 18–64	108	0.69	Goldfarb (196)
Otis (20 min.)	Male adults, ages 18–64	108	0.73	Goldfarb (196)
Raven Prog. Matrices	Adolescent deaf, male and female	41	0.55	Levine and Iscoe (311)
Raven Prog. Matrices*	Brain-damaged male adults	82	0.72	Hall (223)
Morgan Mental Ability	College freshmen, male and female, ages 16–23	125	0.62	Fishbein (159)

* Correlation with WAIS.
† Correlation with W–B II.

0.70 or even 0.80, while indicating that the tests compared measure essentially the same thing, do not warrant the assumption, sometimes made, that tests showing this order of correlation are equivalent or interchangeable one for another. Not only does the correlation of 0.80 still have a limited predictive value, but it is precisely this deviation from complete agreement between two tests that can account for the differential suitability or particular merit of the one or the other. Thus, the chances are 1 in 3 that an individual obtaining an IQ of 100 on the W–B I or the WAIS will obtain an IQ which may differ by as much as 10 points or more on the Stanford-Binet. The occurrence of such a discrepancy also raises the question of whether one test or the other is not a more valid measure of the individual's "true capacity." The answer to this question will depend in part on what one believes the Scales as a whole measure, and in part on the difference in type of ability called for by the tests comprising the respective Scales. A similar question will confront the examiner when he deals with discrepancies between the Verbal and Performance IQ's encountered in the administration of the W–B I and WAIS Scales. The relatively high correlations between the Verbal and Performance parts of the Scales also show that both measure essentially the same thing although in different ways. But, of course, even if the correlation between them were perfect one might still find discrepancies between them as regards *absolute* level of IQ. This would occur if the individual measures entering into the correlation showed systematic and constant differences.

Range and Distribution of IQ's

The usefulness of a scale depends not only upon the validity and reliability of its measures, but also upon the manner in which these measures distribute themselves within the limits of their range. In general, it is desirable that the range be as wide as possible, that the measures be continuous and that there be no piling up of scores at any point. Some authors also believe that the resulting frequency curve ought to be Gaussian or as nearly Gaussian as possible. This requirement seems to be a result of the widespread belief[6] that mental measures usually distribute themselves according to the normal curve of error.

The distribution of the adult IQ's on the W–B I and WAIS, as shown in Figures 3 and 4, conforms to the first three criteria just mentioned: (1) The range of scores is approximately 8 S.D.'s (or in terms of IQ, from IQ of *circa* 35 to an IQ of *circa* 155). (2) The IQ's are continuous within the defined limits. All intervening IQ's are not only possible, but actually occur. (3) There is no piling up of scores at any point of the scale, and particularly not at either extreme. The distribution of the IQ's, however, is

---

[6] The author does not share this belief. On this point see Wechsler (521), p. 127.

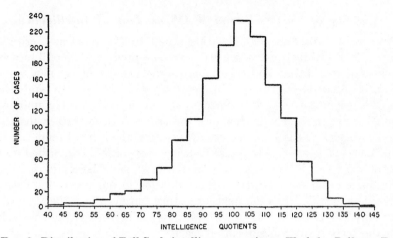

FIG. 3. Distribution of Full Scale intelligence quotients. Wechsler-Bellevue Form I. Ages 10–60 (1508 cases).

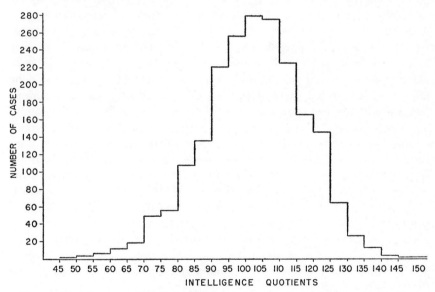

FIG. 4. Distribution of Wechsler Adult Intelligence Scale intelligence quotients. Ages 16–75 and over (2052 cases).

not truly Gaussian. A curve fitted to the data would more nearly approximate Pearson's Type IV,[7] but the difference is not sufficiently great to be of practical significance.

[7] The constants for the W–B I distribution (Figure 3) are as follows:

Mean = 100.11 β_1 = 0.2789 K_1 = 0.3973 $\sqrt{N \Sigma \beta_1}$ = 3.54
S. D. = 14.69 β_2 = 3.6170 K_2 = 0.5668 $\sqrt{N \Sigma \beta_2}$ = 14.00

Validity of the W–B and WAIS as Test of Intelligence

A common procedure for validating a new test is to set as a criterion some well established test which has been accepted as a "good" measure of the trait in question and then appraise the validity of the new one on the basis of the degree to which it correlates with the already established test. The significance of this correlation will depend entirely upon the original criterion, and it is therefore the criterion itself, rather than the new test, which needs examination. In practice, the general tendency has been to accept tests already in use as being more or less established measures of the traits in question, but for the most part these criteria themselves have never been validated. The situation in the case of intelligence tests is not so bad as in other fields of testing, but even here the absence of externally validated criteria imposes serious limitations on the conclusion that the tests really measure intelligence.

The independent criteria that have been used in validating tests of intelligence are primarily of three kinds. The first is that of ratings by selected judges, in the case of children's tests, generally ratings by teachers. A good test of intelligence is thus by implication one that agrees with teachers' ratings. This would seem to be a legitimate approach since it is reasonable to assume that bright children should do well and poor children do poorly in school, and that the competent teacher would be able to make this appraisal. However, this procedure presents a curious paradox. Intelligence tests were first advocated for use in schools because, according to those who proposed them, teachers' judgments of children's intelligence were not very reliable. Nevertheless, intelligence tests were considered as "proving themselves" when they demonstrated their effectiveness in accurately separating the bright from the average and the average from the dull pupil. In other words, teachers' judgments which were at first considered inadequate were subsequently used as validating the tests which were intended to replace their judgments. The same circularity is involved when the criteria used are ratings or judgments by "experts." Thus, one of the main arguments used by psychologists in getting the military services and industry to use tests was by pointing out that ability ratings by officers or personnel managers could not always be trusted; the tests were then "sold" to them because they correlated well with their practical judgments.

A second external criterion for tests of intelligence is the degree to which they reflect or conform to the normal growth curves of mental ability. This criterion can in part be justified when applied to intelligence tests devised for children but is not easily defended in the appraisal of adult intelligence, except in the evaluation of individuals of arrested or impaired development. In the latter instances, norms can be used to show that a mentally retarded adult functions at a level equivalent to the performance of a child of such and such an age, and consequently indicates mental arrest of such and such order.

A third type of criterion available for the evaluation of intelligence tests is comparison with over-all socio-economic achievement. Tests of intelligence seem to correlate positively with almost any kind of positive achievement or socially approved activity. Ministers, doctors, scientists, engineers and businessmen, on the average, attain higher scores on intelligence tests than porters, domestics and unskilled laborers. But even more clear-cut is the agreement of intelligence test scores with estimates of that group of individuals which, on the basis of diverse criteria, are designated as the mentally defective. In fact, it was the effectiveness of mental tests in detecting this group of individuals that first demonstrated their validity as measures of intelligence.

Both the W–B I and the WAIS meet all the above criteria. Whether in terms of degree of agreement with experts' ratings, manifestation of increments with age parallel to those observed in growth curves of mental ability, or in the effective appraisal of mental deficiency, both tests show substantial correlation with the posited criteria as well as with other tests used to appraise intelligence. But these findings must be considered only as the minimum required of any intelligence scale. No new test can be markedly out of line with established criteria and still claim to be a good test of intelligence. But the degree to which a new test correlates with recognized ones cannot in and of itself be accepted as unimpeachable proof of its validity. The test must also be able to stand on its own feet; here, day-to-day trial and evaluation by one's peers is the final arbiter.

Level and Range of W–B I and WAIS IQ

A criticism that has been made of the W–B I is that the IQ's attained on the Scale by older subjects were too high, that is, often significantly greater than those derived from other intelligence scales. This stricture, if it is a stricture, has been met to some extent in the 1955 standardization. Older subjects on the WAIS now need a somewhat greater standard score for the same number of tests to obtain corresponding IQ's on the W–B I. Part of this increase in the required score may be due to the greater number of businessmen and professional subjects included in the WAIS sampling, part possibly due to the over-all increase in functioning ability of older subjects to which we have already referred. It should be emphasized, however, that differences in norms of W–B and WAIS are not due to a change in the difficulty of the Scales; nor is it altogether certain which of the two is "fairer" to the older subjects. The author's provisional view is that the WAIS IQ's may turn out to be a little low just as the W–B I may have been a little high, but further experience with the 1955 revision is necessary before answering the question.

While the WAIS IQ's for older subjects will tend to be a little lower than those obtained with the W–B I, the WAIS IQ's, as a whole, like those of the W–B I, will probably continue to be higher than those generally attained on other scales. This is due primarily to the bonus (credit) which the Wechsler Scales allow for age. Plus differences, that is, differences in favor of the W–B I and WAIS, will be most common and greatest in subjects who test at the dull-normal and lower levels of intelligence on other scales. They will generally be small and negligible for subjects testing at average intelligence; in the case of subjects of superior intelligence the differences will generally disappear and even tend in the opposite direction. The reason for the last trend is that neither the WAIS nor the W–B I has so high a "ceiling" as some other scales, as for example, the 1937 Terman Merrill revision of the Binet.

The lower ceiling of the W–B and the WAIS is no accident but represents the author's deliberate attempt to eschew measuring abilities beyond points at which he feels they no longer serve as a valid measure of a subject's general intelligence. IQ's of 150 or more may have some discriminative value in certain fields, such as professional aptitude, but only as measures of unusual intellectual capacity. Intellectual ability, however, is only partially related to general intelligence. Exceptional intellectual ability is itself a kind of special ability.

W–B I and WAIS IQ's will also be found delimited at the lower end of the Scale. But here the limitation is occasioned by purely practical considerations, namely, the need for continuity both as to mode of presentation and as to type of material presented. The testing of low grade mental defectives (imbeciles and idiots) generally requires special items and modes of administration. Some tests, like Similarities, are just too difficult for low grade defectives, while others like the Picture Arrangement cannot be easily presented in a way that will be comprehensible to them. For this reason it seemed better to leave the testing of this group to more suitable scales.[8] Nevertheless, the W–BI and the WAIS have a "floor" sufficiently low to discriminate between the higher grades of mental retardation (IQ's of 50 to 70). This is generally sufficient for the testing of most adult defectives.

[8] For adults testing below 50 IQ, the author's Children's Scale (WISC) will often be found a useful supplement or substitute. The methods of equating scores and obtaining IQ's for adult performance on this scale have been outlined elsewhere (522).

Difficulty of Test Items

The order of difficulty of test items on the W–B I and WAIS were for the most part derived from frequency tables of items passed or failed by the standardizing population. In this respect, a more careful check was possible on the WAIS standardization, where statistical studies of actual frequencies were made on the subtests.[9] But, of course, no matter how comprehensive the check, an order of difficulty applies primarily to the original group for which it was established. Its reference value depends essentially upon how faithfully it corresponds to the larger groups which it is intended to represent. In the case of the W–B I the original standardization group was constituted by a population sampling drawn mostly from the New York area and to this extent may have shown some particularities referable to the testing locus. A number of investigations (16, 273) have in fact been able to show differences as regards order of difficulty in certain subtest items between those given in the measurement book and in their own studies. The significance of these differences have to be evaluated rather carefully, since most of the population samples in these studies were considerably more restricted than those of the original standardization.

In addition to geographic locus there are at least three factors that can influence order of difficulty: education, sex and level of intelligence. Along with these is the ever present variable of age. None of these was specifically investigated as regards possible effect, but in the course of analysis of test variables with age some interesting data regarding the order of difficulty came to light on the Vocabulary test. In general, the *order* of difficulty for words was roughly the same at all ages, but interestingly enough the harder words were much more frequently passed by the older than the younger subjects (Appendix Table 66). The implication of this finding was that in presenting the words one had to proceed further down the Vocabulary List with older subjects. The finding did not affect the general results but did suggest the possibility that it might influence individual test scores. Much of this concern centers about doing injustice to subjects who may tend to "scatter." In such cases the possible source of error may be circumvented by proceeding beyond the stopping point prescribed by the test instructions. In the case of the Picture Completion test this contingency is automatically provided for, since all items are presented to the subject. In the case of the older subtests a certain amount of leeway is left to the examiner. But, of course, this leeway must not be interpreted as a privilege to continue indefinitely after the subject has reached the number of allowed failures, since to do so is generally not only a waste of time but also does violence to the norms as established.

[9] As an illustration, see Appendix Table 61, which gives an analysis of data for the Information test.

Scale Abbreviations and Short Forms

Since the initial publication of the Wechsler Bellevue Scales many attempts (408, 409) have been made to set up 'short forms' through various 'best' combinations of the subtests. The usual justification for these procedures, apart from the fact that they greatly reduce the time required to administer the Scale in its entirety, is that they furnish correlations with the Full Scale, of a sufficiently high order to be used as substitutes for it. The high correlations of most of these short scales with total score derived from empirical studies could, of course, be anticipated from the high inter-test correlations, and might be derived directly from them by appropriate multiple correlation techniques. McNemar (337) has in fact established in this manner correlation tables for best pairs, triads, quartets and quintets for the W–B I. Maxwell (358) applying a like technique to obtain comparable abbreviated scales for the WAIS contrasted them with corresponding combinations of the W–B I. A table of contrasting validities of the Short Scale combinations is given in Table 27. A more extensive study of the correlations of the WAIS subtest with total score was recently done by Doppelt (146). In this study Doppelt calculated the correlations for the Verbal and Performance subtests separately[10] and again for optimal correlations of the sum of a combination of 4 of the subtests (Arithmetic, Vocabulary, Block Design and Digit Span) with Full Scale. Doppelt's findings are given in Table 28.

It should be noted, as McNemar has pointed out, that the usefulness of all abbreviated scales depends upon the accuracy with which total IQ scores can be estimated. This involves taking into consideration the error of estimate in IQ points of the test combinations employed as well as standard deviation of the Full Scale IQ. The confidence which an examiner can have in the abbreviated scale will then depend on the leeway which he will allow himself for the anticipatable error of prediction. More important, however, as regards legitimate employment of an abbreviated scale, is the use to which the examiner intends to put his results. If he merely wants an IQ for screening purposes, any of the triad or even some of the diad test combinations listed in the tables may suffice. For anything beyond that, the author would not recommend short scales. His point of view is that an intelligence test should and can give the examiner much more than an IQ. What one wants from a meaningful intelligence examination is an evaluation of an individual's special as well as over-all capacity, his strengths and weaknesses and an indication of how these contribute to or influence his global functioning. For this purpose not fewer but more tests are needed, and the Full Scale W–B I or WAIS should be looked upon as a minimal rather than a maximal battery.

---

[10] Also for different age groups.

TABLE 27

*Validities of abbreviated WAIS and W–B I Scales (Maxwell)**

The correlation coefficients of the abbreviated W–B Scales recommended by Mc-Nemar as contrasted with the coefficients for corresponding combinations of the WAIS subtests.

Scale Length	Subtests†	W–B *r*	WAIS *r*
Duads.............	I–BD	0.884	0.917
	C–BD	0.881	0.885
	S–BD	0.880	0.885
	S–DS	0.864	0.855
	C–DS	0.853	0 870
	S–PC	0.851	0.889
	I–S	0.844	0.903
	DS–BD	0.844	0.852
	A–BD	0.841	0.855
	A–DS	0.840	0.849
Triads.............	C–DS–BD	0.912	0.927
	I–S–BD	0.912	0.942
	S–DS–BD	0.911	0.915
	I–C–BD	0.910	0.939
	S–PC–DS	0.907	0.917
	S–D–BD	0.906	0.913
	C–A–BD	0.903	0.932
	I–DS–BD	0.903	0.935
	C–S–BD	0.902	0.926
	S–D–PC	0.898	0.917
Tetrads............	C–A–DS–BD	0.932	0.953
	C–S–DS–BD	0.929	0.949
	I–S–DS–BD	0.928	0.954
	C–A–DS–PC	0.928	0.954
	A–S–PC–DS	0.928	0.946
	I–C–DS–BD	0.928	0.959
	S–D–PC–BD	0.927	0.944
	S–DS–PC–BD	0.927	0.941
	C–DS–PC–BD	0.926	0.947
	A–S–DS–BD	0.926	0.942

* Correlations of some clinically validated scales and correlations cited by Maxwell show systematic equivalent differences for W–B I and WAIS combinations.

Abbreviated scales of WAIS have higher correlations with Full Scale than abbreviated W–B I for both clinical as well as normal population. Some changes undergone for best abbreviated scales increased correlations because of the increased reliability of subtests.

Abbreviated scales reduce time necessary for obtaining IQ; they also reduce the effectiveness of individual examination. The loss of qualitative observations and discreqancies in individual subtest performances is particularly significant.

TABLE 28

Validities of Abbreviated WAIS

Correlations between 2 WAIS Verbal Tests and Total Verbal Score (Doppelt)		Correlations between 2 WAIS Performance Tests and Total Performance Score	
Ages 25–34*		Ages 25–34	
Subtests	r	Subtests	r
Inf., Voc.	0.940	Bl.Des., P.Arr.	0.917
Inf., Sim.	0.936	D.Sym., Bl.Des.	0.917
Arith., Voc.	0.934	P.Comp., Bl.Des.	0.914
Sim., Voc.	0.924	P.Comp., Obj.Assem.	0.909
Inf., Comp.	0.921	P.Arr., Obj.Assem.	0.906
Comp., Arith.	0.914	P.Comp., P.Arr.	0.906
Inf., Arith.	0.913	Bl.Des., Obj.Assem.	0.902
Comp., Voc.	0.912	D.Sym., P.Comp.	0.900
D.Sp., Voc.	0.912	D.Sym., Obj.Assem.	0.897
Arith., Sim.	0.911	D.Sym., P.Arr.	0.880
Comp., Sim.	0.908		
Inf., D.Sp.	0.905		
Comp., D.Sp.	0.894		
Sim., D.Sp.	0.891		
Arith., D.Sp.	0.843		

Correlation of Sum of 4 Subtests (Arith., Voc., Bl.Des., P.Arr.) with Full Scale.

Age group	No.	r
18–19	200	0.960
25–34	300	0.954
45–54	300	0.958
60–64	101	0.968
65–69	86	0.963
70–74	80	0.957
75 and over	85	0.962

* For additional and separate correlations for age groups 18–19 and 45–54, see Doppelt (146).

Comparison of WAIS and W–B I

Thus far there have been only a few studies comparing the WAIS with the W–B I. Of the three available to the author, the first by Goolishian and Ramsay (203) was a serial study of 546 white, psychiatric patients, 392 of whom were given the W–B I, and 154 the WAIS. The subjects were not the same individuals but the two groups were preliminarily equated for age and education. Comparisons were made between IQ scores of the

TABLE 29

*Comparison of W–B I and WAIS IQ's**

Scale	W–B I†		WAIS‡		Significance of Difference	
	Mean	S.D.	Mean	S.D.	*t*	*P*
Verbal IQ................	103.42	15.53	100.68	19.47	1.87	—
Performance IQ...........	101.82	17.60	94.99	13.97	4.76	<0.01
Full Scale IQ.............	102.94	18.13	98.53	15.01	2.91	0.01

* Goolishian and Ramsay (203).

† 392 subjects (different subjects from WAIS group).

‡ 154 subjects (different subjects from W–B I group).

two groups on the Verbal, Performance and Full Scales and between mean scores on the various subtests. The results showed a mean difference of 2.7 points on the Verbal, 6.8 on the Performance and 4.4 points on the Full Scale, respectively. All the differences, though small, were in favor of the W–B I; those for the Verbal and Performance parts were significant at the 0.01 level. The findings are summarized in Table 29. All of the subtests showed relatively small differences in absolute score but in five of them (Arithmetic, Digit Span, Digit Symbol, Picture Arrangement and Block Design) the differences were significant at the 1 per cent level. The authors correctly conclude that the differences need to be taken into account when comparisons are made between the subject's performance on the WAIS and W–B I. Although the subjects in this study were equated for age and sex, the fact that the investigation was not a test-retest evaluation of the same subjects and that it was carried out on psychiatric patients needs to be considered in interpreting the results.

The other two studies reported involve test-retest or concomitant administration of both Scales but they involve relatively small population samples (college students). In one by Cole and Weleba (113), 46 subjects were given both the W–B I and the WAIS alternately and successively and the correlations between Verbal, Performance and Full Scale separately reported. These were as follows: W–B I Verbal × WAIS Verbal = 0.87, W–B I Performance × WAIS Performance = 0.52 and W–B I Full Scale × WAIS Full Scale = 0.82. The corresponding changes in IQ were: 0.38, 0.92 and 0.52 points, respectively. While differences for the Scale as a whole or the major parts of it were quite negligible, differences between some of the subtest scores reached levels of significance. The Vocabulary "ran significantly and consistently higher" in favor of the WAIS. The investigators also reported noticeable practice effects on Picture Arrangement, Object Assembly and Digit Symbol subtests.

The third study by Dana (126) was limited to a comparison of a quartet of subtests, namely, Similarities, Comprehension, Information, Vocabulary. Subjects were 208 college students. Results showed no significant differences between the WAIS and the W–B I on Information, Comprehension and Similarities tests, and a barely significant difference (at the 0.5 level) between the two Vocabularies. This difference varied on the average of 1 to 2 points in favor of the WAIS. One reservation that may be made in the findings of both the Dana and Cole and Weleba studies is that they do not seem to have taken into account the problem of overlapping contents or of the variations that might result from the differences in mode of presentation of some of the subtests.

In addition to the above, we add the results of an unpublished investigation by Rabourn[10a] (419) in which the possible sources of error considered in the foregoing studies appear to have been avoided. This was achieved by presenting the test questions for both the W–BI and WAIS in a single administration. Each scale was given to half of the subjects, and completed by adding the unique items from the other instrument. The 50 subjects used came from the University of California Counseling Center intake. Their age range was from 17–27, with a mean age of 20.2. The mean Full Scale IQ's for the W–B and WAIS were, respectively, 118.3 and 115.2 with corresponding S.D.'s of 9.04 and 8.47. A comparison of the Means, S.D.'s and levels of significance of the difference between the Full, Verbal and Performance IQ's of the respective scale differences is given in Table 30. The findings show small but significant test differences between the Full and Performance Scales but not between the respective Verbal Scales of the WAIS and W–B I. There were also significant differences between the subtest scores of the two scales. For the range of IQ's comprehended,

TABLE 30
*Comparison of W–B I and WAIS IQ's**

Scale	W–B I†		WAIS†		Significance of Difference	
	Mean	S.D.	Mean	S.D.	t	P
Verbal IQ	115.36	9.43	116.30	8.75	1.88	—
Performance IQ	116.98	10.14	111.78	9.72	8.14	0.01
Full Scale IQ	118.34	9.04	115.22	8.47	7.80	0.01

* Rabourn (419).
† The same 50 subjects tested for both tests.

[10a] The author wishes to thank Mr. Rabourn, and Miss Barbara A. Kirk, Manager of the University of California Counseling Center, for permission to use the data contained in a copy of Mr. Rabourn's paper.

subjects attained lower[11] WAIS scores on the Similarities, Picture Completion, Block Design, Picture Arrangement and Object Assembly, and lower W–B I scores on Information, Comprehension, Digit Span and Vocabulary. No significant differences were found between the Arithmetic and Digit Symbol tests. A comparison of t scores and level of significance for average and superior subjects (IQ's 110 and below and 120 and above) indicated that the WAIS might be more discriminating at the upper end of the IQ range than the W–B I.

[11] And, hence, indicating that these tests were somewhat harder.

Chapter 8

Factorial Composition of the Wechsler
Bellevue I and Wechsler Adult
Intelligence Scales

As advanced in the first chapter, general intelligence is not a unique entity but a complex constellation of interacting factors, and, if regarded as a capacity or trait, is most satisfactorily interpreted as a composite aggregate resulting from the interaction of a varying number of primary abilities. It is these abilities that are measured in the first instance by an intelligence scale, but by virtue of this fact alone an intelligence scale is not equivalent to a differential aptitude test, although one can, if one wishes, so treat it.[1] In so far as they enter into some global measure of intelligence, the individual subtests that compose a battery lose their separate identities. They then become different measures of whatever it is presumed the scale measures. For this very reason it is of particular importance to know the factorial composition of the tests one is using, not only because some may be better measures of intelligence than others, but also because they serve to define the abilities one is presumably measuring.

The ensuing discussion of the factorial composition of the W–B I and WAIS is presented in order to illustrate the points just made as well as to bring together the actual findings of the several factorial analyses that have been done on the two scales.

Nearly all the factorial studies reported on the W–B I have used Thurstone's centroid method of factor extraction, but some are limited to simple orthogonal solutions while others proceed to oblique solutions. The Australian school (182, 235) in analyzing the W–B I has employed Burt's modified orthogonal bifactor procedure, and Cohen (112) supplemented the complete centroid solution of the WAIS with a comparable analysis. The differences with regard to fitting hyperplanes account in

---

[1] This is what is done when one uses an intelligence scale for differential diagnosis, but doing so does not demand that the tests be regarded as pure measures. The author does not believe in pure abilities any more than he believes in pure intelligence.

TABLE 31

Comparison of factor pattern of two age levels of the Wechsler Intelligence Scale for Children and the Adult Wechsler Scale*

Subtest	WISC Year 10½					WISC Year 13½					Adult Scale Form I†				
	I	II	III	IV	h^2	I	II	III	IV	h^2	I	II	III	IV	h^2
Inf..........	69	−07	48	21	76	69	−03	51	10	74	70	−10	40	25	69
Comp........	65	−01	44	15	64	54	−09	48	01	53	71	−03	43	12	72
Arith.........	57	04	31	42	60	53	−11	36	30	50	63	−01	34	14	54
Sim..........	58	−09	43	22	59	66	05	48	03	66	75	06	40	06	72
Voc..........	75	08	42	18	79	66	01	51	01	70					
D.Sp.........	34	11	10	55	45	39	−08	25	24	28	49	−07	14	44	45
P.C..........	57	31	15	−17	47	49	49	09	−01	47	60	35	08	08	50
P.A..........	51	12	22	34	45	51	33	00	38	52	52	22	03	26	39
B.D..........	61	49	00	22	65	60	56	11	−02	69	69	44	02	16	70
O.A..........	49	51	−02	16	54	49	55	00	06	54	48	51	05	−07	49
Coding B....	33	05	16	38	28	43	13	14	24	28	59	06	02	54	64
Mazes.......	50	42	00	13	45	44	17	−01	55	53					
Mean contribution to variance (%)															
	32	7	8	8	55	30	9	10	6	55	39	6	6	7	58

* Gault (182).
† From Hammer's analysis.

part for the difference in the definition of the first reference variable, and to some extent the differences in factor loadings of the various factors extracted.

Since publication of the W–B I there have been at least six factorial studies of the scale, some done on the original standardization data (34), others on newly collected data, including material from both normal (235) and abnormal (109) subjects, and one study (131) in which a number of other reference variables were combined with the 11 subtests of the W–B Scale. The number of factors identified in most of the analyses has seldom exceeded 4, of which 3 are recurrently described. These are a broad verbal factor (verbal comprehension), a non-verbal organization factor (variously identified as performance, non-verbal, space and visual-motor organization) and *g* (sometimes referred to as the eductive or general reasoning factor). Depending upon the method employed, the general factor emerges either as the first reference variable or as the prime second order factor in the extended analysis. Table 31, illustrative of the findings on W–B I, shows the order and range of the factors as obtained with a bifactor analysis. Table 31 also gives the factor pattern at two age levels of the WISC and shows the equivalence and continuity of the factors entering into both Scales. Table 32 shows the factor structure of neuropsychiatric groups on the W–B I Scale, after oblique rotation (109).

TABLE 32

*Common factor and second-order factor loadings of the Wechsler Bellevue subtests
in psychoneurotic, schizophrenic and brain-damaged groups**

Test	Factor A Verbal			Factor B Non-Verbal			Factor C Distractibility			Second Order Factor g		
	Psy	Sch	BrD	Psy	Sch	BrD	Psy	Sch	BrD	Psy	Sch	BrD
I	59	61	68	−06	04	−03	06	04	03	74	63	67
C	57	49	58	13	−10	−02	−03	11	−08	71	50	47
DF	−01	−07	−01	−09	04	00	52	51	54	57	60	53
DB	−04	02	00	05	−11	−07	51	55	69	59	62	64
A	17	33	32	−14	18	09	45	11	34	67	57	72
S	43	55	64	03	05	03	14	07	−04	69	62	61
V	68	66	49	−13	−01	−09	02	02	−01	77	57	40
PA	10	25	18	36	42	60	23	−06	−11	57	62	53
PC	41	39	22	44	53	33	−10	−21	03	58	61	50
BD	00	05	00	44	60	73	36	14	05	65	67	61
OA	−04	01	−21	71	64	83	04	00	−04	35	49	40
DS	02	−02	04	13	15	40	44	44	22	62	64	57
										84 (A)	68 (A)	76 (A)
										45 (B)	60 (B)	64 (B)
										84 (C)	83 (C)	78 (C)

(A) = Factor A.   (B) = Factor B.   (C) = Factor C.
* Cohen (109).

Thus far, there has been only one factorial study of the WAIS, that of
Jacob Cohen (112). Dr. Cohen's obliquely rotated solutions are presented in Table 33, and have been supplemented with a bifactor analysis
done at the request of the author.[2] The factor structure of this analysis is
given in Table 34.

With the above data in view, let us now consider the various factors which
enter into the scales and the respective contribution of each of the tests
to the total variance of the scales. The first and most important is the
general eductive factor *g*. This emerges, as already noted, either as a first
reference or as the calculated second order factor, depending upon the
type of solution employed. It shows large loadings in all tests, which do
not vary too much with age. It accounts for about 50 per cent of the total

[2] The author wishes to express special indebtedness to Dr. Cohen (Psychiatric
Evaluation Project, Veterans Administration Hospital, Montrose, New York) for
his assistance in evaluating the *ad hoc* W–B factorial studies and for his aid in the
clarification of various problems presented in this chapter. The conclusions drawn
by the author do not necessarily coincide with Dr. Cohen's points of view.

TABLE 33

*Comparative factor analysis of WAIS Performance for ages 18 to 75 and over with oblique primary factors for 4 principal age groups**

Age	Factor A, Verbal				Factor B, Non-Verbal				Factor C, Memory			
	18–19	25–34	45–54	60–75+	18–19	25–34	45–54	60–75+	18–19	25–34	45–54	60–75+
Inf...........	30	21	36	29	09	−06	05	−09	04	10	10	41
Comp.........	33	45	27	39	08	03	−04	01	09	−10	08	38
Arith.........	09	01	06	04	10	00	02	06	32	32	33	52
Sim...........	23	20	32	42	−07	−10	06	10	05	−02	−10	10
D.Sp.........	−10	−05	−06	00	−09	03	00	09	28	24	35	45
Voc..........	24	48	37	37	−09	07	−03	−02	09	−02	03	51
D.Sym.......	08	04	01	−06	14	09	04	29	08	−02	09	21
P.C..........	07	03	04	07	09	02	05	04	−01	−06	02	01
B.D..........	−03	−01	00	00	34	30	35	58	12	07	01	09
P.A..........	14	06	00	30	24	22	−03	20	−10	09	−02	−09
O.A..........	−08	00	00	−01	34	45	31	56	05	−01	00	−03

Age	Factor D, Picture Completion				Factor E, Digit Symbol		
	18–19	25–34	45–54	60–75+	18–19	25–34	45–54
Inf..................	04	15	−08	10	01	02	−03
Comp...............	−02	11	09	−10	−08	−07	−10
Arith...............	−05	06	00	08	00	−09	−04
Sim.................	21	15	02	−02	00	17	06
D.Sp...............	08	−05	02	03	26	10	06
Voc................	16	−09	−03	−09	07	02	10
D.Sym.............	−08	01	00	20	24	25	31
P.C................	29	34	21	38	−06	06	00
B.D................	03	04	−03	00	00	00	02
P.A................	06	−03	22	10	04	04	22
O.A................	04	−06	04	03	08	00	−06

* Cohen (109). For interpretation of factors, see text.

contributed by all the tests, and from 66 to 75 per cent of the *communal* variance, that is ⅔ to ¾ of all the variance shared by two or more tests.

The interpretation of the general factor is at once both easy and difficult to expound. It is clearly similar to, if not identical with Spearman's g.[3] By general consensus, it involves broad mental organization; it is independent of the modality or contextual structure from which it is elicited; g cannot be exclusively identified with any single intellectual ability and for this reason cannot be described in concrete operational terms. Statisti-

[3] Sometimes designated as G.

TABLE 34

Bifactor analysis of WAIS Performance for ages 18 to 75+ with primary factors for 4 principal age groups*

	Ages 18-19						Ages 25-34					
	I	II	III	IV	V	VI	I	II	III	IV	V	VI
Inf.	83	35	12	04	05	01	84	22	-08	10	18	02
Comp.	69	38	11	09	-02	-09	71	47	04	-10	13	-08
Arith.	68	10	13	34	-06	00	71	01	00	31	07	-10
Sim.	81	27	-09	05	24	00	75	21	-13	-02	18	18
D. Sp.	63	-12	-12	29	09	29	59	-05	04	23	-06	11
Voc.	86	28	-12	09	18	08	79	50	09	-02	-11	02
D. Sym.	66	09	19	08	-09	27	64	04	11	-02	01	27
P.C.	76	08	12	-01	33	-07	72	03	03	06	41	06
B.D.	71	-03	46	13	03	00	71	-01	38	-07	05	00
P.A.	66	16	32	-11	07	04	69	06	28	09	-04	04
O.A.	65	-09	46	05	05	09	59	00	56	-01	-07	00
Mean Contrib. to Variance, %	52.7	4.5	6.0	2.3	2.1	1.7	50.0	5.2	5.3	1.7	2.5	1.3
	(Total = 69.3%)						(Total = 66.6%)					

	Ages 45-54						Ages 60-75+ (K.C.)				
	I	II	III	IV	V	VI	I	II	III	IV	V
Inf.	82	37	06	10	08	-03	73	29	-08	40	07
Comp.	76	27	-05	08	08	-10	60	39	01	37	-07
Arith.	74	06	02	32	00	-04	63	04	05	51	05
Sim.	75	32	07	-10	07	06	65	42	09	10	-01
D. Sp.	65	-06	00	34	02	06	48	00	08	44	02
Voc.	83	38	-03	03	-03	10	66	37	-02	50	-06
D. Sym.	65	01	05	09	00	30	71	-06	26	21	13
P.C.	77	04	06	02	20	00	75	07	04	01	25
B.D.	69	00	40	01	-03	02	65	00	53	09	00
P.A.	74	00	-03	-02	21	22	65	30	18	-09	07
O.A.	68	00	36	00	04	-06	58	-01	51	-03	02
Mean Contrib. to Variance, %	54.3	4.2	2.8	2.3	0.9	1.6	42.1	5.9	6.1	9.7	0.9
	(Total = 66.1%)						(Total = 64.%)				

* Cohen (109). For interpretation of factors, see text.

cally, it is somewhat easier to define. Perhaps the most general and straight-forward interpretation of g is the one given by G. Thomson (490 a). According to Thomson, g is a recurrent statistical quantity arising from the fact that every test of any complexity (and all tests of intelligence are) contains common elements. Hence, if a battery is made up of any consider-able number of tests or even a small number containing many common elements, the tests so combined will inevitably permit the extraction of an embracingly common or universal factor. The factor will be all-embracing, because it derives from the collective influence of the common elements germane to the tests. In brief, g is a measure of a collective communality which necessarily emerges from the intercorrelation of any broad sample of mental abilities.

Other suggestive interpretations of g have been offered by Adcock et al. (2) in discussing the nature of the general factor which they extracted from the W–B Scale. One interpretation of g which they give is that it is a factor of common function, in the sense that the same or similar operations may be involved in a variety of different activities. For example, a person with good neuromuscular endowment may be expected to excel in various manipulative skills or athletic abilities. Similarly, speed of perception may, without much differentiation, be involved in solving an arithmetical problem, in retaining memory for words or in getting the "hang" of a puzzle. Their second[4] interpretation of g is that it is "a factor resulting from vicarious function," or the fact that one type of ability may substitute for another in a variety of situations, for example, trial and error for methodical analysis, rote memory for logical inference, use of mechanical aids for brute strength, etc. This interpretation is in line with the concept of the functional equivalence of mental abilities advanced in this volume, namely, the view that any ability may be substituted for any other ability in the intellective process, provided it contributes to the same end effect; g is the factor which best accounts for this potential and explains its systematic high communality in all tests of intelligence. As in "skinning a cat," there are many ways of solving a problem, and if the criterion is successful achievement (attaining a high test score) it makes little difference in most cases how a task is accomplished, provided it is completed satisfactorily. For this reason an intelligence scale should comprehend a large variety of tests so as to afford the individual as many alternative ways as possible to evidence his basic endowment. By the same token, it makes little difference what type of task is involved, provided it permits of substitutive solutions.

The last and perhaps the most important interpretation of g is that it is

[4] The writers also offer a third interpretation of g as "a measure of concomitant endowment," but this would not differentiate g from any other broad factor or merely from the assertion that all mental abilities tend to be positively correlated.

not a factor at all in the sense that verbal comprehension, memory, etc., are factors of the mind. To be sure, we have repeatedly referred to g as a factor, but only in the sense of its being one of the variables which accounts for a large part of the communal variance in a battery of intelligence tests. One should note, however, that unlike all other factors it cannot be associated with any unique or single ability; g is involved in many different types of ability; it is in essence not an ability at all, but a property of the mind. It is the property of the mind which in terms of Stern's conceptualization (478) determines its capacity for *collective coupling*.[5]

The other broad factors which have been invariably extracted from the W–B I and WAIS are: (1) a verbal comprehension and (2) a performance or non-verbal (visual motor, space-perception, etc.) organization factor. Verbal comprehension[6] is the ability to derive meaning from words singly or in combination. It is best represented in such tests as Vocabulary, Information, Comprehension and Similarities. Its high correlation with g represents its substitutive potential, but its specific characteristics leave it open to ambiguous interpretation. Vocabulary, for example, may involve an inherent capacity for verbal concept formation but may also be the result of acquired verbal information. For this reason, many have often been suspicious of the verbalizer. Another interesting fact about verbal comprehension is that it is seemingly the one broad factor that shows cortical localization as inferred from recurrent types of defects observed in aphasic disorders. However, the high intercorrelation of the primary factors would not make this finding so serious as it might at first appear. The aphasic patient, as Hughling Jackson once pointed out (530), may be wordless but not speechless. If our concept of the substitutive nature of factors and abilities is correct, even a speechless subject has hope for rehabilitation, since it may be possible to replace verbal comprehension by other noetic processes.

Non-verbal organization, variously interpreted as performance (Balinsky), closure (Birren), space perception (Hammer) or visualization (Davis), is the third broad factor systematically identified in both W–B I and WAIS. The tests which most consistently load on this factor in all age groups are the Object Assembly and Block Design tests. Picture Arrangement and Picture Completion are also comprehended by this factor, though usually with much lower loadings. In the factorialization of the WAIS, however, Picture Completion disappears from the non-verbal column. Its major contribution to the Scale's variance only appears when an additional fifth factor is extracted (Table 34). Since it is the only test under this factor,

[5] See section on the physical constructs of intelligence, p. 20.
[6] In contradistinction to verbal fluency.

Cohen temporarily omitted defining it.[7] Non-verbal organization thus appears to be a more complex factor than verbal comprehension, a fact supported by its multiple interpretations by different authors. Its main determinant seems to be a capacity to organize discrete spacially perceived units into larger wholes or configurations.

The fourth major factor systematically identified in both the WAIS and the W–B I is an undifferentiated memory factor. The tests which show highest loadings on this factor are Digit Span, Digit Symbol[7] and, depending upon the age group, Arithmetic and Information. The first three of these were comprehended by Cohen in his analysis of W–B I performance by neuropsychiatric subjects under a factor interpreted as freedom from distractibility, but later reinterpreted by him as a Memory Factor. The identification of an undifferentiated memory factor in intelligence is, in a sense, a challenge to the historic concept of the memory function, which was divided into different types, such as visual vs. auditory, logical vs. rote, immediate vs. remote, etc. The memory factor as extracted does not seem to be any of these in particular.

The emergence of a general memory factor on the W–B I and WAIS is perhaps surprising in view of the relatively low correlations of the one clear reference test (Digit Span) with the rest of the subtests of the Scales. Nevertheless, it is quite clear that it is present and that its contribution to the total variance of the Scale is considerable, being almost equal to that of the verbal and non-verbal organization factors. Equally interesting is the fact that it contains loadings of test performance ordinarily not considered as dependent upon memory, e.g., arithmetical reasoning. As a factor in intelligence it is negligibly identifiable with any historic memory types, such as visual, auditory, recent, remote, etc. The memory required for intellectual functioning, as represented by the extracted factor, is a kind of general retentiveness, perhaps operationally identified as associative memory, where associative does not stand for a type but an over-all description.

Another finding worthy of special note is the increasing role which the memory factor plays in the older age groups. This again would seem to be explicable on the basis of the broad substitutive nature of the primary factors.[8] The older person depends more and more on past experience (stored information), far more than upon the utilization of primary abilities. A

[7] A similar situation occurred in the case of the Digit Symbol test which, though frequently comprehended under the memory factor in other studies, failed to appear in Cohen's analysis of this factor, and only showed a significant loading when still another factor (VI, Table 34) was extracted.

[8] Another possible explanation is that there is a change in the nature of the factor with age. In this case one should re-name the factor.

good memory is much more important in old age than in youth; where it fails altogether, as in senility, the individual presents indeed a sad picture.

In addition to the factors mentioned above, several other independent factors have been reported for the W–B I and the WAIS. Some of these are merely alternative interpretations of those already named, as, for example, closure for verbal organization, eduction of conceptual relations or general reasoning for g. But others are distinctly different, such as numerical facility and mechanical knowledge for the W–B I (Davis), and some still unidentified, such as the two derived by Cohen from the WAIS. The former were obtained through the addition of supplementary reference tests to the 11 W–B subtests, the latter by extending the factorialization of the WAIS beyond points where other authors might have stopped. It should also be noted that these additional factors account for a very small fraction of the total variance (less than 2 per cent) and generally involved the interpretation of a single test or, as in the case of Davis' study, loadings derived from alternate forms of almost identical tests.

The two "new" factors extracted by Cohen on the WAIS are difficult to interpret because of the absence of any reference abilities and the lack of clear-cut implications of the tests which uniquely load under these factors. Some clues, however, are available from the alignment which the Picture Completion and Digit Symbol occasionally show with some of the other subtests under other factor columns. On the basis of this association, which is far from systematic but supplemented by a number of clinical clues, we shall venture the following tentative interpretations of the two unidentified factors.

Factor E (Factor VI in the bifactor analysis) appears to be a measure of the individual's capacity to resist distraction. This is in part suggested by occasional substantial, though not necessarily significant loadings on the same factors as Digit Span, Picture Arrangement and Arithmetic. It appears similar to but not quite identical with Cohen's freedom from distraction factor,[9] and for practical purposes could be identified with it. Factor D (Factor V in the bifactor analysis) we propose to interpret as, and provisionally call, a *relevance* factor. By relevance we mean appropriateness of response. This is perhaps best illustrated by instances when appropriateness is lacking. For example, many schizophrenics and other subjects, instead of noting the called for and essential missing part of a picture, respond with an irrelevant detail. Thus, in the "water" item (WAIS PC, item 6), instead of noting the absence of poured water, a subject may say, "The hand should be there"; in the picture of the man's head (WAIS PC 7), where the bridge of the spectacles is missing, the subject will say, "The rest of the body"; or again in the picture of the pig minus a tail (WAIS PC 2), the subject

---

[9] It is so interpreted in the case of pathological subjects.

may say, "Food in the pail." The same sort of irrelevancy can occasionally be forthcoming on most of the other subtests of the Scale, especially the Verbal ones. For example, to the Similarities "Dog-lion" item, a subject may respond with, "Dog can be kept as a pet, lion can't"; "Coat-dress," "They conserve modesty." To Comprehension, "Why does a train need an engine?" . . . "Because a train needs a whistle; a whistle is on the engine and it is needed to prevent accidents." Arithmetic, "A man buys 6 cents worth of stamps and gives the clerk 10 cents, how much change should he get back?" Subject asks, "Does he buy 1 cent or 3 cent stamps?" Information, "In what direction would you travel if you went from Chicago to Panama?" The subject asks, "By plane or train?" "What is the population of the United States?" Subject says, "I can't say; it changes from day to day."

Irrelevancies of the type just noted may arise from inner preoccupation or from impairment of the subject's perceptual or cognitive processes. This interpretation is based on clinical leads derived, curiously enough, from the opposite kind of performance by subjects similarly diagnosed, namely schizophrenics. Schizophrenics either do very badly (as a rule) or surprisingly well (but not frequently) on the Digit Symbol Test. Some seemingly fail because of inner distraction; others do well because of obtuseness to outer stimulation. The former cannot "concentrate" on the task for a sufficient length of time to perform the test; the latter are so little involved that doing the test becomes a perseverative task which they carry out without concern. It would, of course, be desirable to find some objective criteria with which to validate this hypothesis. The only support comes from recent correlations obtained between the Taylor Manifest Anxiety Scale and certain of the subtests of the WAIS and W–B I (Arithmetic, Digit Span and Digit Symbol) which have been clinically described as subject to anxiety. The correlations are not very high, and are generally one-sided. Subjects with high anxiety scores tend to have significantly lower scores on the designated subtests, but not vice versa. The Digit Symbol is the test most affected.

In discussing the factors that have been extracted from both Scales, as indeed those extracted from other intelligence test batteries, there is need to take cognizance of the difference in the amount of variance which the factors contribute. It is possible by using a great number of tests, or even a smaller number of specially selected tests, to extract additional factors. Guilford in his paper on *The structure of intellect* (216) now includes some 40 different factors that have been "identified." Most of these would hardly occur in any standard test of intelligence but, even from a theoretical point of view, their admission presents some serious problems. The first is that the profusion of factors discovered seems to contradict the intent or purpose of the factorial technique, the generally stated aim of which is to account for the major variance of a large battery of tests in terms of a minimal number of primary abilities or factors. Actually, there seem to be more factors than available tests, certainly than good tests of intelligence. This paradox is in part resolved if one examines the percentage of variance most of these newly discovered factors contribute to the total variance extracted from the factorial matrices in which they appear. Quantitatively, they often contribute less than 1 or 2 per cent, and their "independence" is often attested by only a single loading of acceptable magnitude or at best by two.[10]

But even as regards the more solidly established factors, there is considerable difference in the percentage of variance which they contribute, respectively, to the total. Consider, for example, the variance contribution made by the major factors that have been extracted from the WAIS and W–B I Scales. There is first a general factor that appears in any intelligence test battery, which accounts for roughly 50 per cent of the variance. Then there are at most 3 or 4 other principal factors which account for anywhere from 5 to 8 per cent. Finally, depending upon the point to which the factorialization has been carried and the number of tests included, a number of other factors may emerge which contribute at most 1 to 3 per cent to the total. One can conclude from this finding that the factors obtained are of quite a different order and perhaps need to be differently designated. In the opinion of the writer, factors contributing less than 2 per cent might well be regarded as specifics, those contributing between 3 and 10 per cent as broad factors and only those contributing 35 per cent or more as truly general. The factorial composition of the WAIS involves all three types, although in most discussions it is only the general (*g*) and three or four broad common factors (Verbal, Comprehension, Memory, etc.) that are emphasized.

Stability of Factorial Composition in Relation to Age

In the first factorial analysis of the W–B I, Balinsky (34) found that the same factors did not appear in every age group and that the same tests did not enter into the same factors. This has not been substantiated by other authors (2, 112) and may be due to limitations of the samples used.[11] The comparative study of Gault and Hammer, with both the WISC and W–B I (Table 31), showed remarkable consistency in the emergence of the same four factors over the broad age levels compared (7½, 13½ and 25–39 years), and this finding is corroborated by Cohen's complete analysis of the WAIS (Table 33). *g*, Verbal Comprehension and Non-Verbal Organi-

---

[10] In the latter instance, they generally turn out to be alternate forms of the same est, as for example, Davis' Similarities Doublet on the W–B I (131).

[11] In the Balinsky study, the *N*'s were not always so large as desirable; in a number of the age groups not all the tests were administered.

zation ability appear at all ages studied by these two investigators. In addition, Cohen extracted two more factors (the "Picture Completion" and the "Digit Symbol" factors), as yet uninterpreted. But two types of variation still remain: (1) significant differences in the degree of communality of the factors and (2) significant differences in the magnitude of factor loadings contributed by the different tests at different ages. Thus, whereas the total communality contributed by the memory factor is 2.26 per cent at age level 24–35, it reaches 15.1 per cent at age level 60–75 (Table 33). Vocabulary, which has a loading on Factor II (Verbal Comprehension) of 0.28 at year level 18–19, rises to a loading of 0.50 in ages 25–34. Picture Arrangement which has a loading of 0.32 on Factor III all but drops out at ages 45–54. Of course, part of this discrepancy may be accounted for by error variance, but not enough to explain the large changes. Also to be noted are differences in the subtest specificities which, while small, are not negligible. Thus, comprehension at age 18–19 shows a specificity of 0.15, whereas at age 45 specificity is only 0.08. Finally, while the basic four, g, Verbal Comprehension, Non-Verbal Organization and Memory, appear at all ages, some of the lesser general ones fluctuate, and one, the "Digit Symbol" factor, disappears entirely in the age group 60–75.

Of particular interest is the factorial alteration in the oldest age group (Kansas City Sample, ages 60–75). The most striking change is the reduction in the contribution of the general factor and the concomitant increase in the other three principal factors, particularly the memory factor. One explanation might be that the older person is better able to use various abilities for different tasks. Another possibility is that the younger adult[12] relies more on g because he has not yet specialized. Finally, there is always the question whether, as the writer believes, the oldster just does not have as much g and therefore must substitute other abilities for it (particularly, his exploitation of stored experience). In any event, it is fairly evident that the substitutive potential of the various factors plays different roles in the mental organization of the individual at different ages.

The discussion thus far has concerned itself primarily with the factorial composition of the W–B I and WAIS as a whole. The following section will be devoted to a discussion of the factorial characteristics of the individual subtests. The discussion will be based on a composite evaluation of the several analyses reported.

Factorial Composition of Subtests

INFORMATION. The highest test loading for Information other than g is consistently in verbal comprehension, but in a number of studies (112, 235) the test also shows considerable loadings on the memory factor.

---

[12] This is not true of children.

Occasionally it is allied with certain "specifics" and sometimes has been otherwise interpreted (131). In the W–B and WAIS analyses it showed significant loadings, particularly in the older age groups, under the memory factor. As clinically observed, the impact of the factors on the Information Test seems to vary considerably with the individual case. It is also influenced to a degree by pathological conditions; in schizophrenics, for example, by "awareness of environment," in impaired organics by memory defect.

COMPREHENSION. The Comprehension Test, in normal subjects, is mostly dependent on Verbal Comprehension and g. In the case of pathological groups, however, it shows much variability as regards both factors (112). Clinically, one gets the impression that it is much more complexly determined, and that it probably includes factors that could be demonstrated by the use of other reference tests. Davis, by use of such reference tests, found Comprehension to have loadings in verbal fluency, visualization and numerical facility as well as general reasoning. Even more suggestive are certain capacities which, though as yet not actually demonstrated factorially, seem on the basis of clinical experience to influence performance on this test. One of these is a "factor" that may be termed "social stereotypy"; another, "common sense judgment." But here again one must await further analysis to substantiate these clinical hunches. On the basis of findings thus far reported, one can only say that the main variance for the test is substantially accounted for by the g and Verbal Comprehension.

ARITHMETIC. One of the surprises of the Arithmetic Test is its high loading on the Memory factor, although as one might expect, it also shows good g saturation. But here again we are in for a surprise; it rates less well on the g factor than any of the Verbal tests except Digit Span. Moreover, its total communality is relatively low. Even more than in the case of Comprehension, one suspects that with the addition of other reference tests it might show substantial loadings on other factors. One finds support for this in Davis' analysis of the W–B, where the W–B Arithmetic not only showed significant loadings on general reasoning but also on the factors identified as numerical fluency, mechanical knowledge and information. The writer regards these as specifics, but they are nevertheless of an order that needs to be taken into account in interpreting the abilities involved in this test. The high memory factor loading which Arithmetic has at all age levels, particularly in the age group of 60–75, makes one question some of the "abilities" often posited by teachers as necessary for proficiency in mathematics. Reasoning ability seems to have been considerably overestimated and, if our findings are correct, sheer memory substantially underestimated.

SIMILARITIES. The Similarities Test systematically shows the highest loadings on the g factor at all age levels of the WAIS and W–B I. Allowing for the concomitant contribution of the Verbal factor, the test would seem to be primarily a measure of generalizing or abstract ability. For this reason it has been repeatedly designated as a test of concept formation. Still it is not so unique in this respect as certain authors have suggested; nor is it so exclusively dependent on verbal capacity as its content would suggest. This interpretation is supported by its consistently good correlation with tests of abstract reasoning which do not necessarily involve language. Nevertheless, there remains the fact that the test does show conspicuous loadings in Verbal Comprehension in practically all the factorial analyses.[13] One suspects other contributing abilities would emerge from more extended factorialization. Davies found a specific in what he termed the *Similarities Doublet*, without further interpreting its meaning. There is also some indication that the Similarities Test shares with Picture Completion some elements peculiarly common to both, as evidenced by the fact that the test shows very nearly significant loadings on the Picture Completion factor, albeit only at 2 of the 4 age levels of the WAIS analysis. The possible meaning of this posited factor will be considered in the discussion of the Picture Completion Test.

DIGIT SPAN. Operationally defined, facility in repeating numbers would seem to be almost a specific or even unique ability. It is certainly true that a good auditory memory does not go with a good visual memory. Persons who can repeat a poem after one hearing often have difficulty in reproducing a picture or a design, and great chess players who are known to have extraordinary powers of visualization have not shown unusual memory span for digits (157[a]). Nevertheless, the combination of Digit Symbol with Digit Span, the two tests which show the highest loadings on the memory factor, would seem to indicate that both modalities have something in common, perhaps a general or neutral memory function. It is a neutral memory of this sort which is apparently important in intelligence, particularly in later adulthood where it plays a substantial role.

The correlation of Digit Span with g, whether as seen in the factorial analysis or inferred from its correlation with other tests, is systematically low. At the same time, its relative uniqueness is consistently high. This fact may be the reason why other factors have been frequently posited to explain the test's otherwise unaccounted for variance. One factor commonly posited is the ability to attend and concentrate. This is a factor which closely resembles the one Cohen provisionally identified as freedom from distraction in his analysis of the test performance of mentally disturbed

---

[13] But in the case of abnormal subjects, the Similarities Test has been shown to be only a moderately good measure of verbal ability (112).

subjects. The writer strongly suspects that the ability (or the inability) to repeat digits both backward and forward is even more dependent upon what he has called the non-intellective factors of intelligence; perhaps freedom from distraction is one of these.

VOCABULARY. This test at first glance appears to be self-defined. The ability to acquire new words obviously involves Verbal Comprehension, and the Vocabulary does in fact show highest loading of any test on this factor. The puzzling question that remains, however, is why it should also systematically rank highest in g. In the writer's opinion, this is largely due to the test's substitutive potential. This view is supported by Cohen's findings on organics, in which the brain-damaged subjects showed not the highest but the lowest loadings on both the g and Verbal Comprehension factors of any of the Verbal tests. This would suggest that the relatively high score of the brain-damaged patient is in a certain sense an artifact. The words retained are like empty shells. They reflect probable past level of performance but not actual functioning ability. But this very fact makes the Vocabulary a useful test for clinical diagnosis, since it enables the examiner to appraise premorbid functioning. For this reason too, it has generally been used as a base for estimating mental deterioration.

DIGIT SYMBOL. Apart from g, the Digit Symbol test shows its most consistent factorial loadings in Non-Verbal Organization and Memory. Occasionally it has also shown a substantial loading on a Verbal factor. In the Cohen analysis of the WAIS, it appears uniquely under still another unidentified factor (E in the oblique and VI on the bifactor solutions). In the Davis W–B I analysis, it is coupled with numerical facility and perceptual speed. Perceptual speed might be looked upon as an aspect of Non-Verbal Organization but Numerical Fluency would certainly have to be considered as a separate factor—a conclusion which is supported by the fact that certain occupational groups such as accountants and clerical workers generally do well on this test. Because of its multiple determinants, Digit Symbol is factorially ambiguous, and for this reason its inclusion in the Scales has sometimes been questioned. Its other merits, however, more than compensate for this limitation.

PICTURE COMPLETION. Factorially, this test presents an anomalous situation. In most of the analyses, it has shown significant loadings on the non-verbal factors; in some, as in the Cohen analysis of mentally disturbed patients, it divides its communality with the Verbal factor. In the WAIS it fails to show up with any significant loadings on either. Here, most of the test variance is accounted for by a new factor as yet unidentified—the factor labelled E in the oblique and V in the bifactor solution. The factorial ambiguity and inconsistency suggest that Picture Completion should be a poor test to include in an intelligence scale. But this would be a hasty conclusion. In the first place, it shows the highest g loading of any of the Performance tests, at least in normal subjects and, in the second place, it emerges with a new unique factor that seems to be important in intelligent behavior. This is the relevance factor whose significance for the test has already been discussed. Along with other findings, it would seem to substantiate the original description of Picture Completion as a test which measures the individual's ability to differentiate essential from non-essential details.

BLOCK DESIGN. Block Design next to Object Assembly loads most consistently on the Non-Verbal Organization factor. It differs from Object Assembly by the fact that it has a much higher saturation in g. Apart from g, almost its entire communality is accounted for by the non-verbal factor. This holds true for normal, organic and schizophrenic subjects, but not for neurotic subjects (111), in which group it shares its communality to some degree with Freedom from Distraction (Memory) factor. This finding prompted Cohen to express the opinion that "a knowledge of a patient's diagnosis is necessary to approach one's understanding of the score on this test." The same observation could be made regarding the scores on any test. Our own view is that the Block Design is no more subject to this stricture than most of the other subtests of the Scale. Special conditions like mental illness can influence test performance, but changes in the factorial composition of a test are more likely due to the emergence of previously undetected factors than to the suppression of already demonstrated ones. It is clear that Non-Verbal Organization may involve not only closure, perceptual speed, etc., but also depend on certain other capacities which might be discovered by more extended factorialization and especially through the inclusion of other reference abilities. This has actually been shown to be the case by Davis, who found the Block Design to show considerable loadings not only on visualization but on factors which he called Mechanical Knowledge and Information. Taken separately, each of these factors do not contribute much to the test's total variance, but collectively they can be significant. Moreover, in individual cases, even factors with low loadings may considerably influence a subject's performance on a test.

PICTURE ARRANGEMENT. Picture Arrangement loads consistently at all ages on the Non-Verbal Organization factor but generally less than either the Block Design or the Object Assembly. It also shows a significant loading on the Memory factor, and is seemingly interlarded to a significant degree with specific (non-intellective) factors. None of these has been extracted, but one that is seemingly operative as reported by clinicians is what, for want of a better term, might be called "social awareness." In the case of schizophrenics and neurotics, the test appears to be a rather poor measure of non-verbal organization, but it holds up fairly well in the brain-damaged group. It should also be noted that Picture Arrangement has the lowest communality of any tests of the Scale.

An interesting finding is the test's relatively high loading, although not at the level of significance, on Factor E (V on the bifactor oblique) in one of the age groups (45–54). This is the factor which we have provisionally interpreted as *relevance* (see p. 126). Lack of relevance on the Picture Arrangement is indicated when a subject fails to get the point of a story even though he may produce correct sequence or, contrariwise, when he seemingly gets the story and completely misplaces the sequence. For example, a subject is completely stymied by the "Flirt" cartoon because he cannot see why the Little King has to carry a bundle on his head.

OBJECT ASSEMBLY. Object Assembly is a test that gladdens the heart of the factor analyst. Apart from g, almost all its variance is accounted for by the Non-Verbal Organization factor, and only that. The clinician, however, is likely to be less impressed by its factorial purity than by its diagnostic possibilities; for it is the one test on which a low score is almost invariably associated with pathology. Of this, more later on. For the time being, one must note that, unlike Caesar's wife, the Object Assembly Test, in spite of its purity, is not without blemish. It runs with the hare and hunts with the hounds. Regrettably also, the Digit Span Test excepted, it correlates least with g and systematically low with all the subtests of the Scale. For this reason, it is best omitted from any abbreviated battery. By the same token, it is often useful in aptitude evaluation. It correlates well with mechanical interest (228) though not necessarily with mechanical knowledge (229).

Chapter 9

Changes in Intelligence and Intellectual
Ability with Age

At several points in our previous discussion we have had occasion to refer to the posited changes of intellectual ability with age. These were considered primarily from the point of view of their bearing on the establishment of test norms. In this chapter we shall consider the major reported findings from the point of view of their bearing on the question as to whether or not intellectual abilities, and hence intelligence, may be said to decline with age.

Beginning with the investigation by Galton in 1883 (435) and continuing up to and including the most recent studies of Pacaud (383), nearly all studies dealing with the age factor in adult performance have shown that most human abilities, in so far as they are measurable, decline progressively, after reaching a peak somewhere between ages 18 and 25. The peak age varies with the ability in question, but the decline occurs in all mental measures of ability, including those employed in tests of intelligence. This finding, it should be noted, is based on cross-sectional and not longitudinal studies, that is, studies derived from the comparison of test scores of successive age groups and not from scores derived from the successive examination of the same individuals at different ages. The results obtained with intelligence tests have been reviewed on numerous occasions, among others by Shock (455a), Jones (282), Lorge (325), Bayley (43), and this author (521). With few exceptions the reviewers agree as to the findings but not as regards their significance or interpretation.

Four main objections have been raised against the conclusion that intellectual ability declines with age. The first is that the tests used in intelligence scales are generally unfair to the older subject because they are heavily weighted for speed. Lorge (325) first raised his objection to the original findings of Jones and Conrad, and sought to demonstrate that by making allowance for the speed factor the scores of the older subjects in the Jones and Conrad study could be made to approximate the level of performance of the younger ones. Both Jones (282) and this author (521) have elsewhere indicated the limitation of Lorge's analysis. A less controversial approach to the question of the influence of speed on test performance of older subjects is now offered by a more direct study.

The study in question included the administration of five of the WAIS tests to a group of 465 older men and women both with and without time limits. The subjects consisted of random samples of the older population of Kansas City,[1] ages 60 and over, to whom the Full Scale was administered in two ways. The subjects were first allowed the usual time to complete the task assigned, and then allowed to continue the test until they said they had finished or indicated they could do no more. This procedure enabled the investigator to obtain two scores for each subject and to compare the resulting performance on the same tests, timed and not timed.

The results for approximately half of the population tested (male) are shown in Table 35. The average increment in raw score per test, when subjects were allowed unlimited time, was approximately 5 per cent. None of the mean differences between the compared scores was statistically significant. The differences between timed and untimed performance of the other age groups tested (not shown in table) were of the same order. Altogether, the findings show that the older subjects were negligibly penalized by a speed factor, at least so far as the indicated tests of the Wechsler Adult Scale are concerned.

A second objection to the reported data on variations of ability with age is that the scores attained on the tests are largely dependent upon the subjects' acquired and stored knowledge. Older subjects, it is argued, are not only penalized because at the time of testing they are more remote from their school days, but also because they are likely to have had less formal education than younger subjects. That level of education is correlated with level of performance on intelligence tests is well established. The question at issue here is not whether education influences test scores but how this factor enters differentially to affect performance at successive age levels. Age and education affect each other reciprocally; simple analysis of variance or partial correlational methods alone are insufficient to disentangle the *interaction* between them. To equate this interaction it is almost imperative to keep one or the other of the variables constant. Since the possible effect of age alone is here at issue, it is the educational factor that needs to be accounted for. Unfortunately, studies of adult test performance in which education as such has been kept relatively constant for any considerable age range have been almost entirely lacking. But there is one recently published investigation in which the author did manage to eliminate the educational factor to a fairly satisfactory degree and thereby make

[1] For a complete description of this experiment, see Doppelt and Wallace (147).

TABLE 35

Comparisons of timed and untimed performance* by older persons on subtests of the Wechsler Adult Intelligence Scale

Subtests	Age Group†	No. Tested	M_t	M_u	$S.D._t$	$S.D._u$	C.R.
Arithmetic	60–64	52	10.13	10.27	2.91	2.85	0.28
	70–74	51	8.78	8.76	3.51	3.48	0.32
Picture Completion	60–64	50	9.50	9.82	3.98	3.97	0.40
	70–74	47	8.88	9.18	4.86	4.73	0.29
Block Design	60–64	46	23.43	25.57	10.21	10.64	0.72
	70–74	44	18.77	21.18	9.30	9.21	0.92
Picture Arrangement	60–64	45	16.10	16.72	5.78	6.11	0.36
	70–74	41	14.16	14.65	5.86	6.13	0.33
Object Assembly	60–64	46	22.72	23.28	7.88	7.68	0.24
	70–74	40	19.55	20.55	8.26	8.43	0.59

* M_t , mean scores on tests when timed; M_u , mean scores on tests when not timed; $S.D._t$ and $S.D._u$, corresponding standard deviations.

† Male subjects only.

possible appraisal of changes in test score with age alone. This is the study by Mlle. Pacaud (383) who tested some 4000 subjects employed in the French Railways with an extensive battery of tests. Because of the constricted range of formal education of the subjects tested she was able to divide her entire population at each age level into two comparatively homogeneous groups, those who had received their *Certificat d'Études*, and those who had completed only the *Instruction Primaire.*[2] The findings showed: (1) almost identical rates of decline of score with age in most of the abilities tested, and (2) no substantial score difference between the groups at the different ages reported. This indicates that decline of ability with age is real, regardless of influence education may have on it.

A third argument against accepting the indicated decline of intellectual ability with age proceeds from the view that the cross-sectional method on which the finding is based is invalid. The results are rejected because the scores compared are not scores of the same individuals retested at successive ages, but the scores of different individuals tested at different ages. Longitudinal studies, of course, need also to be made, but the fact that results thus obtained might not coincide with findings derived from horizontal studies do not necessarily controvert this evidence. Actually, only a few longitudinal studies have been reported, and the two most frequently cited, namely, those of Owens (382) and Bayley (43), were done on special

[2] Levels of education roughly equivalent to 9th and 6th grades in American schools. Separate age curves were drawn for the two groups with each of the battery of tests administered and then compared.

population samples. Both the Owens and the Bayley studies dealt with select populations in that the subjects for the studies were individuals of superior intelligence.[3] The subjects of the Owens study were college students with estimated IQ's of 110 and above; those in the Bayley study, the parents of gifted children, with a mean IQ of at least 120 or better. Now it is well known that intelligence test scores of persons of superior intellectual ability tend to hold up or even improve for some time beyond age 25. Moreover, the tests employed in both studies consisted primarily of tests measuring verbal ability, and these are again precisely the types of tasks which have been shown to fall off least with age. The subjects in the Bayley study were a particularly selected group since they comprised a large percentage of individuals engaged in vocations and professions (teaching, etc.) whose day to day activity might well exercise or involve some practice in the kinds of ability called for by the tests.

Apart from the sampling limitation of the hitherto published longitudinal investigations, one should note that the arguments used in rejecting the findings obtained with the cross-sectional studies may be marshalled with equal force against the longitudinal studies themselves. For, if education, experience, stored knowledge, etc., play the role assigned to them one should also expect that the extended exposure of the adult to these factors, as he grows older, would similarly serve to raise the level of his later performance. Thus, assuming that an individual, at age 40–45, is able to learn as well[4] as an individual at age 20–25, then one may presume that the older subject at the time of taking the test will have the advantage of some 20 years of exposure to the educative process, whatever that may be. Of course, the objection may be interposed that the things which the older subject may have learned are not the kinds of items which enter into intelligence tests, and that is in part true. If so, why should the older adult not do as well as the younger adult on such a test as arithmetical reasoning despite the fact that the average man or woman, even when not engaged in a mercantile occupation, has both reason and opportunity to practice this skill.[5]

This brings us to the last and perhaps most cogent reason for the refusal of some psychologists to accept the indicated decline of intellectual ability with age, and by implication of intelligence: namely, their belief that the tests used in our intelligence scales are as a whole not suited to older subjects. There are two parts to this argument. The first part is that our current

[3] For interpretation of findings regarding changes of IQ with age in mental defectives, see Kuhlmann (303) and Charles (96).

[4] As well, though admittedly not so quickly. This is one of the main arguments used to refute the decline of test scores with age (326).

[5] For the differential performance of younger and older subjects on different tests, see Jones and Conrad (281).

TABLE 36

*Correlation of WAIS Scale scores with age**

Sex		Verbal Scale	Perform- ance Score	Full Scale Score	Age
Male (710 subjects)............	r	−0.233	−0.509	−0.391	
	Mean	58.275	41.120	99.317	48.873
	S.D.	16.259	13.660	27.927	15.148
Female (792 subjects).........	r	−0.305	−0.551	−0.440	
	Mean	55.807	40.646	96.535	49.827
	S.D.	15.877	13.245	26.963	15.245
Total (1502 subjects)........	r	−0.271	−0.530	−0.416	
	Mean	57.014	40.877	97.895	49.366
	S.D.	16.112	13.452	27.472	15.205

* Based on subjects 25 years and over from National Standardization Sample and all the cases from Old Age Study.

tests, modeled as they are after those originally devised for children, are stacked with items depending upon school information which no longer concerns the older adult or which he may have forgotten. The other objection is that the abilities tapped by the tests are not valid measures of the abilities the tests purport to measure, and in particular not of general intelligence. Both claims, in the writer's opinion, are essentially incorrect, and in any case not pertinent to the points at issue. One may allow that our present tests are not altogether suited for adults and even concede that they do not measure what has been defined as intelligence. But whatever it is that the tests measure, the argument advanced does not controvert the fact that the abilities involved alter with the aging process. The least one can say is that for most persons intellectual ability, after reaching a peak in early maturity, declines progressively with age. The correlation between age (after age 25) and scores on tests of intelligence is always negative (Table 36).

The findings with the Wechsler Adult Intelligence Scales are in line with and support the above generalizations. The curve of changes in intelligence test scores with age for the 1939 standardization (W–B I) was shown in Figure 1 (p. 31); that for the 1955 (WAIS)[6] standardization, in Figure 2 (p. 96). As can be seen, the curves are essentially similar, but they also show two noteworthy differences. The first is that the maximum for the 1955 curve falls in the age interval 25–29, whereas that of the 1939 curve

[6] The difference in absolute scores of the two standardizations is due to the fact that in the WAIS 11 subtests were used to obtain a full scale score, whereas on the W–B I only 10 tests were used.

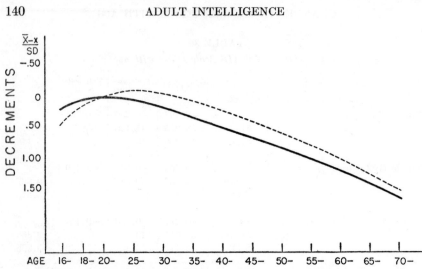

FIG. 5. Curve of decline of mental ability with age. Ages 16–74. *Solid line*, 1939 W–B I Standardization; ages 60–74 (1000 cases) extrapolated on basis of regression equation of score on age. *Dash line*, 1955 WAIS Standardization (1700 cases); ages 60–74 (450 additional cases) derived from Kansas City Study. $\bar{\bar{X}} - x$ = Mean of peak group minus mean of specified age group (x).

in the age interval 20–24. The second difference is that the rate of decline, at least up to age 50, is noticeably less in the case of the 1955 standardization than it is in the 1939 standardization. These changes are more clearly seen in Figure 5 where the two curves, drawn to scale, are presented simultaneously. The original test scores[7] have been equated and rendered statistically comparable by expressing them as deviations in terms of S.D. units from a common base reference age group.

Accepting the observed differences between the 1939 and 1955 standardizations as reliable, one can posit several factors to account for the differences in the curves' maxima as found in the two standardizations. The first has to do with the possible role played by the sampling factor. Although equated with the estimated national population for 1934, as regards sex, age, occupation and educational levels, the 1939 revision was based on populations drawn primarily from the metropolitan New York area; the 1955 revision is based on a sampling of the entire national population, with close approximation for urban-rural proportions, occupation and educational level of the country as a whole as described in the 1950 United States Census. There is also some indication that the 1939 standardization may have contained smaller proportions of individuals falling into the more skilled, business and

---

[7] The test scores from which the curves have been derived are given in Tables 13 and 14. For more detailed discussion of the WAIS age data and in particular of those obtained from the Kansas City Study, see article by Doppelt and Wallace (147).

high professional groups. The second, and perhaps more clear-cut factor that must be taken into account, is the difference in the educational level of the individuals tested in the respective standardizations. The educational level of the American population between 1930 and 1950 has risen about two years, or from approximately the 7.5 to 9.5 grade level. In view of the consistently high correlation (0.65 to 0.70) between last grade completed in school and intelligence test scores, there is some reason to suspect that the differences between educational level of subjects tested may account in part for the lesser test score decline in the 1955 standardization. A third possible consideration is the fact that the American people have become more test-wise over the past 15 to 20 years. Not only may this be the result of the increasing role which achievement and aptitude tests have played in the curriculum of our schools, but also of the ever increasing number of quiz programs which now seem to be part and parcel of the American way of life.

The factors thus far discussed, while undoubtedly important, do not seem sufficient to account completely for the changes observed. In the opinion of the writer, part of the improvement in test performance may be due to the enhanced general health of the adult population, and with it an extension of the period during which the individual can function effectively. People not only live longer but, as a result of medical and social progress, can carry on longer. For example, not only has there been a lessening in the incidence of senile diseases in the age period 35–50, but there also appears to be some diminution in the debile conditions that have been associated with the so-called male as well as the normal female climacteric.[8] In industry, management has discovered that older people can keep on working efficiently beyond ages formerly thought possible and is accordingly extending the age limits set for retirement. These and similar facts may be accepted as evidence of an increasing intellectual vigor of the average adult, a vigor which is not only greater but is maintained over a longer period than it was a generation ago. This does not mean that the average adult is now brighter than his father or grandfather was at his age (although the younger generation, as always, seems to think so), anymore than his increased life expectancy testifies to a greater biological life span. It merely indicates that we may indeed be "adding more life to years as well as years to life."[9]

In line with the title of this chapter we have thus far concerned ourselves primarily with the question of the changes of ability with age. Undoubtedly,

[8] General practitioners as well as gynecologists have reported, for example, a delay of from 5 to 10 years in the onset of the female menopause within the last generation or two.

[9] Caption on the cover of the Journal of Gerontology.

what the reader is more desirous of knowing is what bearing these findings have on the problem of intelligence itself. Specifically, does intelligence, like the abilities by which it is now measured, also reach a peak in early maturity and then decline with increasing years? If the answer is an unqualified yes, one has to face the fact that it does not jibe with work-a-day appraisals, whether made in terms of achievement, leadership, success in dealing with complexities of everyday life and, more generally, in terms of what has been historically defined as wisdom. On the other hand, if one admits that intelligence, unlike ability, does not decline with age, every user of an intelligence scale is in the paradoxical position of having to disavow the claims which he made for his test to begin with. The fact of the matter is that no unqualified answer can be given. What is definitely established is: (1) that our intelligence tests can and do measure intelligence in older as well as younger subjects to a substantial, although not necessarily an equal, degree; (2) that the abilities by which intelligence is measured do in fact decline with age; and (3) that this decline is systematic and after age 30 more or less linear (Figures 1, 2 and 5).

In spite of the above findings, intelligence when appraised by other criteria does not always manifest the same decline with age as do the abilities (test scores) by which it is measured. Two principal reasons would seem to account for this discrepancy. The first is that while intellectual ability is the basic "factor" in intelligent behavior, it does not constitute all of intelligence; the second, that intellectual ability whether expressed in terms of g or specific factors does not enter equally at all ages.[10] To these must be added yet a third factor, namely, that with increasing age, experience plays an ever increasing role in the individual's capacity to deal effectively with his environment.

The problem may be summed up as follows. General intelligence as evaluated by pragmatic criteria appears to maintain itself unimpaired over a much greater portion of adult life, and to decline at a much slower rate than do the mental abilities by which it is inevitably[11] measured. Our general answers have been that sheer ability enters as only one of several factors of intelligence, that factors like drive, interest and motivation also operate in varying degrees as determinants and that learned responses, stored information and general experience may substitute for, or better serve the individual than original aptitude. To these may be added the fact that at different ages different skills or abilities contribute varying amounts of whatever is needed for effective performance.

[10] The second fact is partially taken care of in the WAIS and W–B Scales by allowing a bonus for age. A lesser test score is required for an older than a younger subject to obtain the same IQ rating.

[11] Perhaps not inevitably, but only currently.

What we are proposing then is that general intelligence is a multivariate construct, the differentiae of which may and do alter with successive periods in the individual's life. There will be differences in how we define intelligence at different ages, and these differences will depend in a great measure on which of the elements entering into the construct one wishes to emphasize and how consistent an evaluation one wishes to maintain. One cannot, operationally, attach a unique or fixed meaning to the term intelligence because at different times and under different circumstances we are compelled to appraise it from different points of view. In the case of older people it seems that one thing we wish most to include under the term intelligence, is what William James long ago referred to as *sagacity*, a trait which may be broadly defined as the ability to deal with life's situations in terms of past experience. This is understandable, even desirable, but sagacity cannot be equated to intellectual ability or general intelligence. Intellectual ability, intelligence and wisdom are not identical. We cannot safely substitute one for the other. Wisdom and experience are necessary to make the world go round; creative ability to make it go forward.

Chapter 10

Sex Differences in Intelligence

In trying to arrive at an answer as to whether there are sex differences in intelligence much depends upon how one defines intelligence, and on the practical side, on the type of tests one uses in measuring it. The contemporary approach, contrary to the historical point of view, adopts a sort of null hypothesis. Unfortunately this procedure turns out to be a circular affair since the nature of the tests selected can prejudice or determine in advance what the findings will be. In constructing an intelligence scale it is possible by initial selection to combine one's test in such a way as to minimize or cancel out sex differences. This has been the usual procedure of most test constructors. The principal reason for adopting such a procedure is that it avoids the necessity of separate norms for men and women.

As regards the W–B I, the original standardization data showed small but positive sex differences on Full Scale scores in favor of female subjects. Subsequent studies (73, 263) again revealed sex differences, but this time in favor of men. In attempting to account for the discrepancy the author at first was inclined to interpret the observed findings as due primarily to sampling differences, but the consistent findings of the later studies showed that men may be expected to do better than women on the W–B I as a whole, and on the Performance part of the Scale in particular. The differences are not large but for the most part significant.

The same trend is now revealed in the WAIS data. Here again, the differences are small, at least small enough to make unnecessary separate sex norms, but sufficient to warrant further analysis of test findings. The WAIS mean and standard deviations for Verbal, Performance and Full Scale by age and sex are given in Table 37.

Table 37 shows that there are systematic, but for the most part negligible differences in Verbal, Performance and Full Scale scores in favor of the male subject. But while this holds for the Scale as a whole, the question arises whether it is equally true for the individual subtests of the Scale. The data which enabled us to answer this question are given in Table 38.

TABLE 37

WAIS means and standard deviations on Verbal, Performance and Full Scale Scores of national and old age samples by age and sex*

National Sample			Verbal		Performance		Full Scale	
Age	Sex	No.	Mean	S.D.	Mean	S.D.	Mean	S.D.
16–17	M	100	55.21	14.82	48.84	11.19	104.05	24.80
16–17	F	100	53.96	12.79	48.72	11.31	102.68	22.33
18–19	M	100	56.90	16.17	48.54	13.48	105.44	28.22
18–19	F	100	57.72	13.45	50.31	9.83	108.03	21.59
20–24	M	100	60.02	15.18	51.15	10.89	111.17	24.36
20–24	F	100	58.91	15.21	50.12	12.94	109.03	26.91
25–29	M	84	63.46	14.39	51.94	11.16	115.40	24.11
25–29	F	68	60.85	14.81	50.40	12.26	111.25	25.64
30–34	M	66	58.02	15.03	46.21	11.35	104.23	24.69
30–34	F	82	60.35	13.85	49.04	11.54	109.39	23.73
35–39	M	84	61.44	16.53	47.37	12.29	108.81	27.68
35–39	F	84	60.63	13.09	48.10	10.42	108.73	22.13
40–44	M	66	59.88	12.37	44.50	9.89	104.38	20.64
40–44	F	66	58.59	16.72	43.36	11.78	101.95	26.96
45–49	M	83	60.54	18.32	42.47	12.36	103.01	29.26
45–49	F	84	58.02	15.46	42.04	10.01	100.06	24.55
50–54	M	67	57.61	14.34	40.22	10.99	97.84	23.77
50–54	F	66	55.29	15.73	38.83	11.22	94.12	25.54
55–59	M	61	57.25	17.19	36.15	12.02	93.39	28.09
55–59	F	60	54.45	15.49	37.80	10.06	92.25	24.28
60–64	M	39	57.49	15.73	38.41	9.24	95.90	23.33
60–64	F	40	53.90	16.59	36.28	10.85	90.18	26.17
Old Age Sample								
60–64	M	44	56.66	14.71	34.80	11.08	91.45	24.62
60–64	F	57	54.14	14.27	35.11	10.82	89.25	23.74
65–69	M	42	55.17	15.29	35.31	9.99	90.48	23.88
65–69	F	44	52.36	13.60	33.52	10.03	85.89	21.73
70–74	M	38	49.53	14.24	29.11	10.98	78.63	23.60
70–74	F	42	45.98	13.03	29.90	7.80	75.88	19.14
75+	M	36	44.53	15.08	23.56	9.94	68.08	22.78
75+	F	49	43.65	13.42	25.51	9.14	69.16	20.60

* These age groupings do not correspond to groupings used in the WAIS Manual, in which 10-year age groupings were used, starting with age 25.

This table gives means and standard deviations of the WAIS subtests by age and sex in terms of scaled scores for the various reference groups. The data show that although the mean test scores of men are generally higher than those of women there are a number of subtests on which women do

TABLE 38

Means and standard deviations of WAIS subtests by age and sex, and critical ratios between sex means

Age Group	Sex	No.	Information Mean	S.D.	C.R.	Comprehension Mean	S.D.	C.R.	Arithmetic Mean	S.D.	C.R.	Similarities Mean	S.D.	C.R.
16–17	M	100	9.41	2.94		9.55	3.03		9.36	2.97		9.24	2.89	
	F	100	8.82	2.63	1.50	9.09	2.80	1.12	8.56	2.41	2.09	9.61	2.75	0.88
18–19	M	100	9.78	3.15		9.71	3.08		9.72	3.34		9.27	3.22	
	F	100	9.59	2.67	0.46	9.66	2.83	0.12	9.24	2.63	1.13	9.67	2.92	0.92
20–24	M	100	10.15	2.93		10.14	3.04		10.45	3.12		10.03	3.03	
	F	100	9.38	3.06	1.82	9.79	3.29	0.78	9.51	3.22	2.10	10.32	3.09	0.67
25–34	M	150	10.39	2.88		10.11	3.03		10.61	3.28		9.89	3.07	
	F	150	10.16	2.80	0.69	10.27	3.00	0.46	9.55	2.82	2.22	10.26	2.87	1.08
35–44	M	150	10.49	2.95		10.36	2.82		10.73	3.23		9.46	3.02	
	F	150	10.09	3.03	1.16	9.93	2.90	1.30	9.57	2.90	3.27	8.94	3.27	1.04
45–54	M	150	10.27	3.07		10.35	3.24		10.65	3.39		8.91	3.50	
	F	150	9.62	3.00	1.28	9.49	3.13	2.34	9.39	3.07	3.34	9.17	3.31	0.66
55–64	M	100	10.46	3.35		9.68	3.02		10.26	3.39		9.33	3.33	
	F	100	9.31	3.04	3.57	9.47	2.98	0.50	8.57	3.22	3.62	8.59	3.33	0.55

Age Group	Sex	No.	Digit Span Mean	S.D.	C.R.	Vocabulary Mean	S.D.	C.R.	Digit Symbol Mean	S.D.	C.R.	Picture Completion Mean	S.D.	C.R.
16–17	M	100	9.26	2.93		8.39	2.56		9.08	2.39		9.79	2.72	
	F	100	9.39	2.94	0.31	8.49	2.36	0.29	10.61	2.76	4.19	9.97	2.22	2.11
18–19	M	100	9.48	3.14		8.94	2.95		8.88	2.85		9.87	3.04	
	F	100	10.00	2.90	1.22	9.56	2.61	1.57	10.66	2.92	4.36	9.60	2.47	0.71
20–24	M	100	9.69	2.85		9.56	3.01		9.71	2.46		10.41	2.91	
	F	100	10.19	2.65	1.29	9.72	3.02	0.38	10.57	3.06	2.22	9.57	2.99	2.01
25–34	M	150	10.13	2.91		9.95	2.99		9.26	3.12		10.25	2.96	
	F	150	9.79	3.09	0.98	10.55	2.92	1.74	10.47	2.95	3.55	9.70	2.87	1.64
35–44	M	150	9.57	2.86		10.15	3.22		8.07	2.65		10.09	2.75	
	F	150	9.61	3.17	0.11	10.69	3.14	1.47	9.01	3.05	2.97	9.45	2.60	2.07
45–54	M	150	9.00	2.99		10.05	3.49		6.90	2.63		9.15	3.05	
	F	150	8.91	2.97	0.26	10.23	3.27	0.49	8.07	2.93	3.76	8.08	2.38	3.39
55–64	M	100	8.70	3.26		9.91	3.46		6.11	2.68		8.34	2.93	
	F	100	8.10	2.59	1.44	10.19	3.58	0.56	6.49	2.58	1.05	7.73	2.50	1.58

Age Group	Sex	No.	Block Design Mean	S.D.	C.R.	Picture Arrangement Mean	S.D.	C.R.	Object Assembly Mean	S.D.	C.R.
16–17	M	100	10.08	3.28		10.12	2.90		9.77	3.11	
	F	100	9.40	3.06	1.52	10.53	3.09	0.99	9.11	3.10	1.50
18–19	M	100	9.96	3.42		10.04	3.38		9.79	3.10	
	F	100	9.70	2.72	0.60	10.23	2.39	0.46	10.12	2.44	0.84
20–24	M	100	10.18	2.95		10.56	2.98		10.29	2.98	
	F	100	9.65	3.13	1.23	10.34	3.36	0.49	9.99	3.14	0.69
25–34	M	150	10.22	3.13		9.77	2.59		9.92	2.91	
	F	150	9.77	3.10	1.25	9.70	2.87	0.22	10.01	2.96	0.27
35–44	M	150	9.65	2.98		9.05	3.02		9.26	2.91	
	F	150	9.15	2.94	1.51	9.07	2.82	0.06	9.33	2.81	0.21
45–54	M	150	8.79	2.93		7.88	2.69		8.75	2.94	
	F	150	8.17	2.42	2.00	8.03	2.79	0.47	8.27	2.96	1.41
55–64	M	100	7.51	2.71		7.54	2.46		7.53	2.59	
	F	100	7.88	2.78	0.95	7.06	2.09	1.54	8.03	2.91	1.28

TABLE 39

Means, S.D.'s and C.R.'s between male and female performance on subtests of the WAIS (ages 16–64)*

Test	Sex	Mean	S.D.	C.R.
Information................	M	10.18	3.04	
	F	9.64	2.94	3.72
Comprehension,.............	M	10.04	3.17	
	F	9.71	3.02	2.20
Arithmetic.................	M	10.35	3.29	
	F	9.25	2.94	7.28
Similarities................	M	9.32	3.21	
	F	9.66	3.14	2.21
Digit Span.................	M	9.43	3.02	
	F	9.43	3.00	0.00
Vocabulary.................	M	9.65	3.19	
	F	10.02	3.10	2.42
Digit Symbol...............	M	8.25	2.97	
	F	9.37	3.25	7.42
Picture Completion..........	M	9.72	2.99	
	F	9.04	2.69	4.93
Block Design...............	M	9.50	3.18	
	F	9.09	2.97	2.75
Picture Arrangement........	M	9.21	3.04	
	F	9.22	3.03	0.07
Object Assembly............	M	9.33	3.05	
	F	9.26	3.01	0.47

* Total number, 1700, 850 male and 850 female. For subtest differences age by age, see Table 38.

consistently better. The differences are again small and the critical ratios significant at only certain age levels. However, inspection of the table indicates that the lack of consistency might be due to the relative smallness of the numbers when the groups are broken down by age. To check this hypothesis critical ratios were calculated between the subtests for the *total* male and female population. The results are given in Table 39. As anticipated, certain of the subtests which showed only slight differences now reveal critical ratios which are clearly significant. Of the 11 WAIS subtests, 8 now show clear-cut sex differences; men do better on 5 of the subtests, women on 3.

It thus appears that among the tasks which may be used for tests of intelligence there are some which are easier (or more difficult) for one or the other of the sexes. Whether these differences are presumptive of a better or poorer endowment in intellectual ability still remains to be decided, but the fact that they exist cannot be questioned.

The differences found in the analysis of the WAIS subtests are not unique. Systematic differences in scholastic and other abilities have been repeatedly reported (498a), but these have generally been regarded as evident sex differences in acquired aptitudes; for example, women do better in language, men better in arithmetic, etc. But the present findings, taken together with certain others, seem to call for a more fundamental interpretation. The fact that women are better in rote learning and men in arithmetical reasoning is, so far as appraisal of intellectual endowment is concerned, of no greater significance than would be the fact that women have better eye-hand co-ordination and men greater vital capacity. The facts are only important if they represent basic differences in intellectual capacities or in so far as they may enter into effective intelligent behavior.

The findings on the WAIS suggest that women seemingly call upon different resources or different degrees of like abilities in exercising whatever it is we call intelligence. For the moment one need not be concerned as to which approach is better or "superior." But our findings do confirm what poets and novelists have often asserted, and the average layman long believed, namely, that men not only behave but "think" differently from women. This difference could probably be more clearly demonstrated if our intelligence scales included a greater variety of tests than now employed, and included a fair number of the kind previously referred to as non-intellective.[1] In the absence of such study it seemed worth while to make a comparison between male and female performance based on a selective combination of the WAIS subtests on which men and women did respectively better. This was achieved as follows. With Table 39 as a base for 3 of the tests on which men did consistently better and the 3 tests on which women did consistently better,[2] we provisionally designated the former as "masculine" (M) and the latter as "feminine" (F) tests. Separate scores were then obtained for each of 600 (300 men and 300 women) subjects by the following formula. Sum of weighted scores for the M tests minus the sum of the weighted scores of the F tests = plus or minus MF score, where a plus difference signified a masculine, and a minus a feminine trend. These differences for all subjects male and female (age sample 20–44) were then distributed and compared in the usual manner. The mean scores by sex and the critical ratios are given in Table 40.

The distribution of MF scores for both sexes is shown in Figure 6. From

---

[1] There is no doubt in the author's mind that a factorial study of a battery of tests of this sort would reveal a sex factor.

[2] The tests designated as feminine (F) are Vocabulary, Similarities and Digit Symbol; the masculine (M) tests are, Information, Arithmetic and Picture Completion.

TABLE 40

MF scores expressed as difference between sum of Information, Arithmetic and Picture Completion and sum of Similarities, Vocabulary and Digit Symbol

Sex	No.	Mean	S.D.	C.R.
M	300	+2.84	4.40	
F	300	−1.34	4.51	11.6

this figure and the data given in Table 40, it is clear that there exist significant sex differences in at least certain aspects of intelligence, and that these differences become significant when cumulatively weighted. Thus, one can obtain an MF score on the WAIS comparable to MF scores on standard masculinity-femininity tests like the Miles-Terman or the MMPI, with possible comparable interpretation. Using 2 P.E. as cut-off criterion, one might say that a score of minus 3.5 or lower is feminine for men and a score of plus 5.0 or higher is masculine for women. Table 41 gives the percentile equivalents for WAIS masculinity-femininity scores for men and women respectively.

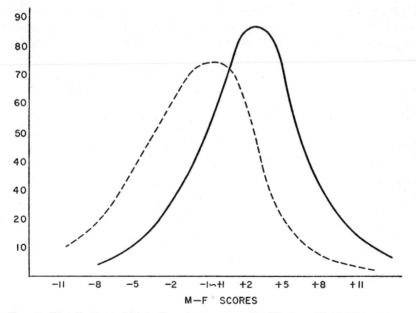

Fig. 6. Distribution of Male–Female scores on WAIS. Ages 25–44 (300 male, 300 female). *Solid line*, male. *Dash line*, female.

TABLE 41

Percentile equivalents for composite MF test scores on WAIS
(300 male, 300 female, ages 25–44)*

M	%	F
+10.6	95	−9.0
+9.0	90	−7.0
+7.1	80	−5.0
+5.8	70	−3.2
+4.6	60	−1.8
+3.5	50	−0.5
+1.8	40	+0.7
+0.2	30	+2.0
−0.9	20	+3.5
−3.7	10	+5.4
−6.5	5	+7.1

* + scores indicate masculinity; − scores femininity.

To obtain an M − F score on the WAIS one proceeds as follows: Sum weighted scores on Information, Arithmetic and Picture Completion, and designate total as subject's M score; sum Vocabulary, Similarities and Digit Symbol scores, and designate same as F score. Subtract F total from M total; the algebraic difference is the subject's M − F score. Look up the obtained difference in Table 41 which gives the percentile equivalents

Subject A—Male, Age 25		Subject B—Female, Age 28	
Inf..	11	Inf.	15
Comp.	9	Comp.	16
Arith..	9	Arith.	13
Sim.	11	Sim.	13
D. Sp.	10	D. Sp.	9
Voc.	10	Voc.	16
D. Sym.	14	D. Sym.	11
P. Comp.	9	P. Comp.	16
Bl. Des.	10	Bl. Des.	17
P. Arr.	12	P. Arr.	12
Obj. Ass.	9	Obj. Ass.	14

M Scores		F Scores		M Scores		F Scores	
Inf.	11	Sim.	11	Inf.	15	Sim.	13
Arith.	9	D. Sym.	14	Arith.	13	D. Sym.	11
P. Comp.	9	Voc.	10	P. Comp.	16	Voc.	16
	29		35		44		40

M − F = 29 − 35 = −6   M − F = 44 − 40 = +4

Rating = 5%tile   Rating = 17%tile

for these scores, being careful to select the proper column (males under men, females under women). The percentile equivalent is the subject's rating.

The two cases, Subjects A and B, demonstrate the procedure used. When the M − F differences are close to values given in the table, one takes the nearest percentile as the approximate equivalent. When they are not close, the exact percentile may be obtained by interpolation. It should be noted that the M − F scores are independent of the subject's level of performance.*

* One could take this level into account by dividing the subject's M − F by his M + F score.

PART III

Diagnostic and Practical

Applications

Chapter 11

Diagnostic and Clinical Features

Although the primary purpose of an intelligence examination is to give a valid and reliable measure of the subject's global intellectual capacity, it is reasonable to expect that any well conceived intelligence scale will furnish its user with something more than an IQ or M.A. In point of fact, most intelligence examinations, when administered individually, make available a certain amount of data regarding the testee's mode of reaction, his special abilities or disabilities and, not infrequently, some indication of his personality traits. At present, the amount of this sort of adjuvant data which may be derived from an intelligence examination is in a large measure dependent upon the individual examiner's clinical experience and sagacity. No doubt this will always remain true to a greater or lesser degree. But much also depends upon the character and projective possibilities of the tests themselves. In this respect different tests show wide variations. For example, one is more likely to elicit qualitative material from an open-end comprehension question ("What is the thing to do when . . .") than from an information or arithmetic problem requiring a unique response ("How far is it from New York to Paris?"). However, no one test is ever so good but that, on a different occasion or for a different subject, another will not be more effective. For this reason a composite scale calling for a variety of performance, such as the W–B I or the WAIS, is likely to be more productive than one confined to a specific mode of response. An individual reveals himself not only by the way he takes in the world but how he reacts to it, not only by the way he perceives but by the way he thinks, that is, cognizes his experience.

The qualitative data one obtains from an intelligence test, as indeed from any other, are largely inferential; they depend upon the interpretation of the examiner as to what the tests allegedly measure, as well as to what particular responses are presumed to signify. In both cases the examiner is treading on thin ice, not only because his personal interpretations are unlikely to have been sufficiently validated, but because all behavior is

155

multi-determined. One cannot always be sure that a given effect (a test performance or response) is necessarily the consequence of a particular referable cause. For example, a low score on arithmetic may be due to a special disability in dealing with numbers, a lack of educational opportunity, momentary anxiety or to just low over-all intellectual ability. Which of these obtains in any given instance must be worked out anew with each recurring case rather than by any rigid formulation. To be sure, for practical purposes it is useful to associate a particular kind of performance with a particular type of defect or diagnostic group. But in doing so one must remember that in most instances the association is at best only occasional and partial. When one reads that adolescent psychopaths tend to do better on Performance than on Verbal tests, that schizophrenics do poorly on tests of social comprehension and organics do worst on tests involving visual-motor organization, one should subsume the term "sometimes" or at most "often." Whether one can use this *quondam* association as a basis for individual diagnosis will depend not only on its incidence and overlap, but on its unique relationship to other subtests of the Scale. Thus, a very low Picture Completion test score associated with a high Picture Arrangement, though occurring rarely in this combination, is nevertheless strongly pathognomonic of schizophrenia.

In the following pages we shall discuss various features of the W–B I and WAIS which have shown themselves to be of diagnostic value. But prior to doing so it will be useful to stop long enough to review a number of ever vexing questions which are repeatedly put to the clinician, and for which some answer, however tentative, must be made. The first of these has to do with the reliability and value of the IQ, particularly when obtained from a mentally ill or disturbed subject.

Reliability and Value of IQ's

An individual's IQ, in the first instance, is an index number defining his relative brightness as compared to persons of his own age, but in a broader and more meaningful sense it is also a comprehensive statement about a person's over-all intellectual functioning ability. In view of this fact, one might suppose that it would generally be considered the most important single bit of information to be derived from an intelligence examination. Unfortunately, that is not so. In recent years the IQ has lost caste. There has been a growing tendency among clinical psychologists to pay only scant attention to the IQ as such, presumably because in many cases it is undifferentiating[1]—a statement which in part is true, or because it is believed to be inconstant and unreliable—a generalization that, in the

---

[1] For the reason that two persons with an identical IQ may be quite different in other respects.

main, is false. Particularly misleading are such statements as "the days are past in which an individual was presumed to have been born with a certain IQ which he bore throughout his life and died with" (420). Actually no responsible group of psychologists has ever maintained that a person is born with an IQ, much less dies with it, or that it is eternally unchangeable. On the contrary, almost from the start, careful investigators have sedulously pointed out that the IQ an individual attains on a test may be influenced by many factors, that it has an expected variability and that correlations between test-retest IQ's are much lower than one would wish for long range predictive purposes. The so-called "myth of the unchanging IQ" is largely a rigged straw man. What has been asserted, and adequately demonstrated, is that when individuals are retested with the same or similar intelligence scales, the IQ's obtained by most individuals will show relatively little change. 'Relatively little' means an *average* IQ difference of approximately 5 points between successive retests, after intervals of from several weeks to several years. The term 'most individuals' will vary with the size of the IQ differences one wishes to consider practically negligible. A difference of 5 IQ points between retests will ordinarily include about 50 % of the cases, a difference of 10 points, 75 % or more of the cases, and so on. In terms of prediction, the chances are 1 in 2 that a subject's IQ on retest will not differ by more than 5 points; 1 in 4 that it will not differ by more than 10, and 1 in 20 by more than 15 points. These probabilities are approximately of the order one can infer from test-retest studies done with the W–B I (409), from comparisons of results obtained with alternate administrations of the W–B II (240) and from obtained reliability coefficients of the WAIS (525). The size of the change in IQ will depend in part on the recency of the earlier examination and the age level[2] at which the initial test was administered. It will also depend in a measure on the degree to which the test items of the scales used lend themselves to practice. For example, the Performance section of the W–B and WAIS are much more subject to practice than the Verbal section. When these factors are taken into consideration and allowances made for special cases such as the handicapped or emotionally disturbed individual, the IQ variations from test to test for the preponderant number of individuals examined is surprisingly small. They are, in the opinion of the writer, much smaller than the variations reported in physiological and biological measures which are accepted without much question.

Though the reliability and constancy of the IQ is not predicated on findings obtained with disturbed individuals it is legitimate to ask how much trust one may place in the test scores obtained by such subjects.

[2] IQ's determined prior to age 6, and particularly in infancy, have been shown to be not too reliable (42).

In brief, is an IQ obtained from a test administered to a mentally disturbed individual valid? In any event, of what value is it when you get it? The question (and answer) needs to be broken down into two parts, depending upon whether what one is seeking is an intelligence evaluation of the subject prior to his illness or an evaluation of his actual level in his present and immediate predictable future. If the former is the examiner's intent, the answer is not too difficult and, in instances where a good case history is available, will not even require a systematic intelligence examination. However, this can also be achieved in several ways by the use of intelligence test scores. One is to use only types of tests, such as Vocabulary and Information, which have been found to decline but little with age or to stay relatively unimpaired in cases of mental disorder. Another possible procedure is to use only those test scores for calculating an IQ on which a subject scores maximally, on the assumption that an individual's potential is most adequately represented by what he can do best. Such a procedure has been recommended by W. Jastak (272), who obtains an IQ for what he terms the subject's *altitude* or basic intelligence level. He does this by calculating a subject's IQ on the basis of the three tests on the W–B Scale on which the subject makes the highest scores. The procedure substitutes what might be termed a selective for the global concept of intelligence, and implies that an accurate evaluation of intelligence may be obtained from the appraisal of a small, rather than a large sample of the subject's abilities. This is like trying to estimate a man's annual income on the basis of the highest salary he may have received in any calendar month.

The usual way of dealing with the dilemma of the variable IQ in disturbed subjects has been to fall back on the distinction between present functioning and potential intelligence. This might seem a satisfactory solution except that the terms potential and functioning are highly ambiguous. To some, potential is equivalent to native ability; to others it signifies what a person might be able to do if he had the opportunity to acquire the skills tested; and again, what the individual might have been able to do prior to his sickness or how we might expect him to perform after he recovers. The term functioning seems more clear-cut but is equally mischievous. If by functioning ability one merely means a subject's level of performance at the moment he is being tested, the statement is straightforward enough, but the data of such a temporally delimited performance are of no great value. An estimate of intelligence, expressed as an IQ or otherwise, can only have significance if it purports to be a statement of how the subject has been able to function at least in the immediate past and even more of how he will continue to do so for some reasonable period in the anticipated future. Hence, the qualifying phrase "present functioning," to have useful meaning must imply not only that a subject is not functioning maximally, but that one anticipates an early change and return to a previous level of performance. A post-encephalitic, a chronically deteriorated schizophrenic or a patient with Alzheimer's syndrome who attains an IQ of 60 is not merely functioning at the defective level but is mentally defective, although for nosological and practical reasons he may be otherwise classified.

The intent of the foregoing remarks is to emphasize the fact that the IQ of an individual, though neither invariant nor infallible, nevertheless is in and of itself an important datum for diagnosis. Like all quantitative measures it needs to be interpreted, but interpretations must be based on objective findings and not upon reiterated misconceptions. Its primary aim is not, as sometimes assumed, to define a person's special abilities and disabilities or how these combine with his interests and training, although this information may sometimes be obtained from the way an individual performs on the subtests of the Scale. Its aim is rather to define his over-all functioning. It defines a person's general assets and liabilities. The fact that a subject has an IQ of 110 rather than 90 is ordinarily more important than whether he does well or poorly on a particular test, and this holds for the mentally ill as well as for the normal individual.

Verbal versus Performance

One of the more useful features of the WAIS and W–B Scales is their dichotomy into Verbal and Performance subtests. This grouping was originally based not on the theory that there are different kinds of intelligence, but on the hypothesis that either through habit, training or endowment some individuals are able to deal better with objects than with words. Factorial analysis of the Scales, however, has revealed that the grouping may deal with a more fundamental dichotomy although the tests themselves show considerable overlap. In any event, the abilities inferred from tests will be found to constitute functional clusters of sorts, the separation of which is often useful in vocational guidance and in the evaluation of personality constellations.

As regards the diagnostic implications of differences between verbal and performance ability as a whole, the findings are that in most mental disorders impairment of function is generally greater in the performance than in the verbal sphere. With occasional exceptions, this holds for psychoses of nearly every type, for organic brain disease and to a lesser degree for psychoneuroses. The order of difference in favor of the Verbal score varies with the disease entity and in the case of organic brain disease with the type of impairment. The findings for some organic brain diseases will be discussed in Chapter 13.

In appraising the significance of the differences between Verbal and

Performance scores one must naturally allow for variability even among normal individuals. The standard deviation of the mean difference between Verbal and Performance for the normal population is 10.02. This means that a V–P difference greater than 10 points will be encountered in less than 32 cases in 100, a V–P difference of 15 points in 13 cases in 100, a difference of 20 points two times in 100, and so on. Depending upon one's criteria of abnormality, one can set cut-off points at different levels of deviancy. In most instances a difference of 15 or more points may be interpreted as diagnostically significant.

In the analysis of the W–B I standardization data the intelligence level of individuals seemed to have been an important factor in determining both the direction and the degree of difference found. Subjects of superior intelligence generally did better on Verbal; subjects of inferior intelligence did better on the Performance part of the tests. This was not confirmed by analysis made of the WAIS data (see p. 102), except in the cases of subjects at the upper extreme of the distribution. It would seem that level of intelligence often needs to be taken into consideration in the evaluation between a Verbal minus Performance difference, but no general rule can be laid down since many other factors will influence it. Among these is the educational and vocational history of the subject. Occupation is frequently an important factor, so that carpenters, mechanics and engineers will do better on Performance, and clerical workers, school teachers and lawyers better on Verbal items. There also appears to be cultural and possibly racial differences which in individual cases may have to be taken into consideration, but owing to the large overlap between such groups, this fact alone cannot be used as an unfailing criterion. All this means, of course, that the significance between a subject's Verbal and Performance score cannot be interpreted *carte blanche*, but only after due weight is given to the various factors which may have contributed to it.

A significant Verbal minus Performance constellation (V–P), frequently met with in subjects roughly labeled as "acting-out" individuals, is the systematic high Performance scores which these subjects attain. This "pattern" was first noted by Levi and this author in the test performance of adolescent psychopaths, and has since been reported for other groups (139, 194). One of the reported studies, that of the Gluecks (194), is especially impressive because it was carried out with a large number of subjects carefully matched for a number of variables including age and IQ. A summary of the Gluecks' findings is given in Table 42. As will be seen, the observed Verbal minus Performance differences in favor of Performance are statistically significant at a high level of confidence. The only question that arises is whether the Verbal minus Performance difference is due primarily to the lowering of the Verbal or increase in Perform-

TABLE 42

Comparison of mean weighted scores of delinquents and non-delinquents on the W–B I*

Subtest	500 Delinquents		500 Non-Delinquents		Difference	
	M	S.D.	M	S.D.	SEm	C.R.
Information.................	6.84	3.10	8.10	2.64	−1.26	7.02
Comprehension..............	8.08	2.88	8.60	2.68	−0.52	3.02
Digit Span.................	7.58	2.72	7.46	2.52	−0.12	0.76
Arithmetic.................	6.34	2.90	6.54	2.60	−0.20	1.17
Similarities................	7.20	2.70	7.44	2.42	−0.24	1.43
Vocabulary.................	7.22	2.46	7.62	2.12	−0.40	2.81
Picture Arrangement........	9.64	2.76	9.50	2.76	0.14	0.80
Picture Completion..........	9.30	2.94	9.44	2.74	−0.14	0.78
Block Design...............	9.46	2.94	8.92	2.98	0.54	2.88
Object Assembly............	9.46	2.88	9.22	3.06	9.42	2.25
Digit Symbol..............	7.96	2.12	8.70	2.08	−0.74	5.67

Mean Verbal weighted score minus mean Performance weighted score, W–B I

Subtest	500 Delinquents		500 Non-Delinquents		Difference	
Mean Verbal minus mean Performance, weighted score.....................	−9.55	10.10	7.65	8.60	−2.30	3.84

* Adapted from *Unraveling Juvenile Delinquency* by Glueck and Glueck (194). Above table combines data given in several separate tables.

ance score, and whether we are dealing with basic or environmentally conditioned factors. It is probable that both factors are operable. The subjects of the Glueck study, for example, while matched both for age and IQ and other variables, nevertheless showed significant differences in the level of education attained. The delinquent group, on the average, were one to two grades below the non-delinquent both in school placement and on scholastic achievement tests. On the other hand, they also reveal basic differences in certain character traits as shown both by case history and projective tests. Whatever the cause, the Verbal minus Performance differences are sufficiently consistent and significant to be of diagnostic value.[3]

[3] Another study supporting this conclusion is that of L. Diller in which he compared female delinquents with non-delinquents (139). The subjects were not so well controlled as in the Gluecks' study, the delinquents on the average being some two years younger and with a mean IQ some 15 points lower than the controls. Here again the Verbal minus Performance difference between the two groups was clear-cut and indicated significance in association between high performance and delinquents. On the other hand, Vane and Eisen (499) comparing a group of delinquent with non-delinquent girls matched for age, education and socio-economic status found no sig-

Test Variability and Scatter

The term test variability has been used to define two types of erraticism in performance: (1) inter-test and (2) intra-test variability. The former is indicated when a subject does very well on certain tests and at the same time very poorly on others; the latter when a subject fails easy and succeeds on hard items of one and the same test. In this section we shall be concerned primarily with inter-test variability, which is sometimes referred to as "scatter."

Evaluation of inter-test variability may be effected in a number of ways, the most generally accepted being some summative measure involving a standard or average deviation score from the subject's mean test performance.[4] When such measures or indices are used, the findings have not always confirmed the large differences in test variability between disturbed and normal subjects which the clinician has generally posited. Several reasons may be ventured for this lack of concordance. The most general is the lack of adequate controls. This may involve such items as insufficiency of number of cases, the heterogeneity of either the normal or abnormal groups used and finally an implicit delimitation in the characteristics or type of subjects entering into the experimental group. Thus, when the clinician speaks of the greater variability of schizophrenics (or any other abnormal group) he may have in mind only a very small segment of this group which shows certain features. As regards scatter on the WAIS or W–B, for example, he may be thinking primarily of cases which deviate on any given subtest, by at least three or more weighted score units from their own mean score. Individuals showing such extreme deviations must, in a sense, be treated apart if they are not to be lost in the crowd. Their appraisal requires the examination of an unusually large number of individuals to make possible the emergence of the exceptional case. The problem it presents is similar to that one is confronted with when attempting to inquire into the effectiveness of a drug for a particular disease or

---

nificant difference between Verbal and Performance W–B IQ's. It should be noted, however, that the subjects of both groups were from a Vocational High School, and this fact may have attenuated the differences observed, on the assumption that the subjects of both groups in the study were selected on the basis of better performance or at least limited verbal ability (actually both groups in the Vane and Eisen study had significantly higher Performance than Verbal IQ's). It should be further noted that the association between high performance and psychopathic personality made by both Levi and the author referred specifically to *male* adolescent psychopaths, and we may be dealing here with a possible sex difference.

[4] A number of authors have preferred other measures of deviation; thus, Rapaport and Schafer (420) in their diagnostic studies used no less than five different types of "scatter" mesures, among them Vocabulary scatter, modified Mean scatter, composite Verbal scatter, etc.

TABLE 43

Comparison of variables of controls and schizophrenics in terms of average deviation of subtests from subjects' own mean matched for sex, age, educational level and IQ*

Group	Sex	No.	M_{AD}	SD_{AD}	SE_m	C.R.
Schizophrenic..........	M	30	1.91	0.60	0.1095	
Normal................	M	30	1.43	0.33	0.0602	3.84
Schizophrenic..........	F	28	2.05	0.81	0.1531	
Normal................	F	28	1.35	0.29	0.0548	4.41
Schizophrenic..........	M and F	58	1.98	0.72	0.0945	
Normal................	M and F	58	1.40	0.31	0.0407	5.63

* The subjects were 58 consecutive patients examined on the semi-disturbed wards of Bellevue Psychiatric Hospital. The "normals" were drawn from our master standardization sample, matched for the variables indicated.

symptom which occurs only two or three times per thousand subjects. The situation is not quite so extreme as regards the incidence of aberrant psychological test scores, but how to deal with the unusual or unique individual as part of the group still remains an unsolved problem. One can only say that in spite of the many negative results thus far reported, the clinician is essentially correct in concluding that schizophrenics, like other mentally disturbed persons, show greater inter-test variability. To verify this conclusion it will be necessary to make a comparative study with subgroups carefully matched with controls for as many variables as possible. The results of one such study done on the WAIS are given in Table 43.

One of the problems in practical diagnosis is the definition of what constitutes an abnormal deviation. This definition will depend on the conditions of the study; for most purposes, a deviation of two or more scaled score units on any subtest from the mean is a convenient cut-off point. The magnitude of the difference used will depend upon the level of significance the examiner wishes to set for himself. Differences of significance at the 15 per cent level or better between pairs of scores on the WAIS and W–B I have been calculated by F. B. Davis (130) and are given in Tables 44 and 45.

Patterning and Pattern Analysis

The phrases pattern analysis, test patterning and similar rubrics have appeared with increasing frequency in psychometric literature, but while the terms have some common underlying implications they have seldom been strictly defined. Sometimes the terms have been used to describe a particular statistical technique, sometimes to illustrate a diagnostic formulation and sometimes a combination of the two. In general, the intent of

TABLE 44

Differences significant at the 15 per cent level, or better, between pairs of scores derived from the Wechsler-Bellevue Scales, Forms I and II* (F. B. Davis)†

Tests	Scaled Score Units										
	1	2	3	4	5	6	7	8	9	10	11
Information........................		3	3	3	3	3	3	4	3	4	3
Comprehension.......................			4	3	4	3	4	4	3	4	3
Digit Span..........................				3	4	3	4	4	3	4	3
Arithmetic..........................					3	3	3	3	4	3	4	3
Similarities........................						3	4	4	3	4	3
Vocabulary..........................							3	4	3	4	3
Picture Arrangement.................								4	3	4	3
Picture Completion..................									4	5	4
Block Design........................										4	3
Object Assembly.....................											4
Digit Symbol........................											

* Based on test intercorrelations of 355 cases, ages 20–34, reported in *Measurement of Adult Intelligence* (517). Standard deviations were obtained from recomputation of data for 355 cases, ages 20–34 in Table 39, p. 222. Reliability coefficients are reported by L. Cronbach (121). The reliability coefficients were corrected for range to match variability of intercorrelation sample.

† From personal communication to author.

TABLE 45

Differences significant at the 15 per cent level, or better, between pairs of scores derived from the Wechsler Adult Intelligence Scale* (F. B. Davis)†

Tests	Scaled Score Units										
	1	2	3	4	5	6	7	8	9	10	11
Information........................		3	3	3	3	2	2	3	3	3	3
Comprehension.......................			3	3	4	3	3	3	3	4	4
Arithmetic..........................				3	4	3	3	3	3	4	4
Similarities........................					3	2	3	3	3	3	3
Digit Span..........................						3	3	3	3	4	4
Vocabulary..........................							2	2	2	3	3
Digit Symbol........................								3	3	3	3
Picture Completion..................									3	3	3
Block Design........................										3	3
Picture Arrangement.................											4
Object Assembly.....................											

* Based on 200 cases, ages 18–19, from *WAIS Manual* (524), Table 6, p. 13.

† From personal communication to author.

"pattern analysis" is to find a way or formula for identifying diagnostically different groups, and eventually the individuals composing them, on the basis of their differential performance on a number of tests administered as a battery. Implicit in all such attempts is the assumption that test scores can be combined into and identified as unique combinations. Statistically this requires a method of unique coding and, more important, a technique for discovering the few relevant from the enormous number of possible combinations that may emerge from a battery consisting of even a small number of tests. For example, if one starts with 10 tests and 3 dichotomies the total number of test combinations, one or more at a time, is $3^{11} - 1$, or better than 175,000.[5] If the tests are intercorrelated to any degree, the number of combinations may be considerably smaller, but even when thus reduced, the number will generally be too great for practical evaluation. Actually, no such type of analysis has been employed; instead, some circumscribed procedures have been used which, though put forward under the title "patterning," are not patterns at all in the strict sense of the term.

Among the procedures denoted as patterning techniques, perhaps the oldest and the one most commonly used is that of profile analysis. This consists essentially of the graphic representation of comparable test scores sequentially arranged in which the high and low points indicate high and low test performance on the tests in question. The form or shape of the graph is then taken to give a "picture" of the characteristic idiosyncrasies of the individual's over-all test performance. Unfortunately, the resultant profile is easily altered by changing the order of the tests so that the configuration or picture obtained is both arbitrary and ephemeral. It should also be noted that in test profiling it is essentially the magnitude of the test score rather than their configuration with which the investigator is ostensibly concerned. Nevertheless, for certain clinical purposes, the method can be used with advantage since it can tell us at a glance on which of a given battery of tests an individual does relatively poorly or well.[6]

A second procedure to which the term patterning has been applied is one in which the scores on the individual tests of a battery are not treated separately but summed up into a hoped-for discriminating total. This method has often been used in constructing aptitude and personality scales. The usual procedure here is to correlate each test or test item with a differential criterion, and then maximalizing the contributions of each

[5] The general formula for the sum of total possible patterns is $S_p = (N + 1)^m - 1$, where S = the total number of combinations, N = the number of alternates (dichotomies) and m = number of tests used (494).

[6] Assuming, of course, that the tests compared have been previously equated to a common denominator.

of the tests by means of an appropriate regression equation. The more recently invoked "discriminant function" technique (341) is a refined and special application of this method.

A third procedure sometimes drafted into the service of pattern analysis is factor analysis. Here the implication is that mere identification of a subject's performance in terms of the defined group factors rather than in terms of individual subtests of the battery from which the factors have been extracted constitutes a pattern of his abilities. Actually, much more is required. To obtain a true pattern, the factors themselves still need to be combined in ways other than by summation of factor loadings.

Patterning involves not merely identification or maximalization of test scores but their separation into uniquely significant configurations. No mere sum, however arrived at, can attain this end, because an identical score can be arrived at in a great many different ways.

The foregoing considerations do not imply that groups may not in some cases be matched by summation methods. For certain purposes such a type of matching is altogether appropriate. Indeed, one such method using an interclass correlation technique recently described by Haggard (222) promises some interesting and useful applications. Among the examples given by Haggard are two applications to data presented in the third edition of the *Measurement of Adult Intelligence*. One shows the similarity between the W–B test performance of neurotics, the other the dissimilarity between the W–B test performance of an "organic *vz.* psychopath."[7] It should be noted, however, that this method applies only to a type of performance in which the necessary combination of test scores has already been determined; it does not enable us to discover which test scores will be high and which low in any given diagnostic group but only the level of variance that must be found in order to identify them as like or unlike.

The intent of the foregoing discussion has been to point out the inherent difficulties of obtaining true statistical configurations from test score data in any simple fashion.[8] Profiles, summation of weighted scores, discriminant functions and even configurational scoring will not do it. Statistically, what we are looking for are uniquely identifiable combinations which at the same time are diagnostic of clinical entities. The chance of discovering such combinations at random from any considerable assembly of tests with even a limited number of dichotomies, is infinitesimally small. The chances can be significantly increased either by reducing the number of tests or the number of dichotomies. The first is not possible until we know which tests are associated with which clinical syndromes, and generally requires that one start out with more tests than one hopes eventually to

---

[7] *Measurement of Adult Intelligence* (517) pp. 161–166.
[8] For further discussion of patterning problems, see Meehl (360).

use. The second condition may be more easily met, but only if one has previously established reliable cut-off points.

The job of finding unique combinations for diagnostic purposes will have to be a piecemeal procedure. The author has thus far confined himself to the task of discovering what test may be significantly associated with what diagnostic syndrome. As an initial attempt, based on his own and reported data, he has tried to list the tests in which schizophrenics, psychopaths, organics, etc. tend to do relatively well or relatively poorly as compared with "normals." This is *not* patterning, although it is often so referred to in the literature. It is a preliminary step which is necessary in any attempts at patterning, in the sense that it gives us clues to tests which might in combination yield significant configurations. An example of such a potential combination now being revealed in a study with the WISC on childhood schizophrenics is the pattern, high Picture Completion, low Picture Arrangement, high Object Assembly, low Digit Symbol. The four tests are treated as a unique group, and the subject to be considered as showing the indicated pattern, must have scores on each of the individual subtests of the tetrad which agree as to sequence as well as relative order of magnitude.

A fact to be taken into consideration when one deals with some, and not all of one's data, is that along with the increase in the chances of obtaining unique combinations are the increased chances for overlap. This results in a drastic reduction of the number of subjects in any population to which one can apply any posited pattern. This may be a serious limitation but one must always bear in mind that in differential diagnosis one should be more concerned with the question of how well rather than how many. This last fact is often lost sight of. For example, in one of the earlier attempts to use the "W–B subtest signs" for schizophrenia an investigator was greatly disappointed because she was able to detect only some 20 per cent of the schizophrenics tested by means of the combinations of signs she employed, and consequently concluded that her findings were of no great value. This is somewhat like concluding that a test for cancer is of no value because only a small percentage of cases are picked up with it. It is almost inevitable that when one looks for unique patterns which are both highly reliable and valid, any selected combination will detect only a small percentage of the individuals tested. This fact has led the writer to turn increasingly in his attempt at psychological diagnosis to what may be termed the *method of successive sieves*.

The method of successive sieves is based on the hypothesis that one can arrive at diagnostic combinations more easily by dealing successively with selected parts of one's data than by trying to deal with them as a whole. Such approach, as already suggested, will reduce the number of individuals in a given population detected by any one test pattern. But the possible number that may be eventually detected can be increased considerably by successive applications of second, third and fourth sieves to the same population. Thus, if one test combination picked up 18 per cent of schizophrenics (with, to be sure, only a very narrow band of false positives), another combination 15 per cent, still another 12 per cent, and so on, it is clear that by the use of several sieves a very substantial percentage of the patients will have been diagnosed. An example illustrating the application of the method of successive sieves for distinguishing schizophrenics from normal subjects is summarized in Table 46.

One of the serious problems in psychological diagnosis is the fact of overlap, and in particular, the matter of the so-called "false positive." False positives are "normal" subjects whose test scores or sign count fall within the range of the designated abnormal. A certain amount of this is inevitable, first, because of the uncertainty of our criteria, and second, because of the unreliability of our measures. Not only, for example, is schizophrenia a changing concept, but there are always atypical cases which cannot be encompassed in a single rubric. But the risk of misdiagnosis can be greatly reduced by lowering one's cutting point or restricting

TABLE 46

Illustrative application of the method of successive sieves

Group†	No.	Sieve A		Sieve B		Sieve C		Sieve D		Total	
		%	t*	%	t	%	t	%	t	%	t
Male schiz.‡	30	27		13		10		3		43	
Male normal	30	0	3.06	0	2.04	0	1.79	0	0.97	0	4.06
Fem. schiz	30	27		7		17		10		61	
Fem. normal	30	0	3.06	7	—	3	1.82	0	1.79	10	4.07
Total schiz	60	27		10		13		7		52	
Total normal	60	0	4.33	3	2.23	2	3.24	0	2.12	5	5.73

* t of 2.58 is significant at the 1 per cent level.

Sieve A: A difference of at least 20 points between Verbal IQ and Performance IQ.

Sieve B: PC and OA scores lower than PA and DSym; the difference between PC and PA at least 3 weighted scale points.

Sieve C: Vocabulary and Comprehension scores higher than Similarities and Digit Span; the difference between Vocabulary and Similarities at least 3 points.

Sieve D: The reverse of Sieve C. Similarities and Digit Span higher than Vocabulary and Comprehension; a difference of at least 3 points between Similarities and Vocabulary.

† The groups were equated for age and IQ.

‡ In this group there was some slight overlap between the sieves.

one's area of operation. For example, one can be sure of not misdiagnosing mental deficiency by using a minimal IQ of 50 instead of the usual 65 or 70, or, again, one may insist that a patient fail on at least two or three of the successive schizophrenic sieves (see above) rather than only one before he is definitively diagnosed as schizophrenic. Similarly, a differential diagnosis is very much easier if one is confronted with situations which do not present too many alternatives.

Actually, the task of differential diagnosis is much less difficult for the experienced clinician than *a priori* considerations would suggest. This is because the experienced examiner generally deals not with hypothetical but real cases in which he makes use of other information besides the obtained test data. It is true, for example, that there is a great deal of overlap in the psychometric signs encountered in organics and schizophrenics, but if the examiner is confronted with a case in which he already knows (from the case history) that the patient is not a schizophrenic, then this question of overlap between the disease entities is of no great consequence in this particular case. What he has to determine from the subject's test performance is whether the signs presented are or are not consistent with an organic brain syndrome. Conversely, some unique test performance may be definitely diagnostic irrespective of whether other signs are present or absent. For example, a very high Similarities along with a very low Picture Completion is definitely indicative of schizophrenia, because no other type of patient, so far as we have been able to determine, shows this combination. Of course, this situation may not occur very often and thus may not be a very useful sign, but the experienced examiner should be acquainted with this fact so that when it does occur he is able to use it in the absence of any other relevant symptoms.

With the above considerations in mind, we shall now proceed to describe the test characteristics manifested by various clinical groups. The subtests are listed under each diagnostic category with indications as to how subjects of the indicated category tend to perform on each of the tests. As already mentioned, these lists *are not patterns*. They are only bases from which patterns may be evolved from tried test combinations. The significance of the notation that follows each subtest score is explained on page 170. In general, the more nearly a subject's test performance resembles the score profile of a particular diagnostic group, the greater the probability that he belongs in that clinical category. This, of course, does not mean that an individual, to be diagnosed as a schizophrenic, organic, etc., will show all or even a majority of the signs characteristic of a particular category; it only suggests that he will show more of these signs than one would find in a non-organic or non-schizophrenic test protocol, etc.

On the other hand, owing to the considerable overlap between the performance profiles of different clinical groups, single signs are rarely differentially diagnostic. As in medicine, a single sign or symptom cannot be utilized without regard to the presence or absence of other symptoms. Thus, a high temperature plus labored breathing, plus pleuritic infiltration point to a probable pneumonia; high temperature plus inflammation of the skin and a butterfly rash over the eye, erysipelas, etc. One is confronted with similar situations in interpreting overlap of test performance. Low Digit Symbol plus low Arithmetic plus poor Digit Span may, other things equal, merely indicate neurotic anxiety; low Digit Span plus low Picture Arrangement and very low Block Design, organicity; low Digit Span plus low Similarities and low Picture Completion possible schizophrenia, etc. Some of these combinations have already been sufficiently verified to prove their value but most for which claim has been made have not been substantiated.

We now turn to a discussion of the data which give the test characteristics of various diagnostic groups. These are summarized below. They show how well or how poorly subjects in each of the listed groups tend to do on the subtests of the W–B I and WAIS.

The meanings of the symbols used are as follows: + and ++ signify relatively good, high or considerably above the mean of the subject's remaining subtest scores; − and − −, relatively poor, low or considerably below the mean of the subject's remaining subtest scores; 0, no significant deviation from the mean of the remaining subtest scores. The combined symbols + to 0, − to 0, etc., signify that the deviation in subtest scores may be either above or approximately at the mean of the remaining subtests, etc. In general, the symbol placed first represents the general tendency. Thus, Object Assembly under Organic Brain Disease is marked 0 to − −. This means that, in general, the organic subject's score on Object Assembly is not outstanding but that in some cases it may be extremely low.

On a quantitative basis the symbols have approximately the following significance:

+ a deviation of from 1.5 to 2.5 units above the mean subtest score
++ a deviation of 3 or more units above the mean subtest score
− a deviation of from 1.5 to 2.5 units below the mean subtest score
− − a deviation of 3 or more units below the mean subtest score
0 a deviation of +1.5 to −1.5 units from the mean subtest score

All deviations are in terms of weighted score units.

Test Characteristics of Various Clinical Groups

Organic Brain Disease

Information...	+
Comprehension*..	+
Arithmetic...	−
Digit Span†...	− −
Similarities...	−
Vocabulary...	++
Picture Arrangement.......................................	0 to −
Picture Completion...	0
Object Assembly‡..	0 to − −
Block Design‡..	− − to 0
Digit Symbol...	− −

Verbal higher than Performance

Inter-test variability: omitting the 2 or 3 tests on which subject is likely to
  do very badly, scatter of remainder generally small.

* Except in paretics.

† Particularly digits backward.

‡ Depending on type of impairment.

Schizophrenia

Information...	+ to ++
Comprehension*..	+ to −
Arithmetic...	0 to −
Digit Span...	+ to 0
Similarities*..	+ to − −
Vocabulary...	++
Picture Arrangement.......................................	− to 0
Picture Completion*..	0 to − −
Object Assembly...	−
Block Design...	0 to +
Digit Symbol...	−

Verbal generally higher than Performance.

Sum of Picture Arrangement plus Comprehension less than Information
  and Block Design.

Object Assembly much below Block Design.

Very low Similarities with high Vocabulary and Information, definitely
  pathognomonic.

Inter-test variability: marked, and in most cases greater between subtests of
  the Verbal than of the Performance part of the Scale.

* Depending on type of schizophrenia.

Anxiety States

Information	+
Comprehension	+
Arithmetic	0 to −
Digit Span*	−
Similarities	+
Vocabulary	+
Picture Arrangement	0
Picture Completion	−
Object Assembly	−
Block Design	0
Digit Symbol	−

Verbal generally higher than Performance.

Inter-test variability: moderate, less than in psychoses but greater than in "normals".

* But unpredictable.

Adolescent Sociopaths (Delinquents)

Information	− to − −
Comprehension	0 to −
Arithmetic	−
Digit Span	0 to −
Similarities	− to 0
Vocabulary	0
Picture Arrangement	++ to +
Picture Completion	+ to 0
Object Assembly	++ to +
Block Design	+ to 0
Digit Symbol	0 to −

Performance generally higher than Verbal.

Sum of Object Assembly plus Picture Arrangement nearly always greater than the sum of Block Design and Picture Completion test scores.

Mental Defectives

Information	0 to −
Comprehension	+
Arithmetic	− −
Digit Span	− to 0
Similarities	0 to +
Vocabulary	+ to 0
Picture Arrangement	0 to −
Picture Completion	0
Object Assembly	++
Block Design	0 to +
Digit Symbol	− to 0

Digits backward almost systematically − to − −; very frequently subject unable to comprehend what is wanted.

A combination of high Arithmetic plus high Block Design, independent of any other score, is counter-indicative of mental deficiency.

High inter- as well as intra-test variability suggestive of emotional disturbance, more likely previous or concomitant psychosis.

Our test characteristics are composite appraisals representing mean trends derived from the literature and from the author's own studies. In some instances they are at variance with previously reported findings, but on the whole represent rather broad over-all agreement. Various factors account for discrepancies encountered among the findings of individual authors. Probably the most important are due to the limitations of the research methods employed. Others include the low numbers tested, heterogeneity of population samples grouped under the same diagnostic rubrics and, last but not least, unreliability of individual psychiatric diagnoses. Considering the many possible sources of error, the over-all agreement in the findings on most of the subtests is rather substantial. This is not equally true for all the syndromes. The consensus is much better for organic brain disease than for schizophrenia, better for schizophrenia than psychopathic personality, and generally poor for the category neuroses, whether treated as a broad category or broken down to sub-groups, like conversion hysteria, obsessions, etc.

In view of the limited agreement as regards the neurotic signs as originally described in the earlier editions of the *Measurement of Adult Intelligence*, and also their limited usefulness in practice, this category has been dropped from our present summaries. In its place we have substituted the category *Anxiety Reaction Types*, which though less specific, shows more consistent findings. The category adolescent psychopath, about which there was also some question, has been retained in essence, but the title of the category has been altered to *Adolescent Sociopaths* (and delinquents) which was basically the group on whom the test descriptions were worked out. No attempt has been made to establish a pattern for depression because, apart from the general slowing up and significantly lower Performance scores on the W–B Scale, we were unable to find any consistent differences between the depressive and other groups, or such as reported by Shafer and Rapaport (420).

The test characteristics for the various groups are based primarily on studies with the W–B I. They have, however, been confirmed by the writer as applying to the WAIS for at least two of the major groups, namely, schizophrenic and organic reaction types. On the other hand, the evaluation of anxiety reaction types has been derived primarily from analysis of WAIS protocols and particularly from the reported study by Siegman (456).

Comments on Diagnostic Groups

ORGANIC BRAIN DISEASES. This category covers a large group of syndromes ranging all the way from brain tumors to chronic alcoholism. The cases cited are not intended as examples of differential diagnoses between any specific disease entities but rather as illustrations of the disorganization of the intellectual processes observed in most organic brain cases, irrespective of type. The most general symptoms in organic brain cases are disturbances in the visual-motor spheres, a loss of shift, memory defects and a falling off of capacities involving organization and synthetic ability.

Organic brain patients, with few exceptions, do consistently better on verbal than on performance tests. The greatest and most consistent falling off is on the Digit Symbol test, but even more diagnostic, though not necessarily the most adversely affected, is the organic's inability to do the Block Design test, which is systematically associated with disturbances in visual-motor organization. Next in order of frequency to a low score on the Digit Symbol and the Block Design are low scores on the Picture Arrangement and, depending on the type of organic involvement, the Object Assembly Test. Memory defect is reflected in low Memory Span score, particularly on digits backward. Certain patients also do poorly on the Similarities Test, and this may reflect either a loss in conceptual thinking or, more frequently, an increasing rigidity in the thought processes. All new learning is markedly affected. This accounts mainly for the organic's low score on the Digit Symbol Test, although visual-motor disturbances also play a role.

Some groups, as the paretics and arteriosclerotics, often show a generalized deterioration, that is, do badly on nearly all tests. These patients even though they do better on Verbal than on Performance, show no great variability as regards the tests which constitute each part of the Scale. This fact is often of value in differential diagnosis, for example, as between traumatic brain injury where the defects are uneven and general paresis where the intellectual processes are more or less equally impaired.

SCHIZOPHRENIA. Schizophrenia or dementia praecox comprises a related group of affections rather than a single disease entity. Although the classical division of dementia praecox into the four types, catatonic, paranoid, hebephrenic and simple, is more theoretical than factual, it does suggest, what experience demonstrates, that schizophrenics may vary widely among themselves as to both symptoms and general picture. Moreover, the general diagnosis of schizophrenia itself is often contingent upon the orientation of the psychiatrist or the school to which he may belong. A case which in one hospital is diagnosed as schizophrenia may be labeled manic depressive at another, and vice versa. In view of this situation it is obvious that no single list of signs can be either sufficiently comprehensive or free from exceptions.

Intellectually, the most general effect of the schizophrenic process is the impairment of the subject's mental efficiency. This loss is evidenced by the low scores which he makes on most tests calling for immediate and directed effort. Occupationally, this is shown by the fact that the schizophrenic's vocational adjustment and life adaptations are often considerably inferior to what might be expected of a person with his original endowment. In addition to the impairment of mental efficiency, the schizophrenic is further characterized by a marked slowing up of his thinking, a loss in mental shift and a tendency toward perseveration. As often noted, he does much better on verbal tests. This relative superiority of the schizophrenic is of special interest because ordinarily one does not think of him as a verbalist. Clinically, he is continually being referred to as a shut-in uncommunicative person. The inconsistency, however, between the two findings is explained when it is discovered that the verbal tests, on which the schizophrenic does well (Information, Word definitions), are precisely those which do not require spontaneous verbalization. When they do make this demand, as in the case of the Similarities test, he is likely to fail. This failure is not due to a lack of either understanding or linguistic facility, but to a distortion in the patient's ideational processes. The schizophrenic misinterprets words just as he misinterprets reality, and his incongruent replies, like his bizarre ideas, are a product of this misinterpretation.

Another characteristic of the schizophrenic is his inability to deal with concrete and specific situations. He is oblivious to details and does not perceive ordinary likenesses and differences, difficulties which are often reflected by the poor scores he attains on either the Similarities or Picture Completion tests or both. Last but not least is the schizophrenic's unpredictability, so that now and again one finds some schizophrenic patients who do well on one or several of the tests which are characteristically failed by the typical schizophrenic. A thorough acquaintance with a particular case generally makes it possible to account for the contradictory findings, but the occurrence of such exceptions show that the diagnosis of schizophrenia through psychometric "signs" or "patterns" is not a cut and dried affair. The cases we have used as illustrations are typical only in the sense that they are of individuals who manifest most or many of the signs characteristic of the schizophrenic group as a whole.

ANXIETY REACTION TYPES. Anxiety is a state that occurs in many mental disorders and is not necessarily diagnostic of any one of them. While most often associated with certain neurotic conditions and depressions, it is also an important symptom in organic brain disease and schizophrenia. As a transient manifestation it may be observed in normal persons when under severe stress or threat.

Anxiety may be either a cause or symptom. In either case it is generally disruptive or disabling. It may interfere with the individual's functioning in a variety of ways. On the physical side it may reflect itself in tremor, restlessness, physiological inhibition, dryness of mouth, palpitation, etc.; mentally, by inability to concentrate, fluctuations in attention, moodiness and erraticism. In test performance any or all of these manifestations may be present. There are, however, some tests which are more sensitive to impairment than others, *e.g.*, Arithmetic, Digit Span and Digit Symbol. Thus, Siegman (456) found that subjects with high anxiety scores on the Taylor Scale made systematically lower scores on these three tests than on the other subtests of the Wechsler Scales,[9] and this is a finding which is in line with clinical experience. Other tests which occasionally reflect anxiety are the Object Assembly and Picture Arrangement, in which instances the low score seems to be due to temporary loss of goal, occasional awkwardness or unnecessary persistence. Individuals under anxiety, like neurotics in general, will tend to have lower Performance than Verbal scores, but the failures of these subjects, unlike those of organics, are not systematic or consistent. On the other hand, anxiety states seldom occur in isolation, and it is always necessary to take into consideration other aspects of the personality structure or attending conditions which can influence the individual's test performance.

MENTAL DEFECTIVES. The diagnostic problems encountered in the mental defective group have been detailed in Chapter 4. In most instances, the diagnosis of mental deficiency is most safely made on the basis of a reliably established IQ. Nevertheless, individual cases present special problems. The test characteristics of the mental defectives given above are primarily an aid for differential diagnosis in doubtful cases. The major characteristics of the mental defective's performance are relatively limited intra- as well as inter-test variability, consistently low scores on Arithmetic, Digit Span and Digit Symbol and relatively good scores on Comprehension and Object Assembly. A distinction must be made between the "familial" and the traumatic groups, and between the defectives with and without psychosis. A not infrequent problem, particularly with younger subjects, is the differentiation between the childhood schizophrenic with low IQ and the true mental defective. Examples illustrating the differences in type of performance that may be met with in the two are given at the end of the chapter.

SOCIOPATHS. The most outstanding single feature of the sociopath's test profile is his systematic high score on the Performance as compared to the Verbal part of the Scale. Occasional exceptions occur but these generally reflect some special ability or disability. Also worthy of note is the good score frequently made by the sociopath on the Picture Arrangement Test, a finding that is surprising because this test has been interpreted as measuring social intelligence. If this interpretation is correct, a

[9] However, subjects with low anxiety score on the Taylor Test did not necessarily show the expected concomitant difference.

distinction must be made between intellectual understanding and affective acceptance of conventional behavior.

Sociopaths generally have a grasp of social situations, but they are inclined to manipulate them to their own advantage in an antisocial way. The point cannot, however, be pushed too far because there are many exceptions to the rule, particularly in the case of extreme sociopaths who are not only perverse in their behavior, but distorted in their social comprehension. The sociopath's test performance as a whole is characterized by a breeziness and self-assurance which contrasts markedly to that of a neurotic. He is not bothered by contradictions and, when not ornery, takes everything in his stride. His abstract thinking is generally below average, and this is frequently indicated by a low score on the Similarities test. He also tends to do poorly on arithmetical reasoning, but in this connection it must be noted that the mean Arithmetic subtest score for the normal adolescent (ages 12 to 16) is systematically lower than his mean score on the remaining tests of the scale.

The test pattern just described is based primarily on the performance of male adolescent sociopaths. Further experience has shown that it is also applicable to the adult male psychopath, but a study recently completed (499) indicates that it may not have the same diagnostic value in the case of the female psychopath. There is seemingly an important sex difference. One feature, however, common to both male and female adolescent sociopaths is a relatively low score on the Information Test. This may reflect in part educational retardation or the tendency of many psychopaths to disregard those aspects of available knowledge (reality) which do not lead to the satisfaction of his immediate needs.

Comments on Test Interpretation

Performance on any test is multi-determined, and for this reason it is not always possible to posit a single explanation for any given response. Nevertheless, of the many potential factors that may have to be taken into account, success and failure on a given task are most often found to depend on the degree to which a subject possesses or lacks the ability or abilities implicit in or required by the task. This presupposes that one knows what a test measures or purports to measure. Our knowledge in this respect still leaves much to be desired, but it is fair to say that the most reliable indicators we have are those derived from factorial studies. In general, the abilities entering into a test are best defined in terms of the reference factors which account for its major variance. Accordingly, an examiner will be on safest ground if, to begin with, he assumes that a subject's successes or failures are probably due to strength or weakness in the major abilities as defined by the attested factors.[10] Thus, a low score on the Vocabulary or Similarities test should, in the first instance, be interpreted as due to limited verbal ability, a low score on the Digit Span to poor memory, a high score on the Block Design to superior visual-motor organization, etc. But, in any given case any one factor may act as a major determinant. Thus, a low score on Digit Span may be primarily due to an individual's greater distractability rather than poor memory, a high score on the Comprehension to stereotypy rather than verbal facility, etc.

The assumption that high and low scores on tests are primarily determined by amount of ability does not negate the fact that non-intellective factors, special training (or lack of it), developed interests and personal involvement may also influence test performance. Thus, a poor score on the Information and Arithmetic tests may be due primarily to limited schooling, a better than average score on Picture Arrangement to familiarity with comics, and a high score on the Block Design to occupational experience (*e.g.*, in commercial art). Sometimes environmental background will account for particular successes or failures. Thus, people who are *more* familiar with the Bible will *more* often give a correct answer to the question "What is the theme of the Book of Genesis" than those who are not. Again, women more frequently detect the missing eyebrow (on P.C., Item 21) than do men.

More challenging, at least for diagnostic purposes, are the failures and successes on a type of test performance or usually on individual test items which are seemingly due to the individual's personality and emotional conditioning. For example, a subject who may do rather well on most of the Performance subtests and even parts of the Picture Arrangement will unexpectedly have extreme difficulty with the Taxi item (on the Picture Arrangement). Here, one may reasonably assume that it is the content of this particular series that is the disturbing factor. Since the picture concerns itself with a sex theme, one may presume that the difficulty is due to some preoccupation with sex, and such is not infrequently the case. A patient with an IQ of 112 misses completely the first and easiest item on the Picture Completion test (card showing nose missing). This card is passed by nearly 100 per cent of adults, and one would normally not expect a person with this level of intelligence to be stumped by it. Moreover, the subject succeeded on several much harder cards, including the most difficult of all (Item 21 on WAIS). Since failure was not due to limited intelligence or defective perception, one is led to the conclusion that some special fact or circumstance must account for it.

Instances of the kind just noted might be interpreted as merely testifying to the unreliability of certain test items and, if occurring in the case of

[10] That is, by the fact of showing the highest test loadings.

any considerable number of items, as pointing to the unreliability of the test as a whole. Actually, such anomalous failures do not occur very often. But conceding that failures of this kind might materially alter a subject's score, there still remains the question whether the "loss" to the test's reliability might not be more than compensated for by the gain in insight one may get regarding the subject's personality. In the case described above, the subject's failure to detect the missing nose called the examiner's attention to the possibility that he might be dealing with a schizophrenic or with a subject who was much concerned about her body image.[11] This is the projective aspect of the test. Clinicians look upon it as a positive factor; many test constructors, as a source of error; to a degree both are correct. An intelligence test gains in value in proportion to the amount of information it gives, other than over-all rating of intellectual level; at the same time it suffers if it is at the mercy of factors other than the basic abilities which it is trying to measure. The question, of course, is to what extent these factors influence the final results or contribute to the better understanding of the individual. In the writer's opinion, both the over-sensitized clinician and the matter-of-fact statistician are likely to over-estimate the impact of personality variables on test performance. This does not mean that these variables are of no importance. They are, and indeed a large part of the discussion to follow will be concerned with their possible significance. Emotionality, anxiety, motivation, etc., can influence test scores, but only seldom do they influence performance to such a degree as to invalidate the test findings as a whole. More important than either of the above considerations, however, is the fact that the impacts of these personality factors, far from being sources of error, must be looked upon as significant aspects of the individual's global intellectual capacity. If an individual, because of compulsions, lack of drive, uncontrolled anxiety, etc., is *continually* unable to utilize his intellectual resources and, in general, acts stupidly because of these disabilities, he is for all practical purposes mentally defective.

Diagnostic Significance of the Individual Subtests

The following remarks are intended to supplement our previous evaluation of the W–B I and WAIS subtests, and to consider more specifically a number of points bearing on their rationale and suggested interpretations.

INFORMATION. Apart from its factorial determinants, the conditions which most often influence level of information are schooling, cultural background and specific interests. From a strict psychometric point of view these facts

[11] Actually, the case mentioned is that of a young woman referred for examination as a possible schizophrenic, one of whose main complaints was that her nose was too large.

may be considered "sources of error", but since they are factors which must inevitably be taken into account it is important that the items of a test tend to bring to light rather than to hide their presence. When this obtains, it is often possible to convert the "source of error" into a useful diagnostic indicator. Thus, we may infer something about the background and interest of a subject from a comparison on types of items he tends to fail with those he passes with ease. Of particular interest are failures and successes which are contrary to what one may expect from the knowledge of a person's background, for example, answers to such questions as "What is the theme of the Book of Genesis?" "Who is the Author of Faust?" and "Who wrote the Iliad?" from persons with limited schooling, and failures on such items as "the number of weeks in a year?" "Height of the average American woman?" and "the population of the United States?" from persons with good schooling or high IQ level. In the first instance we are likely to find that we are dealing with an alert and socially interested individual; in the latter, with an impractical individual, and in pathological cases, an individual with a tendency toward withdrawal and avoidance of reality.

Large discrepancies between the Information and other subtests of the Scale are clinically important. Of particular significance is a large discrepancy between Information and Vocabulary (V–I, 2 or more Scale points). A discrepancy of this order is generally not to be expected because of the high correlation between the two tests. When it does occur, especially in individuals of good schooling, one may suspect limited interest in or tendency to withdraw from the environment. Even more pathognomonic are bizarre responses. Bizarre responses are given most often by schizophrenics and manic depressives, occasionally also by psychopaths, although not in quite the same manner. The following are some examples.

"Distance from Paris to New York."—"I don't know, I never walked that far." (adolescent psychopath)

"Capital of Italy."—"Rome, but it could have changed." (manic depressive)

Population of the United States."—"The population is 10,000." (involutional depression, IQ 96)

"Where Egypt is."—"It is in the southeast corner of the Mediterranean, southwest of Palestine, east of North Africa, south of the Suez Canal and the Red Sea." (schizophrenic)

"Function of the heart."—"Invigorates the blood by putting red and white corpuscles in the blood stream." (schizophrenic)

"Why dark-colored clothes are considered warmer than light-colored clothes."—"Light clothes are lighter, dark clothes heavier." (schizophrenic)

"How yeast causes dough to rise."—"Something takes place in the bacteriological *context*. When heat is applied molecules become active and cause it to rise." (schizophrenic)

"In what direction you would travel if you went from Chicago to Panama?"—"I'd take a plane and let the pilot worry about the direction." (psychopath)

"What the Koran is."—"Like a chorus or a piece of cord." (schizophrenic)

"Colors in the American flag."—"I don't remember." (response of a subject of superior intelligence, charged with espionage)

VOCABULARY. Words have orectic as well as noetic connotations; hence, the way an individual defines a word often tells us something more than how fluent he may be verbally or how extensive his vocabulary. One can judge a person by what he says (and thinks) as well as by what he does. This is an assumption which underlies personality inferences based on verbal productions. In the case of the Vocabulary Test, the exact verbalization as well as the form and content of a subject's definition is often revealing. And where there are several choices or alternative definitions possible the particular meaning of the word which a subject chooses to define is also of some significance. For example, one may reasonably assume some difference in background or interests between the individual who defines a diamond as a "precious stone" and the individual who first thinks of it as a "baseball field", or between the individual who defines a sentence as "a group of words, etc." and the person who says "it means a penalty meted out by a judge." Definitions do not have to be incorrect or bizarre to be of interest diagnostically, although bizarre answers are usually pathognomonic.

The common dichotomy of definitions in terms of concrete *vs.* abstract, or as descriptive, functional or conceptual, although of value for certain purposes, is generally not too useful diagnostically. By contrast there are certain unusual modes of response found in thinking disturbances for which clinicians should be on the lookout. Among the more important of these are the following.

Over-elaboration. The tendency to give alternate meanings and irrelevant details, or to be overly and unnecessarily descriptive. Thus, for "diamond", "A gem; part of jewelry which consists of precious stones; what you give to a girl when you are engaged."

Ellipsis. The omission of one or more words (sometimes only syllables) necessary to complete the meaning in a phrase or sentence. Thus, for "microscope," "Germs" (omitted or implied, an instrument for magnifying small objects, as germs).

Self-Reference. Incorporation into a definition of personalized elements or of details reflecting self-involvement. Thus, for "conceal", "To hide away from peeking eyes."

Bizarreness. Definitions involving markedly idiosyncratic associations or the juxta-position of disconnected ideas. Thus, for "plural", "A way of thinking in grammer." For "impale", "Not blanched" (im = not, pale = blanch).

Of the above categories, the one needing most discrimination because it is sometimes not too different from otherwise common definitions is the response type designated as over-elaboration. The others are generally easily recognized as deviant (and usually encountered in psychotics). But the over-elaborated response because it might be quite acceptable score-wise can be readily missed. Sometimes, over-elaboration may only indicate a mild tendency toward pedantism, at other times a basic insecurity and ambivalence and at still others a tendency toward over-intellectualization. In the last instance, it often represents one of the early signs of schizophrenia. Occasionally it is the one sign in evidence when others are seemingly lacking.

The following examples are illustrative of one or another of the categories just described. A single definition may, of course, simultaneously include several of them.

Join.	To enlist, combine, to make a connection. Join two elements.
Bacon.	A variety of meat obtained from the lumbar region of a pig. A part of pig associated with breakfast.
Fur.	A kind of attire which comes from the skin of an animal. Clothing. (Omitted or implied: the skin of an animal which is used for clothing). Wooly covering of an animal to protect it from weather.
Seclude.	To go off in a corner, to be alone. A trapper lives in seclusion.
Espionage.	The act of obtaining information secretly from an enemy, in the service of your country.
Nail.	A hammer (Implied: what you use to put together with a hammer).
Stanza.	Stands up.
Guillotine.	Like gelatin. Either ammunition or a dessert.
Pewter.	Something that smells (phew).
Fortitude.	Like a fortress.
Regulate.	Control. You can regulate a life (self-reference).
Tolerate.	Pay no attention to.
Revenge.	Trouble (subject explains it is what you do to a person who causes you trouble).
Donkey.	An ass in a class by itself. A democratic animal.
Brim.	Aroundness; circular topness.

SIMILARITIES TEST. The Similarities Test is often designated as a test of abstraction or concept formation, and to the extent that it calls for perception of broad, common or universal elements between the terms compared, its designation as such is altogether justified. But it should be remembered that the mere presence of a universal element does not in and of itself constitute conceptualized relationship. The essence of a concept requires a generalization or deduction drawn from particulars,[12] and one is never quite sure whether a subject in giving even a superior (2 credit) response has actually done just that. Some of the responses awarded maximum credit turn out in many instances to be merely verbal associations— for example, Banana–Apple, "Both fruit"; or even Fly–Tree, "Both liv-

[12] A distinction is also sometimes made between a general and an abstract concept, for example, as between the terms Man and Truth. On this point see Baldwin (33). Most of the terms used in the Similarities test, it should be noted, call for general concepts. For example, Dog-Lion, Wood-Alcohol, rather than such an abstract idea as Statue-Poem.

ing things." Here additional questioning is necessary to find out whether we are dealing with a true concept formation or merely an associative recall.

Individuals who perform well on the Similarities Test may do so because they are either over-ideational or very logical. Conversely, subjects who perform poorly on the Similarities Test may do so not because of intellectual lack but because of an inner need for concretistic thinking. Sometimes both defects are shown by the same subject, as in certain schizophrenics who are at once over-ideational and concrete.

Another point that needs to be borne in mind is that, genetically, abstraction is to a degree an adaptive function of the organism. Accordingly, difficulties in making abstractions will often be consequent or related to faults of an adaptation rather than limitations in reasoning ability. This is most clearly seen in the case of many schizophrenics whose "bizarre answers" reflect not so much poor logic as idiosyncratic ideation.

As in the case of the Vocabulary Test, the dynamisms of over-elaboration, condensation and ellipsis often enter into the Similarities response. Finally, as in the case of the F-Rorschach response, the subject's misunderstanding of the terms compared seems to go back to defective perception rather than to a faulty cognition.

The following responses to various Similarities items culled from the protocols of mental patients illustrate some of the points just discussed.

Dog–Lion.	Both forms of life. (over-abstract)
	Both have hair. (over-concrete)
	Depends on heredity. (bizarre)
	Dog can be kept as a pet. (idiosyncratic)
Coat–Dress.	A man or woman would be naked without them. Both undergarments—you can take a coat off and you can take a dress off.
	Natural items for men and women for comfort and warmth.
	Standard articles of clothing.
Orange–Banana.	Both grow in hot climate—both products of nature.
Wagon–Bicycle.	Instruments to get around with.
Table–Chair.	Both built upright and have legs.
	Both contribute to comfort of people in the home.
Air–Water.	Both rotate.
Wood–Alcohol.	Same substance in different form.
	Both natural products.
Praise–Punishment.	Methods in dealing with dominant-subordinate relations.
	Both begin with letter P; both words.
Eye–Ear.	Not alike—the eye is easily fooled, the ear is not.
Egg–Seed.	Vehicles of reproduction.
Nos. 49–121 (W–B II).	Both equally distant from 85.
Fly–Tree.	You can kill both.
	Fly lives in tree and tree can breed flies.

A type of response that one frequently gets from both normal (usually dull-normal) and disturbed patients is a difference rather than a likeness. In such instances one may encourage a subject by saying, "Now tell me the way in which they are *alike*." Usually the subject persists in denying any likeness; sometimes he will alter the response. The schizophrenic may start out with a difference as a manifestation of his negativism but eventually builds up to a correct concept. Thus, Orange–Banana: "They are both yellow; both round, both food, both fruit," Axe–saw: "Axe is used for chopping wood, saw for sawing wood—both used in carpentry, both tools."

PICTURE ARRANGEMENT. Grasping and following the ideas or the "stories" exploited in the pictures that make up this test would, *a priori*, seem to depend to a large extent on the subject's familiarity with the cultural setting from which the "stories" were drawn. Actually, this dependency is much less than anticipated; the finding may be a consequence of the type of situation depicted or due to the fact that the humor of "funnies," as is sometimes claimed, is more or less universal. The W–B and WAIS pictures, in spite of their local origin, seem readily understood by persons of quite different cultural backgrounds. This is attested by the fact that in the foreign adaptations of our Scales the Picture Arrangement items have been generally reproduced with negligible modifications.[13]

Cultural background does, however, play a role in the *interpretation* of the picture series. Thus, comparing identical arrangements of Caucasian and Japanese subjects on the Flirt and Taxi items, Brieger (65) found significant group differences in their respective story elaborations. A very high proportion of the Caucasian group (German refugees) entitled the Flirt sequence as a "pick-up" and projected some flippant romantic story into it; the Japanese (Nisei), on the other hand, entitled the story "chivalry" and by-passed or rejected the romantic aspects of it. In the case of the Taxi item, many Nisei preceived the central character as being concerned about the possibility that some member of the protagonist's family might have observed his actions, whereas very few of the Caucasians made any reference to such concern. On the other hand, the Caucasians tended to project an "abnormal" sexual theme into the *Taxi* series, much more often than the Nisei group.

[13] Thus, in the Japanese adaptation of the WISC, the only change made in the "Garden" item was a substitution of a young *boy* for a *man* as the main character in the picture. In the original, this item depicts a man who has ostensibly been asked by his wife to do some gardening but who, as the story proceeds, changes his efforts to a more enjoyable chore. In the first picture he starts by cultivating the garden, in the second he spades up a worm, and eventually, inspired by the season of the year, goes off fishing instead. The substitution of a boy for a man as protagonist of the story was seemingly made because in Japan wives do not send their husbands on chores.

More frequent than variations in interpretation referable to differences in socio-cultural background are those due to the personal reactions, attitudes and affective involvement of the individual subject. This, of course, represents the projective aspect of the test, which is elicited not so much by the particular arrangements which the subject makes of the pictures, as by how he interprets what has happened. To elicit this information the examiner may ask the subject either to tell a story at once or to wait until the end of the test and then re-present the pictures as initially arranged by the subject; the examiner than asks him to say what has happened, card by card. The story may be treated as a whole or supplemented by a TAT type of inquiry. Generally, the Flirt and Taxi are the most productive items, but almost any of the series can, on occasion, furnish illuminating diagnostic material. The following are a few illustrations.

Taxi.

He walks along the street, gets into a cab, looks at her and looks back to see if someone is watching him. Perhaps he stole a statue and is trying to get away. (paranoid schizophrenic)

The man carries a dummy—she changes into a woman in the taxi and he gets very hot and excited. (fluidity and magical thinking in a schizophrenic)

The man calls a taxi because he is embarrassed to walk with a statue. (a "normal," shy, sexually inhibited adolescent with sex preoccupation)

A guy and girl are driving along in a car. The driver is alone in the front seat. I assume it's a cab but I don't see the taxi sign on it. He is carrying a female model but moves away as if he has undergone shock at what he has seen. (perceptual distortion and confusion in a schizophrenic with compulsive trends)

This is a man and woman in a car. The man looks around now but holds the woman. Now they sit apart, he is perspiring like mad.

A guy walks down the street with the head of a woman; he might have killed her. (Subject charged with homicide)

Flirt.

He gets out to help woman carry her bundle. He carries it to the place of destination but gets back into the car and goes on his way. (a person who tells a story without changing the order of the cards as presented)

He's walking down street carrying dirty linen—package gets too heavy and gives it back to her—gets into car because he's tired—drives a while—when police are gone gets out of car. (schizophrenic functioning at a defective level)

Fish.

Somebody put a fish on a line for him; first he gets a small fish so he throws it back and the diver puts a bigger one on for him.

The man is fishing but is frightened away by the diver.

This guy didn't catch anything—he is cursing the water—he jumps in. (alcoholic with severe depression)

A man fishing and he lands a catch and the catch stirs up such a rumpus that the line and pole falls out of his hand. He sees something that he doesn't quite believe—a sea monster. (a confused paranoid schizophrenic)

He is hollering to the fish and telling the fish he is going to catch him. (manic)

PICTURE COMPLETION. A type of response often elicited by the Picture Completion items is one which has no obvious relevancy to the immediate percept. The subject sees things which he thinks ought to belong but which are not called for by the sense of the picture. A simple example would be the response, "The hand is missing" to the Pitcher item, or "Bow is missing" to the Violin item. Responses of this kind are sometimes given by normal persons, but when they occur more than once or twice, or when particularly bizarre, are pathognomonic. Examples of bizarreness are: Item 1 (door without a knob), "The rest of the aeroplane is missing"; Item 17, (man with one finger lacking), "His wife is missing." Responses of this type are in a sense confabulatory and generally only elicited from schizophrenics. Also diagnostically significant is the "nothing" answer. In subjects who respond in this manner, the rejection generally represents either negativism or hostility, but sometimes may be indicative of a phobic reaction. For example, an adolescent girl with symptoms of conversion hysteria responded as follows to the Crab item. "Nothing . . . I hate crabs, never eat them; take this card away." Further examples of deviant responses are given below.

W-B I

Item   1: Rest of body missing.
       2: Teeth are missing.
       4: Red is missing.
       7: Anchor or rudder missing.
       9: Watch chain.
     10: Should have more water in it.
     11: Lipstick missing.
     14: She should have two eyes.

WAIS

Item   1: Rest of the aeroplane is missing.
       2: No food in the trough.
       4: No person in car.
       8: The person who is fiddling is missing.
     10: Filament is missing.
     11: The flagpole is missing.
     12: The leash is missing.
     13: The states aren't filled in.
     17: The man's wife not with him.
     18: No path.

Assets vs. Liabilities

In discussing the significance of subtests we have emphasized primarily negative and inadequate performance. This is because, like most clinicians, we have been concerned in the first instance with problems of diagnosis. It would be regrettable, however, to conclude that the WAIS and W–B I can only be used for finding out what is wrong with an individual. The tests can reveal a person's assets as well as his liabilities. It is important to know in what areas an individual functions above as well as below average. Information of this kind has been most generally used by psychologists engaged in selection and vocational guidance, and an illustration of its application in these areas will be given in Chapter 14. But it should be noted that even in dealing with maladjusted and mentally ill patients it is important to know the patient's strong as well as weak points; these give us indications both as to his potential and his resources. Here, as elsewhere, it is the total functioning of the individual that must be appraised. Clinical psychologists are becoming increasingly aware of this fact, but much more remains to be done to make the average clinician's report more of a total appraisal than an inventory of the patient's disabilities.

Illustrative Cases

Organic Brain Disease

W–B I

Information	14
Comprehension	12
Arithmetic	9
Digits	13
Similarities	11
Verbal	59
Picture Arrangement	9
Picture Comparison	8
Block Design	4
Object Assembly	1
Digit Symbol	3
Performance	25
Verbal IQ	115
Performance IQ	74
Digits forward	8
Digits backward	6

Case 0–1. Male, age 34, showing definite neurological signs including marked hydrocephalus, facial weakness, slight tremor, absent abdominals. Also suggested Babinsky on left side with mild postural deviations on same side. Diagnosis—post-meningo-encephalitic syndrome. At age of 6 months patient had an injury with sequelae lasting 6 months, which was diagnosed as meningitis. This case illustrates the four most conspicuous signs of organic brain disease: large discrepancy between Verbal and Performance in favor of the former, very low Blocks combined with even lower Object Assembly and very low Digit Symbol. While all of the test scores on the verbal part of the examination are average or above, the two lowest are Similarities and Arithmetic, which are in line with the organic picture. The only exception is the Digit Span which is good for both forward (8) and backward (6).

W–B I

Vocabulary	7
Information	8
Comprehension	9
Arithmetic	7
Digits	6
Similarities	9
Verbal	39

Case 0–2. White, male, adolescent, age 14. Brought to hospital because of marked change in personality. Had been normal boy until 6 months prior to admission. Illness first manifested by failure at school and increased irritability. Physical and neurological examination on admission essentially negative. Case presented to illustrate value of Scale in detecting possible organic brain condi-

Picture Arrangement......	6
Picture Comparison.......	1
Block Design.............	1
Object Assembly.........	2
Digit Symbol.............	5
Performance............	15
Verbal IQ................	91
Performance IQ..........	50
Digits forward..........	6
Digits backward........	3

WAIS

Information..............	5
Comprehension..........	6
Arithmetic...............	6
Similarities..............	3
Digit Span...............	4
Vocabulary..............	8
Digit Symbol.............	0
Picture Completion.......	6
Block Design.............	2
Picture Arrangement......	4
Object Assembly.........	3
Verbal IQ................	77
Performance IQ..........	71
Full IQ..................	73

WAIS

Information..............	12
Comprehension..........	12
Arithmetic...............	10
Similarities..............	12
Digit Span...............	14
Vocabulary..............	16
Digit Symbol.............	5
Picture Completion.......	7
Picture Arrangement......	6
Object Assembly.........	5

tions prior to manifestation of neurological symptoms. Psychometric organic signs are: Verbal much higher than Performance; very low scores on *both* Object Assembly and Block Design; large discrepancy between Digits forward and Digits backward. On the qualitative side, subject showed common organic manifestation of being able to reproduce designs if presented with a model of assembled blocks (200), after failing completely with the usual form of presentation.

Case 0–3. 55-year-old housewife was admitted with a history of vomiting, diarrhea, loss of appetite and complaints of pain in abdomen. Stomach content analysis showed lack of hydrochloric acid. X-ray of chest normal; red and white blood count normal. Patient was disoriented and confused with mild signs of pellagra. Alcoholism denied. General over-all picture was that of chronic brain disease. Final diagnosis: chronic brain syndrome associated with pellagra.

WAIS protocol showed over-all impairment of type met with in organic brain syndrome. On the verbal part of the test her worst performance was on the Digit Span and Similarities tests. As expected Vocabulary held up. On the Performance she did systematically poorly on all the tests. Lowest scores were on the Digit Symbol and Block Design. Note that in spite of low scores on the Performance, IQ is not much below the Verbal IQ. This is due to bonus given for age. WAIS Deterioration Index showed loss of 42 per cent.

Case 0–4. 65-year-old housewife, formerly secretary. Three years high school. History of cerebral vascular accident. Admitted to hospital for study and rehabilitation. Five years prior to accident diagnosis of rheumatic heart disease. On admission she was diagnosed left hemiplegia, embolus middle cerebral artery and rheumatic heart disease with auricular fibrillation.

WAIS protocol revealed person of bright normal intelligence with considerable difference between Verbal IQ of 122 and Performance IQ of 94. Vocabulary and general information as well as Memory

Verbal IQ.................. 122
Performance IQ.......... 94
Full IQ.................... 111

Span intact. Performance scores fairly even, except Digit Symbol and Object Assembly below the mean. Some qualitative disturbances in visual organization on fusion of parts of the picture. On Picture Completion failed easy items: (1) the knob on the door and (6) water pouring from the pitcher, but noted the absence of oarlock on the boat (9) and the missing finger on the man (17). WAIS Deterioration Index showed no loss. This case is interesting in that it illustrates the possibility of organic brain syndrome without deterioration. An individual may show impairment without deterioration and also over-all deterioration without an organic picture.

Schizophrenia

W–B I

Information.............. 10
Comprehension.......... 6
Arithmetic............... 6
Digits................... 6
Similarities.............. 1
    Verbal................. 29

Picture Arrangement...... 4
Picture Comparison....... 10
Block Design............ 1
Object Assembly......... 1
Digit Assembly.......... 2
    Performance........... 19

Verbal IQ................ 83
Performance IQ.......... 71

Case S–1. White, male, age 39, elevator operator. This patient showed marked deterioration, generally seen only in old cases but occasionally also in cases of relatively short duration. In his case, reported onset of disease was about six months prior to administration of test. First indication that something was radically wrong with patient occurred when he left his job for no apparent reason; he said he was nervous and had no peace of mind. Later complained police were after him. On admission to hospital was bewildered, kept to himself but was passively co-operative. Although diagnosed as paranoid schizophrenic, general behavior was that of a simple or mixed type. Psychometrically, he showed the following schizophrenic signs: Verbal higher than Performance, low Digit Symbol with much better Digit Span, low Object Assembly, zero scores on Similarities and Block Design, high Information. Most outstanding of all, very large inter-test variability ranging from a score of zero to a score of 10. The very low scores on the Object Assembly and Digit Symbol together with zero score on the Block Design taken alone would suggest organic brain disease, but in that case we would also get a low Picture Completion and not an average score on this test. The inconsistency here is what definitely shows this case to be schizophrenic. Similarly, only a schizophrenic would give an average score on Information and a zero score on Similarities,

W–B I

Vocabulary	10
Information	10
Comprehension	7
Arithmetic	9
Digits	11
Similarities	6
Verbal	43
Picture Arrangement	11
Picture Comparison	10
Block Design	13
Object Assembly	6
Digit Symbol	13
Performance	53
Verbal IQ	97
Performance IQ	113

WAIS

Information	11
Comprehension	4
Arithmetic	9
Similarities	10
Digit Span	10
Vocabulary	12
Digit Symbol	7
Picture Completion	3
Block Design	6
Picture Arrangement	7
Object Assembly	5
Verbal IQ	95
Performance IQ	72
Full IQ	84

Case S-2. White, female, age 38. Admission following arrest for refusing to take shelter during blackout raid and causing commotion. History of previous commitment to State Hospital. On admission agitated, hallucinatory, seclusive, manneristic; threatens to kill doctor. Psychometrically of interest as a case of schizophrenia with Performance higher than Verbal; also as a patient who though failing to show many of the listed signs, nevertheless revealed a test pattern which is definitely schizophrenic. The diagnostic signs present were a combined low Similarities and low Comprehension; Object Assembly much below Block Design; sum of Comprehension and Object Assembly much lower than sum of Information and Block Design; large inter-test variability.

Case S-3. Female, 27, white, 2 children, became disturbed soon before admission. Would sit about house with baby in arms and cling to Bible. Began to speak about magic numbers and symbolic language in which "blue" was "love," "white," "pure," etc. While on ward continued confused, affect flat and inappropriate, speech illogical and disconnected. Recommended for commitment but signed out to husband for private care.

WAIS protocol showed a 23-point difference between Verbal and Performance and a large inter- and intra-test variability (range of scores from 3 on Picture Completion to a Vocabulary of 12). The Picture Completion revealed perceptual disorganization and poor object reality testing. She failed on the first item (knob) saying, "rest of airplane missing." She perseverated the answer "dot" from item 4 to item 6. To item 9 she said, "someone ought to be there to row it"; to 19 (horse), a rider and to 17, (man), a wife.

Her lowest score on the Verbal was on the Comprehension Test. To the "bad company" question her reply, "It's up to us to choose. There's good and bad in everyone—butter and salt go together." Again her answer to the first proverb "Strike while the iron is hot" was, "It means we are able to project our minds when we want to. It means that it burns."

Subtest scatter showed following pattern: high Vocabulary, low Comprehension, high Information, Arithmetic and low Picture Completion.

WAIS

Information	15
Comprehension	10
Arithmetic	14
Similarities	12
Digit Span	14
Vocabulary	18
Digit Symbol	5
Picture Completion	11
Block Design	13
Picture Arrangement	10
Object Assembly	10
Verbal IQ	125
Performance IQ	110
Full Scale IQ	120

Case S-4. Male, age 47. Brought by friend after an "attempt" to jump out of window. On admission patient stated that he thought there was a plot against his life; later he asserted it was just imagination. "I had delirium tremens. I was drinking for a week." On the morning of his admission patient was visited by an acquaintance whom he recognized as a "Village character" and whom he knew as a friend of a man recently involved in a shooting in a nearby tavern. The assailant had been apprehended but a second man had escaped. "They were going to get me . . . because I was known to have a loose tongue."

Patient was 1 of 2 children of divorced parents. Father deserted mother over 30 years ago. As a child he went to radical school, in which he said he learned nothing. Actually, patient has unusual fund of information. At 17 left home, took to "road" and lived the life of a hobo for 14 years. In 1943 he was drafted but was CCD'd after 9 months on a medical discharge. In the interim he had married a "hunchback" girl because the family offered him security. He deserted her after 6 months, went West, did odd jobs and worked as carpenter. Returned to New York after a few years. On the way East patient stopped at Las Vegas, married a feeble-minded girl after only a one day acquaintance. Left her 2 days later. During the last 10 years he lived with mother who was receiving $100 per month through welfare. Occasionally worked as carpenter, odd jobs. Patient gave long history of inadequacy, and active homosexuality. Referred to self as "small-time male prostitute."

Patient is an individual of superior endowment (IQ 125). On the basis of case history patient would pass as a typical psychopath. Analysis of WAIS, however, shows clear-cut schizophrenic patterning on both the Verbal and Performance parts of the examination. The Information is greater than the Comprehension; Vocabulary greater than Similarities, Picture Completion greater than the Picture Arrangement, Block Design greater than Digit Symbol. In addition to the usual sign of Verbal higher than Performance, patient shows high test variability with a range of scores from 5 to 18. He also gives a number of qualitatively deviant responses. Thus, to the "Bad Company" question his reply was, "You can be in bad company if you are under the supervision of a psychiatrist."

This case is of particular interest because it calls attention to a type of schizophrenia in which the symptoms reflect themselves in an acting out rather than withdrawal, internalization and regressive behavior.

Anxiety States

WAIS

Information	15
Comprehension	18
Arithmetic	8
Similarities	13
Digit Span	7
Vocabulary	13
Digit Symbol	10
Picture Completion	13
Block Design	12
Picture Arrangement	12
Object Assembly	9
Verbal IQ	114
Performance IQ	107
Full IQ	112

Case An. 1. A 21-year-old white male college student who was referred to the psychiatric section of the Student Health Center much worried about impending failure in college and uncertainty about marriage plans. Patient gave a history of acute abdominal pain on two occasions, with no organic etiology being found. He related many lesser episodes of abdominal discomfort. In spite of fairly good study habits his grades continued to be very poor and he was about to flunk out of school. He stated that he became anxious when he heard of someone sick or when he saw "cancer" mentioned. There had been no frankly abnormal behavior and he seemed to get along with others fairly well. Planed to marry that summer. Diagnosis: anxiety reaction.

Patient showed typical picture of low scores on anxiety triad: Arithmetic, Digit Symbol and Digit Span. The low scores on the 3 tests is particularly noteworthy because we are dealing with an individual at college level in whom we should expect at least average functioning in these areas. The fact, however, that he was failing in college, in spite of his good native endowment, brings out the impact of anxiety measured by these tests. It is probable that this was a temporary reaction in a basically neurotic individual occasioned by the need for making decision about marriage. Under psychotherapy much sexual material came out and after a relatively few sessions he showed marked improvement. Excerpts from staff conference revealed patient no longer bothered by somatic complaints and showing greatly diminishing anxiety.

WAIS

Information	12
Comprehension	14
Arithmetic	7
Similarities	12
Digit Span	10
Vocabulary	17

Case An. 2. 35-year-old female, married, mother of two children. Referred to psychiatrist because of inability to sleep, stomach trouble and feeling of inadequacy and inferiority. Married to a physician, felt concerned because she couldn't measure up to her husband's expectations. She was afraid husband was going to leave her and marry someone

Digit Symbol 7
Picture Completion 11
Block Design 9
Picture Arrangement 8
Object Assembly 5

Verbal IQ 112
Performance IQ 92
Full IQ 103

else. Her family was moving away from the small town in which she was living and she felt she was being deserted. As a child very obedient, now conflict about her mother. Preoccupation with failure but unable to do anything about the feeling of inadequacy and inferiority.

Patient showed a majority of anxiety signs: low Arithmetic, low Digit Span, and Digit Symbol and a wide discrepancy between the Verbal and Performance IQ's. In addition the patient did very badly on the Object Assembly—a sign which may be associated with schizophrenia depending on the nature of the subject's performance. If low score is due to poor juxtaposition of parts or bizarreness of arrangement one may suspect a schizophrenic process. On the other hand, if poor performance is due to hesitation and uncertainty, particularly on the "Hand" and "Face" items, it is more likely the results of dynamic repression. In either case it reflects unchannelized anxiety. In this patient it seems to be the latter. The additional discrepancy between Information and Vocabulary suggests that we may be dealing with a pseudoneurotic schizophrenic. The case is, however, presented to show the evidence of anxiety on performance.

W-B I

Information 11
Comprehension 12
Digit Span 7
Arithmetic 9
Similarities 11
Vocabulary 10
    Verbal 60

Picture Arrangement 14
Picture Completion 8
Block Design 11
Object Assembly 12
Digit Symbol 16
    Performance 61

Verbal IQ 104
Performance IQ 114
Full IQ 109

Case An. 3. Female, age 22, stenographer by occupation. Came in for counseling because always under tension, anxious and unable to deal with problems in mature manner. Characterized herself as labile, and with mood swings between elation and depression. Histrionic person who dramatized her emotions. Patient showed typical low Digit Span and Arithmetic encountered in anxiety states in contrast to high social awareness as revealed in good Comprehension and Picture Arrangement scores. On the other hand, she did well on Digit Symbol, possibly because of her business experience (stenographer) and did better on Performance than Verbal, but this situation is sometimes met with in anxiety states. On the Digit Span test she sometimes failed on the first then succeeded on the second trial of the series and when coming to the more difficult she gave up completely; when she came to Arithmetic, after passing the first seven with ease she started to complain and lost her composure. This patient showed hysterical and schizoid features along with her anxiety.

WAIS

Information	12
Comprehension	11
Arithmetic	10
Similarities	15
Digit Span	10
Vocabulary	14
Digit Symbol	11
Picture Completion	15
Block Design	11
Picture Arrangement	14
Object Assembly	11
Verbal IQ	118
Performance IQ	116
Full IQ	121

Case An. 4. 16-year-old white male student who was admitted to a psychiatric out-patient clinic; revealed the typical adolescent problems: tension with his family, particularly in his relationships with his mother and sibling, difficulty in school, and struggling to find a value system, perhaps a sense of identity. His difficulties in school forced him to leave school shortly before his admission to the out-patient clinic.

On admission patient gave a two year history of epigastric pain with an ulcer demonstrated radiologically at different stages of healing or activity. The present episode began three weeks prior to admission when an active ulcer was demonstrated by x-ray and was treated medically. He was referred to a psychoanalyst who saw him 3 times prior to admission. He was admitted in a state of acute anxiety. Diagnosis: anxiety state.

Psychometrically, this patient did not show too large inter-test variability but it is significant that the lowered scores on the Verbal part of the examination were on Arithmetic and Digit Span. The Digit Symbol was not so much out of line on the Performance part of the examination but was still one of the lower scores. In this case we seem to be dealing with an individual with chronic anxiety and a great deal of aggression directed inward. This would be better indicated by his projective technique tests. The high scores on the Similarities in contrast with the low score on Comprehension aslo suggests a possible schizoid trend. This case suggests a much more complicated diagnosis than the one assigned it clinically; it has been added to illustrate the presence of anxiety (along with other symptoms) revealed by the psychometric pattern.

Mental Defectives

Most mental defectives are diagnosed on the basis of IQ level. A low IQ, however, may be due to a variety of reasons, and one not infrequent problem is to distinguish between true mental deficiency, schizophrenia and organic brain disease. Of the three examples given below one is that of a "typical" defective, the second of a psychosis with mental deficiency, and the third of an unrecognized schizophrenia in a child who for a long time had been labeled as a mental defective.

WAIS   *"Typical" Defective*

Information	3
Comprehension	4
Arithmetic	2
Similarities	5

Case D-1. Female, age 17. Patient had been in institution several years. She was committed at mother's request because of her habitual wandering away from home and sex play with boys. Parents

Digit Span................ 1
Vocabulary............... 3

Digit Symbol............ 4
Picture Completion....... 2
Block Design............. 3
Picture Arrangement...... 0
Object Assembly.......... 5

Verbal IQ................ 64
Performance IQ.......... 55
Full Scale IQ............ 58

    Digits Forward........ 3
    Digits Backward....... 2

WAIS

Information............... 4
Comprehension............ 5
Arithmetic................ 3
Similarities............... 3
Digit Span............... 9
Vocabulary............... 4

Digit Symbol............ 0
Picture Completion....... 8
Block Design............. 4
Picture Arrangement...... 4
Object Assembly.......... 7

Verbal IQ................ 71
Performance IQ.......... 66
Full Scale IQ............ 67
    Digit Forward......... 5
    Digits Backward....... 5

of dull-normal intelligence. Father a chronic alcoholic who gambled away most of his money. Mother emotionally unstable, once committed to a state hospital for 7 weeks. Physical and neurological examinations of patient, including EEG, reported as negative.

Psychometrically, apart from the low IQ, the case represents the following features of a typical defective: low inter-test variability and failure on performance of those tests in which defectives generally have most difficulty: Picture Arrangement, Digit Span and Arithmetic. The protocol does not show a single test performance above the Borderline Defective level. She had extreme difficulty in understanding directions and, in the case of the Picture Arrangement, failed to grasp the idea altogether.

Psychosis with Mental Deficiency

Case D-2. Male, age 17. Patient's present admission followed a long history of aberrant behavior. At age of 8 committed by court to institution for mental defectives because of antisocial behavior. At that time considered by the court to be a "psychopath." Discharged after about two years, but soon recommitted for stealing. Mother of dull-normal intelligence; likewise father, who had frequent incarcerations in penal institutions for various crimes, and had been diagnosed as paranoid schizophrenic. Reported psychometric, is a re-test given on admission to present institution. On examination patient reported to be very distractible and showing generally poor attention. Impression of examiner was that one was dealing with a psychotic rather than a defective individual, and same was confirmed by projective tests. Patient was preoccupied with sexual fantasies, many of a primitive sort. During examination he asked examiner if she would have sexual intercourse with him.

Psychometrically, the patient's test performance was in sharp contrast to that of patient *D-1.* Most outstanding difference is the large inter-test variability. His scores range from 0 on the Digit Symbol to 9 on the Digit Span. He was hardly able to get started on the Digit Symbol Test; his attention wandered. He was at once confused and frustrated by the task. At first approach, one might suspect that the over-all low performance might be ascribed to the psychotic process but while this undoubtedly served to interfere with his "efficiency," the systematic poor performance on the Vocabulary and Similarities, as well as the Block Design, support the view that in addition to any mental disturbance we are dealing with an individual of basically limited mental endowment. Diagnosis of psychosis with mental deficiency would seem accurately to sum up his mental status. Whether this patient might not do better at a state mental hospital rather than an institution for mental defectives needs to be considered. In this connection it should be noted, however, that a substantial percentage of patients in feeble-minded domiciliaries are undoubtedly also psychotic.

W–B I

Information	10
Comprehension	8
Arithmetic	4
Similarities	5
Digit Span	4
Vocabulary	11
Picture Completion	8
Picture Arrangement	4
Object Assembly	5
Block Design	3
Digit Symbol	4
Verbal IQ	89
Performance IQ	81
Full IQ	84

Pseudodefective Childhood Schizophrenia

Case D–3. 44-year-old male admitted when parents died. Sister who tried to take care of him was unable to tolerate his temper outbursts and afraid to leave him alone with her children. Considered mentally defective all his life; but kept at home by his parents. Had only gone a few grades in school.

Admitted for possible commitment and considered defective by examining psychiatrist, on the basis of his past history, but was referred for psychological testing. Indications contradicting the tentative diagnosis are: (1) an IQ now falling in the dull-normal category, (2) large inter-test variability, (3) two of the test scores (Information and Vocabulary) far above what one would expect in a straight mental defective, (4) high deterioration index. Comparing the Hold-Don't Hold Tests (see p. 221) shows a deterioration loss of 45 per cent. It is probable that we are dealing here with an unrecognized childhood schizophrenia who deteriorated as he grew older. Patient was committed to State Hospital.

Adolescent Sociopaths (Delinquents)

W–B I

Comprehension	11
Arithmetic	6
Information	10
Digits	6
Similarities	5
Verbal	38
Picture Arrangement	12
Picture Comparison	10
Block Design	15

Case P–1. White, male, age 15, 8th grade. Continuous history of stealing, incorrigibility and running away. Several admissions to Bellevue Hospital, the last one after suicidal attempt. While on wards persistently created disturbances, broke rules, fought with other boys and continually tried to evade ordinary duties. Psychopathic patterning: Performance higher than Verbal, low Similarities, low Arithmetic, sum of Picture Arrangement plus Object Assembly greater than sum of scores

Object Assembly.......... 16   on Blocks and Picture Completion.
Digit Symbol............. 12
   Performance............ 65

Verbal IQ................. 90
Performance IQ........... 123

W–B I

Information...............	6
Comprehension............	9
Arithmetic................	7
Digit Span................	10
Similarities...............	6
Verbal..................	38
Picture Comparison.......	12
Picture Arrangement......	13
Block Design.............	11
Object Assembly..........	13
Digit Symbol.............	9
Performance............	58
Verbal IQ.................	90
Performance IQ...........	115

Case P–2. White, male, school-boy, age 14, 8th grade. Boy a behavior problem since age of 3. Never responded to either cajoling or punishment. Brought to court for stealing, staying away from home days at a time, and continued incorrigibility. Psychiatric diagnosis: psychopathic personality. This subject showed almost all the psychometric signs for this diagnosis. Performance higher than Verbal; sum of Picture Arrangement and Object Assembly greater than sum of Picture Completion and Block Design. Information low and similarities low. Digit Symbol just at mean of all subtest scores but still lower than any of Performance. Highest Verbal score on Digit Span. This is not typical of all psychopaths but rather characteristic of a certain group who have "good memory."

While the sociopath "pattern" was first derived from and applied to the adolescent group one frequently meets a similar test configuration in adult psychopaths.

WAIS

Information...............	5
Comprehension............	5
Arithmetic................	4
Similarities...............	6
Digit Span................	4
Vocabulary..............	3
Digit Symbol.............	4
Picture Completion.......	4
Block Design.............	2
Picture Arrangement......	9
Object Assembly..........	10
Verbal IQ.................	67
Performance IQ...........	73
Full IQ..................	68

Case P–3. Female, 32, employed as a packer. Referred from court with charge of felonious assault. This patient also a mental defective and was in an institution for 3 years. On discharge, she married, had one child. Long history of delinquent behavior, including fire-setting. Since discharge from institution for mental defectives she worked at various non-skilled jobs and generally supplemented her salary by prostitution. She continued this activity even after marriage. Present admission resulted from assault on a neighbor. WAIS protocol showed both defective and sociopathic signs. The latter are represented by the following: Performance IQ higher than Verbal, sum of Picture Arrangement and Object Assembly much higher than Block Design and Picture Completion. Low Block Design combined with low Vocabulary shows we are dealing with a basically mentally defective individual, while Picture Arrangement in this case indicates a capacity for manipulating environment. In this connection her answer to the "Bad Company" question is of interest. Her reply was, "Put it in mail box if it doesn't have anything for me."

WAIS

Information	8
Comprehension	9
Arithmetic	9
Similarities	7
Digit Span	14
Vocabulary	11
Digit Symbol	15
Picture Completion	11
Block Design	11
Picture Arrangement	15
Object Assembly	17
Verbal IQ	99
Performance IQ	124
Full IQ	110

Case P-4. Female, age 24, married, unemployed. History of extra-marital affairs and petty stealing. Admitted to the prison ward of Bellevue Psychiatric Hospital because she set fire to a house in which her paramour lived, after he rejected her. Psychopathic patterning: Performance higher than Verbal, low Similarities, sum of Picture Arrangement plus Object Assembly greater than sum of scores on Blocks and Picture Completion. High Digit Span suggests lack of anxiety.

Qualitatively significant responses: *Envelope*— "Mail it is what you are supposed to do. The average person would open it to see if money was inside." *Axe–Saw*—"Tools . . . to cut; can be used to hurt people." *Table–Chair*—"Needed to eat."

Chapter 12

Mental Deterioration and Its Appraisal

In discussing the problem of mental deterioration it will be useful to distinguish between what may be termed "normal" decline in human abilities and abnormal loss or impairment. The distinction is to some extent arbitrary, and it is not always easy to indicate where one ends and the other begins. In general, the gradual falling off of ability in later age may be considered as an indication of normal decline; a marked and disabling loss, at any age, as a sign of definite impairment. Mental deterioration is mostly associated with the latter, but it may also refer to a cumulative loss which, even though gradual, is nevertheless incapacitating, as in the case of senility.[1] Indeed, it is the disabling effect on mental function as a whole rather than specific decline of any given ability that most characteristically defines the diagnosis of mental deterioration.

Mental deterioration is a falling off from a previous functioning level. A mental defective, no matter how low, is not mentally deteriorated if he never functioned any differently. On the other hand, mental deterioration does not necessarily presuppose any specific disease or localized brain lesion. It is the degree rather than the cause of the decline in ability that is the fact to be considered. Accordingly, an individual can be said to show signs of mental deterioration when in comparison with his own previous functioning he shows a significant loss in ability to perform on tests of intelligence, provided that the decline is greater than the changes that may be expected for a person of his own age.

The definition as just stated would seem to conform fairly well with the majority opinion of those currently concerned with mental deterioration. One should note, however, that the age provision introduces a seeming contradiction in the definition by virtue of the fact that it calls for a dif-

[1] Senility, unlike senile psychosis, is not a clinical entity. Current nosology also qualifies the psychosis in terms of its associated condition—thus, senile psychosis, senile psychosis with Alzheimer's disease, and so on.

ferential evaluation of an identical decline of ability at different ages. Thus, an identical quantitative decline in an individual's test performance at ages 40 and 70 would be differently interpreted. At the former age it might be interpreted as showing mental deterioration, at the latter as merely reflecting the "normal" decline. This approach is similar to the one used in medical evaluation of other capacities. For example, if a physician on examining a man of 70 finds that the patient shows, as he generally would, an increased blood pressure, reduced pulse rate, shortness of breath, etc., unaccompanied by other symptoms, he would in most instances not consider these changes as pathological. Nevertheless, the fact remains that our septuagenarian's physical capacity is considerably below what it was at age 40; not only is his breath shorter and his movements slower; he is probably no longer so agile, cannot remember so well or work so many hours. Should one on this account say that the person has deteriorated? In an absolute sense one might be compelled to say that he has, and from certain points this conclusion is justifiable, but this would fail to consider a very important fact. The 70-year-old in question may neither look, feel, nor act as a deteriorated person. It is undoubtedly this fact which the examining physician takes into consideration in giving the 70-year-old a physical "O.K." The physician's implicit assumption, we may conjecture, is that a certain amount of physical decline goes with age. A similar situation presents itself in the diagnosis of mental deterioration. A certain amount of intellectual decline is allowable before the loss is interpreted as pathological. The question, of course, is how much.

The changes in test performance with age have already been considered in a number of places, but we shall at this point briefly review the basic facts and add a few other findings relevant to the discussion.

Every human capacity after initial growth attains a maximum and then begins to decline. This decline is at first very slow but after a while increases perceptibly. The age at which the maximum is attained varies from ability to ability but seldom occurs beyond 30 and in most cases somewhere in the mid 20's. Once the decline begins it progresses uninterruptedly. Between the ages of 30 and 60 it is more or less linear. In the case of most abilities the decline between these ages may be described with good approximation by an equation of the first degree. Two curves typical of the course of decline are shown in Figure 7. One illustrates the decline of intelligence test scores (W–B I) for subjects aged 15 to 65; the other, that of vital capacity for the same age period. Both have'been reduced to comparable scale units.[2] As will be seen the maximum of both curves occurs in the age

[2] The test score means were derived from an abbreviated 8 test scale; the actual means for the Full Bellevue Scale are given on page 95. Those for vital capacity will be found in article by Ruger and Stoessiger (435).

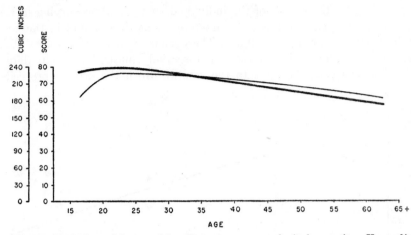

Fig. 7. Variation with age of intelligence scores and vital capacity. *Heavy line*, intelligence scores. *Fine line*, vital capacity.

period 20 to 25. Another point of interest is that the intelligence test curve declines at a faster rate than the curve of vital capacity. This is not an artifact. Contrary to common belief, some intellectual abilities show greater impairment with age than do physical ones.[3] The actual decline in any given case, however, varies with the ability in question.

The general curve of decline of mental ability with age as reflected in test performance is shown in Figure 8. This curve is a composite curve based on W–B I and WAIS standardizations.[4] It is a composite curve not only in the sense that it is based on the data derived from a large number of individuals but also by virtue of the fact that the mean scores are averages of a number of different abilities. The abilities which entered into these averages are those measured by the subtests of the WAIS and W–B I Scales. Scores obtained from a different set of tests might be expected to produce a curve which differed from the one presented. Indeed, scores derived from a special combination or selection of the subtests of a scale would furnish age curves showing varying rates of decline. This is illustrated, for example, by comparing the age curves derived from the subtests on the WAIS designated, respectively, as Verbal and Performance (Figure 9). Even greater variability in rates of decline is manifested by the individual subtest curves. A number of these are shown in Figures 10, 11, and 12. Comparable curves derived from the W–B I standardization are shown in Figures 13 and 14.

[3] The most conspicuous decline of all is shown in the sensory field. Vision and hearing fall off rapidly after 30. Their curves of decline, however, are far from straight lines. See Ruger and Stoessiger, *op. cit.*

[4] The individual curves for the separate standardizarion are given on pages 31 and 96.

The form of the curves of the individual subtests while varying in the rate of decline, show the same characteristics as those found in the generalized curves for mental ability. The decline of any given ability, like that of any combination of them, is essentially linear. The main difference between them pertains to the rate at which the decline proceeds.

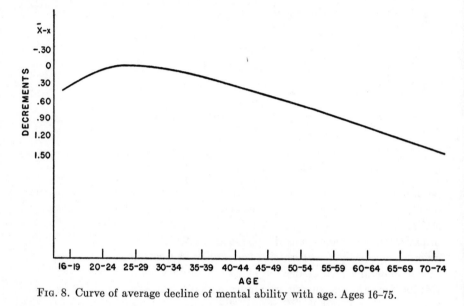

FIG. 8. Curve of average decline of mental ability with age. Ages 16–75.

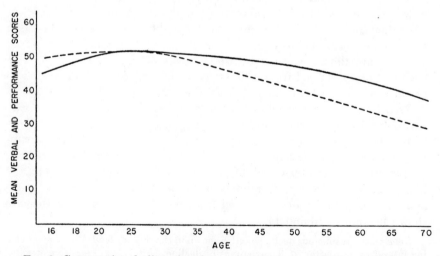

FIG. 9. Comparative decline of verbal and performance subtests on WAIS with age. Ages 16–75 and over (2052 cases). *Solid line*, Verbal. *Dash line*, Performance.

Different mental abilities decline at different rates. That they do is psychometrically fortunate, because these differences can be made use of in determining mental deterioration.

The decline of mental ability with age is part of the general senescent process of the organism as a whole. Hitherto the common view has been that our mental abilities, unlike our physical abilities, remain relatively unimpaired until rather late in life (senility), except as an occasional con-

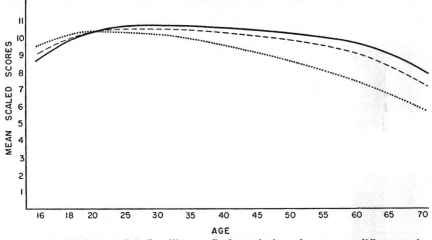

FIG. 10. Wechsler Adult Intelligence Scale variation of scores on different subtests. *Solid line*, Information. *Dash line*, Arithmetic. *Dotted lines*, Block Design.

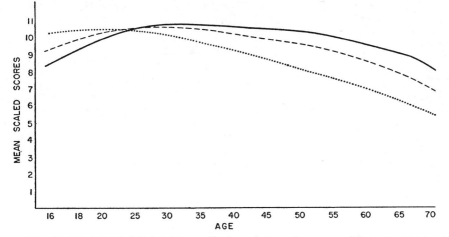

FIG. 11. Wechsler Adult Intelligence Scale variation of scores on different subtests. *Solid line*, Vocabulary. *Dash line*, Similarities. *Dotted line*, Picture Arrangement.

sequence of disease or traumatic injury. This was an unsubstantiated hypothesis tenable only so long as no facts were at hand to oppose it. But the view still persists even though such facts are now available. Most people, including psychologists, are loathe to believe that they are not as mentally alert at 50 as they were at 25. Part of this is due to a confounding of mental with practical ability, that is, a failure to differentiate between intellectual endowment and success in applying it. The latter is naturally dependent in no small measure upon experience. What one has lost through a falling off of native ability one may often replace by acquired knowledge. An old

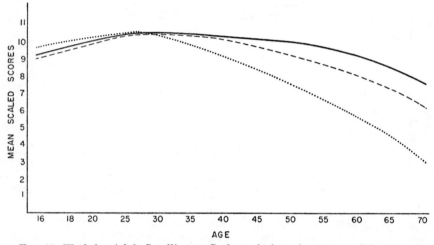

Fig. 12. Wechsler Adult Intelligence Scale variation of scores on different subtests. *Solid line*, Comprehension. *Dash line*, Digit Span. *Dotted line*, Digit Symbol.

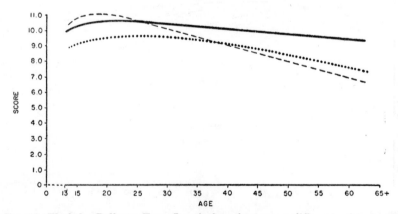

Fig. 13. Wechsler-Bellevue Form I variation of scores on different subtests. *Solid line*, Information. *Dash line*, Block Design. *Dotted line*, Arithmetic.

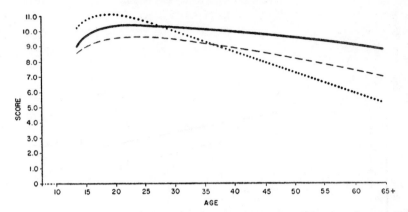

FIG. 14. Wechsler-Bellevue Form I variation of scores on different subtests. *Solid line*, Comprehension. *Dash line*, Digit Span. *Dotted line*, Substitution.

clinician may be a better doctor than a younger one, even though he possesses less actual understanding of disease processes.

Another item which contributes to the biased attitude toward the facts of mental decline is the historical distinction between physical and mental. According to this distinction what is mental is conceived of as being higher, better or more important. Hence, few people are upset when told that at 40 they cannot hear or run so well as when they were 20, but are quite perturbed when informed that they probably also cannot calculate or reason so well. There also exists a kind of hierarchy of relative values as regards the various mental abilities themselves. J. McKeen Cattell long ago called attention to the fact that people are ever ready to complain about their bad memory, but seldom of their poor judgment or common sense. But it is certain that memory is not the only mental capacity which declines with age, or the one which is always most impaired by it. Conrad and Jones (281), for example, found that older people (individuals over 50) did much better on the Army Alpha Test calling for general information, than on the one calling for abstract reasoning (the Analogies Test), and our own data support these findings.

We have advanced the hypothesis that the decline of mental ability with age is part of the general organic process which constitutes the universal phenomenon of senescence and have insisted upon the fact that the phenomenon begins relatively early in life. The evidence adduced for this hypothesis is the observed parallelism found in the rate of decline of various physical and mental abilities. Another line of evidence is furnished by neurological studies of the brains of senile individuals. These are not always clear-cut cases because they may be associated with special trauma or organic disease. If our hypothesis is correct, however, the same changes,

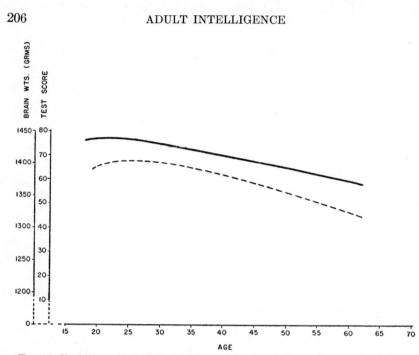

FIG. 15. Variation of intelligence test scores and brain weights with age. *Solid line*, intelligence test scores. *Dash line*, brain weight.

though of course to a lesser degree, ought to be expected much earlier in life, say from 20 years onward. Up to the present, experimental data supporting this view have been lacking. This may be due to the fact that neuropathology has not been particularly alive to the problem, or as is more probable, to the fact that neurological techniques are not sufficiently advanced to detect very small and gradual alterations[5] which may, and undoubtedly do, occur in brain tissue. There is, however, some indirect evidence that alteration of the brain begins at an early age, which may be accepted as supporting our view. We refer to the progressive change in brain weight with age.

It has been known for some time that the mean weight of the adult brain declines with age (389). If one accepts the brain as the organ of the mind, it is reasonable to assume that even gross changes such as alterations of weight may also affect its function. Assuming that to be the case, one should expect that the changes in brain weight show concomitance with alterations in general intellectual ability. A number of studies show that it does. Figure 15 represents the result of such a study and shows what one finds when such comparison is made. In this figure parallel age curves for

---

[5] Probably because most of these are atomic or molecular and therefore not discernible under the microscope.

changes in intellectual abilities and brain weight have been drawn to scale. The age curve for intellectual ability is that obtained from subjects given the tests used in standardizing the W–B I Scale; the brain weight curve is that computed from figures collected by Rössle and Routlet (537) for brain weights of autopsied subjects of comparable ages. Inspection of these curves reveals a close parallelism between loss in brain weight and decline in mental ability with age. It is probable that, with a different series of brain weights and a different series of tests, the similarity between the two curves would not be so marked. But the general parallelism cannot be ascribed either to chance or artifact. It is much better than that found between most physical and mental traits and as good as that found between curves for many mental abilities taken separately. The decline in the weight of brain, like that in intellectual ability, is essentially linear (390). After reaching a maximum, at about age 20, the brain begins to decline in weight, somewhat irregularly at first, but after age 25 or 30 at a fairly constant rate.

It thus appears that various lines of evidence support the view that mental ability does not continue unaltered over any considerable portion of adult life but that it begins to decline at a relatively early age. However, to speak of a person in his early 30's as showing signs of deterioration because he already manifests some measurable decline of ability would be stretching the term beyond its accepted connotation. Clearly that is not what is implied by deterioration. It would seem desirable to restrict the term to only such impairment or losses in ability as are significantly greater than those due to the age factor alone. To do this we must necessarily know what the normal loss of ability is for the average individual and the mean limits of variability at all ages for the normal population. To evaluate deterioration one must be able to measure it quantitatively.

The measurement of mental deterioration involves three separate problems: (1) The reliable measurement of the individual's actual or present functioning ability; (2) the evaluation of his previous functioning level; (3) the expression of the difference between the two in meaningful, quantitative terms. The first of these is now possible through the use of such tests as the WAIS or W–B I, for which we have norms up to age 80.

The second step in the measurement of deterioration, namely, the evaluation of an individual's previous functioning level, presents a more difficult problem. The reason is that in most cases no psychometric data are available by which such evaluation can be made. Few persons examined for mental deterioration have ever had a previous psychological examination. Yet, in order to make an accurate estimate of a person's normal functioning ability, we should have not only one but a series of psychometric examinations taken at various intervals and so far as possible with the same or comparable tests.

In practice, it is necessary to turn to other sources of data that will enable us to appraise the subject's previous functioning ability. The data usually consist of facts gleaned from the subject's educational, vocational and social history. Thus, if from a subject's history we learn that he is a high school graduate, that he has held responsible positions for a number of years and that he attained some social recognition in his community, we can safely assume that he must have been a person of at least average endowment and that he should be able to perform certain mental operations which may be expected of individuals of comparable endowment. But information of this sort is of value only where the discrepancy between an individual's actual and expected functioning is considerable. Thus, if a formerly successful business man, age 45, is unable to do simple calculations or can only repeat 4 digits, one can safely assume that he shows a severe loss from previous functioning. Such obvious evidence of impairment requires no special psychometric technique for its demonstration. It is for the subtler or more insidious indications of deterioration that special techniques are needed.

We do not need tests to discover deterioration in an old paretic. The merit of psychometric tests is that they can detect small differences of ability, and their usefulness in the clinical field depends upon how well they can do this. Their value in determining mental deterioration must reside in their ability to detect changes in mental functioning long before they have so disorganized the behavior of the individual as to make them patent to all. For such purposes a general social and psychiatric history is insufficient as a base for comparison. One must either have records of previous psychometric examination or be able to use the results of present mental tests as a means of inferring the previous functioning. However, few adults come up for a psychological examination with previous psychometric test records, and even fewer with available test data that would make possible accurate comparison of present *vs.* past functioning. Hence what is required is the possible utilization of the individual's test scores at any given time as a measure of change in his functioning ability. It is in this connection that studies of differential changes in ability with age have offered suggestive leads.

One of the more interesting facts revealed by the age curves for different abilities obtained on the same groups of individuals is that certain abilities decline more slowly with age than others. Thus, the abilities called for by Vocabulary and Comprehension tests hold up much better than do the abilities called for by the Substitution, Similarities and Memory Span tests. This difference in the rate of decline of various abilities suggests a possibility of estimating previous functioning levels. Thus, if the abilities which do not decline significantly with age were precisely those which were least affected by the deteriorative process, one could assume that scores which individuals attain on tests measuring these abilities more nearly represented their original or permanent endowment. If one combines a number of these tests into a single measure, such a measure might furnish a means of measuring mental deterioration. All that would be necessary would be to compare the mean score which a subject attained on the tests relatively unimpaired with age, with the scores obtained on tests which tend to be significantly impaired with age. The ratio or difference between these scores would then give us the required measure.

The method just outlined for comparing previous and present functioning ability in terms of test scores obtained in a single examination of a subject may be termed the *differential-test-score method* of measuring mental deterioration. This method makes use of the fact that some abilities decline relatively little during adult life and others to a considerable degree, and assumes that the difference between their rates of decline in any given individual expresses his relative degree of deterioration. The usefulness of the differential-test-score method for evaluating deterioration necessarily depends upon the availability of tests with full age norms. Ideally, one should have available age curves for many different abilities, each measured in as many ways as possible with tests whose validity and effectiveness had previously been established. At present such tests are all too few, but the 11 subtests made available by the standardization of the author's Scales make ït possible to try out the method.

The first step in the application of the differential-test-score method is the optimal allocation of tests to the "Hold" *vs.* "Don't Hold" groups. In general, the tests which drop most markedly with age belong, as might be expected, with the "Don't Hold" and those which drop least, with the "Hold" tests. But another factor must also be considered, namely, the type of ability measured by the tests. There must be some functional similarity between the opposed or contrasted tests. If this is not the case, we risk making test combinations which, though showing significant differences, are likely to give spurious discriminants. For example, most abilities tapped by performance tests decline much more rapidly with age than those involved in verbal tests. At first thought it might appear that this situation could be capitalized on by using verbal tests against performance tests as a ready means of obtaining measures of "Hold" *vs.* "Don't Hold" abilities. To do so might, however, lead to serious error. If we accepted differences between the scores on verbal and performance tests as a criterion of deterioration, all individuals who have relatively good verbal capacity would inevitably show greater mental deterioration as they grew older. This would follow from the fact that the differences between verbal and performance abilities automatically increase with age. On the other hand, people who

TABLE 46

	Hold tests	
W–B I		WAIS
Information*		Vocabulary
Comprehension		Information
Object Assembly		Object Assembly
Picture Completion		Picture Completion
	Don't Hold tests	
Digit Span		Digit Span
Arithmetic		Similarities
Digit Symbol		Digit Symbol
Block Design		Block Design

* Or Vocabulary.

are relatively good in performance tests would show less deterioration or indeed none at all, because the discrepancy between their verbal and performance scores would become smaller and smaller as they grew older. Accordingly, in assembling our "Hold" *vs.* "Don't Hold" batteries we have brought together approximately the same number of verbal as performance tests. The test combinations under the separate categories "Hold" *vs.* "Don't Hold" are somewhat different in the W–B I and WAIS groupings. The tests included in the W–B I and WAIS respectively are shown in Table 46.

To obtain a measure of deterioration, one compares the sum of weighted scores of the "Hold" tests with that of the "Don't Hold" tests. The resulting comparison may be expressed either as a ratio or difference between the two sums. Naturally, if the result is given as a difference it must be expressed as a percentage difference in order to take into account the absolute magnitude of the sums compared. Thus, if the sum of a subject's "Hold" subtest scores is 50 and the sum of his "Don't Hold" subtest scores 40, he shows a deterioration loss of 20 per cent.

The problem, of course, is to define what is meant by considerable or significant loss. In the long run such a definition would have to be statistical in character and be based on a distribution of individual percentages of loss or calculated deterioration quotients of a sufficiently large number of cases both normal and pathological. These data were not available for the W–B I but it was possible to arrive at good approximations by the use of certain tables. These tables contain the mean scores of all the subtests at successive age periods. By summing the subtest scores of the tests composing each of the batteries compared, one obtained the total weighted score that may be expected for the "Hold" and "Don't Hold" batteries at different ages. From these data it was possible to calculate by the method described in the earlier editions of the *Measurement of Adult Intelligence*

TABLE 47

Means and standard deviations of deterioration quotients for WAIS by age
National Sample*

Age	No.	Mean	S.D.
16–17	200	−0.02	0.16
18–19	200	0.00	0.13
20–24	200	−0.02	0.16
25–34	300	−0.01	0.15
35–44	300	−0.01	0.17
45–54	300	−0.02	0.15
55–64	200	−0.01	0.13
Kansas City Sample			
60–64	101	−0.05	0.15
65–69	86	0.00	0.13
70–74	80	0.00	0.13
75 and over	85	0.02	0.17
Total	2052	−0.01	0.15

* Deterioration quotient $= \dfrac{\text{Hold} - \text{Don't Hold}}{\text{Hold}}$ (using *age* scaled score equivalents). Hold Tests: Vocabulary, Information, Picture Completion and Object Assembly; Don't Hold Tests: Similarities, Digit Span, Digit Symbol and Block Design.

the normal percentage of loss to be expected at each age. An individual was said to show a sign of possible deterioration if he showed loss of above 10 per cent and of definite deterioration if he showed a loss greater than 20 per cent than that allowed by normal decline with age. This delimitation is based on the fact that the intervals 10 and 20 per cent correspond roughly to the deviation of 1 P.E. and 2 P.E. from the mean at age 25.

In the case of the WAIS, deterioration indices (percentage of loss) were so calculated as to avoid the need for any extrapolation or bonus for age. This was done as follows. Additional tables were established to give separate scaled scores for each of the main age groups, which enabled the examiner to compare an individual's performance on each test with that of his age peers. These tables are given and described in detail in the appendix of the WAIS Manual (524). With these new tables, deterioration quotients were calculated on all subjects of the standardization population (total of 2052) by the method already indicated, *i.e.*,

$$\text{Deterioration loss} = \frac{\text{Hold} - \text{Don't Hold}}{\text{Hold}}.$$

The findings for each of the major age groups are given in Table 47, and the distribution of the percentages of loss for the entire population is shown in Figure 16. It should be noted that the mean percentage of loss for any age group and the entire population approximates zero, as was to be expected. If one defines a normal limit of variation by the interval 1 S.D. or 2 P.E. from the mean, a mean loss of more than 15 or 20 per cent may be considered significant. It should be noted that the level of percentage of loss which becomes significant is practically identical with that derived by approximation figures as given for the W–B I.

The value of using percentage of loss as an indicator of deterioration depends, of course, upon its discriminating potential in clinical diagnosis. In this respect the studies reported thus far give, on the whole, not too encouraging findings. Furthermore, correlations between deterioration indices derived from the W–B Scales and those of other mental deterioration tests indicate that the several measures cannot be interchanged. The inconsistencies that have appeared have led several investigators to try different test combinations than those recommended by the author. For example, W. L. Hunt (267) has suggested that Information and Comprehension might be contrasted with Block Design and Digit Symbol for a better measure of normal deterioration. But it is unlikely that a deterioration ratio based on fewer rather than a larger number of tests will prove more reliable (251).

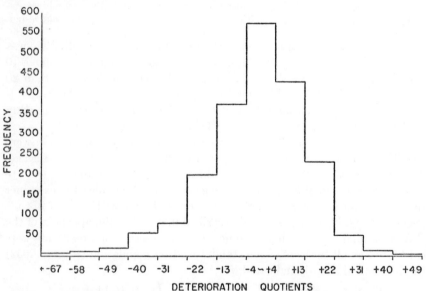

Fig. 16. Distribution of deterioration quotients (Wechsler Adult Intelligence Scale). Ages 16–75 and over (2052 cases). Mean, 1.22 per cent. Standard deviation, 15.14.

In spite of the lack of supporting data from other studies the writer can report that in his own experience the *"Hold"—"Don't Hold" Index* is very useful in clinical diagnosis. The discrepancies between the reported and the author's findings seem to be the result of the fact that many investigators have tried to use the deterioration quotient as an either/or discriminant. In clinical practice, the numerical value of the ratio is only one of the facts that determines eventual diagnosis. Besides taking into account a subject's obtained percent of loss, one must evaluate the rest of his psychometric pattern; for example, whether the Picture Arrangement and the Comprehension test scores are comparatively low or high, whether the difference between the Information and Vocabulary is significant, and so on. To be sure, a certain number of false positives and false negatives are bound to occur, but judicious evaluation of the subject's test performance as a whole will generally enable the examiner to detect them.

In summary, while published studies have not given too much support to the claims of the author regarding the validity of the *Hold—Don't Hold Index*, it has proved of diagnostic value in clinical practice and merits further study. Particularly indicated are new studies with the WAIS which offer an improved and more reliable method of determining the percentage of loss, independent of the age factor. In this connection it should also be noted that the WAIS deterioration loss is based on test scores derived from separate age norms and consist of somewhat different test combinations.

A point of general interest regarding the utilization of the percentage of loss indices, however calculated, is how to interpret what may be called a negative deterioration score, that is, instances where the sum of the *Don't Hold* tests is greater than the sum of the *Hold* tests. In a normal population, approximately one-half of the cases may be expected to fall within this category. For the present they are disregarded in the evaluation process. Nevertheless, there is reason to suppose that negative indices do have some significance, although what it is remains to be investigated.

Chapter 13

Changes in Intelligence Consequent
to Brain Damage

Psychological changes consequent to brain damage have been the object
of much investigation during the past two decades, and the literature on the
subject has been comprehensively reviewed from various aspects by a
number of authors (287, 288, 366). In this chapter we shall deal with only
a limited portion of the findings, namely, those relating to reported changes
in general intelligence as measured by standardized tests. The findings as a
whole show that intellectual impairment may result from almost any insult
to the brain, whether vascular accident, traumatic injury, space-occupying
lesions or degenerative diseases. So far as effect on functioning is concerned,
sequelae may range from negligible changes in IQ, as from localized missile
wounds or delimited ablations of certain portions of the cortex, to marked
impairment or deterioration, as in extensive temporoparietal lesions
(speech areas) or in degenerative diseases of the brain (Alzheimer's or
Pick's Disease). For the most part, correlations between specific localized
brain lesions and performance on particular tests are both limited and inconstant (288). This finding has been ascribed to various factors, the most
important of which are: (1) differences in brain pathology consequent to
similar brain lesions, (2) the heterogeneity of the groups compared and (3)
the absence of adequate controls. In the case of brain surgery there is often
the additional difficulty of the exact definition of locus of injury or extent
of the presumed insult to the parts involved.

Psychosurgery

The psychological consequence of brain lesions and ablations has recently
been reviewed by Klebanoff, Singer and Wilensky (288). The findings, as
a whole, show that there are fairly significant, though not necessarily large
changes in intelligence test performance following the usual types of operations performed for psychotherapy. Table 48 condensed from the study of
Klebanoff et. al., indicates the order of change one may expect. The smallest

TABLE 48

Summary of studies presenting pre- and postoperative IQ's for psychosurgery patients (Klebanoff et al.)

Author	No.	Diagnostic Category	Surgical Technique	Test	Mean Preoperative IQ	Time of Postoperative Test	Mean IQ Change	Remarks
Porteus and Kepner	18	Psychotic	Lobotomy	SB	83.9	Varied	−3.2	Modified Stanford-Binet
Rylander	5	Neurotic	Lobotomy	SB	116.2	Varied	−11.6*	Calculation by the author
Strom-Olsen et al.	11	Psychotic	Lobotomy	SB	94.3	6 wks.	−2.2	Calculation by Crown
Yacorzynski et al.	1	Psychotic	Lobotomy	SB	118.0	3 mos.	−21.0	Patient received 2 preoperative WB's.
Koskoff et al.	5	Normal with intractable pain	Lobotomy	WB	104.5	3 mos.	−17.5	
				WB	87.2	3 mos.	−20.4*	
Malmo	6	Neurotic	5 Lobotomy, 1 gyrectomy	WB	107.8	1–3 mos.	−8.3*	W-B II on re-test
McCullough	10	Psychotic	Lobotomy	WB	83.4	2 mos.	2.9	Mean IQ change calculated from 2nd postoperative test
Petrie	20	Neurotic	Lobotomy	WB	105.8	2–3 mos.	−5.0*	
Vidor	21	Neurotic and psychotic	Lobotomy	WB or S.B.	111.5	Varied	0.6	16 received SB, 5 received W-B I
King		Psychotic	Topectomy	WB	101.7	3 wks.	3.9	Surgical group gained 3.7 points less than control group
Sheer et al.	20	Psychotic	Miscellaneous	WB	79.3	6 mos.	3.4	W-B II on re-test; surgical group gained 4.5 points less than control group

* Significant at 0.05 level of confidence.

changes are those encountered in lobotomies and lobectomies performed on psychotic patients of long duration, usually the more deteriorated schizophrenics. Similar operations on neurotics and otherwise intellectually intact subjects seemingly result in varying but significant degrees of impairment. This impairment is particularly striking if, in addition to drop in IQ, one takes into consideration the often reported loss of initiative and drive, decrease in planning ability, etc., which are, of course, also important aspects of intelligence. Altogether, the evidence at hand supports the conclusion that the effects of psychosurgery on measured intelligence are not inconsequential. From a therapeutic point of view, the loss in intellectual ability may be unimportant in comparison with the gain afforded the patients as regards possible alleviation of symptoms, reduction of anxiety, etc., but this gain does not controvert the negative results so far as general intelligence is concerned.

Removal of Large Areas of the Brain (Hemispherectomy)

More impressive than the findings consequent to the cutting or excision of the small areas usually involved in lobectomies and topectomies are the reported intellectual changes following the removal of extensive areas of the brain. These have already been considered from the point of view of their general implications as regards the role of the brain in intelligence. They will now be discussed from the point of view of the actual impairment in intelligence level reported. Here there is some difference of opinion among investigators. Considering only the most radical operations, removal of an entire hemisphere, the findings, as reviewed by Mensh, Schwartz and Matarazzo (361), show that in most of the cases reported (41 since 1921) the investigators were of the opinion that the patients on whom the operations were performed showed little and sometimes no loss at all after removal of the hemispheres. Statements such as, "there did not seem to be any obvious mental impairment"—"no demonstrable intellectual loss," and the like, seem to be the rule rather than the exception. However, these evaluations were based almost entirely on clinical impressions and seemingly did not take into consideration the possibly decreased efficiency of the patients occasioned by the diseased process which necessitated the operation. There seldom was any systematic pre- as well as postoperative testing. In the case reported by Mensh et al. (361), of a man 54 years old (with right-sided glioblastoma) who was tested repeatedly postoperatively, the hemisherectomy resulted in serious loss and disturbance in mental functioning as reflected in impaired performance on a variety of tests including parts of the W–B I, the Wechsler Memory Scale and the Rorschach. The implication of these findings was that the effect of the operation was to produce clearcut deficits in almost all areas tested. However, test protocols of four additional hemispherectomies subsequently collected by Matarazzo (565) failed to support this conclusion. The patients when re-tested postoperatively approximately one year after surgery showed no marked changes in status; indeed one patient showed considerable improvement. Still, all cases, even the one that showed considerable improvement in IQ, continued to show a typical organic test pattern.

At this point it is well to call attention to the distinction that must be made between levels of functioning designated as preoperative and premorbid, respectively. When a patient is tested preoperatively he is generally considerably disturbed and disorganized. It is indeed for this reason that he is generally operated upon; he is not normal, but an already impaired individual. Any changes thus found are not as between the individual's pre- and postmorbid abilities but as between his morbid and postoperative functioning. If the changes are to be interpreted as reflecting no loss in normal functioning, they should show not negligible but marked increase in test scores over preoperative levels. This is generally not the case. The most that can be said about the hemispherectomized subject, so far as intellectual ability is concerned, is that he has not been made worse than he was with his impaired hemisphere *in situ*. The remarkable thing, of course, is that he seemingly does not "miss" half of his brain. If so, one might conclude that the "extra" hemisphere, like the second eye, is biologically speaking, a luxury. This conclusion is probably false, but what the function of the non-dominant hemisphere may be, other than that of a "spare," still remains to be discovered.

Cortical Lesions and Space-Occupying Tumors

We have already referred to the fact that correlations between neurological and intelligence test findings are often inconstant, but a number of studies do indicate certain associations between locus of lesion and type or degree of resulting defect (533). These studies, however, deal mostly with special functions or disabilities rather than global deficit. More relevant to our present considerations is the study by Morrow and Mark (371). These investigators administered the W–B Intelligence Scale to 44 neuropsychiatric patients, 22 with pathological brain disease who later came to autopsy, and 22 psychiatric (non-organic) patients used as controls. From a comparison of the subtest scores of the two groups on the W–B II, the authors concluded that there was a more or less typical W–B "patterning" on the organic cases as compared with the psychiatric. The organic patients were consistently poor on the following subtests: Digit Symbol, Digit Span, Block Design, Arithmetic and Similarities. In addition they showed consistently lower Performance than Full Scale and Verbal IQ's. There was no significant difference between the groups as regards Vocabu-

TABLE 49

Wechsler-Bellevue Intelligence Scale scores of brain-damaged and psychiatric control patients (Morrow and Mark)

Variable	Brain-Damaged (22)	Psychiatric (22)	t*	P
Age....................................	40.91	39.82	0.305	—
Education.............................	10.00	10.09	0.075	—
Wechsler-Bellevue				
Full Scale IQ........................	91.95	108.85	3.647	0.001
Verbal IQ...........................	97.67	106.76	1.897	—
Performance IQ......................	87.49	109.67	4.804	0.001
Subtest weighted scores				
Information.........................	9.41	10.86	1.571	—
Comprehension......................	9.86	11.00	1.356	—
Digit Span (total weighted).........	6.68	9.14	2.081	0.01
Digits Forward (no. correct)........	5.73	6.36	1.518	—
Digits Backward (no. correct).......	3.91	5.04	2.211	0.05
Arithmetic.........................	7.09	10.41	2.781	0.01
Similarities........................	7.64	9.82	2.390	0.05
Vocabulary.........................	11.05	10.89	0.173	—
Picture Arrangement................	7.05	10.38	3.112	0.01
Picture Completion.................	7.32	10.27	3.292	0.01
Block Design.......................	7.00	10.00	2.988	0.01
Object Assembly....................	7.05	10.36	2.971	0.01
Digit Symbol.......................	4.23	9.14	4.610	0.001

* $df = 35$–45.

lary, Information and Comprehension (Table 49). These findings are consistent with those of other investigators (9), (21), and may be said to present the "typical organic test picture." In addition, Morrow and Mark found that patients whose lesions were located anterior to the Rolandic fissure showed far less intellectual impairment than those with lesions that were post-Rolandic. Like most previous investigators they found that subjects with lesions in the dominant hemispheres showed greatest defects and greater loss in both Verbal and Performance IQ's. Interestingly enough, subjects with bilateral lesions showed only lowered Performance scores, possibly because of less extensive (restricted) midline lesions.

As regards the over-all relation of locus of injury to extent of ensuing defect, as it pertains to measures of general intelligence, most[1] recent studies agree on at least three points. The first is that, other conditions being equal, trauma or lesion to the left (dominant) cortex always carries greater loss in intellectual ability and intelligence level than that to the right (nondominant) cortex. The only question is whether this may not be due in

[1] Exceptions are Rylander (439), Halstead (230) and Goldstein (200).

part to the nature of the tests employed and the type of function usually tested, namely, those involving language and verbal comprehension. Since persons with left-sided lesions are most likely to have special difficulty in communication they will most generally fall down in test situations, depending upon this factor. Some support for this possibility is suggested by test findings in certain brain lesions following cerebrovascular accidents (see below). Second, lesions of the posterior and intermediate cortex (post-Rolandic) produce more serious intellectual impairment than those of the anterior (pre-Rolandic) cortex, including the frontal lobes. Combining these two general findings, the order (most to least) of seriousness or degree of intellectual impairment following brain injury has been estimated as follows (533): (1) left temporal and/or left parietal, (2) left occipital and/or left frontal, (3) right parietal and/or right occipital lobes, (4) right frontal lobe. This order appears to hold for global functioning as measured by composite tests of intelligence as well as delimited functions (specific disabilities) as measured by tests of specific abilities. (533)

Cerebrovascular Accidents (CVA)

As in other kinds of cortical damage, this type of patient generally shows greater defects when the lesion is on the left than on the right side. This is, of course, particularly true when the lesion is accompanied by marked aphasic disturbances, but there are numerous and challenging exceptions. In some cases of left (dominant) cortical damage with aphasia, the patient may do much better on performance tests than the patient with right-sided damage and no aphasic symptoms. The finding is all the more surprising because patients with left cortical damage are individuals who have lost the use of their practiced and educated side (being right hemiplegics), whereas the right cortical damaged patient (left hemiplegics) have retained the function of their favored limbs. Observations of this sort are commonly reported by persons engaged in rehabilitation who have noted the contrasting rates of progress which these patients make in re-acquiring elementary motor functions needed in daily life. Illustrative examples of test findings on the two types of patients are given in Tables 50 and 51. While the examples cited are not necessarily typical of all cases of CVA with and without aphasia, they are fairly representative of a large group of these patients, and warrant special study.[2]

Changes in the test (and other) behavior of CVA patients of the type just described again bring up the question of the relative roles of the hemispheres. Bauer and Becka (41), on the basis of similar observations made on a group of CVA patients, concluded that the type of deficit ob-

[2] Cf. Reitan, R. M., *Certain differential effects of left and right cerebral lesions in human adults* (428).

right out

TABLE 50

W–B test scores of 2 patients with left hemiplegia following cerebrovascular accident

Man (aged 56)		Man (aged 58)	
Information	13	Information	12
Comprehension	13	Comprehension	11
Digit Span	7	Digit Span	7
Arithmetic	9	Arithmetic	9
Similarities	12	Similarities	7
Vocabulary	12	Vocabulary	—
Picture Arrangement	4	Picture Arrangement	1
Picture Completion	7	Picture Completion	3
Block Design	3	Block Design	1
Object Assembly	0	Object Assembly	0
Digit Symbol	2	Digit Symbol	2
Verbal IQ	117	Verbal IQ	105
Performance IQ	79	Performance IQ	71

Dentist; College 6 yrs.; CVA 6 mos. prior to testing. Made little progress in rehabilitation, although under treatment for many months.

Upholsterer; 8th grade; CVA 4 mos. prior to testing.

left out

TABLE 51

W–B test scores of 2 patients with right hemiplegia following cerebrovascular accident

Man (aged 54)		Woman (age p 27)	
Information	—	Information	—
Comprehension	—	Comprehension	—
Digit Span	—	Digit Span	—
Arithmetic	—	Arithmetic	—
Similarities	—	Similarities	—
Picture Arrangement	11	Picture Arrangement	10
Picture Completion	9	Picture Completion	9
Block Design	12	Block Design	6
Object Assembly	12	Object Assembly	10
Digit Symbol	—	Digit Symbol	—
Verbal IQ	—	Verbal IQ	—
Performance IQ	124	Performance IQ	94

Assistant office manager; high school 4 yrs.; tested 14 mos. after CVA. Residual sensory aphasia with moderate perceptive difficulties. Able to walk; partial use of right arm.

Housewife; high school 2 yrs.; CVA during childbirth with moderate to severe aphasia. Tested about 1 yr. after accident. Good progress in rehabilitation.

served in their aphasic patients did not support the Goldstein hypothesis that such patients showed greater impairment of abstract ability than patients with other brain lesions. On the other hand, the recurrent and persistent difficulties which non-aphasic patients have in tests of visual motor planning and organization, as reflected in such tests as the Block Design and Object Assembly, indicate strongly that the right hemispheres play some significant role in these functions. No doubt motivation plays some part; the aphasic patient has perhaps greater need to compensate for his loss of ability to communicate and therefore may make greater efforts to overcome his disability by substitutive use of the motor modalities. Still, the fact remains that the right cerebrally damaged patient also falls down on Arithmetic and Digit Span, and not infrequently also on the Similarities test. An observation made by Anderson (20) is that the patients with left cortical lesions (those showing loss of language) have seemingly forgotten "what to do", whereas patients with right brain lesions, "how to do." The implied hypothesis would call for assignment of differential memory functions in the two hemispheres, which is doubtful; in any case, it would not entirely explain the differences observed. The effect of laterality on intellectual function is still an unresolved problem.

Another investigation relative to the present discussion is the study of Kahn (282a) on the relation between the degree of cerebral electroencephalographic pathology and the patterns of intellectual disturbance. This investigation was based on the study of patients with space-occupying tumors showing a variety of symptoms. In spite of the heterogeneity of the population, the subjects consistently showed the "organic test-syndrome": Verbal higher than Performance, low Digit Symbol, Digit Span, Picture Arrangement, etc. But when he divided his patients into two groups, those with abnormal EEG's and those with relatively "normal" EEG's, he found no significant difference between the two groups as regards Full Scale IQ. Kahn interpreted his findings as supporting Hebb's hypothesis, that the abnormal EEG is primarily an indicator of cortical dysfunction rather than intellectual deficit. Nevertheless, when patients with the abnormal EEG's were further subdivided into high and low abnormals, he found significant differences between the Verbal and Performance IQ's of these patients as well as between their respective scores on Similarities and certain other tests of organization. This finding he interpreted as confirming the observation made by Polatin, Strauss and Altman (400a) regarding the correlation between the abnormality of the EEG and the loss of capacity in abstract reasoning.[3]

The subjects of Kahn's study were too heterogeneous a group to be

[3] A similar difference in conceptual ability was found by Kahn (282a), between patients with normal and abnormal EEG's.

evaluated in other respects, and his findings are indecisive because of lack of experimental controls. But they did bring into focus certain problems regarding the nature of the impairment of intelligence in patients with space-occupying lesions. Some of these problems were further investigated with a subsequent study by Pollock (401), apparently on the same group of patients. The study again showed that patients with these occupying-lesions tended to show the typical organic test syndrome. Of further interest was his observation as regards some of the factors which seemingly influenced the test performance of the patient studied. One of these was the factor of spatial inattention, a factor previously reported by Teuber and his co-workers, in which the subject either disregarded or failed to perceive objects in the visual field contralateral to the side of their reported lesion. Thus, patients with right-sided lesions would be unaware of cards on the left side of the Picture Arrangement sequence although they could be made to notice the cards when directed toward them by prodding.

Effects of Chronic Alcoholism

In discussing the effects of alcoholism on intelligence it is necessary to distinguish between the transitory changes in psychological functions following the ingestion of restricted amounts of alcohol and those ascribed to its continued use. Apart from information available from common observation, the former have been evaluated primarily on the basis of controlled experiments under conditions of subclinical intoxication. The latter are descriptions of long-range effects inferred primarily from terminal and pathological cases of chronic drinking. The reported observations are mutually supportive, but not always interchangeable.

The changes in psychological functions observed under experimental conditions have been comprehensively summarized by Jellinek and McFarland (279). Their survey shows that while much of the work done thus far is inconclusive, and some of it contradictory, the results as a whole leave little doubt that the effect of alcohol is to lower the functioning level of nearly all mental abilities that have been tested. The immediate effect of alcohol is to impair the efficiency of the individual. The degree of impairment is dependent on the amount of alcohol absorbed, the time interval following ingestion, the specific susceptibility of the subject, and to some degree, on the mental functions of the tasks involved. Sensory discrimination in nearly all modalities is decreased, and thresholds of perception raised. Retention and recall are adversely affected with loss in rote memory generally less than that for logical material. Frequently there are disturbances in associative processes as shown by a lengthening of reaction time and the augmentation of superficial and clang associations.

Mental changes observed in the chronic drinker include many or all the above, plus certain other sequelae. There is general loss in mental efficiency, and in severe cases, as in Korsakoff's psychosis, there is definite evidence of mental deterioration. Memory for recent events and the ability to form new associations are especially affected. So far as over-all intellectual ability is concerned, the general rule seems to be progressive impairment of nearly all intellectual abilities. But there are great differences due to variation in individual tolerance to alcohol. Moreover, most investigations reported have dealt with cross-sectional studies, whereas what is needed for evaluation of individual differences are longitudinal studies in which the age as well as other factors can be taken into account. The two studies presently reported suffer similarly from this defect, but nevertheless indicate the type of impairment that may be expected, at least in tests of general intelligence. The data in these instances were test scores obtained with the W–B I and the WAIS.

The first study was done in 1940 and previously reported (518). It consisted in the administration of the W–B I to 29 ambulant patients who were diagnosed as alcoholics without psychosis, in fair physical condition (neurologically negative). The second study was on a comparable group from the same institution, similarly diagnosed, who were given the WAIS in 1955. The results, giving the Full Scale IQ's and mean subtest scores for both groups on the respective Scales are given in Table 52. The table shows that irrespective of age and IQ level, the chronic alcoholics showed almost identical performance as regards the tests they failed and passed. This is seen more clearly in a rank-order comparison of the subtests for the two parts of the Scales respectively (lines 5 and 6). As will be seen the chronic alcoholic presents essentially the organic test pattern. On the Verbal part he does best on Information and Comprehension and worst on Digit Span and/or Arithmetic and Similarities. On the Performance part he does best on Picture Completion, worst on Digit Symbol and Object Assembly. It differs somewhat from the typical organic pattern in that the Object Assembly is particularly low, and when accompanied by a relatively good Picture Arrangement and Block Design is almost pathognomonic of the chronic alcoholic. The test findings, especially those in the younger group, are of particular interest because they give evidence of organic brain pathology often long before the appearance of neurological symptoms. Irrespective of the psychodynamics, excessive use of alcohol has a deteriorative effect on intellectual capacities.

In summary, brain injury, irrespective of origin, if sufficiently extensive, results in a more or less typical organic test syndrome. On the W–B and the WAIS it is characterized by a marked difference between Verbal and Performance and by special deficit or dysfunction in certain of the Verbal as well as most of the Performance subtests. There is some evidence of

TABLE 52

Performance of chronic alcoholics on W–B I and WAIS

Scale	Age Group	Mean Age	Mean IQ*	No.	Verbal Test Mean Score						Performance Test Mean Score			
					Inf.	Comp.	Arith.	Sim.	D. Span	D. Symp.	P.C.	B.D.	P.A.	O.A.
(A1) W–B I..........	36–42	38.7	98.8	16	10.0	10.7	9.2	8.3	7.2	6.8	8.1	8.2	8.4	7.8
(A2) W–B I..........	45–55	48.9	98.5	13	9.5	8.8	7.7	6.8	7.1	5.2	9.2	8.5	7.3	7.2
(B1) WAIS..........	35–44	40.3	91.9	14	9.6	10.1	9.6	8.7	8.4	5.6	7.9	7.5	7.7	6.6
(B2) WAIS..........	45–55	50.1	103.1	17	11.9	11.6	10.4	10.4	10.6	4.7	9.1	7.5	7.7	6.6
Rank Order† of Subtest														
W–B I (A1 + A2)............	36–55	43.1	98.6	29	1½	1½	3½	3½	5	5	1	2	3	4
WAIS (B1 + B2)............	35–55	45.6	97.7	31	1	2	3½	3½	5	5	1	2½	2½	4

* Full Scale.

† Verbal and Performance treated separately. In the case of the WAIS, the Vocabulary was also given but is omitted from evaluation so that the order of the subtests would be strictly comparable.

correlation between particular disabilities and certain lesion loci but the correlations are generally of small order. In appraising the resulting disability there seems to be some need for bearing in mind Hebb's distinction between intellectual deficit and cortical dysfunction. Notwithstanding this distinction there is clear-cut evidence that the effect of brain damage, irrespective of presence or absence of other sequelae, generally involves some loss in general intelligence, however measured.

Chapter 14

Utilization of W–B I and WAIS
in Counseling and Guidance

Selection, guidance and counseling are complex processes involving many areas of appraisal. These include assessment of the individual's abilities, awareness of his personal problems and evaluation of his needs and interests. An area that is always relevant is the level of the individual's intelligence. In selection and vocational guidance, knowledge of this level is important because it sets broad limits to the kind of occupation which an applicant or a client may be expected to pursue with reasonable success. In spite of the wide overlap, different kinds of occupations may, and often do, require different levels of intelligence.

I Q Differences Between Occupational Groups

The most extensive studies on relation between test scores and occupational levels have been obtained with group tests (56a). But in recent years there have also become available data derived from individual examinations. In general, the results of individual tests of intelligence give findings similar to those of group tests, although with occasional changes in the hierarchical order in the occupations listed. A study by Simon and Levitt (458) discusses the relationship between W–B IQ's and various occupational levels with norms for major descriptive categories. The Mean Full Scale W–B I IQ's for nine of the occupational groups listed by these authors are shown in Table 53.

A general finding in the Simon and Levitt study is that most of the occupational groups studied showed a systematic 2 to 5 point higher Verbal than Performance IQ. The exceptions were the groups designated as artists and skilled laborers, where the reverse was obtained. The differences reported, while not large, suggest a possible selectivity in the population[1] tested or may reflect the increasing emphasis on verbal facility and comprehension in job selection.

[1] Although the numbers tested for most of the groups in the reported study were substantial and selected randomly from a larger population (8000), neither the age nor the sex factor appears to have been considered.

TABLE 53

*IQ scores on the Wechsler Bellevue Form I in relation to occupation**

	No.	Median	Q	Range
Engineers...................	52	133	4.0	116–148
Accountants, etc...........	61	128	5.0	106–143
Teachers....................	421	126	6.0	94–152
Business managers and executives...................	134	125	5.0	92–146
Sales people................	153	122	8.0	95–142
Bookkeepers...............	55	117	8.0	99–137
Clerks.....................	128	116	8.5	74–140
Skilled labor...............	107	115	6.5	87–139
Personal service............	57	106	10.5	54–130

* Adapted from Simon and Levitt (458). The authors also give separate norms for the Verbal and Performance IQ's (as Q1 and Q3) but these have been omitted to save space. For definition of range of occupations included under list of main groups, see author's article.

Intelligence tests have been most generally used in guidance and counseling to rule out intellectual inadequacy or to call attention to superior potential. Some attempts have been made to relate IQ or M. A. levels to employability. Thus, on the basis of earlier studies it has been found that an M. A. of about 10 years (equivalent to an IQ of about 65 on the WAIS and W–B I) is sufficient for jobs such as assembling parts, wrapping and certain types of filing. At the opposite end of the IQ range there are studies giving "norms" for college students and mean scores for professional (and graduate) students in various specialties. The implication of the findings is that different specialties or types of graduate work may require a particular level of performance. For this reason, among others, many colleges have in the past few years begun to require minimal IQ's for admission. These standards have varied from place to place and, of course, are not the sole basis for admission but do indicate the growing appreciation of the importance of intelligence level in college success. So far as the WAIS and W–B are concerned a number of studies would indicate that individuals with IQ's below 110 have poor chances of completing the average course within the usual four-year period. A representative distribution of W–B IQ's of students at the average college is reproduced in Table 54.

Of equal and sometimes great importance for guidance is evidence of assets and liabilities as revealed in the subject's over-all general functioning. Here a composite intelligence scale which is composed of different subtests has a considerable advantage over the omnibus type of scale. It should be emphasized, however, that the purpose of an intelligence test even when composed of a variety of subtests is not primarily that of discovering special

TABLE 54

*Mean and range of IQ scores (W–B I) for a sample of 100 college students**

	Men		Women		Total	
	M	Range	M	Range	M	Range
Full Scale						
Freshmen.............	115.0	131–99	118.1	136– 98	116.6	136– 98
Sophomores.........	119.1	138–101	117.0	134–106	118.2	138–101
Juniors..............	119.2	136–107	121.2	129–112	120.2	136–107
Seniors..............	116.5	133–104	121.8	140–111	118.8	140–104

* A Midwestern State University.

aptitudes. For this, specific aptitude tests are required. But the fact that a scale does consist of a varied battery makes it useful in calling attention to those perceptual and other areas in which the subject may show certain strengths or weaknesses, and in general assets or liabilities. Considered in terms of broad functional areas or factors, the various subtests of the W–B I and the WAIS, particularly when taken in combination, are often useful in furnishing indications of potential aptitudes and pertinent interests or both. Thus, Risch (429a) found that the Performance part of the W–B I correlated as well with the Bennett Mechanical Comprehension Test and mechanical interests on the Kuder Preference Record, as the latter two did with one another (Table 55).

Manifestation of assets or liabilities on test performance must, of course, be considered in relation to the individual's total problem. Above all, one must bear in mind the relevance of one's findings to the particular problem presented by the subject. For example, an unusual facility in repeating digits (high Digit Span) or a high score on arithmetical reasoning may be of no great consequence if the occupation in question has no requirement at all for this aptitude. On the other hand, one must make a clear distinction

TABLE 55

*Correlations between W–B I Performance and Bennet Mechanical Comprehension and Kuder Mechanical Interest Scales** (Risch) (N = 94 or 97)

	r	Sig.
		%
W–B × Bennet Mech. Comp........................	0.350	1
W–B × Kuder Mech. Int............................	0.310	1
Kuder Mech. Int. × Bennet Mech. Comp..............	0.348	1

* Correlations with Full Scale or Verbal part alone were of zero order. However, the r between the W–B Verbal and literary interest on the Kuder was 0.30 ± 0.068, significant at the 1 per cent level.

between aptitude and interest. What a person can do and what he likes or thinks he can do are two different vectors. Manifestation of interest in a particular field or occupation one wishes to pursue is, of course, desirable but is no substitute for aptitude. Competence in a given field is determined by particular abilities and if an individual does not possess them to a sufficient degree, no amount of interest can compensate for a lack of them.[2]

With the above considerations in mind, there are often broad vocational inferences one can make from the way a subject performs on the WAIS (or W–B I) subtests or combinations of them. For example, a subject who does poorly on the performance part of the Scales might well be advised to re-evaluate his interests in pursuing occupations calling for manipulative and mechanical ability. This does not mean that the Performance IQ must always be higher than the Verbal but does imply at least moderate ability on the non-verbal test. Much also depends on the level of the occupation considered. For example, engineering calls for good arithmetic and abstract reasoning and interestingly enough a high level of verbal ability. Thus, studies have shown that engineers along with their other abilities generally attain higher Verbal than Performance IQ's. A recent example is furnished by the findings of DeMartino (134) who compared Verbal and Performance IQ's obtained by pre-engineering students on the W–B II as well as various scores on the subtests of the Scale, with college grades and an aptitude inventory. With these subjects, DeMartino found that the Verbal part of the Scale correlated much better with the criteria than the Performance part (0.516 against 0.097). The Means of the W–B II subtests as well as the Verbal, Performance and Full Scale Scores obtained by DeMartino's subjects (100 freshmen engineering students) are shown in Table 56. Mean subtest scores varied from 10.6 on Digit Span to 13.7 for the Block Design. Correlations of subtest scores with grades in engineering courses as well as with percentile scores on the Pre-Engineering Inventory Scale, also showed large differences. The Arithmetic subtest, while far from representing the highest mean score made by the students, correlated best with most of the criteria variables (grades in freshman subjects), e.g., 0.34 with grades in chemistry and 0.30 with mathematics. This might have been anticipated, but why Arithmetic also correlated 0.33 with Religion is a mystery.

Executive Appraisal

Appraisal of top-level management personnel is an ever-increasing concern of industrial organizations and governmental agencies, not only

[2] The wide and indiscriminate use of Vocational Interest Inventories would indicate that this fact is not yet sufficiently appreciated. The correlation between abilities and interests is far from the order that authors of inventories imply; nor should we expect them to be any higher than those reported.

TABLE 56

Means and standard deviations of the Wechsler-Bellevue Scores (W–B II) for 100 freshmen engineering students (DeMartino)

Instrument	Mean	S.D.
W–B subtests		
Information...................	12.50	1.71
Comprehension................	12.49	2.27
Digit Span...................	10.64	3.09
Arithmetic...................	11.70	2.26
Similarities..................	12.52	1.42
Vocabulary...................	12.42	1.27
Picture Arrangement...........	12.35	2.42
Picture Completion............	11.18	1.71
Block Design.................	13.69	1.97
Object Assembly..............	13.53	1.77
Digit Symbol.................	11.46	2.48
W–B IQ scales		
Verbal......................	118.31	8.13
Performance..................	115.22	9.71
Full........................	120.02	8.00

because executives of high ability are hard to find but also because we know too little about what makes for high executive ability. Many factors obviously enter into it, among which certain personality traits such as leadership and energy level are admittedly important. In this section, however, we will only discuss the role of intelligence and consider more particularly how tests, like the W–B and WAIS, may be of value in the appraisal of executive personnel. Here the problem is not so much the elimination of persons of limited endowment as the selection of individuals of greatest ability and promise; occasionally, also the detection of decline or breakdown of individuals previously functioning at an adequate level but who for one reason or another have fallen off in performance. We shall begin by discussing the first of these problems.

Top executives in business and industry, contrary to the belief in certain circles, will generally be found to be individuals of superior intelligence. Individuals in this category obtain, on the average, IQ's equal to the mean of college graduates (*e.g.*, WAIS Full Scale IQ's of 120 or better) with a systematic difference from 5 to 10 points in favor of Verbal as against Performance IQ's. Thus, in a recent study by Balinsky and Shaw (36) of executives in a medium-sized company dealing with a basic industry, the mean IQ's for the group were respectively 125 for the Verbal, 117 for the Performance and 124 for the Full Scale IQ (Table 57). Correlations with

TABLE 57

*Level of WAIS scores of executives and correlations of same with performance
ratings (N = 39) (Balinsky and Shaw)*

	Mean	S.D.	r
Information	13.62	1.43	0.257
Comprehension	15.85	1.96	0.005
Arithmetic	14.51	2.21	0.424*
Similarities	12.56	2.07	0.240
Digit Span	12.28	3.39	0.173
Vocabulary	15.00	1.98	0.129
Digit Symbol	10.21	2.04	0.046
Picture Completion	13.62	2.83	0.175
Block Design	11.26	2.30	0.150
Picture Arrangement	10.59	2.23	0.052
Object Assembly	10.74	2.96	0.047
Verbal IQ	125.1	8.09	0.318†
Performance IQ	117.1	9.81	0.076
Full Scale IQ	124.1	7.90	0.238

* Significant at 1 per cent level.

† Significant at 5 per cent level.

ratings of performance on the job varied with both parts of the Scale as
well as with the individual subtests. The highest correlation was with the
Verbal part of the Scale, significant at the 5 per cent level, and least with
the Performance which was only slightly better than chance. As regards
the subtests, the highest correlation was with Arithmetic (0.42) significant
at the 1 per cent level; modest correlations, approaching but not quite
reaching the significant 5 per cent level, were also found for the Information
(0.26) and Similarities (0.24) Tests. The order of these correlations is in
accord with other observations, but the lack of significant correlation with
Vocabulary is not in accord with views met with in the literature. The
executives in the Balinsky and Shaw study do, as one would expect, make
high scores on the Vocabulary Test, but level of Vocabulary *per se* fails to
show significant correlation with Performance on the job. On the other
hand, arithmetical reasoning on which executives do only moderately well
does appear to be an important criterion for successful performance.

Level of intelligence for different types of administrative functioning
no doubt varies with different types of positions but as in the case of professional success, plays a much greater role than generally acknowledged.
Strikingly enough, people in business are often more alert to this fact than
academicians. An interesting example is furnished by Holt's (257) study on

the prediction of performance in residency training. In this study, Holt used a large number of variables in the hope of obtaining significant correlations with ultimate criteria of successful performance on the job in psychiatric residency. Among the test variables included was the W–B Intelligence Scale regarding which he had this to say: "We had little hopes that any of the W–B measures would yield anything because it is widely considered to have little 'top,' and does not contain enough difficult items to give an estimate of intelligence at the upper levels that is reliable enough to distinguish between the 'very superior' and 'absolutely brilliant.' " As a good investigator, however, Holt proceeded to try out the tests, and after comparing the results with those obtained with other instruments came up with some surprising findings: The W–B Verbal IQ of the psychiatric residents tested, far from being inconsequential, predicted performance on the job much better than most other variables including a host derived from personality tests.

Holt's comment on the above finding was as follows: "This array of validities for the Verbal IQ is quite astonishing, particularly in view of the validities reported in the previous chapter. There are few better predictors

TABLE 58

Validities of Wechsler-Bellevue Verbal Intelligence Quotients in evaluation of psychiatric residents* (Holt and Luborsky)

Supervisors' Evaluations (Major)	Verbal IQ	Supervisors' Evaluations (Minor)	Verbal IQ
Over-all competence	0.38	Warmth for patients	0.31
Psychotherapy	0.29	Ability to inspire confidence	0.39
Diagnosis	0.45	Empathy	0.35
Management	0.28	Freedom from over-identifica-	
Administration	0.29	tion	0.16
		Interest in patients and psy-	
Peer's Evalvtions (Major)		chiatry	0.40
		Spontaneity *vs.* inhibition	0.28
Over-all competence	0.36	Acceptance of responsibility	0.25
Psychotherapy	0.28	Tolerance for patient's aggres-	
Diagnosis	0.47	sion	0.32
Management	0.27	Tolerance for stress	0.28
Administration	0.37	Freedom from hostility toward	
		patients	0.16
		Firmness *vs.* vacillation, etc.	0.33
		Sensitivity	0.38
		Judiciousness *vs.* impulsivity	0.30
		Effective communication	0.30

* $N = 64$. The sample represents only a part (Classes V and VI) of residents studied. I am grateful to Drs. Holt and Luborsky for permitting me to use these data prior to publication in their forthcoming volume (257).

of a half-dozen of the minor variables, and even over-all competence is predicted just about as well as the MSP tester could do with all of the rest of the information in the standard battery in addition to this measure of verbal intelligence!" Cross-validation of the findings did not quite support this initial result, but the final validity values of the Verbal IQ were still among the best obtained. These values as they pertained to the more important criteria of on the job performance by psychiatric interns are shown in Table 58. The cited results are not presented as unchallengeable, but rather to emphasize again the all too prevalent tendency of under-estimating the role of intelligence in professional as well as other fields.

Illustrative Cases

We shall conclude the present chapter with four cases illustrating the use of the W–B I or WAIS in counseling and guidance, and one in the selection of a top-level executive. It is, of course, understood that for thorough counseling or selection, other instruments including a comprehensive interview would be employed.[3] The following cases are cited primarily to illustrate the contributions that may be expected from the inclusion of a comprehensive test of general intelligence.

W–B I

Information	10
Comprehension	13
Digit Span	11
Arithmetic	13
Similarities	16
Vocabulary	12
Picture Arrangement	16
Picture Completion	12
Block Design	16
Object Assembly	13
Digit Symbol	13
Verbal IQ	121
Performance IQ	126
Full IQ	127

Case C–1. Male, age 18. Referred by his high school counselor because he wanted to become an electrical engineer but had taken a commercial course in high school and had failed bookkeeping.

C–1 maintained a steady, absorbed interest in all of the test tasks, although he stated that the testing made him anxious. He spoke in a high, strained voice, rushed through timed tests, and was constantly dissatisfied with the level of his response. He recognized the fact that his drive for perfection was somewhat disabling. On the W–B Form I, he achieved ratings of "superior" intellectual ability on the Verbal, Performance and Full Scales. Although the scores on all the subtests were at least average, there was some variability with his performance. His score on Information seemed to reflect a lack of consolidation of previous learning. His high score on the Similarities test showed exceptional ability in formulating abstract concepts. General comprehension was also superior, as was

---

[3] The cases cited are from actual reports furnished the author by several organizations. The author wishes to express his indebtedness to these organizations for permitting their publication. The cases are reproduced essentially as reported but have been slightly edited both to avoid individual identification and to conform to a single general format.

his arithmetical reasoning. In solving some of the arithmetical problems he appeared tense but performed computations rapidly.

Highest score on the Performance part was on Picture Arrangement and Block Design. On the former he was extremely quick to recognize and correlate situation factors and to interpret the social interplay. On the Block Design, while occasionally fumbling because of his eagerness, he nevertheless completed the tasks in rapid time and showed excellent spatial perception and ability for visual-motor organization. The remaining subtest scores were not so high, although still above average.

In summary, C–1's performance on the Wechsler-Bellevue placed him in the superior category of intellectual functioning in both verbal and performance areas. His handling of the various test situations was somewhat inhibited by self-doubt, but he displayed a well integrated approach to problems and exceptionally fine powers of analysis. In spite of his tension, he was able to maintain a responsive, stimulating social relationship and to view his problems objectively.

Recommendation: C–1 should return to school and get credits he needs for an engineering course.

WAIS

Information	18
Comprehension	18
Digit Span	15
Arithmetic	16
Similarities	16
Vocabulary	19
Picture Arrangement	12
Picture Completion	13
Block Design	12
Object Assembly	17
Digit Symbol	11
Verbal IQ	141
Performance IQ	120
Full IQ	134

Case C–2. Male, age 25, referred by employment service to evaluate discrepancy between interest and ability and type of job he was holding. He had been working as a shipping clerk and loader, and at the same time studying music at night. On testing, C–2 appeared rather submissive, shy, and at the same time rather formal in his manner. He approached his tasks seriously, always putting forth maximum effort. In spite of this he was often displeased with his own performance. All his subtest scores on the Verbal were at the superior level. His Performance test scores were not so high but still above average, and showed some unevenness. His highest score was on the Object Assembly which he performed in almost errorless fashion. On the other hand he only did moderately well on the Block Design which likewise involved visual-motor organization but more planning. His relatively poorest performance was on the Digit Symbol on which he attained a score of only 11; he was slowed down by unnecessary painstaking. This is in line with his need for precision and accuracy. Manner of test responses suggested emotional involvement. His tendency to submissiveness was indicated by some of the questions he asked the examiner. For example, in doing Digits, he asked the examiner if it were permissible for him to rehearse the numbers in his mind before repeating them.

In summary, C–2 is an individual of superior intelligence who has been functioning much below what one would expect of a person of his endowment. Probably some personality limitations as well as individual circumstances have contributed to his present vocational maladjustment. He seems, however, definitely capable of functioning at higher and more adequate levels. In view of his limited formal scholastic achievements it is recommended that he be encouraged to complete his high school education. Further planning may be deferred until he gets his diploma. In the meantime he might also continue with his music as an avocational interest and source of personal satisfaction.

WAIS

Information	6
Comprehension	4
Arithmetic	2
Similarities	8
Digit Span	4
Vocabulary	5
Digit Symbol	6
Picture Completion	3
Block Design	3
Picture Arrangement	4
Object Assembly	3
Verbal IQ	71
Performance IQ	60
Full IQ	64

Case C–3. Defective female (cretin), 28 years old. Client has been under continuous treatment with thyroid medication for some time. Attended CRMD classes from 5th grade until age 16. Now voluntarily attends an evening elementary school three nights a week where she learns reading and writing. She seems to have made considerable progress in reading in the last five years. Her employment history consists of two jobs which lasted for 2 days and 3 days. She was discharged from both because of slowness. C–3 is now attending a sheltered workshop for adult retardates where she is considered as potentially employable.

C–3's current testing resulted in a considerably higher IQ than that reported for her in 1951. She now achieves a Verbal score of 71, a Performance score of 60 and a Full Scale IQ of 64. The higher rating is much more likely in view of her relative competence in expressing herself and her accomplishments in reading. She reads at the level of an average first year high school student and uses the library as a source of stimulation and satisfaction. Most of her subtest scores are clearly defective, and she indicates only a limited potential for improving beyond her present levels. Her most serious weaknesses are in areas requiring the ability to relate parts to each other to form a meaningful whole. On such tasks, she becomes confused and disorganized and is unable to shift appropriately or make the necessary adjustments in thinking. She tends to perseverate her errors and exercises limited judgment. Her verbal abilities are considerably better than her handling of concrete objects and she is likely to make a better social impression than she can maintain in work.

In summary, C–3 is currently functioning in the upper defective range and shows clear signs of organic impairment that affect her reasoning ability and judgment. Although she is able to learn and has achieved marked success in reading, she has particular difficulty in seeing relationships between objects or people. Her skills with concrete objects are considerably below her verbal abilities and she is likely to make a better first impression than she can maintain in practice. Job training should concentrate on developing a skill in a routine, repetitive task where she might acquire enough speed to be in a competitive position. Additional training in social skills leading to greater independence is necessary but is not likely to result in any marked characterological changes.

WAIS

Information	14
Comprehension	13
Arithmetic	12
Similarities	17
Digit Span	12
Vocabulary	16
Digit Symbol	9
Picture Completion	13
Block Design	10
Picture Arrangement	9
Object Assembly	9
Verbal IQ	123
Performance IQ	105
Full IQ	116

Percentile equivalents:

Verbal IQ	93%
Performance IQ	63%
Full IQ	85%

Case C–4. Male, 40 years. Two years college. Referred by industrial organization for evaluation as top-level executive.

Compared with the general population C–4 has bright normal intelligence. However, he is in the lower end of the average range of executive personnel. Analysis of his test performance indicates that he is much more highly developed verbally than in dealing with objects and things.

Examination of the distribution of verbal scores shows a very highly developed abstract ability together with very high vocabulary. These were the two areas in which he showed real depth of understanding. However, he was somewhat detached in expressing himself. This attitude of detachment was specifically notable in the comprehension test. He did not seem able to relate intellectual understanding of a situation to the more practical. Ordinarily one finds higher comprehension and arithmetical reasoning test scores in an individual who has such high similarities and vocabulary. In the case of C–4 his relatively low comprehension and arithmetic scores, and possibly also information, would indicate some lack of facility in articulating his highly developed reasoning ability with its applications.

There is probably some inability to tackle and cope effectively with situations where he has to come up with practical answers. In the test situation, the examiner found that C–4 could verbalize freely in those areas where he had some familiarity but in other areas, such as arithmetic, he showed a good deal of anxiety and hesitation. It was also necessary for C–4 to have instructions gone over very completely before he would answer.

In the Picture Completion test, he rated above average but was easily satisfied with incorrect responses. He did not seem to push himself. There were other instances where he demonstrated uncertainty in coping with problems, and at such times he tended to block badly.

In summary, C–4's performance on intelligence test's evaluation reveals an individual of above average endowment but below the mean expected of executive personnel. He is inclined to be over-abstract; he also showed some lack of scope in his over-all intellectual development.

Recommendation: Candidate does not meet optimal requirements for position.

APPENDICES

Appendix 1

Special Statistical Methods

Method Used to Calculate IQ's and IQ Tables for W-B I

1. Mean and S.D. of *weighted* score distributions obtained for each age level.

2. All weighted scores for each age level converted in z scores by usual formula

$$z = \frac{X - M}{\sigma}$$

where M's and σ's are the constants of the different age level distributions. Charts drawn up for each age level giving the weighted scores and their corresponding z scores.

3. z scores for the different age distributions equated against P.E. limits, such that the score 0.6745 σ (1 P.E.) below the mean would in all age levels give an IQ of 90. This was carried through as follows.

(a) For each age level locate the weighted score at 0.6745 σ below the mean of the group.

(b) Calculate zero point for each age level by the formula

$$\frac{Y + z'}{Y} = \text{IQ}$$

where Y = zero point, $z' = -0.6745$ and IQ' = 0.90). Obviously, when IQ' is set at 90, the zero point then will be equal to 6.745.

(c) With the zero point at 6.745, get IQ for every weight score in each age level (1) by looking up charts containing z scores and their corresponding weighted scores and then (2) by solving the formula

$$\text{IQ}_a = \frac{6.745 + z_a}{6.745}$$

where IQ = IQ for particular weighted score at any age and z = z score for particular weighted score at any age.

Method Used to Construct IQ Tables for WAIS

While the method for calculating IQ's for WAIS may appear different from that used for the W–B I, the two methods give essentially the same results. With a mean IQ of 100, and S.D. of 15, a P.E. of 10, will set the limits of normality at an IQ of 90 (see above).

Tables of Verbal, Performance and Full Scale IQ's were constructed separately for each of the seven age groups in the national standardization and for three age groups of the Old Age Study. The method consisted of equating the mean and standard deviation of the appropriate sum of scaled scores to a mean of 100 and a standard deviation of 15 for the IQ scale. This was done by means of the following equation

$$(1) \qquad \frac{X_1 - M_{ss}}{\text{S.D.}_{ss}} = \frac{X_2 - M_{IQ}}{\text{S.D.}_{IQ}}$$

where X_1 = any sum of scaled scores

  M_{ss} = mean of the sum of scaled scores

  S.D.$_{ss}$ = standard Deviation of sum of scaled scores

  X_2 = IQ corresponding to X_1

  M_{IQ} = mean of IQ scale, which is 100

  S.D.$_{IQ}$ = standard deviation of IQ scale, which is 15.

Equation (1) can be written as follows

$$(2) \qquad X_2 = \frac{\text{S.D.}_{IQ}}{\text{S.D.}_{ss}} (X_1 - M_{ss}) + M_{IQ}$$

or

$$(3) \qquad X_2 = \frac{\text{S.D.}_{IQ}}{\text{S.D.}_{ss}} X_1 + \left[M_{IQ} - M_{ss} \left(\frac{\text{S.D.}_{IQ}}{\text{S.D.}_{ss}} \right) \right]$$

Substituting the values of 100 and 15 for M_{IQ} and S.D.$_{IQ}$, respectively,

$$(4) \qquad X_2 = \frac{15}{\text{S.D.}_{ss}} X_1 + \left[100 - M_{ss} \left(\frac{15}{\text{S.D.}_{ss}} \right) \right]$$

To compute the Verbal IQ table for age groups 25–34, for example, we substituted in equation (4) the mean sum of Verbal scaled scores of that group for M_{ss}. For S.D.$_{ss}$ we used one value for all age groups as described in the WAIS Manual. Then by putting in all possible values for X_1 (i.e., all possible sums of scores), we determined the corresponding IQ or X_2.

Equations for Predicting Mean W–B I Test Scores for Any Age 25 Years or Over.

1. From equation obtained by method of least squares.

$$y = 0.764x + 81.63$$

Where y = mean (most representative) score at any age and x = difference between 47.5 and the chronological age (A) at which score is desired.

Illustration. Required mean score for age 57.5.

$$y = 0.746 \ (47.5 - 57.5) + 81.63 = 74.2$$

2. From regression equation of the two variables, age on test score.

$$y = 0.735x + 85.77$$

where y = mean (most representative) score at any age, and x = difference between 40 and the chronological age (A) at which score is desired.

Illustration. Required mean score at age 70.

$$y = 735 \ (40 - 70) + 85.77 = 63.7$$

Note: Equation (1) seems to give better values, but the discrepancies in score obtained by the two methods are very slight (seldom more than 1 or 2 points).

On the other hand, one may use the above equations to calculate the age for which any given score is the mean. The case which is of particular interest is the age beyond which no further decline is possible. For our adult scale this age turns out to be approximately 150 years. This value may be obtained from either equation. Thus from equation (1)

$$4 = 0.746 \ (47.5 - A) + 81.63$$

setting $y = 4$ (lowest possible score). Whence, $A = 151.5$.

Appendix 2

Efficiency Quotients

An individual's efficiency quotient is his mental ability score on the Full Scale when compared with the score of the average individual of the peak age group. In the case of the W–B I, this is age group 20–24; in the WAIS it is the age group 25–34.

TABLE 59

W–B I *efficiency quotients*

Weighted Score	EQ	Weighted Score	EQ	Weighted Score	EQ	Weighted Score	EQ
5	34	35	56	65	77	95	98
6	35	36	56	66	77	96	99
7	35	37	57	67	78	97	99
8	36	38	57	68	79	98	100
9	37	39	58	69	79	99	101
10	37	40	59	70	80	100	101
11	38	41	59	71	81	101	102
12	39	42	60	72	81	102	103
13	40	43	61	73	82	103	104
14	40	44	62	74	83	104	104
15	41	45	62	75	84	105	105
16	42	46	63	76	84	106	106
17	42	47	64	77	85	107	106
18	43	48	64	78	86	108	107
19	44	49	65	79	86	109	108
20	44	50	66	80	87	110	109
21	45	51	67	81	88	111	109
22	46	52	67	82	89	112	110
23	47	53	68	83	89	113	111
24	47	54	69	84	90	114	111
25	48	55	69	85	91	115	112
26	49	56	70	86	92	120	116
27	49	57	71	87	92	125	119
28	50	58	72	88	93	130	123
29	51	59	72	89	94	135	126
30	52	60	73	90	94	140	130
31	52	61	74	91	95	145	133
32	53	62	74	92	96	150	137
33	54	63	75	93	96	155	141
34	55	64	76	94	97	160	144

TABLE 60
WAIS efficiency quotients

Scaled Score	EQ	Scaled Score	EQ	Scaled Score	EQ	Scaled Score	EQ
21	47	61	71	101	94	141	118
22	47	62	71	102	95	142	119
23	48	63	72	103	96	143	119
24	49	64	72	104	96	144	120
25	49	65	73	105	97	145	121
26	50	66	74	106	97	146	121
27	50	67	74	107	98	147	122
28	51	68	75	108	99	148	122
29	52	69	75	109	99	149	123
30	52	70	76	110	100	150	124
31	53	71	77	111	100	151	124
32	53	72	77	112	101	152	125
33	54	73	78	113	102	153	125
34	55	74	78	114	102	154	126
35	55	75	79	115	103	155	127
36	56	76	80	116	103	156	127
37	56	77	80	117	104	157	128
38	57	78	81	118	105	158	128
39	58	79	81	119	105	159	129
40	58	80	82	120	106	160	130
41	59	81	83	121	106	165	133
42	59	82	83	122	107	170	135
43	60	83	84	123	108	175	138
44	61	84	84	124	108	180	141
45	61	85	85	125	109	185	144
46	62	86	86	126	109	190	147
47	62	87	86	127	110	195	150
48	63	88	87	128	110	200	153
49	63	89	87	129	111		
50	64	90	88	130	112		
51	65	91	88	131	112		
52	65	92	89	132	113		
53	66	93	90	133	113		
54	66	94	90	134	114		
55	67	95	91	135	115		
56	68	96	91	136	115		
57	68	97	92	137	116		
58	69	98	93	138	116		
59	69	99	93	139	117		
60	70	100	94	140	118		

Difficulty (*p*) Values of Individual Items of WAIS Subtests Based on 1700 Cases of National Standardization

TABLE 61
Information

Item	Passing
	%
1. Flag	100
2. Ball	100
3. Months	99
4. Thermometer	98
5. Rubber	91
6. Presidents	86
7. Longfellow	86
8. Weeks	85
9. Panama	75
10. Brazil	74
11. Height	70
12. Italy	57
13. Clothes	56
14. Washington	61
15. Hamlet	53
16. Vatican	48
17. Paris	38
18. Egypt	36
19. Yeast	34
20. Population	29
21. Senators	29
22. Genesis	28
23. Temperature	24
24. Iliad	21
25. Blood vessels	16
26. Koran	15
27. Faust	7
28. Ethnology	3
29. Apocrypha	1

TABLE 62
Comprehension

Item	Passing*
	%
1. Clothes	100
2. Engine	99
3. Envelope	98
4. Bad company	95
5. Movies	80
6. Taxes	83
7. Iron	75
8. Child labor	74
9. Forest	73
10. Deaf	62
11. City land	53
12. Marriage	52
13. Brooks	38
14. Swallow	22

* Passing percent includes answers for which only partial credits were given.

TABLE 64
Similarities

Item	Passing*
	%
1. Orange—Banana	93
2. Coat—Dress	90
3. Axe—Saw	90
4. Dog—Lion	86
5. North—West	73
6. Eye—Ear	69
7. Air—Water	56
8. Table—Chair	55
9. Egg—Seed	46
10. Poem—Statue	38
11. Wood—Alcohol	21
12. Praise—Punishment	25
13. Fly—Tree	18

* Passing percent includes answers for which only partial credits were given.

TABLE 63
Arithmetic

Item	Passing	Item	Passing
	%		%
1	100	8	76
2	100	9	74
3	99	10	56
4	97	11	52
5	88	12	38
6	81	13	28
7	87	14	20

TABLE 65
Vocabulary (total sample, 1700, ages 16–65)

Item	Passing*	Item	Passing
	%		%
1. Bed	100	21. Terminate	55
2. Ship	100	22. Obstruct	58
3. Penny	100	23. Remorse	51
4. Winter	99	24. Sanctuary	49
5. Repair	98	25. Matchless	47
6. Breakfast	99	26. Reluctant	50
7. Fabric	92	27. Calamity	50
8. Slice	94	28. Fortitude	36
9. Assemble	90	29. Tranquil	36
10. Conceal	87	30. Edifice	22
11. Enormous	89	31. Compassion	29
12. Hasten	87	32. Tangible	30
13. Sentence	83	33. Perimeter	26
14. Regulate	80	34. Audacious	20
15. Commence	79	35. Ominous	20
16. Ponder	64	36. Tirade	17
17. Cavern	68	37. Encumber	19
18. Designate	63	38. Plagiarize	13
19. Domestic	65	39. Impale	14
20. Consume	61	40. Travesty	5

* Passing percent includes answers for which only partial credits were given.

TABLE 66
Vocabulary (3 age groups, Male)

Item	Passing*			Item	Passing		
	Ages 16–19 (189)	25–34 (142)	55–64 (94)		Ages 16–19 (189)	25–34 (142)	55–64 (94)
	%	%	%		%	%	%
1. Bed	100	100	100	21. Terminate	28	62	63
2. Ship	100	100	100	22. Obstruct	46	63	64
3. Penny	99	100	99	23. Remorse	30	46	49
4. Winter	100	97	99	24. Sanctuary	38	44	55
5. Repair	97	98	100	25. Matchless	38	54	54
6. Breakfast	99	100	100	26. Reluctant	35	50	54
7. Fabric	86	92	88	27. Calamity	32	41	64
8. Slice	93	94	88	28. Fortitude	25	34	39
9. Assemble	87	94	87	29. Tranquil	24	38	37
10. Conceal	82	90	87	30. Edifice	5	14	35
11. Enormous	88	89	88	31. Compassion	11	22	44
12. Hasten	76	88	86	32. Tangible	20	28	31
13. Sentence	88	83	76	33. Perimeter	27	36	22
14. Regulate	75	85	76	34. Audacious	9	13	29
15. Commence	65	87	78	35. Ominous	11	19	21
16. Ponder	47	58	67	36. Tirade	6	21	34
17. Cavern	67	70	65	37. Encumber	10	19	26
18. Designate	53	73	56	38. Plagiarize	4	15	18
19. Domestic	51	59	68	39. Impale	8	18	22
20. Consume	46	67	45	40. Travesty	1	3	13

* Passing percent includes answers for which only partial credits were given.

TABLE 67
Picture Completion

Item	Passing
	%
1. Knob	98
2. Tail	95
3. Nose	91
4. Handles	78
5. Diamond	76
6. Water	70
7. Nose piece	69
8. Peg	64
9. Oarlock	63
10. Base thread	63
11. Stars	57
12. Dog tracks	55
13. Florida	54
14. Stacks	51
15. Leg	49
16. Arm image	48
17. Finger	46
18. Shadow	42
19. Stirrup	42
20. Snow	23
21. Eyebrow	22

TABLE 69
Block Design

Item	Passing
	%
1.	99
2.	95
3.	97
4.	94
5.	88
6.	75
7.	75
8.	41
9.	35
10.	24

TABLE 68
Object Assembly

Item	Passing†
	%
1. Manikin	97
2. Profile	73
3. Hand	70
4. Elephant	67

† Percent passing includes cases which received full accuracy credit, but not necessarily any time bonus.

TABLE 70
Picture Arrangement

Item	Passing
	%
1. Nest	100
2. House	100
3. Hold up	88
4. Louie	56
5. Enter	54
6. Flirt	62
7. Fish	54
8. Taxi	35

Appendix 4

TABLE 71

Correlation between education and WAIS subtests,
Verbal, Performance and Full Scale Scores

	Age Group 18–19 (200)	Age Group 25–34 (300)	Age Group 45–54 (300)
Information	0.658	0.655	0.714
Comprehension	0.574	0.511	0.625
Arithmetic	0.522	0.490	0.585
Similarities	0.600	0.522	0.612
Digit Span	0.476	0.421	0.471
Vocabulary	0.624	0.649	0.688
Digit Symbol	0.609	0.590	0.586
Picture Completion	0.473	0.441	0.486
Block Design	0.465	0.397	0.451
Picture Arrangement	0.453	0.476	0.516
Object Assembly	0.409	0.349	0.427
Verbal Score	0.688	0.662	0.733
Performance Score	0.597	0.570	0.614
Total Score	0.688	0.658	0.718
Mean	10.73	10.90	9.37
S.D.	2.09	2.88	3.28

TABLE 72

Correlation of WAIS Scale Scores with age*

Sex	No.	Verbal Score	Performance Score	Full Scale Score	Age
M	710	−0.233	−0.509	−0.391	
	Mean	58.275	41.120	99.317	48.873
	S.D.	16.259	13.660	27.927	15.142
F	742	−0.305	−0.551	−0.440	49.837
	Mean	55.807	40.646	96.535	15.245
	S.D.	15.877	13.245	26.963	
Total	1452	−0.271	−0.530	−0.416	
	Mean	57.014	40.877	97.895	49.366
	S.D.	16.112	13.452	27.472	15.205

* Cases 25 years and over from National Standardization and complete cases from Old Age Study.

251

Appendix 5

TABLE 73

*Frequency distributions WAIS of Verbal, Performance and Full Scale IQ's
of National Sample and Old-Age Sample combined (Total, 2052 subjects)*

IQ's	Verbal	Performance	Full Scale
148–152..................	—	—	1
143–147..................	1	1	—
138–142..................	7	1	3
133–137..................	17	12	12
128–132..................	32	28	26
123–127..................	78	63	64
118–122..................	128	102	145
113–117..................	156	188	165
108–112..................	211	250	224
103–107..................	255	275	274
98–102..................	277	283	278
93–97..................	258	268	255
88–92..................	229	205	220
83–87..................	149	123	135
78–82..................	114	103	107
73–77..................	76	58	55
68–72..................	33	44	49
63–67..................	17	21	18
58–62..................	9	13	11
53–57..................	4	9	6
48–52..................	1	3	3
43–47..................	—	2	1
Mean..................	99.95	99.82	99.91
S.D..................	14.82	15.03	14.74

Appendix 6

TABLE 74

Intercorrelation of the subtests of the WAIS (ages 16–17,* 100 males and 100 females)

Test	In-formation	Compre-hension	Arithmetic	Similari-ties	Digit Span	Vocabu-lary	Digit Symbol	Picture Comple-tion	Block Design	Picture Arrange-ment	Object Assembly
Comprehension	0.71										
Arithmetic	0.68	0.61									
Similarities	0.67	0.66	0.62								
Digit Span	0.50	0.49	0.57	0.49							
Vocabulary	0.83	0.72	0.66	0.71	0.54						
Digit Symbol	0.48	0.43	0.42	0.44	0.43	0.51					
Picture Completion	0.63	0.58	0.52	0.52	0.47	0.63	0.42				
Block Design	0.58	0.55	0.60	0.60	0.52	0.58	0.44	0.61			
Picture Arrangement	0.53	0.58	0.51	0.54	0.44	0.57	0.50	0.54	0.60		
Object Assembly	0.35	0.34	0.38	0.41	0.30	0.42	0.32	0.51	0.56	0.48	
Verbal Score†	0.81	0.76	0.75	0.75	0.60	0.84	0.54	0.67	0.69	0.64	0.44
Performance Score†	0.66	0.64	0.63	0.65	0.56	0.69	0.51	0.67	0.71	0.68	0.59
Full Scale Score†	0.79	0.75	0.74	0.75	0.62	0.82	0.57	0.72	0.75	0.70	0.53
Mean	9.1	9.3	9.0	9.4	9.3	8.4	9.8	9.4	9.7	10.3	9.4
S.D.	2.8	2.9	2.7	2.8	2.9	2.5	2.7	2.5	3.2	3.0	3.1

* Intercorrelations of subtests of other age groups will be found in WAIS Manual (524) and Doppelt and Wallace article on standardization of WAIS for older persons (147).

† Verbal Score: sum of 6 tests; Performance Score: sum of 5 tests; Full Scale Score: sum of 11 tests

BIBLIOGRAPHY

1. ACKLESBERG, S. B. Vocabulary and mental deterioration in senile dementia. J. abnorm. soc. Psychol., 1944, **39**, 393–406.
2. ADCOCK, C., MCCREARY, J., RITCHIE, J., AND SOMERSET, H. An analysis of Maori scores with the Wechsler Bellevue. Aust. J. Phychol., 1954, **6**, 16–30.
3. AEPPLI-TANNER, L. Anwendung des Wechsler Bellevue Tests in der Schweiz. Schweiz. Z. Psychol., 1954, **13**, 136–145.
4. AITA, J. A., ARMITAGE, S. G., REITAN, R. M., AND RABINOWITZ, A. The use of certain psychological tests in the evaluation of brain injury. J. gen. Psychol., 1947, **37**, 25–44.
5. ALDERDICE, E. T., AND BUTLER, A. J. An analysis of the performance of mental defectives on the Revised Stanford Binet and the Wechsler-Bellevue Intelligence Scale. Amer. J. ment. Defic., 1952, **56**, 609–614.
6. ALEXANDER, R. S., CRUTCHLOW, E., AND HOFFMANN, M. A selective survey of the Wechsler Bellevue section of Rapaport's Diagnostic Psychological Testing. Canad. J. Phychol., 1951, **7**, 289–290.
7. ALEXANDER, W. P. Intelligence, concrete and abstract. Brit. J. Psychol., Monog. Suppl., 1935, No. 19.
8. ALIMENA, B. Norms for scatter analysis on the Wechsler Intelligence Scale. J. clin. Psychol., 1951, **7**, 289–290.
9. ALLEN, R. M. The test performance of the brain injured. J. clin. Psychol., 1947, **3**, 225–230.
10. ALLEN, R. M. The test performance of the brain diseased. J. clin. Psychol., 1948, **4**, 281–284.
11. ALLEN, R. M. A note on the use of the Wechsler Bellevue Scale; Mental deterioration index with brain injured patients. J. clin. Psychol., 1948, **4**, 88–89.
12. ALLEN, R. M. A comparison of test performances of the brain injured and brain diseased. Amer. J. Psychiat., 1949, **106**, 195–198.
13. ALLEN, R. M. An analysis of the comparative evaluation of Allen's brain injured patients and of normal subjects. J. clin. Psychol., 1949, **5**, 422.
14. ALLEN, R. M., AND KRATO, J. C. The test performance of the encephalopathic. J. ment. Sci., 1949, **95**, 369–372.
15. ALLEN, R. M., THORNTON, T. E., AND STENGEN, C. A. Ammons and Wechsler Test performances of college and psychiatric subjects. J. clin. Psychol., 1954, **10**, 387–381.
16. ALTUS, W. D. The differential validity and difficulty of subtests of the Wechsler Mental Ability Scale. Psychol. Bull., 1945, **42**, 238–239.
17. ALTUS, W. D. Adjustment and subtest variation on the Army Wechsler for the mentally limited. J. genet. Psychol., 1949, **40**, 167–176.
18. ALTUS, W. D., AND CLARK, J. H. Subtest variation of the Wechsler Bellevue for two institutionalized behavior problem groups. J. consult. Psychol., 1949, **13**, 444–447.
19. ANASTASI, A. *Psychological Testing.* New York: The Macmillan Co., 1954.
20. ANDERSEN, A. L. The effect of laterality localization of brain damage on Wechsler Bellevue indices of deterioration. J. clin. Psychol., 1950, **6**, 191–194.
21. ANDERSEN, A. L. The effect of laterality localization of focal brain lesions on the Wechsler Bellevue subtests. J. clin. Psychol., 1951, **7**, 149–153.

22. ANDERSON, E. E., *et al.* A comparison of Wechsler Bellevue, Binet, ACE at college level; Wilson College Studies in Psychology I. J. Psychol., 1942, **14,** 317–326.

23. ANSBACHER, H. L., AND ANSBACHER, R. Social interest and intelligence; Adler's contribution to the theory of intelligence. Unpublished lecture, New York, 1953.

24. ARMITAGE, S. G. An analysis of certain psychological tests used for the evaluation of brain injury. Psychol. Monog., 1946, 60–277.

25. ARMSTRONG, C. P. Tests as diagnostic aids in clinical practice. Amer. J. ment. Defic., 1943, **47,** 270–276.

26. ARMSTRONG, R. G. A comparison of the comprehension subtests of the Wechsler Bellevue Intelligence Scale, Forms I and II. J. clin. Psychol., 1953, **9,** 172–176.

27. Memoirs of the National Academy of Sciences. 1921, **15,** 189–404.

28. ARONOV, B. Education and intelligence variables in the psychopath's W–B Intelligence Test achievement. Paper read at Midwest Psychological Association, Cleveland, April, 1952.

29. ARTHUR, GRACE *A Point Scale of Performance Tests.* Vol. 2, New York: Commonwealth Fund, 1933.

30. ATKEY, R. R. An empirical validation of the Wechsler Bellevue Test for mental deterioration. New York: The Macmillan Co., 1954.

31. ATWELL, C. R. Psychometric changes after lobotomy. J. nerv. ment. Dis., 1950, **111,** 165–166.

32. BABCOCK, H. An experiment in the measurement of mental deterioration. Arch. Psychol., New York, 1930, No. 117.

33. BALDWIN, J. M. *Dictionary of Philosophy and Psychology.* New York: The Macmillan Co., 1902.

34. BALINSKY, B. An analysis of the mental factors of various age groups from 9 to 60. Genet. Psychol. Monogr., 1941, **23,** 191–234.

35. BALINSKY, B., ISRAEL, H., AND WECHSLER, D. The relative effectiveness of the Stanford Binet and the Bellevue Intelligence Scale in diagnosing mental deficiency. Amer. J. Orthopsychiat., 1939, **9,** 798–801.

36. BALINSKY, B., AND SHAW, H. W. The contribution of the WAIS to a Management Appraisal program. Personnel Psychol., 1956, **9,** 207–209.

37. BARBEAU, G. L., AND PINARD, A. Épreuve individuelle d'intelligence générale. Le Centre de Psychologie et de Pedagogie, Montreal, 1941.

38. BARNETT, I. The use of the Z-scores in equating the Wechsler Bellevue subtests. J. clin. Psychol., 1950, **16,** 184–188.

39. BATTERSBY, W. S., TEUBER, H. L., AND BENDER, M. Problem solving behavior in man with frontal and occipital brain injuries. J. Psychol., 1953, **35,** 329–351.

40. BATTERSBY, W. S., KRIEGER, H. P., AND BENDER, M. Visual and tactile discriminative learning in patients with cerebral tumors. Amer. J. Psychol., 1955, **68,** 562–574.

41. BAUER, R. W., AND BECKA, D. M. Intellect after cerebral vascular accident. J. nerv. ment. Dis., 1954, **120,** 379–384.

41a. BAY, M., AND BERKS, M. Comprehension, similarities and digit symbols of the Wechsler Bellevue Scale used in a court clinic. Amer. Psychologist, 1948, **3,** 365–372.

42. BAYLEY, N. Consistency and variability in the growth of intelligence from birth to 18 years. J. genet. Psychol., 1949, **75,** 165–196.

43. BAYLEY, N. On the growth of intelligence. Amer. Psychologist, 1955, **10,** 805–818.

44. BAYLEY, N. Data on the growth of intelligence between 16 and 21 years as measured by the Wechsler Bellevue Scale. J. genet. Psychol., 1957, **90,** 3–15.

45. BECKER, G. J. The relationship between the Thurstone SRA Primary Mental Abilities Tests and the Wechsler Bellevue Scale. Unpublished doctoral dissertation, Fordham University, New York, 1948.

46. BENDER, L. The Visual Motor Gestalt Test and its clinical use. Research Monograph No. 3. New York: American Orthopsychiatric Association, 1938; Arch, Neur. & Psychiat., 1933, **30,** 514–537.

47. BENSBERG, G. J., AND SLOAN, W. A study of Wechsler's concept of normal deterioration in older mental defectives. J. clin. Psychol., 1950, **6,** 359–362.

48. BENTON, A. L., AND HOWELL, L. I. The use of psychological tests in evaluation of intellectual function. Psychosom. Med., 1941, **3,** 138–151.

49. BENTON, A., WEIDER, A., AND BLAUVELT, J. Performance of adult patients on Wechsler Bellevue Intelligence Scale and Revised Stanford Binet. Psychiat. Quart., 1941, **15,** 802–806.

50. BERNSTEIN, R., AND CORSINI, R. J. Wechsler Bellevue patterns of female delinquents. J. clin. Psychol., 1953, **9,** 176–179.

51. BERKOWITZ, B. The Wechsler Bellevue performance of white males past age 50. J. Geront., 1953, **8,** 76–80.

52. BIJOU, S. W. The psychometric pattern approach as an aid to clinical analysis; a review. Amer. J. ment. Defic., 1942, **46,** 354–362.

53. BINET, A. Nouvelles recherches sur la mesure de niveau intellectual chez les enfants d'école. Ann. Psychol., 1911, **17,** 145–201.

54. BINET, A., AND SIMON, T. Le dévelopment de l'intelligence chez les enfants. Ann. Psychol., 1908, **14,** 1–94.

55. BIRREN, J. E. A factorial analysis of the Wechsler Bellevue Scale given to an elderly population. Amer. Psychologist, 1951, **6,** 398–399; J. consult. Psychol., 1952, **16,** 399–405.

56. BLAKE, R., AND MCCARTY, B. A comparative evaluation of the Wechsler Bellevue mental deterioration index distribution of Allen's brain injured patients and normal subjects. J. clin. Psychol., 1948, **4,** 415–418.

56a. BLUM, M. J., AND BALINSKY, B. *Counseling and Psychology.* New York: Prentice-Hall, 1951.

57. BOEHM, A. E., AND SARASON, S. B. Does Wechsler's formula distinguish intellectual deterioration from mental deficiency? J. abnorm. soc. Psychol., 1947, **42,** 356–358.

58. BOTWINICK, J. Wechsler Bellevue split-half subtest reliabilities; differences in ages and mental status. J. consult. Psychol., 1953, **17,** 225–228.

59. BOTWINICK, J., AND BIRREN, J. E. The measurement of intellectual deterioration in senile psychosis and psychosis with cerebral arteriosclerosis. Amer. Psychologist, 1951, **15,** 145–150.

60. BOTWINICK, J., AND BIRREN, J. E. The measurement of intellectual decline in the senile psychoses. J. consult. Psychol., 1951, **15,** 145–150.

61. BOTWINICK, J., AND BIRREN, J. E. Differential decline in the Wechsler Bellevue subtests in the senile psychoses. J. Geront., 1951, **6,** 365–368.

62. BRADWAY, K., AND BENSON, S. The application of the method of extreme deviations to Rapaport's Wechsler Bellevue Data. J. clin. Psychol., 1955, **11,** 285–291.

63. BRECHER, S. The value of diagnostic signs for schizophrenia on the Wechsler Bellevue Adult Intelligence Test. Psychiatr. Quart. Suppl., 1946, **20**, 58–64.

64. BRIEGER, B. Cultural differences as indicated by an analysis of W–B with special references to problems of clinical diagnosis and acculturation. Unpublished doctoral dissertation, University of Illinois, 1952.

65. BRIEGER, B. The use of the Wechsler Bellevue Picture Arrangement as a projective technique. J. consult. Psychol., 1956, **20**, 132.

66. BRODY, A. B. A factorial study of intellectual functioning in normal and abnormal adults. Unpublished doctoral dissertation, Columbia University, New York, 1950.

67. BRODY, M. B. A survey of the results of intelligence tests in psychosis. Brit. J. med. Psychol., 1942, **19**, 225–261.

68. BRODY, M. B. Mental testing. J. ment. Sci., 1944, **90**, 127–151.

69. BROOKS, L. E. The application of the Hunt-Minnesota Test for organic brain damage and the Wechsler Bellevue Test to psychotic patients before and after shock therapy. Unpublished doctoral dissertation, Fordham University, New York, 1946.

70. BROWER, D. The relations of visuo-motor conflict to personality traits and cardiovascular activity. J. genet. Psychol., 1948, **38**, 69–99.

71. BROWER, D., AND ABT, L. E. *Progress in Clinical Psychology*. Grune & Stratton, Inc., New York, 1952.

72. BROWN, M. N. A critique of the Wechsler Bellevue system of weighted scores. J. clin. Psychol., 1949, **5**, 170–173.

73. BROWN, M. N., AND BRYAN, E. Sex difference in intelligence. J. clin. Psychol., 1955, **11**, 303–304.

74. BROWN, M. N., AND BRYAN, E. The interpretation of the Wechsler Bellevue Intelligence Scale in terms of altitude scores. Amer. Psychologist, 1955, **8**, 431.

75. BROWN, J. F., RAPAPORT, D., DUBIN, S., AND TILLMAN, C. G. The scatter on the Bellevue Adult Intelligence Scale. Paper read at Meeting of Mid West. Psychol. Ass., Athens, Ohio, April, 1941.

76. BROWN, J. F., RAPAPORT, D., DUBIN, S., AND TILLMAN, C. G. An analysis of scatter in a test battery used in clinical diagnosis. Psychol. Bull., 1941, **38**, 715.

77. BROWN, R. R., AND PARTINGTON, J. E. The intelligence of the narcotic drug addict. J. genet. Psychol., 1942, **26**, 175.

78. BROWN, R. R., AND PARTINGTON, J. E. A psychometric comparison of narcotic addicts with hospital attendants. J. genet. Psychol., 1942, **27**, 71–79.

79. BRYAN, G. C., AND BROWN, M. H. The use of Wechsler Bellevue ratio scores in the differential diagnosis of brain damaged adolescents. Amer. Psychologist, 1955, **8**, 337–338.

80. BURIK, T. E. Investigation of the learning involved in the Digit Symbol subtest of the Wechsler Bellevue Intelligence Scale. Unpublished doctoral dissertation, Fordham University, New York, 1949.

81. BURIK, T. E. Relative roles of the learning and motor factors involved in the Digit Symbot Test. J. Psychol., 1950, **30**, 33–42.

82. BURNHAM, C. A. A study of the degree of relationship between Rorschach H% and Wechsler Bellevue Picture Arrangement scores. Rorsch. Res. Exch., 1949, **13**, 206–209.

83. Buros, O. K. *The 1940 Mental Measurements Yearbook.* The Gryphon Press, Highland Park, N. J., 1941, pp. 264–267.

84. Buros, O. K. *The Third Mental Measurements Yearbook.* Rutgers University Press, New Brunswick, N. J., 1949, pp. 297–303.

85. Buros, O. K. *The Fourth Mental Measurements Yearbook.* The Gryphon Press, Highland Park, N. J., 1953, pp. 361–366.

86. Burt, Cyril. *Mental and Scholastic Tests.* Staples Press, London, 1933.

87. Burt, Cyril. The structure of mind; a review of the results of factor analysis. Brit. J. educ. Psychol., 1949, **19**, 100–111, 176–199.

88. Burton, A. The use of the psychometric and projective tests in clinical psychology. J. Psychol., 1949, **28**, 451–456.

89. Butler, A. Test-retest and split-half reliabilities of the Wechsler Bellevue Scales and subtests with mental defectives. Amer. J. ment. Defic., 1954, **59**, 80–84.

90. Canepa, G. La valutazione dell'intelligenza nell'adulto. Adattamento italiano alla scala Wechsler Bellevue. Sistema Nervoso, 1951, Anno III, **5–6**, 392–482.

91. Canter, A. H. Direct and indirect measures of psychological deficit in multiple sclerosis. J. gen. Psychol., 1951, **44**, 3–50.

92. Carp, A. Psychological test performance and insulin shock therapy. Unpublished doctoral dissertation, Stanford University, California, 1948.

93. Carp, A. Performance on the Wechsler Bellevue Scale and insulin shock therapy. J. abnorm. soc. Psychol., 1950, **45**, 127–136.

94. Cattell, R. B. The measurement of adult intelligence. Psychol. Bull., 1943, **40**, 153–193.

95. Catterall, C. D. Reading pupils through the Wechsler Bellevue Intelligence Test. Claremont College Reading Conference, Fourteenth Yearbook, 1949, Claremont Curriculum Laboratory, 1949, pp. 136–141.

96. Charles, D. C. Ability and accomplishments of persons earlier judged mentally deficient. Genet. Psychol. Monogr., 1953, **47**, 3–71.

97. Chesrow, E. J., Wozika, P. H. and Reinitz, A. H. A psychometric evaluation of aged white males. Geriatrics, 1949, **4**, 169–177.

98. Clark, J. H. The relationship of Wechsler Bellevue pattern to psychiatric diagnosis of army prisoners. Amer. Psychologist, 1950, **5**, 462; J. consult. Psychol., 1950, **14**, 493–495.

99. Clark, J. H. The diagnosis of a patient with limited capacity. J. Person., 1946, **15**, 105–112.

100. Clark, J. H. Intelligence test results obtained from a specific type of Army AWOL. Educ. psychol. Measmt., 1948, **8**, 677–682.

101. Clark, J. H. Subtest variation on the Wechsler Bellevue for two institutionalized behavior problem groups. Amer. Psychol., 1949, **4**, 395.

102. Clark, J. H. An investigation of certain relationships between the California Test of Mental Maturity and Wechsler Bellevue Intelligence Scale. J. gen. Psychol., 1949, **41**, 21–25.

103. Cleveland, D. E., and Dysinger, D. W. Mental deterioration in senile psychosis. J. abnorm. soc. Psychol., 1944, **39**, 368–372.

104. Cohen, B. Validity of the short form of the Wechsler Bellevue on four psychiatric groups. Unpublished doctoral dissertation, University of Iowa, 1945; Amer. Psychologist, 1946, **1**, 464.

105. Cohen, B., and Steilsel, I. M. An evaluation of the various short forms of the Wechsler Bellevue Test. Proc. Iowa Acad. Sci., 1947, **54**, 221–226.

106. COHEN, D. Wechsler Bellevue Test score patterns in anxiety state and situation reactions due to combat. Unpublished doctoral dissertation, University of Pittsburgh, 1947.

107. COHEN, E. Is there examiner bias on the Wechsler Bellevue? Proc. Okla. Acad. Sci., 1950, **31**, 15–153.

108. COHEN, J. A comparative analysis of the factors underlying intelligence test performance of different neuropsychiatric groups; multiple factor analysis of the Wechsler Bellevue Intelligence Scale performance of schizophrenic, psychoneurotic and brain damaged groups. Unpublished doctoral dissertation, New York University, 1950.

109. COHEN, J. A factor analytic comparison of intelligence test performance of different neuropsychiatric groups. Amer. Psychologist, 1951, **6**, 334–335.

110. COHEN, J. A factor analytically based rationale for the Wechsler Bellevue. J. consult. Psychol., 1952, **16**, 272, 277.

111. COHEN, J. Factors underlying Wechsler Bellevue performance of three neuropsychiatric groups. J. abnorm. soc. Psychol., 1952, **47**, 359–365.

112. COHEN, J. A comparative factor analysis of WAIS performance for 4 age groups between 18 and 80. Amer. Psychologist, 1956, **11**, 449.

112a. COLE, E., BAGGETT, M., AND MACMULLEN, M. Mental and performance testing of neurologic patients. Arch. Neurol. Psychiat., 1947, **58**, 104–107.

113. COLE, D., AND WELEBA, L. Comparison data on the Wechsler Bellevue and the WAIS. J. clin. Psychol., 1956, **12**, 198–200.

114. COLLINS, A. L. Epileptic intelligence. J. consult. Psychol., 1951, **15**, 392–399.

115. COPPLE, G. E. Senescent decline on the Wechsler Bellevue Intelligence Scale. Unpublished doctoral dissertation, Univer. Pittsburgh Bull., 1949, **45**, 8.

116. CORNELL, E. L., AND COXE, W. C. *A Performance Ability Scale.* New York: World Book Company, 1934.

117. CORSINI, R. J., AND FASSETT, K. K. The validity of Wechsler's Mental Deterioration Index. J. consult. Psychol., 1952, **16**, 462–468.

118. CORSINI, R. J. Intelligence and aging. J. genet. Psychol., 1953, **83**, 249–264.

119. COTZIN, M., AND GALLAGHER, J. The Southbury Scale; a valid abbreviated Wechsler Bellevue Scale for mental defectives. J. consult. Psychol., 1950, **14**, 358–364.

120. COTZIN, M., AND GALLAGHER, J. Validity of short forms of the Wechsler Bellevue Scale for mental defectives. J. consult. Psychol., 1949, **13**, 357–365.

121. CRONBACH, L. J. *Essentials of Psychological Testing.* New York: Harper & Brothers, 1949.

122. CROWN, S. Psychological changes following prefrontal leucotomy; a review. J. ment. Sci., 1951, **97**, 49–83.

123. CUMMINGS, S. B., MACPHEE, H., AND WRIGHT, H. A rapid method of estimating the IQ's of subnormal white adults. J. Psychol., 1946, **21**, 81–89.

124. CUTTS, R. A., AND LANE O'KELLY, M. The effect of hospitalization on Wechsler Bellevue subtest scores by mental defectives. Amer. J. ment. Defic., 1947, **51**, 391–393.

125. CUTTS, R. A., AND SLOAN, W. Test pattern of adjusted defectives on the Wechsler Bellevue Test. Amer. J. ment. Defic., 1945, **50**, 98–101.

126. DANA, R. H. A comparison of 4 Verbal subtests of Wechsler Bellevue Form I and the WAIS. J. clin. Psychol., 1957, **13**, 70–71.

127. DANDY, W. E. Removal of the right cerebral hemisphere for certain tumors with hemiplegia. J. A. M. A., 1928, **90**, 823–825.

128. DAUMEZON, M. G., AND MOOR, L. Remarques sur l'utilisation du test de Wechsler deterioration et inefficience. Ann. medico-psychologique, 1955, **1**, 94–98.

129. DAVIDSON, K. S., GIBBY, R. G., McNEIL, E. B., SEGAL, S., AND SILVERMAN, H. A preliminary study of negro and white differences on Form I of the Wechsler Bellevue Scale. J. consult. Psychol., 1950, **14**, 489–492.

130. DAVIS, F. B. Significant difference between pairs of scores derived from Wechsler Bellevue and Wechsler Adult Scales, 1956 (personal communication).

131. DAVIS, F. B. A factor analysis of the Wechsler Bellevue Scale. Educ. psychol. Measmt., 1956, **16**, 127–146.

131a. DAYTON, N. A. Report of the Mental Deficiency Committee 1939. Public Document 117. Commonwealth of Massachusetts.

132. DECROLY, I. Épreuve nouvelle pour l'examination mental. Ann. Psychol., 1914, **20**, 140–159.

133. DELATTRE, L., AND COLE, D. A comparison of the WISC and the Wechsler Bellevue. J. consult. Psychol., 1952, **16**, 228–230.

133a. DELP, H. A. Correlations between the Kent EGY and the Wechsler batteries. J. clin. Psychol., 1953, **9**, 73–75.

134. DEMARTINO, H. A. The Wechsler Bellevue Intelligence Scale as a predictor of success in a college of engineering. Mich. Acad. Sci., 1954, **39**, 459–465.

135. DERNER, G. F., ABORN, M., AND CANTER, A. H. The reliability of the Wechsler Bellevue subtests and Scales. J. consult. Psychol., 1950, **14**, 172–179.

136. DESAI, M. M. The relationship of the Wechsler Bellevue Verbal Scale and the Progressive Matrices Test. J. consult. Psychol., 1955, **19**, 1–19.

137. DIAMOND, S. The Wechsler Bellevue Intelligence Scale and certain vocational aptitude tests. J. Psychol., 1947, **24**, 279–282.

138. DIERS, W. C., AND BROWN, C. C. Psychometric patterns associated with multiple sclerosis. I. Wechsler Bellevue Patterns. Arch. Neurol. Psychiat., 1950, **63**, 760–765.

138a. DIERS, W. C., AND BROWN, C. C. Rorschach "organic signs" and intelligence level. J. consult. Psychol., 1951, **15**, 343–345.

139. DILLER, L. A comparison of the test performances of delinquent and non-delinquent girls. J. genet. Psychol., 1952, **81**, 167–183.

140. DORKEN, H., AND GREENBLOOM, G. Psychological investigation of senile dementia; the Wechsler Bellevue Adult Intelligence Scale. Geriatrics, 1953, **8**, 324–333.

141. DOLL, EDGAR Improper use of the IQ. J. Delinquency, 1920, **5**, 67–70.

142. DOLL, EDGAR A genetic scale of social maturity. Amer. J. Orthopsychiat., 1935, **5**, 180–188.

143. DOLL, EDGAR Notes on the concept of mental deficiency. Amer. J. Psychol., 1941, **54**, 116–124.

144. DOLL, EDGAR The essentials of an inclusive concept of mental deficiency. Amer. J. ment. Defic., 1946, **50**, 503–511.

145. DOLL, Edgar Feeble-mindedness vs. intellectual retardation. Amer. J. ment. Defic., 1947, **51**, 450–459.

146. DOPPELT, J. Estimating the Full Scale score on the Wechsler Bellevue Adult Intelligence Scale from scores on 4 subtests. J. consult. Psychol., 1956, **20**, 63–66.

147. DOPPELT, J., AND WALLACE, W. Standardization of the WAIS for older persons. J. abnorm. soc. Psychol., 1955, **51**, 312–330.

148. DOPPELT, J., AND WALLACE, W.   The performance of older people on Wechsler Adult Intelligence Scale. Amer. Psychologist, 1955, **8**, 338–339.

149. DUBIN, S., AND THALER, M.   The use of psychological tests on schizophrenic patients before and after shock treatment. Amer. Psychologist, 1947, **2**, 283.

150. DUNCAN, J. O.   Correlation between the Wechsler Bellevue and Stanford Binet vocabulary lists. Med. Tech. Bull., 1953, **4**, 45–47.

151. DUREA, M. A., AND TAYLOR, G. J.   The mentality of delinquent boys appraised by the Wechsler Intelligence Scales. Amer. J. ment. Defic., 1948, **52**, 342–344.

152. Edrington, T. C.   The Wechsler Bellevue Test in relation to the demonstrated academic performance of the Naval R.O.T.C. midshipmen in Tulane University. Unpublished doctoral dissertation, Tulane University, New Orleans, 1950.

153. EGLASH, A.   Validation of the Wechsler "shoes" item. J. abnorm. soc. Psychol., 1950, **45**, 733–734.

154. ELONEN, A., AND KORNER, A.   Pre- and postoperative psychological observations on a case of frontal lobectomy. J. abnorm. soc. Psychol., 1948, **43**, 532–543.

155. ESTES, S. G.   Deviations of Wechsler Bellevue subtest scores from vocabulary level in superior adults. J. abnorm. soc. Psychol., 1946, **41**, 226–228.

156. FELDMAN, F., AND CAMERON, D. E.   Speech in senility. Amer. J. Psychiat., 1944, **101**, 64–67.

157. FICCA, S. C.   Relationship of autonomic blood pressure pattern types of subject's performance on the Wechsler Bellevue and the Rorschach Test. Unpublished doctoral dissertation, Pennsylvania State College, 1950; State College, Pa., 1951, **13**, 398–400.

157a. FINE, R.   Psychoanalytic observations on chess and chess masters. Psychoanalysis, 1956, 4.

158. FINKELSTEIN, M., GERBOTH, R., AND WESTERHOLD, R.   Standardization of a short form of the Wechsler Vocabulary subtest. J. clin. Psychol., 1952, **8**, 133–135.

159. FISHBEIN, S.   An evaluation of the Wechsler Bellevue Intelligence tests on the college level. Unpublished doctoral dissertation, Temple University 1941.

160. FISHER, K. A.   Changes in test performance of ambulatory depressed patients undergoing electric shock therapy. J. gen. Psychol., 1949, **41**, 195–232.

161. FISHER, S., AND SUNUKJIAN, H.   Intellectual disparities in abnormal groups and their relationship to disturbance. J. clin. Psychol., 1950, **6**, 288–290.

162. FOSTER, A.   Age and the Wechsler Bellevue Scattergraph. J. clin. Psychol., 1947, **3**, 396–397.

163. FOSTER, C.   A study of the Wechsler Bellevue Intelligence Scale as a vocational guidance indicator of engineering aptitude. Unpublished doctoral dissertation, University of Southern California, 1947.

164. FOX, C., AND BIRREN, J. E.   The differential decline of subtest scores of the Wechsler Intelligence Scale in 60–69-year-old individuals. J. genet. Psychol., 1950, **77**, 313–317.

165. FOX, C., AND BIRREN, J. E.   The differential decline of Wechsler subtest scores in 60–69-year-old individuals. Amer. Psychologist, 1950, **5**, 467.

166. FOX, C., AND BIRREN, J. E.   Intellectual deterioration in the aged; agreement between the W–B and the Babcock-Levy. J. consult. Psychol., 1950, **14**, 305–310.

167. FRANDSEN, A. N. Wechsler Bellevue Intelligence Scale and high school achievement. J. appl. Psychol., 1950, **34**, 406–411.
168. FRANK, G. H. Patterning of the schizophrenic on the Wechsler Bellevue Intelligence Test. Psychol. Newsltr., 1953, **46**, 7–12.
169. FRANK, G. H., CORRIE, C. C., AND FOGEL, J. An empirical critique of research with the Wechsler Bellevue in differential psychodiagnosis. J. clin. Psychol., 1955, **11**, 3, 291–293.
170. FRANKLIN, J. C. Discriminative value and patterns of the Wechsler Bellevue Scales in the examination of delinquent negro boys. Educ. psychol. Measmt., 1945, **5**, 71–85.
171. FREEMAN, A. V. Wechsler Bellevue scatter in schizophrenics and normal controls. Amer. Psychologist, 1948, **3**, 280–821.
172. FRENCH, E., AND HUNT, W. A. The relationship of scatter in test performance to intelligence level. J. clin. Psychol., 1951, **7**, 95–98.
173. GAIER, E. L., AND LEE, M. C. Pattern analysis; the configural approach to predictive measurement. Psychol. Bull., 1953, **50**, 140–148.
174. GARFIELD, S. L. A preliminary appraisal of Wechsler Bellevue scatter patterns in schizophrenia. Med. J. Aust., 1947, **1**, 243–244.
175. GARFIELD, S. L. An appraisal of the Wechsler Bellevue scatter patterns in schizophrenia. Amer. Psychologist, 1947, **2**, 425.
176. GARFIELD, S. L. A note on Patterson's article "The W–B Scale as an aid in psychiatric diagnosis." J. clin. Psychol., 1947, **3**, 198–200.
177. GARFIELD, S. L. Wechsler Bellevue patterns in schizophrenia. J. consult. Psychol., 1948, **12**, 32–36.
178. GARFIELD, S. L. An evaluation of Wechsler patterns in schizophrenia. J. consult. Psychol., 1949, **13**, 279–287.
179. GARFIELD, S. L., AND FEY, W. A comparison of the Wechsler Bellevue and Shipley Hartford Scales as measures of mental impairment. J. consult. Psychol., 1948, **12**, 259–264.
180. GARDNER, W. J. Injection of procaine into the brain to locate speech area in left-handed persons. Arch. Neurol. Psychiat., 1941, **46**, 1035–1038.
181. GARDNER, W. J., KARNASH, L. J., McCLURE, C., AND GARDER, A. K. Residual function following hemispherectomy for tumor and infantile hemiplegia. Brain, 1955, **78**, 487–502.
182. GAULT, U. Factorial patterns on the Wechsler Intelligence Scales. Aust. J. Psychol., 1954, **6**, 85–90.
182a. GEIL, C. A. A clinically useful abbreviated W–B Scale. J. Psychol., 1945, **20**, 101–108.
183. GERBOTH, R. A study of the two forms of the Wechsler Bellevue Intelligence Scale. J. consult. Psychol., 1950, **14**, 365–370.
184. GERSTEIN, R. A. A suggested method for analyzing and extending the use of the Wechsler Bellevue vocabulary responses. J. consult. Psychol., 1949, **13**, 366–370.
185. GIBBY, R. G. A preliminary survey of certain aspects of Form II of the Wechsler Bellevue Scale as compared to Form I. J. clin. Psychol., 1949, **5**, 165–169.
186. GILBERT, J. G. Mental efficiency in senescence. Arch. Psychol., 1935, No. 188.
187. GILBERT, J. G. Memory loss in senescence. J. abnorm. soc. Psychol., 1941, **36**, 73–86.
188. GILHOOLY, F. M. Wechsler Bellevue reliability and validity of certain diagnostic signs of neurosis. J. consult. Psychol., 1950, **14**, 83–87.

189. GILHOOLY, F. M. The relationship between variability and ability on the Wechsler Bellevue Scale. J. clin. Psychol., 1950, **14**, 46–48.

190. GILHOOLY, F. M. Correction on above (189). J. consult. Psychol., 1950, **14**, 329.

191. GILLILAND, A. R., WITTMAN, P., AND GOLDMAN, M. Patterns and scatter of mental abilities in various psychoses. J. gen. Psychol., 1943, **29**, 257–260.

192. GLASER, N. M. A study of the intelligence of immigrants. Amer. Psychologist, 1949, **4**, 211.

193. GLIK, E. E. A comparison of recall and recognition types of measurement on verbal items, and their implications for deterioration testing. J. clin. Psychol., 1954, **10**, 298–299.

194. GLUECK, S., AND GLUECK, E. *Unraveling Juvenile Delinquency.* New York: Commonwealth Fund, 1950.

195. GOLDFARB, W. An investigation of reaction time in older adults. T. C. Contributions to Education, No. 831, New York, 1941.

196. GOLDFARB, W. Adolescent performance on the Wechsler Bellevue Intelligence Scale and the Revised Stanford Binet (L). J. educ. Psychol., 1944, **35**, 503–507.

197. GOLDFARB, W. Note on a revised Block Design Test as a measure of abstract performance. J. educ. Psychol., 1945, **36**, 247–251.

198. GOLDMAN, G. D. A comparison of the personality structures of patients with idiopathic epilepsy, hysterical convulsions, and brain tumors. Paper read at East. Psychol. Ass., Atlantic City, 1952.

199. GOLDMAN, R., GREENBLATT, M., AND COON, G. P. Use of the Wechsler Bellevue Scale in clinical psychiatry with particular reference to cases with brain damage. J. nerv. ment. Dis., 1946, **104**, 144–179.

200. GOLDSTEIN, K., AND SHEERER, N. Abstract and concrete behavior. Psychol. Monogr., 1941, **43**, 1–151.

201. GOLDSTEIN, M. J. A preliminary evaluation of the use of the Wechsler Bellevue Adult Intelligence Scale in South Africa. J. Soc. Res. Pretoria, 1950, **1**, 220–226.

202. GOOLISHIAN, H. A., AND FOSTER, A. A note on sex differences on the Wechsler Bellevue Test. J. clin. Psychol., 1954, **10**, 298–299.

203. GOOLISHIAN, H. A., AND RAMSAY, R. The Wechsler Bellevue Form I and the WAIS; a comparison. J. clin. Psychol., 1956, **12**, 147–149.

204. GOODENOUGH, FLORENCE. *Mental Testing.* New York: Rinehart and Co., 1949.

205. GOTHBERG, L. A comparative study of the Stanford Binet old form test and the Wechsler Bellevue Verbal, Performance and Full Scales as shown in the results of unselected employees. Amer. J. ment. Defic., 1949, **53**, 497–503.

206. GRAHAM, E. E. Wechsler Bellevue and WISC scattergrams of unsuccessful readers. J. consult. Psychol., 1952, **16**, 268–271.

207. GRZYWAK-KACZYNSKA. W–B method as a help in psychological diagnosis. Zdrowie Psychol., 1950, **4**, 53–79.

208. GRAY, C. V. An investigation of the Shipley Hartford and the Wechsler Bellevue Scales as measures of deterioration. Unpublished doctoral dissertation, University of Toronto, 1949.

209. GREENBLATT, M., GOLDMAN, R., COON, G. P. Clinical implications of the Wechsler Bellevue Test with particular reference to cases of injury to the brain. Arch. Neurol. Psychiat., Chicago, 1946, **56**, 714–717.

210. GREENBLATT, M., GOLDMAN, R., COON, G. P. Clinical implications of the Wechsler Bellevue Test (with particular reference to brain damage cases). J. nerv. ment. Dis., 1946, **104**, 438–442.

211. GREENBLOOM, G. C. The psychological investigation of senile dementia; the Wechsler Bellevue Intelligence Scale. Unpublished doctoral dissertation, University of Toronto, 1950.

212. GREENWOOD, E. D., SNIDER, H. L., AND SENTI, M. M. Correlation between the Wechsler Mental Ability Scale, Form B, and Kent Emergency Test administered to Army Personnel. Amer. J. Orthopsychiat., 1944, **14**, 171–173.

213. GROVES, M. H. Some relationship between certain types of mental aberration and the abilities measured by the Wechsler Bellevue Scale. Unpublished doctoral dissertation, University of Chicago, 1951.

214. GUERTIN, W. H., Frank, G. H., AND RABIN, A. I. Research with the Wechsler Bellevue Intelligence Scale, 1950–1955. Psychol. Bull., 1956, **53**, 235–257.

215. GUERTIN, W. H. The effect of instructions and item order on the W–B Arithmetic subtest. J. genet. Psychol., 1954, **85**, 79–83.

216. GUILFORD, J. P. The structure of intellect. Psychol. Bull., 1956, **53**, 267–293.

217. GURVITZ, M. An alternate short form of the Wechsler Bellevue. Amer. J. Orthopsychiat., 1945, **15**, 727–732.

218. GURVITZ, M. An experimental application of the Wechsler Bellevue type tests in an attempt to discriminate and diagnose psychopathic personality types resident in a penal institution. Unpublished doctoral dissertation, New York University, 1949.

219. GURVITZ, M. The Wechsler Bellevue Test and the diagnosis of psychopathic personality. J. clin. Psychol., 1950, **6**, 397–401.

220. GURVITZ, M. The Hillside Short Form of the W–B. J. clin. Psychol., 1951, **7**, 131–134.

221. GURVITZ, M. Some defects of the Wechsler Bellevue. J. consult. Psychol., 1952, **16**, 124–126.

221a. GUTMAN, B. The application of the Wechsler Bellevue Scale in diagnosis of organic brain disorder. J. clin. Psychol., 1950, **6**, 195–198.

222. HAGGARD, E. A. *Interclass Correlation*. New York, 1957, in press.

223. HALL, J. A correlation of a modified form of Raven's Progressive Matrices (1938) with Wechsler Adult Intelligence Scale. J. consult. Psychol., 1957, **21**, 23–26.

224. HALL, K. R. Conceptual impairment in depressive and organic patients of the pre-senile age group. J. ment. Sci., 1952, **98**, 257–264.

225. HALL, K. R., AND CROOKES, T. G. Studies in learning impairment. I. Schizophrenic and organic patients. J. ment. Sci., **97**, 729–737.

226. HALPERN, F. Comparison of Revised Stanford with Bellevue Adult. Psychiat. Quart. Suppl., 1942, **16**, 206–211.

227. HALPERN, F. Studies of compulsive drinker; psychological test results. Quart. J. Stud. Alcohol, 1946, **6**, 468–479.

228. HALSTEAD, W. C. A power factor (p) in general intelligence; the effect of brain injuries. J. Psychol., 945, **20**, 57–64.

229. HALSTEAD, W. C. A power factor (p) in general intelligence; effects of lesions of the brain. Arch. Neurol. Psychiat., 1946, **56**, 234–235.

230. HALSTEAD, W. C. *Brain and Intelligence*. Chicago: University of Chicago Press, 1947.

231. HARPER, A. E. Discrimination between matched schizophrenics and normals by the Wechsler Bellevue Scale. J. consult. Psychol., 1950, **14**, 351–357.

232. HARPER, A. E. *Differential Patterns in Schizophrenics on the W–B Intelligence Test*. The Allahabad Christian Press, Ltd., 1950.

233. HARPER, E. A. Discrimination of the types of schizophrenia by the Wechsler Bellevue Scale. J. consult. Psychol., 1950, **14**, 290–296.

234. HAMISTER, R. The test-retest reliability of the Wechsler Bellevue Intelligence Test for a neuropsychiatric population. J. consult. Psychol., 1949, **13**, 39–43.

235. HAMMER, A. G. A factor analysis of Bellevue Tests. Aust. J. Psychol., 1950, **1**, 108–114.

235a. HARRELL, T. W., AND HARRELL, M. S. Army General Classification Test scores for civilian occupations. Educ. psychol. Measmt., 1945, **5**, 229–239.

236. HARROWER, M. R. *Appraising Personality*. New York: Norton & Co., 1952.

236a. HAYDEN, S. J. The educational significance of the Wechsler Bellevue Test scatter attained by college students of superior, average and inferior academic achievement. Unpublished doctoral dissertation, Fordham University, New York, 1951.

237. HAYES, Cathy. *The Ape in Our House*. New York: Harper & Bros., 1951.

238. HAYES, S. P. Alternative scales for the mental measurement of the visually handicapped. Outlook for the Blind, 1942, pp. 36–225.

239. HAYS, W. A. A comparison of scatter patterning for mental defectives on Wechsler Forms I and II. Amer. J. ment. Defic., 1950, **55**, 264–268.

240. HAYS, W., AND SCHNEIDER, B. A test-retest evaluation of the Wechsler Forms I and II with mental defectives. J. clin. Psychol., 1951, **7**, 140–143.

241. HEATH, R. G., AND POOL, J. L. Bilateral frontal resection of frontal cortex for the treatment of psychoses. J. nerv. ment. Dis., 1948, **107**, 411–429.

242. HEBB, D., AND PENFIELD, W. Human behavior after extensive bilateral removal from the frontal lobes. Arch. Neurol. Psychiat., 1940, **44**, 421–438.

243. HEBB, D. O. Intelligence in man after large removals of cerebral tissue; report of four left frontal lobe cases. J. genet. Psychol., 1939, **21**, 73–87.

244. HEBB, D. O. The effect of early and late brain injury upon test scores and nature of normal adult intelligence. Proc. Amer. Phil. Soc., 1942, **85**, 275-302.

245. HEBB, D. O. Man's frontal lobes; a critical review. Arch. Neurol. Psychiat., 1945, **54**, 10–24.

246. HEBB, D. O. *The Organization of Behavior; A Neurophysiological Theory*. New York: John Wiley & Sons, 1949.

247. HECHT, I. The differentiation of certain psychosomatic groups in terms of psychometric patterns; an evaluation of the Wechsler Bellevue Intelligence Scale and of the Rorschach projective technique to differentiate among the ulcer, colitis and hypertension groups. Unpublished doctoral dissertation, New York University, 1949.

248. HELMICK, J. S. Reliability or variability? J. consult. Psychol., 1952, **16**, 154–155.

249. HERRING, G. An evaluation of published short forms of the Wechsler Bellevue Scale. J. consult. Psychol., 1952, **16**, 119–123.

250. HERRMANN, M., AND HACKMAN, R. B. Distributions of scores on the Wechsler Bellevue Scales and the California Test of Mental Maturity at a VA guidance center. J. appl. Psychol., 1948, **32**, 642–647.

251. HEWSON, L. L. The Wechsler Bellevue Scale and the Substitution tests as aids in neuropsychiatric diagnosis. J. nerv. ment. Dis., 1949, **109**, 158–183, 246–265.

252. HEYER, A. W. "Scatter analysis" techniques applied to anxiety neurotics

from a restricted culture educational movement. J. gen. Psychol., 1949, **40,** 155–166.

253. HILDEN, A., TAYLOR, J., AND DUBOIS, P. Empirical evaluation of short Wechsler Bellevue Scales. J. clin. Psychol., 1952, **8,** 323–331.

254. HILL, A. S. Cerebral Palsy, Mental Deficiency and Terminology. Amer. J. ment. Defic., 1955, **59,** 587–594.

254a. HIMMELSTEIN, P. Evaluation of an abbreviated WAIS in a psychiatric population. J. clin. Psychol., 1957, **13,** 68–69.

255. HODGSON, G. L. An analysis of subtests in the Wechsler Bellevue Verbal Scale Form I administered to 139 delinquent Mexican boys. Amer. Psychol., 1948, **3,** 343.

255a. HOEDEMAKER, E., AND MURRAY, M. Psychological tests in the diagnosis of organic brain disease. Neurology, 1952, **2,** 144–153.

256. HOLLINGWORTH, L. S. *The Psychology of Subnormal Children.* New York: The Macmillan Co., 1920.

257. HOLT, R. R., AND LUBORSKY, L. *Selecting Psychiatric Residents.* New York: Basic Books, in press.

258. HOLZBERG, J. D., ALESSI, S. L., AND TALKOFF, A. Judgments of premorbid intellectual functioning in severely impaired psychiatric patients. J. clin. Psychol., 1954, **10,** 219–224.

259. HOLZBERG, J., AND BELMONT, L. The relationship between factors on the Wechsler Bellevue and Rorschach having common psychological rationale. J. consult. Psychol., 1952, **16,** 23–29.

260. HOLZBERG, J. D., AND DEANE, M. The diagnostic significance of an objective measure of intra-test scatter on the Wechsler Bellevue Intelligence Scale. J. consult. Psychol., 1950, **14,** 180–188.

261. HOMAN, L. B. Intelligence levels in cerebral palsied children. Amer. J. phys. Med., 1953.

261a. HOWARD, A. R. Diagnostic value of the Wechsler Memory Scale with selected groups of institutionalized patients. J. consult. Psychol., 1950, **14,** 376–380.

262. HOWELL, R. J. Changes in Wechsler subtest scores with age. J. consult. Psychol., 1955, **19,** 1, 47–50.

263. HOWELL, R. J. Sex differences and educational influences on a mental deterioration scale. J. Geront., 1955, **10,** 190–193.

264. HOYT, R., ELLIOT, H., AND HEBB, D. O. The intelligence of schizophrenic patients following lobotomy treatment. Queen May Vet. Hosp. Serv. Bull., Montreal, 1951, **6,** 553–557.

265. HUNT, H. A practical clinical test for brain damage. J. appl. Psychol., 1943, **27,** 375–387.

266. HUNT, J. McV., AND COFER, C. N. Psychological deficit. In *Personality* and the *Behavior Disorders.* New York: Ronald Press, 1944, Vol. 2, pp. 971–1032.

267. HUNT, W. L. The relative rates of decline of Wechsler Bellevue "hold" and "don't hold" tests. J. consult. Psychol., 1949, **13,** 440–443.

268. HUTTON, E. L., AND BASSETT, M. Effect of leucotomy on creative personality. J. ment. Sci., 1948, **94,** 332–350.

268a. ISON, M. G. Effect of "thorazine" on Wechsler scores. Amer. J. ment. Defic., 1957, **62,** 543–547.

269. JACKSON, C. V. Estimating impairment on W–B subtests. J. clin. Psychol., 1955, **11,** 137–143.

270. JACKSON, J. H. *Selected Writings of J. Hughlings Jackson.* London: Hodder & Stoughton, 1931–1932.

271. JASTAK, J. Problems of psychometric scatter analysis. Psychol. Bull., 1949, **46,** 177–197.

272. JASTAK, J. Psychometric personality traits. Delaware State Med. J., 1949, **21,** 165–169.

273. JASTAK, J. An item analysis of the Wechsler Bellevue. J. consult. Psychol., 1950, **14,** 88–94.

274. JASTAK, J. Psychological tests, intelligence and feeblemindedness. J. clin. Psychol., 1952, **8,** 107–112.

275. JASTAK, J. Ranking Bellevue subtest scores for diagnostic purposes. J. consult. Psychol., 1953, **17,** 403–410.

276. JASTAK, J., AND GORDON, G. J. Verbal polarity in dementia praecox. Delaware State Med. J., 1946, **18,** 131–136.

277. JASTAK, J., AND ROBINSON, R. K. The clinical application of factorial measure. Delaware State Med. J., 1949, **26,** 168–174.

278. JEFFRESS, LLOYD A. *Cerebral Mechanisms in Behavior.* New York: The Hixon Symposium, 1951.

279. JELLEINK, E. M., AND MacFARLAND, R. A. Analysis of psychological experiments on effects of alcohol. Quart. J. Stud. Alcohol, 1940, **1,** 272–371.

279a. JOHNSON, L. C. Wechsler Bellevue pattern analysis in schizophrenia. J. consult. Psychol., 1949, **13,** 32–33.

280. JOHNSON, T. F. Some needs in research with the Wechsler Bellevue Scale. J. gen. Psychol., 1949, **41,** 33–36.

281. JONES, H. E., AND CONRAD, H. S. The growth and decline of intelligence, etc., Genet. Psychol. Monogr., 1933, **13,** 223–298.

282. JONES, H. E. Age changes in mental ability. In *Old Age in the Modern World.* London, Livingstone, Ltd., pp. 267–274.

282a. KAHN, R. L. The relation of patterns of electrophysiologic abnormality to patterns of intellectual functioning. Unpublished doctoral dissertation, New York University, 1953.

283. KALDEGG, A. The Wechsler Test in clinical practice; comparison of psychiatric and psychosomatic disorders with a control population. J. Ment. Sci., 1950, **96,** 908–922.

284. KASS, W. Wechsler's Mental Deterioration Index in the diagnosis of organic brain disease. Trans. Kansas Acad. Sci., 1949, **52,** 66–70.

284a. KELLEY, T. L. *Crossroads of the Mind.* Palo Alto, California: Stanford University Press, 1928.

285. KELLEY, E. W–B I Test Scores of College Students. Unpublished Master's Thesis, Bowling Green State University, 1955.

285a. KESSLER, L. Intellectual changes in schizophrenic patients following electroshock therapy. Unpublished Master's Thesis, New York University, 1947.

286. KITZINGER, H., AND BLUMBERG, E. S. Supplementary guide for administering and scoring the Wechsler Bellevue Intelligence Scale Form I. Psychol. Monogr., 1951, **65,** No. 319.

287. KLEBANOFF, S. G. Psychological changes in organic brain lesions and ablations. Psychol. Bull., 1945, **42,** 585–623.

288. KLEBANOFF, S. G., SINGER, J. L., AND WILENSKY, H. Psychological consequences of brain lesions and ablations. Psychol. Bull., 1954, **51,** 1–41.

289. KLEIN, G. A. A differentiation of schizophrenics and normals on the Wechsler Bellevue Intelligence Test by means of a multiple correlation technique. Amer. Psychologist, 1946, **1,** 263–264.

290. KLEIN, G. S. An application of the multiple regression principle to clinical prediction. J. gen. Psychol., 1948, **38**, 159–179.

291. KLINE, M. V. Hypnosis and age progression; a case report. J. Genet. Psychol., 1951, **78**, 195–205.

292. KLUGMAN, S. F. The effect of placement of the digits tests in the Wechsler Bellevue Intelligence Scale. J. consult. Psychol., 1948, **12**, 345–348.

293. KNIGHT, R. P., GILL, M., LOZOFF, M., AND RAPAPORT, D. Comparisons of clinical findings and psychological tests in three cases bearing on military selection of personnel. Bull. Menninger Clin., 1943, **7**, 114–128.

294. KNOPF, I. J., MURFETT, B. J., AND MILSTEIN, V. Relationship between the Wechsler Bellevue Form I and the WISC. J. clin. Psychol., 1954, **10**, 261–263.

295. KNOTT, J. R., AND CANNICOTT, R. The application of brief tests of intelligence in psychiatric clinic. Amer. Psychol., 1948, **3**, 365.

296. KNOTT, J., CANNICOTT, R., UMBERGER, J., AND BILODEAU, I. Brief tests of intelligence in the psychiatric clinic. J. clin. Psychol., 1951, **7**, 123–126.

297. KÖHLER, W. Relational determination in perception. In Jeffress, L. A. (Ed.) *Cerebral Mechanisms in Behavior*. New York: John Wiley & Sons, 1951, pp. 200–230.

298. KOGAN, W. An investigation into relationships between psychometric patterns and psychiatric diagnosis. J. gen. Psychol., 1950, **43**, 17–46.

299. KOGAN, W. Wechsler patterns and psychiatric diagnosis; a reevaluation through a new approach. Amer. Psychologist, 1950, **5**, 471.

300. KOSKOFF, Y. D., DENNIS, W., LAZOVIK, D., AND WHEELER, E. T. The psychological effects of frontal lobotomy performed for alleviation of pain. In ARNMD: *The Frontal Lobes*. Baltimore, The Williams & Wilkins Co., 1948. (Research Publication No. 27) pp. 723–753.

301. KRIEGMAN, G., AND HANSEN, F. WIBS; a short form of the Wechsler Bellevue Intelligence Scale. J. clin. Psychol., 1947, **3**, 209–216.

302. KROUT, M. H. Is the brain-injured a mental defective? Amer. J. ment. Defic., 1949, **54**, 81–85.

303. KUHLMANN, F. Results of repeated mental re-examination of 639 feeble-minded over a period of 10 years. J. appl. Psychol., 1921, **5**, 192–224.

304. KUTASH, S. B. A comparison of the Wechsler Bellevue and the Revised Stanford Binet Scale for Adult Defective Delinquents. Psychiat. Quart., 1945, **19**, 677–685.

305. LADD, A. H. The differential predictive value of the Wechsler Bellevue for certain areas of teacher preparation. University of Indiana, School of Education, Studies in Education, Bloomington, Indiana, 1951, Vol. 2, pp. 2–68.

306. LASHLEY, K. S. *Brain Mechanisms and Intelligence. A quantitative Study of Injuries to the Brain*. Chicago: University of Chicago Press, 1929.

307. LA TOURELLE, C. W. A study of the relationship of the subtest deviations of the Wechsler Bellevue Intelligence Scale and the scores of the Minnesota Multiphasic Personality Inventory. Unpublished doctoral dissertation, University of Southern California, 1946.

308. LEVI, J. A psychometric pattern of the adolescent personality. Unpublished doctoral dissertation, New York University, 1943.

309. LEVI, J., OPPENHEIM, S., AND WECHSLER, D. Clinical use of the Mental Deterioration Index of the Wechsler Bellevue Scale. J. abnorm. soc. Psychol., 1945, **40**, 405–407.

310. LEVINE, B., AND ISCOE, I. A comparison of Raven's Progressive Matrices and a short form of the Wechsler Bellevue. J. consult. Psychol., 1954, **18**, 10.

311. LEVINE, B., AND ISCOE, I. The Progressive Matrices (1938), the Chicago Non-Verbal and the Wechsler Bellevue on an adolescent deaf population. J. clin. Psychol., 1955, **11**, 307–308.

312. LEVINE, E. S. *Youth in a Soundless World*. New York: New York University Press, 1956.

313. LEVINE, L. S. Utility of Wechsler's patterns in the diagnosis of schizophrenia. J. consult. Psychol., 1949, **13**, 28–31.

314. LEVINE, L. S. Wechsler's signs in the differential diagnosis of schizophrenia. Amer. Psychologist, 1948, **3**, 345.

315. LEWINSKI, R. J. Performances of naval recruits on the Kent Oral Emergency Test and the Verbal battery of the Wechsler Bellevue Adult Intelligence Scale. Amer. J. Orthopsychiat., 1943, **13**, 138–140.

316. LEWINSKI, R. J. Inter-test variability of subnormal naval recruits on the W–B Verbal Scale. J. abnorm. soc. Psychol., 1943, **38**, 540–544.

317. LEWINSKI, R. J. Discriminative value of the subtests on the Bellevue Verbal Scale in the examination of naval recruits. J. gen. Psychol., 1944, **31**, 95–99.

318. LEWINSKI, R. J. The psychometric pattern in epilepsy. Amer. J. Orthopsychiat., 1947, **17**, 714–722.

319. LEWINSKI, R. J. The psychometric pattern in anxiety neurosis. J. clin. Psychol., 1945, **1**, 214–221.

320. LEWINSKI, R. J. The psychometric pattern in migraine. Psychiat. Quart., 1945, **19**, 368–376.

321. LEWINSKI, R. J. Vocational and mental measurement. J. Genet. Psychol., 1948, **72**, 247–281.

322. LEWIS, E. O. Types of mental deficiency and their social significance. J. ment. Sci., 1939, **79**, 298.

322a. LICKLEY, J. D. *The Nervous System*. London: Longmans, Green & Co., 1916.

323. LINDNER, R. M., AND GURVITZ, M. Restandardization of the Revised Beta Examination to yield the Wechsler type of IQ. J. appl. Psychol., 1946, **30**, 649–658.

324. LIPTON, M. D., TAMARIN, S., AND LOTESTA, P. Test evidence of personality change and prognosis by means of the Rorschach and Wechsler Bellevue Tests on 17 insulin-treated paranoid schizophrenics. Psychiat. Quart., 1951, **25**, 434–444.

325. LORGE, I. Intellectual changes during maturity and old age. Rev. Educ. Res., 1947, **17**, 326–332.

326. LORGE, I. Aging and intelligence. J. Chron. Dis., 1956, **412**, 131–139.

327. LOVE, L. R. An analysis of Wechsler Bellevue items score for assessing the clinical significance of variability of performance. Unpublished doctoral dissertation, University of California, 1953.

328. LUBORSKY, L. Psychometric changes during electric shock treatment. J. nerv. ment. Dis., 1948, **107**, 531–536.

329. LUCHINS, A. S. On certain misuses of the Wechsler Bellevue Scales. J. consult. Psychol., 1946, **10**, 109–111.

330. LUCHINS, A. S., AND LUCHINS, E. H. Effects of varying the administration of the W–B Intelligence Scale. J. gen. Psychol., 1953, **49**, 125–142.

331. LYNN, J. G., LEVINE, K., AND HEWSON, L. R. Psychological tests for the clinical evaluation of the late "diffuse organic," "neurotic" and "normal" reactions after closed head injury. In ARNMD: *Trauma of the Central Nervous System*. Baltimore, The Williams & Wilkins Co., 1945. (Research publication No. 24) pp. 296–378.

332. McClelland, D. S., and Atkinson, J. W.   The projective expression of needs. I. The effect of different intensities of the hunger drive on perception. J. Psychol., 1948, **25**, 205–222.

333. McCulloch, W. S.   Why the mind is in the head. In *Cerebral Mechanisms in Behavior*. (Ed. by L. L. Jeffress). New York: Wiley and Sons, 1951.

333a. McCullough, M. W.   Wechsler Bellevue changes following pre-frontal lobotomy. J. clin. Psychol., 1950, **6**, 270–273.

334. McFarland, R. A.   The psychological aspects of aging. Bull. N. Y. Acad. Med., 1956, **32**, 1, 14–32.

335. McLean, O. S.   Divergent scores on the Wechsler Bellevue Scale as indicators of learning ability. J. clin. Psychol., 1954, **10**, 264–266.

336. McNeal, B. F.   The prediction of psychiatric diagnosis by signs derived from scatter on the W–B Adult Intelligence Scale. Unpublished doctoral dissertation, University of Pennsylvania, 1950; (Diss. Abstr. 1952, **12**, 595).

337. McNemar, Q.   On abbreviated Wechsler Bellevue Scales. J. consult. Psychol., 1950, **14**, 79–81.

338. McNemar, Q.   Review of Rapaport *et al.* Diagnostic psychological testing. Amer. J. Psychol., 1946, **59**, 306–311.

339. McPherson, M. W., and Fisch, R.   Affect in the etiology and maintenance of mental deficiency. J. clin. Psychol., 1955, **11**, 55–60.

340. Machover, S., and Reich, H.   Cross-validation of 2 Wechsler Bellevue regression equations for the diagnosis of schizophrenia (unpublished paper).

341. Machover, S.   Cultural and racial variations in patterns of intellect. New York: Teachers College, Columbia University, Contributions to Education, No. 875, 1943.

342. MacPhee, H. M., Wright, H. F., and Cummings, S. B.   The performance of mentally rural southern negroes on the Verbal Scale of the Wechsler Bellevue Intelligence examination. J. soc. Psychol., 1947, **25**, 217–229.

343. Madonick, M. N., and Solomon, M.   The Wechsler Bellevue Scale in individuals past sixty. Geriatrics, 1947, **2**, 34–40.

344. Magaret, A.   Parallels in the behavior of schizophrenics, paretics, and presenile non-psychotic patients. J. abnorm. soc. Psychol., 1942, **37**, 511–528.

345. Magaret, A., and Simpson, M.   A comparison of two measures of deterioration in psychotics. J. consult. Psychol., 1948, **12**, 265–270.

346. Magaret, A., and Wright, C.   Limitations in the use of intelligence test performance to detect mental disturbance. J. appl. Psychol., 1943, **27**, 387–398.

346a. Magoun, H. W.   The ascending reticular activating system. Proc. Ass. res. nerv. & ment. Dis., 1950, **30**, 480–492.

346b. Magoun, H. W.   Caudal and cephalic influences of the brain stem reticular formation. Physiol. reviews, 1950, **30**, 459–474.

346c. Magoun, H. W.   An ascending reticular activity system in the brain. Arch. neurol. & psychiat., 1952, **67**, 145–154.

347. Maizlish, I. L.   A comparison of Stanford Binet and Bellevue with adult offenders. Psychol. Bull., 1942, **39**, 472.

348. Maleci, O., and Montanari, M.   Some modifications in the scoring of W–B for its uses in the province of Padua. Arch. Psicol. Neurol. Psichiat., 1952, **13**, 584–606.

349. Malmo, R. B.   Reduction in general intelligence following frontal gyrectomy and frontal lobotomy in mental patients. Amer. Psychologist, 1948, **3**, 277.

350. MANSON, M. P. The measurement of intelligence of 102 male paraplegics. J. consult. Psychol., 1950, **14**, 193–196.

351. MARKS, M. R. A criticism of the use of the Wechsler Bellevue as a diagnostic instrument. J. gen. Psychol., 1953, **49**, 143–152.

352. MARKWELL, E. D., WHEELER, W. M., AND KITZINGER, H. Changes in Wechsler Bellevue Test performance following prefrontal lobotomy. J. consult. Psychol., 1953, **17**, 229–231.

353. MATARAZZO, R. G. The relationship of manifest anxiety to Wechsler Bellevue subtest performance. J. consult. Psychol., 1955, **19**, 218.

354. MATARAZZZO, R. G., ULETT, G. A., GUZE, S. D., AND SOSLOW, G. The relationship between anxiety level and several measures of intelligence. J. consult. Psychol., 1954, **18**, 201–205.

355. MAYMAN, M. An analysis of scatter in intelligence test results; a review of the literature. Trans. Kansas Acad. Sci., 1946, **48**, 429–444.

356. MAYMAN, M. Review of the literature on tests treated in this volume (Appendix III) in RAPAPORT, D. *Diagnostic Psychological Testing*, Vol. 1. Chicago: Yearbook Publishing Co., 1945.

357. MAYMAN, M., SCHAFER, R., AND RAPAPORT, D. Interpretation of W–B Intelligence Scale in personality appraisal. In ANDERSON AND ANDERSON. *An Introduction to Projective Technique*. New York: Prentice Hall, 1951.

358. MAXWELL, E. Validities of abbreviated WAIS Scales. J. consult. Psychol., 1957, **21**, 121–126.

359. MECH, E. Item analysis and discriminative value of selected Wechsler Bellevue subtests. J. educ. Res., 1953, **47**, 241–260.

360. MEEHL, P. E. *Clinical vs. Statistical Prediction*. Minneapolis, University Minn. Press, 1954.

360a. MENDOLA, V. S. An investigation of intra-individual variability of a group of schizophrenics on the Wechsler Bellevue Scale. Unpublished doctoral dissertation, Fordham University, New York, 1950.

361. MENSH, I. N., SCHWARTZ, N. G., MATARAZZO, R. G. AND MATTARAZZO, J. D. Psychological functioning following cerebral hemispherectomy in man. Arch. Neurol. Psychiat., 1952, **67**, 787–796.

362. MERRILL, R. M., AND HEATHERS, L. B. Centile scores of the Wechsler Bellevue Scale in a university counseling center group. J. consult. Psychol., 1952, **16**, 406–409.

362a. MERRILL, R. M., AND HEATHERS, L. B. Deviations of the Wechsler Bellevue subtest scores from vocabulary level in university counseling center group. J. consult. Psychol., 1952, **16**, 469–472.

363. MERRILL, R. M., AND HEATHERS, L. B. A comparison of the Wechsler Bellevue and ACE tests on a university counseling center group. J. consult. Psychol., 1953, **17**, 63–66.

364. MILES, W. R. Measurement of certain abilities throughout life span. Proc. Nat. Acad. Sci., 1931, **17**, 627–633.

365. MILES, W. R., AND MILES, C. C. Correlation of intelligence scores, age, etc. Amer. J. Psychol., 1932, **44**, 44–78.

366. MILNER, B. Intellectual function of the temporal lobes. Psychol. Bull., 1954, **51**, 42–63.

367. MILTON, E. O. A difficulty encountered when comparing drug addict scores on the Wechsler Bellevue Scale with norms of the Scale. J. gen. Psychol., 1944, **30**, 271–273.

368. MITCHELL, M. B. Performance of mental hospital patients on the Wechsler Bellevue and the Revised Stanford Binet (L). J. educ. Psychol., 1942, **33**, 535–544.

369. MOLDAWSKY, S., AND MOLDAWSKY, P. C. Digit Span as an anxiety indicator. J. consult. Psychol., 1952, **16**, 115–118.

370. MONROE, J. A statistical analysis of intra-individual scatter on the Wechsler Bellevue Intelligence Scale. Unpublished doctoral dissertation, Purdue University, 1951.

370a. MONROE, J. The effects of emotional adjustment and intelligence on Bellevue scatter. J. consult. Psychol., 1952, **16**, 110–114.

371. MORROW, R. S., AND MARK, J. The correlation of intelligence and neurological findings on 22 patients autopsied for brain damage. J. consult. Psychol., 1955, **19**, 283–289.

372. MUNDY, J. P. The immediate effect of alcohol on intelligence as measured by the Wechsler Bellevue. Unpublished doctoral dissertation, University of Virginia, 1948.

373. MUENCH, G. A. A follow-up of mental defectives after 18 years. J. abnorm. soc. Psychol., 1944, **39**, 407–418.

374. NORMAN, R. D. Sex differences and other aspects of young superior adult performance on the Wechsler Bellevue. J. consult. Psychol., 1953, **17**, 411–418.

375. NADEL, A. B. A quantitative analysis of behavior following cerebral lesions. Arch. Psychol., No. 224, New York, 1938.

376. O'CONNOR, J. P. The Wechsler Bellevue Intelligence Scales as an index of deterioration in psychoneurotics. Unpublished doctoral dissertation, Catholic University, 1949.

377. OLCH, D. R. Psychometric patterns in schizophrenics on the Wechsler Bellevue Intelligence Tests. J. consult. Psychol., 1948, **12**, 127–136.

378. OLIN, T., AND REZNIKOFF, M. The use of Doppelt's short form of the Wechsler Adult Intelligence Scale with psychiatric patients. J. consult. Psychol., 1957, **21**, 27–28.

379. OPPENHEIM, H. Diagnostic limitations of the Adult Wechsler Bellevue Intelligence Scale in cerebral pathology. Univer. North Carolina Rec., 1952, **506**, 223–224.

379a. ORME, J. E. Non-Verbal and Verbal performance in normal old age, senile dementia and elderly depression. J. Geront., 1957, **12**, 408–413.

380. ORTAR, G. Standardizing Wechsler's test for children in Israel. M'gamot, 1952, **53**, 4, 87–100.

381. OSTRANDER, J. M. A report of Rorschach and Wechsler Bellevue records of a man after the removal of tumor from the frontal lobes. Rorsch. Res. Exch., 1948, **12**, 65–71.

382. OWENS, W. A. Age and mental abilities; a longitudinal study. Genet. Psychol. Monogr., 1953, **48**, 3–54.

383. PACAUD, S. Experimental research on the aging of psychological functions. In *Old Age and the Modern World*, London: Livingstone, Ltd., 1955, pp. 279–289.

383a. PAGE, K. Use of the Wechsler Bellevue Scale of Adult Intelligence. Unpublished dissertation, Chico State College, California, 1950.

384. PASCAL, G. R., AND ZEAMAN, J. B. A note on the validity of Wechsler Bellevue scatter. Amer. J. Psychiat., 1949, **105**, 840–842.

385. PATTERSON, C. A comparison of various "short forms" of the Wechsler Bellevue Scale. J. consult. Psychol., 1946, **10**, 260–267.

386. PATTERSON, C. A further study of two short forms of the Wechsler Bellevue. J. consult. Psychol., 1948, **12**, 147–152.

387. PATTERSON, C. *The Wechsler Bellevue Scales. A Guide for Counselors.* Springfield, Ill.: Charles C Thomas, 1953.

388. PATTERSON, C. The W–B Scale as an aid in psychiatric diagnosis. J. clin. Psychol., 1946, **2**, 348–353.

389. PEARL, R. Variations and correlatoin in brain weight. Biometrics, 1905, **4**, 13–104.

390. PEARL, R. *Studies in Human Biology.* Baltimore: The Williams and Wilkins Co., 1924.

391. PEIXOTTO, H. E. Wechsler Bellevue subtest patterns; note of caution. J. clin. Psychol., 1950, **6**, 188–190.

392. PENFIELD, W., AND EVANS, J. The frontal lobe in man. A clinical study of maximum removals. Brain, 1935, **58**, 115–133.

393. PENFIELD, W., AND JASPER, H. *Epilepsy and the Functional Anatomy of the Human Brain.* Boston: Little, Brown & Co., 1954.

394. PENFIELD, W., AND RASMUSSEN, T. *The Cerebreal Cortex of Man.* New York: The Macmillan Company, 1950.

395. PENROSE, L. S. *The Biology of Mental Defect.* New York: Grune & Stratton, 1949.

396. PETRIE, A. Personality changes after pre-frontal leucotomy. Brit. J. Med. Psychol., 1949, **22**, 200–207.

397. PETRIE, A. Preliminary report of changes after pre-frontal leucotomy. J. ment. Sci., 1949, **95**, 449–455.

398. PINTNER, R. *Intelligence Testing.* 2nd ed. New York: Henry Holt, 1931.

399. PINTNER, R., AND PATERSON, R. G. *Scale of Performance Tests.* New York: Appleton & Co., 1925.

400. PLUMB, G. R. The evaluation of the mental characteristics of a reformatory population as revealed by the Wechsler Bellevue and California Test of Mental Maturity. Unpublished doctoral dissertation, University of Nebraska, 1951.

400a. POLATIN, P., STRAUSS, H. AND ALTMAN, L. Transient organic reactions during schock therapy. Psychiat. Quart., 1940, 14, 457–465.

401. POLLACK, M. Effect of brain tumors on perception of hidden figure, sorting behavior and problem solving behavior. Unpublished doctoral dissertation, New York University, 1955.

402. PORTEUS, S. D., AND CORBETT, G. R. Statutory definitions of the feebleminded in the United States. J. Psychol., 1953, **35**, 81–105.

403. PRAGER, D. The performance of adult mental patients on the Revised Stanford Binet L and the Wechsler Bellevue Scale. Unpublished doctoral dissertation, University of Iowa, 1940.

404. PRICE, H. G. The interrelationship among W–B IQ's, reading achievement and college grades. Unpublished doctoral dissertation, University of Iowa, 1945.

405. PTACEK, J. E., AND YOUNG, F. M. Comparison of the Grassi Block Substitution test with the Wechsler Bellevue in the diagnosis of organic brain damage. J. clin. Psychol., 1954, **10**, 375–378.

405a. PURCELL, C. K., DREVDAHL, J., AND PURCELL, K. The relationship between attitude-IQ discrepancy and anxiety. J. clin. Psychol., 1952, **8**, 82–85.

406. PUZZO, F. S. A study of the psychometric signs of anxiety in the Wechsler

Bellevue Scale and the Rorschach test. Unpublished doctoral dissertation, Fordham University, New York, 1947.

407. RABIN, A. I., DAVID, J. C., AND SANDERSON, M. H.   Item difficulty of some Wechsler Bellevue subtests. J. appl. Psychol., 1946, **30,** 493–500.

408. RABIN, A. I., AND GUERTIN, W. H.   Research with the Wechsler Bellevue Test: 1945–1950. Psychol. Bull., 1951, **48,** 211–248.

409. RABIN, A. I., GUERTIN, W. H., AND FRANK, G.   Research with the Wechsler Bellevue Intelligence Scale: 1950–1955. Psychol. Bull., 1956, **48,** 211–248.

410. RABIN, A. I.   Test score patterns in schizophrenic and nonpsychotic states. J. Psychol., 1941, **12,** 91–100.

411. RABIN, A. I.   Psychometric patterns as an aid in differential diagnosis (schizophrenic vs. manic depressive psychosis). Psychol. Bull., 1941, **38,** 536.

412. RABIN, A. I.   Differentiating psychometric patterns in schizophrenia and manic-depressive psychosis. J. abnorm. soc. Psychol., 1942, **37,** 270–272.

413. RABIN, A. I.   A short form of Wechsler Bellevue Test. J. appl. Psychol., 1943, **27,** 320.

414. RABIN, A. I.   Fluctuations in the mental level of schizophrenic patients. Psychiat. Quart., 1944, **18,** 78–92.

415. RABIN, A. I.   Test constancy and variation in the mentally ill. J. gen. Psychol., 1944, **31,** 231–239.

416. RABIN, A. I.   The relationship between vocabulary levels and levels of general intelligence in psychotic and non-psychotic individuals of a wide age range. J. educ. Psychol., 1944, **35,** 411–422.

417. RABIN, A. I.   The use of the Wechsler Bellevue Scale with normal and abnormal persons. Psychol. Bull., 1945, **42,** 410–422.

418. RABIN, A. I.   Effects of electroshock treatment upon some aspects of personality and intellect. Amer. Psychologist, 1947, **2,** 284.

419. RABOURN, R. E.   A comparison of WAIS and W–B Intelligence Scale. Unpublished doctoral dissertation, University of California, 1957.

419a. RAKUSIN, J.   The analysis of scatter on the Wechsler Bellevue Scale in a group of adjusted and a group of maladjusted college students. Unpublished dissertation, Pennsylvania State College, 1949.

420. RAPAPORT, D.   *Diagnostic Psychological Testing.* Vol. 1. Chicago: Yearbook Publishers, 1945.

421. RAPPORT, S. R., AND WEBB, W. B.   An attempt to study intellectual deterioration by premorbid and psychotic testing. J. consult. Psychol., 1950, **14,** 95–98.

422. RASHKIS, H. A.   Three types of thinking disorder. J. nerv. ment. Dis., 1947, **106,** 650–670.

423. RASHKIS, H. A.   The psychometric analysis of a diagnostic problem. Amer. J. Orthopsychiat., 1947, **17,** 529–532.

424. RASHKIS, H., CUSHMAN, J., AND LANDIS, C.   A new method for studying disorders of conceptual thinking. J. abnorm. soc. Psychol., 1946, **41,** 70–82.

425. RASHKIS, H., AND WELSH, G. S.   Detection of anxiety by use of the Wechsler Scale. Amer. J. Orthopsychiat., 1947, **17,** 529–532.

426. REICH, H.   Application of regression equations to W–B Adult Scale and the diagnosis of schizophrenia. Unpublished dissertation, Brooklyn College, New York, 1951.

427. REICHARD, S., AND SCHAFER, R.   The clinical significance of scatter on the Wechsler Bellevue Scale. Bull. Menninger Clin., 1943, **7,** 93–98.

428. REITAN, R. M.   Certain differential effects of left and right cerebral lesions in human adults. J. compar. physiol. Psychol., 1955, **48,** 474–477.

428a. REYNELL, W. R.   A psychometric method of determining intellectual loss following head injury. J. ment. Sci., 1944, **90,** 710–719.

429.   REYNOLDS, G. A.   Investigation of possible relationship of the Object Assembly subtests of the Wechsler Bellevue Intelligence Scale. Unpublished doctoral dissertation, Fordham University, New York, 1950.

429a. RISCH, F.   Tests of intelligence as they relate to interests and attitudes (Unpublished report), 1946.

430.   ROGERS, L. S.   A comparative evaluation of the W–B deterioration index for various adult groups. J. Colorado Acad. Sci., 1949, 4, 53–54; J. clin. Psychol., 1950, **6,** 199–202.

431.   ROGERS, L. S.   Differences between neurotics and schizophrenics on the W–B Scale. J. Colorado-Wyoming Acad. Sci., 1950, 4, 64; J. consult. Psychol., 1951, **15,** 151–153.

432.   ROTHSTEIN, H. J.   A study of the qualitative aspects of the Wechsler Bellevue Intelligence Scale. Psychol. Abstr., 1955, **29,** 8651.

433.   RUBIN, H.   A quantitative study of HTP and its relationship to the W–B Scale. J. clin. Psychol., 1954, **10,** 35–42.

434.   RUBENSTEIN, E.   A note on recording Block Design performance of W–B Scales. J. clin. Psychol., 1948, **4,** 307–308.

435.   RUGER H. A. AND STOESSIGER. B.   On the growth of certain characteristics of man. Ann. Eugenics, 1926, **2,** 85–104.

436.   RUSSELL, G. E.   Wechsler Bellevue Vocabulary subtest items. Med. Tech. Bull., 1954, **5,** 143–148.

437.   RYLANDER, G.   Personality changes after operations of the frontal lobes; a clinical study of 32 cases. London: Oxford University Press, 1939.

438.   RYLANDER, G.   Mental changes after excision of cerebral tissue; a clinical study of 16 cases of resections in the parietal, temporal and occipital lobes. Acta psychiat. Neurol., 1943, Suppl. 20.

439.   RYLANDER, G.   Psychological tests and personality analysis before and after frontal lobotomy. Acta psychiat. Neurol., 1947, Suppl. 47, pp. 383–398.

440.   SABEH, R.   Comparison of the Wechsler Bellevue Adult Intelligence Scale with the Ohio State Psychological Examination in predicting academic success for college freshmen. Unpublished doctoral dissertation, Ohio University, 1950.

441.   SANDS, H., AND PRICE, J. C.   A pattern analysis of the W–B Intelligence Scale in epilepsy. Res. Publ. A. nerv. & ment. Dis., 1947, **26,** 604–615.

442.   SAPPENFELD, B. R.   Rapid method for placement of Wechsler Object Assembly pieces. J. clin. Psychol., 1947, **3,** 301.

443.   SARASON, S. B.   *Psychological Problems in Mental Deficiency.* 2nd. ed. New York: Harper & Bros., 1953.

444.   SARTAIN, A. Q.   A comparison of the new revised Stanford Binet, Wechsler Bellevue Scale, and certain group tests of intelligence. J. soc. Psychol., 1946, **23,** 237–239.

445.   SCHAFER, R.   *The Clinical Application of Psychological Tests.* New York: International Universities Press, 1948.

446.   SCHAFER, R.   Wechsler Bellevue Scale and Word Association Test; the case of Gregor. J. proj. Tech., 1949, **13,** 434–438.

447.   SCHILLO, R. J.   Wechsler Bellevue results of normals and neurotics with obsessive-compulsive features. Unpublished doctoral dissertation, Catholic University, 1951.

448.   SCHLOSSER, J. R., AND KANTOR, R. E.   A comparison of Wechsler's deteriora-

tion ratio in psychoneurosis and schizophrenia. J. consult. Psychol., 1949, **13,** 108–110.

449. SCHMIDT, D. G. Levels of intelligence of prison inmates. Amer. J. ment. Defic., 1946, **51,** 63–66.

450. SCHNADT, R. Certain aspects of Wechsler Bellevue scatter of low IQ levels. J. consult. Psychol., 1952, **16,** 456–461.

451. SCHOFIELD, W. Critique of scatter and profile analysis of psychometric data. J. clin. Psychol., 1952, **8,** 16–22.

452. SEMMES, J., WEINSTEIN, S., GHENT, L., AND TEUBER, H. L. Spatial orientation in man after cerebral injury; analysis by locus of lesion. J. Psychol., 1955, **39,** 227–244.

453. SEMMES, J., WEINSTEIN, S., GHENT, L., AND TEUBER, H. L. Performance on complex tactual tasks after brain injury in man; analysis by locus of lesion. Amer. J. Psychol., 1954, **67,** 220–224.

454. SHANNON, C. E. A chess playing machine. In NEWMAN, J. R. (ed.): *The World of Mathematics*, Vol. 4. New York: Simon & Schuster, 1956, pp. 2124–2153.

454a. SHIPLEY, W. C. Self-administering scale for measuring intelligence impairment and deterioration. J. Psychol., 1940, **9,** 371–377.

455. SHOBEN, E. J. The Wechsler Bellevue in the detection of anxiety; a test of the Rashkis-Welsh hypothesis. J. consult. Psychol., 1950, **14,** 40–45.

455a. SHOCK, N. W. Gerontology (Later maturity). Ann. Rev. Psychol., 1951, **2,** 353–370.

456. SIEGMAN, A. W. The effect of manifest anxiety on a concept formation task, a non-directed learning task and on timed and untimed intelligence tests. J. consult. Psychol., 1956, **20,** 176–178.

457. SIEGMAN, A. W. Cognitive, affective and psychopathological correlates of Taylor MAS. J. consult. Psychol., 1956, **20,** 137–141.

458. SIMON, L. M., AND LEVITT, E. A. The relation between Wechsler Bellevue IQ scores and occupational area. Occupations, 1950, **29,** 23–25.

459. SLOAN, W. Validity of Wechsler's deterioration quotient in high-grade mental defectives. J. clin. Psychol., 1947, **3,** 287–288.

460. SLOAN, W., AND GUERTIN, W. H. A comparison of HTP and Wechsler Bellevue IQ's in mental defectives. J. clin. Psychol., 1948, **4,** 424–426.

461. SLOAN, W., AND CUTTS, R. A. Test patterns of defective delinquents on the Wechsler Bellevue Scale. Amer. J. ment. Defic., 1945, **50,** 95–97.

462. SMYKAL, A., AND WILSON, M. O. Wechsler Bellevue score changes resulting from electric shock convulsive therapy. Proc. Oklahoma Acad. Sci., 1950, **31,** 148–149.

463. SORSBY, F. D. A briefer method for the Wechsler Bellevue Vocabulary subtest. Unpublished doctoral dissertation, University of Pittsburgh, 1949.

464. SPACHE, G. Scoring qualitative responses on the Wechsler Bellevue Scale. Amer. J. Orthopsychiat., 1948, **18,** 360–363.

465. SPANER, F. E. An analysis of the relationship between some Rorschach test determinants and subtest scores on the Wechsler Bellevue Adult Scale. Unpublished doctoral dissertation, Purdue University, 1950.

466. SPEARMAN, C. *The Abilities of Man.* New York: The Macmillan Co., 1927.

466a. SPEARMAN, C., AND JONES, L. *Human Abilities.* London: The Macmillan Co., 1950.

467. SPITZ, J. C. De Wechsler Bellevue Test. Ned. Tijdschr. Psychol., 1950, pp. 126–136.

468. SPRINGER, N. A short form of Wechsler Bellevue Intelligence test and as applied to Naval personnel. Amer. J. Orthopsychiat., 1946, **16**, 341–344.

469. STACEY, C. L., AND LEVIN, J. Performance of retarded individual on Stanford Binet and Wechsler Bellevue Intelligence Scales. Amer. J. ment. Defic., 1950, **55**, 123–131.

470. STACEY, C. L., AND MARKEN, K. E. A study of the differential responses among three groups of subnormals on the Similarities Test of the W–B Scale. Amer. J. ment. Defic., 1951, **56**, 424–428.

471. STACEY, C. L., AND PORTNOY, B. A study of the differential responses on the Vocabulary subtest of the W–B intelligence Scale. J. clin. Psychol., 1951, **7**, 144–148.

472. STANLEY, J. C. Why Wechsler Bellevue Full Scale IQ's are more variable than average of Verbal and Performance IQ's. J. consult. Psychol., 1953, **17**, 419–420.

473. STANTON, J. M. An investigation of the validity of the Mental Deterioration Index of the Wechsler Bellevue Scale in indicating organic brain pathology. Unpublished doctoral dissertation, Fordham University, 1949.

474. STEFIC, E. C. Factors affecting the negative Deterioration Index on the Wechsler Bellevue Scale of psychoneurotics. Unpublished doctoral dissertation, Catholic University of America, Washington, 1950.

475. STEILSEL, I. M. The effect of practice on the various subtests of the Wechsler Intelligence Test. Unpublished doctoral dissertation, University of Iowa, 1945.

476. STEILSEL, I. M. The relation between test and retest scores on the W–B Scale I for selected college students. J. genet. Psychol., 1950, **78**, 155–162.

477. STEILSEL, I. M. Retest changes in W–B scores as a function of the time interval between examinations. J. genet. Psychol., 1951, **79**, 199–203.

478. STERN, A. W. The nature of g and the concept of intelligence. Acta psycholigica, 1956, **12**, 282–289.

478a. STRANGE, R. B., AND PALMER, J. O. A note on sex differences on the Wechsler Bellevue tests. J. clin. Psychol., 1953, **9**, 85–87.

478b. STRAUSS, A. A., AND WERNER, H. Disorders of conceptual thinking in the brain injured child. J. ment. nerv. Dis., 1942.

479. STROTHER, C. R. The performance of psychopaths on the Wechsler Bellevue Test. Proc. Iowa Acad. Sci., 1944, **51**, 397–400.

480. SUPER, D. *Appraising Vocational Fitness by Means of Psychological Fitness.* New York: Harper & Bros., 1949, pp. 142–146.

481. TAGIURI, R. Comparison of results obtained from the Wechsler Bellevue Vocabulary Test with those from the Stanford Binet Vocabulary Test using a population of normal subjects and mental patients. Bull. Canad. Psychol. Ass., 1946, **6**, 181.

482. TAMMINEN, A. W. A comparison of AGCT and the W–B Scales. Educ. psychol. Measmt., 1951, **11**, 646–655.

483. TAMMINEN, A. W. Progress report on AGCT-W–B study. Minn. Counselor, 1948, **3**, 4–5.

484. TATOM, M. H. Relationship between Wechsler Bellevue subtest scores and certain Rorschach test factors in clinical patients. Unpublished doctoral dissertation, Catholic University, 1949.

485. TEICHER, M. I., AND SINGER, E. A report on the use of the Wechsler Bellevue Scales in overseas general hospital. Amer. J. Psychiat., 1946, **193**, 91–93.

486. TENDLER, A. D. The mental status of psychoneurotics. Arch. Psychol., No. 60, 1923.

487. TERMAN, L. M. *Intelligence of School Children*. Boston: Houghton Mifflin Co., 1919.

488. TERMAN, L. M., AND MERRILL, M. A. *Measuring Intelligence*. Boston: Houghton Mifflin Co., 1937.

489. TEUBER, H. L., BATTERSBY, S., AND BENDER, M. Performance of complex visual tasks, after cerebral lesions. J. nerv. ment. Dis., 1951, **114**, 413–429.

490. TEUBER, H. L., AND WEINSTEIN, S. Performance on a formboard task after penetrating brain injury. J. Psychol., 1954, **38**, 177–190.

490a. THOMSON, G. *The Factorial Analysis of Human Ability*. London: University of London Press, Ltd., 1950.

491. THURSTONE, L. L. The absolute zero in measurement of intelligence. Psychol. Rev., Vol. 35, 1928.

492. THURSTONE, L. L. *Multiple-Factor Analysis*. Chicago: University of Chicago Press, 1947.

493. THURSTONE, L. L., AND THURSTONE, T. G. *Factorial Studies in Intelligence*. Psychomtr. Monogr., No. 2, 1941.

494. TOOPS, H. A. A contribution to the theory and technique of classification. Ohio State University, OCA Bull., No. 100, 1935.

495. TREDGOLD, A. F., AND SODDY, K. *A Textbook of Mental Deficiency*, Ed. 5. Baltimore: The Williams & Wilkins Co., 1929.

495a. TREDGOLD, A. F., AND SODDY, K. *A Textbook of Mental Deficiency*, Ed. 7. Baltimore: The Williams & Wilkins Co., 1947.

496. TRIST, E. L. Short tests of low-grade intelligence. Occup. Psychol., London, 1941, **15**, 120.

497. TRIST, E. L., TRIST, V., AND BRODY, M. B. Discussion on the quality of mental test performance in intellectual deterioration. Proc. Roy. Soc. Med., 1943, **36**, 243–252.

498. TURING, A. M. Can a machine think? In NEWMAN, J. R. (Ed.): *World of Mathematics*, Vol. 4. New York: Simon & Schuster, 1956, pp. 2099–2123.

498a. TYLER, L. E. *The Psychology of Human Differences*, 2nd Ed. New York: Appleton-Century-Crofts, 1956.

499. VANE, J., AND EISEN, V. Wechsler Bellevue performance of delinquent and non-delinquent girls. J. consult. Psychol., 1954, **18**, 221–225.

499a. VANDERHOST, L., SLOAN, W., AND BENSBERG, B. Performance of mental defectives on the W–B and WISC. Amer. J. ment. Defic., 1953, **57**, 481–483.

500. VISTICA, N. J. Scatter analysis on the Wechsler Bellevue Scale as an indicator of personality adjustment of normal subjects. Unpublished doctoral dissertation, Fordham University, New York, 1949.

501. VON NEUMANN, J. The general and logical theory of automata. In NEUMAN, J. R. (ed.): *World of Mathematics*, Vol. 4. New York: Simon & Schuster, 1956, pp. 2070–2099.

501a. WALDFOLGEL, S., AND GUY, W. Wechsler Bellevue subtest scatter in affective disorders. J. clin. Psychol., 1951, **7**, 135–139.

502. WALKER, H., AND LEV, V. *Statistical Inferences*. New York: Henry Holt, 1953, pp. 430–431.

503. WARNER, SAMUEL. The Wechsler Bellevue psychometric pattern in anxiety neurosis. J. consult. Psychol., 1950, **14**, 297–304.

504. WATSON, R. I. The use of the Wechsler Bellevue Scales; a supplement. Psychol. Bull., 1946, **43**, 61–68.

505. WATTS, J. W., AND FREEMAN, W. Intelligence following prefrontal lobotomy in obsessive tension states. Arch. Neurol. Psychiat., 1945, **53**, 244–245.

506. WEBB, W. B. The use of the Wechsler Bellevue Intelligence Test in the study of mental deterioration. University of Iowa, Proc. Iowa Acad. Sci., 1942, **49**, 450–451.

507. WEBB, W. B. A note on the Rabin ratio. J. consult. Psychol., 1947, **11**, 107–108.

508. WEBB, W. B. Corrections for variability; a reply. J. consult. Psychol., 1952, **16**, 156.

509. WEBB, W. B., AND DE HAAN, H. Wechsler Bellevue split half reliabilities in normals and schizophrenics. J. consult. Psychol., 1951, **15**, 68–71.

510. WEBB, W. B., AND HANER, C. Quantification of the Wechsler Bellevue Vocabulary subtest. Educ. psychol. Measmt., 1949, **9**, 693–707.

511. WECHSLER, D. The influence of education on intelligence. J. educ. Psychol., 1926, **17**, 248–257.

512. WECHSLER, D. The concept of mental deficiency in theory and practice. Psychiat. Quart., 1935, **9**, 232–236.

513. WECHSLER, D. Mental deterioration; its measurement and significance. J. nerv. ment. Dis., 1938, **87**, 89–97.

514. WECHSLER, D. *Measurement of Adult Intelligence*. Ed. 1. Baltimore: The Williams & Wilkins Co., 1939.

515. WECHSLER, D. Non-intellective factors in general intelligence. Psychol. Bull., 1940, **37**, 444–445.

516. WECHSLER, D. Intellectual Change with Age. Public Health Reports, Washington, D. C., 1942.

517. WECHSLER, D. Effects of alcohol on mental activity. Quart. J. Stud. Alcohol, 1942, **2**, 479.

518. WECHSLER, D. The non-intellective factors in general intelligence. J. abnorm. soc. Psychol., 1943, **38**, 100–104.

519. WECHSLER, D. *Measurement of Adult Intelligence*. Ed. 3. Baltimore: The Williams & Wilkins Co., 1944.

520. WECHSLER, D. *Wechsler Bellevue Intelligence Scale, Form II*. Psychological Corp., New York, 1946.

521. WECHSLER, D. Cognitive, conative and non-intellective intelligence. Amer. Psychologist, 1950, **5**, 78–83.

521a. WECHSLER, D. Intellectual development and psychological maturity. Child Develpm., 1950, **21**, 45–50.

522. WECHSLER, D. Equivalent test and mental age for the WISC. J. consult. Psychol., 1951, **15**, 381–384.

523. WECHSLER, D. Measurement and evaluation of intelligence of older persons. In *Old Age in the Modern World*. London: Livingstone, Ltd., 1954, pp. 275–278.

524. WECHSLER, D. *Range of Human Capacities*. Ed. 2. Baltimore: The Williams & Wilkins Co., 1955.

525. WECHSLER, D. Wechsler Adult Intelligence Scale Manual. Psychological Corp., New York, 1955.

526. WECHSLER, D., HALPERN, F., AND JAROS, E. A psychometric study of insulin treated schizophrenics. Psychiat. Quart., 1940, **14**, 466–475.

527. WECHSLER, D., ISRAEL, H., AND BALINSKY, B. A study of the subtests of the Bellevue Intelligence Scale in borderline and mental defective cases. Amer. J. ment. Defic., 1941, **45**, 555–558.

528. WECHSLER, D., ISRAEL, H., AND BALINSKY, B. The relative effectiveness of

the Stanford Binet and Bellevue Intelligence Scale in diagnosing mental deficiency. Amer. J. Orthopsychiat., 1939, **9**, 798–801.

529. WECHSLER, I. S. The meaning of consciousness. Bull. New York Acad. Med., 1952, **28**, 739–747.

530. WECHSLER, I. S. *Textbook of Clinical Neurology.* Ed. 7. Philadelphia: Saunders, 1952.

530a. WEIDER, A. A comparative study of the performance of psychopathic adults on the Revised Stanford Binet (L) and the Bellevue Intelligence Scale. Psychiat. Quart., 1941, **15**, 802–806.

531. WEIDER, A. Effects of age on the Bellevue Scale in schizophrenic patients. Psyciat. Quart., 1943, **17**, 337–346.

532. WEIDER, A., LEVI, J., AND RISCH, F. Performances of problem children on the Wechsler Bellevue Intelligence Scale and the Revised Stanford Binet. Psychiat. Quart., 1943, **17**, 695–701.

533. WEINSTEIN, S., AND TEUBER, H. L. Effects of penetrating brain injury on intelligence test scores. Science, 1957, **125**, 1036–1037.

534. WEISGERBER, C. A. A note on Diamond's method of scoring the Wechsler Bellevue Intelligence Scale for vocational aptitude. J. clin. Psychol., 1955, **3**, 311.

535. WELLS, F. L. *Mental Tests in Clinical Practice.* New York: World Book Co., 1927.

536. WELSH, G. S. A note on scoring Wechsler Bellevue subtests. J. clin. Psychol., 1949, **5**, 421–422.

537. WERTHAM, F. *The Brain as an Organ.* New York: The Macmillan Co., 1934.

538. WESMAN, A. Standardizing an individual intelligence test on adults; some problems. J. Geront., 1955, **10**, 216–219.

539. WESMAN, A. Separation of sex groups in test reporting. J. educ. Psychol., 1949, **40**, 223–229.

539a. WHEELER, J. I., AND WILKINS, W. L. The validity of the Hewson ratios. J. consult. Psychol., 1951, **15**, 163–166.

540. WHITE, W. A. *The Language of Schizophrenia.* A. Research Nerv. & Ment. Dis. Proc., 1928, **5**, 323–343.

541. WHITEMAN, M. Altitude as a reference point in scatter analysis. J. clin. Psychol., 1950, **6**, 160–164.

542. WHITEMAN, M., AND WHITEMAN, D. B. The application of cluster analysis to the Wechsler Bellevue Scale. Delaware State Med. J., 1949, **21**, 174–176.

543. WINFIELD, D. Intellectual performance of cryptogenic epileptics, symptomatic epileptics, and post-traumatic encephalopaths. J. abnorm. soc. Psychol., 1951, **46**, 336–343.

544. WINFIELD, D. The relationship between IQ scores and Minnesota Multiphasic Personality Inventory Scores. J. soc. Psychol., 1953, **38**, 299–300.

545. WITTENBORN, J. R. An evaluation of the use of Wechsler Bellevue subtest scores as an aid in psychiatric diagnosis. J. consult. Psychol., 1949, **13**, 433–439.

546. WITTENBORN, J. R., AND HOLZBERG, J. D. The Wechsler Bellevue and descriptive diagnosis. J. consult. Psychol., 1951, **15**, 325–329.

547. WITTENBORN, J. R., BELL, E. G., AND LESSER, G. S. Symptom patterns among organic patients of advanced age. J. clin. Psychol., 1951, **7**, 328–330.

548. WITTENBORN, J. R., AND METTLER, F. A. Some psychological changes following psychosurgery. J. abnorm. soc. Psychol., 1951, **46**, 548–556.

549. WORTIS, H., SILLIMAN, L. R., HALPERN, F., AND CUSHMAN, J. F. Studies of Compulsive Drinkers, Part II: Psychological Test Results. New Haven: Hillhouse Press, 1946.

550. WRIGHT, H. F., MACPHEE, H. M., AND CUMMINGS, S. B. The relationship between Kent EGY and the Bellevue Verbal Scale. J. abnorm. soc. Psychol., 1949, **44**, 223–230.

551. YACORZYNSKI, G. K., BOSHES, B., AND DAVIS, L. Psychological changes produced by frontal lobotomy. A. Research Nerv. & Ment. Dis. Proc., 1948, **27**, 642-657.

552. ZIMMERMAN, F. T., BURGMEISTER, B. B., AND PUTNAM, T. J. Effect of glutamic acid on mental functioning in children and adolescents. Arch. Neurol. Psychiat., 1946, **56**, 489–506.

ADDENDA

553. BARRY, J. R., FULKERSON, S. C., KUBALA, A. L., AND SEAQUIST, M. R. Score equivalence of W-B Intelligence Scales I and II. Air Force School of Medicine (Randolph Field) Report No. 56–23.

554. BLACKBURN, H. L., AND BENTON, A. L. Revised administration and scoring of the Digit Span test. J. consult. Psychol., 1957, **21**, 241–5.

555. CALDWELL, M. B., AND DAVIS, J. C. A short form of Wechsler Bellevue Intelligence Scale—Form II for a psychotic population. J. clin. Psychol., 1956, **12**, 402–3.

556. DAVIS, J. C. The scatter pattern of a Southern negro group on the Wechsler Intelligence Scale. J. clin. Psychol., 1957, **13**, 298–300.

557. GALTON, F. *Hereditary Genius*. New York, 1891

558. GOLDFARB, W. Effects of psychological deprivation in infancy and subsequent stimulation. Amer. J. Psychiat., 1945, **102**, 18–33.

559. JONES, H. G. The evaluation of the significance of differences between scaled scores on the WAIS: the perpetuation of a fallacy. J. consult. Psychol., 1956, **20**, 319–20.

560. KARSON, S., AND POOL, K. B. The abstract thinking abilities of mental patients. J. clin. Psychol., 1957, **13**, 126–32.

561. KARSON, S., POOL, K. B., AND FREUD, S. L. The effects of scale and practice on test scores on WAIS and the Wechsler Bellevue Intelligence Scale—Form I. J. consult. Psychol., 1957, **21**, 241–45.

562. KEEHN, J. D. Repeated testing of four chronic schizophrenics on the Bender-Gestalt and Wechsler Block Design Test. J. clin. Psychol., 1957, **13**, 179–182.

563. KOHS, S. C. *Intelligence Measurement*. New York: The Macmillan Co., 1923.

564. MCNEMAR, Q. On WAIS differences scores. J. consult. Psychol., 1957, **21**, 239–40.

565. MATARAZZO, J. Comparisons of pre- and post-operative performance of 4 cases of hemispherectomy on the Wechsler Bellevue Intelligence Scale. 1958. Personal communication to author.

566. MINDESS, H. Psychological indices in the selection of nurses. J. Project. Techniques, 1957, **21**, 37–9.

567. MURPHY, D. B., AND LANGSTON, R. D. A short form of the Wechsler Bellevue and the Army Classification Battery as measures of intelligence. J. consult. Psychol., 1956, **20**, 405.

568. REITAN, R. M. Investigation of relationship between psychometric and biological intelligence. J. nerv. ment. Dis., 1956, **123**, 536–41.

569. ROBERTSON, J. P., AND BATCHELDOR, K. L. Cultural aspects of the Wechsler Adult Intelligence Scale in relation to British mental patients. J. ment. Sci., 1956, 102, 612–18.

570. RUBIN-RABSON, G. Item order and difficulty in four verbal subtests of the Wechsler Bellevue Scale. J. genet. Psychol., 1956, 88, 167–174.

571. SOMER, R. Rorschach animal responses and intelligence. J. consult. Psychol., 1957, 21, 358.

572. THALER, M. Relationships among Wechsler, Weigle, Rorschach, EEG findings and abstract-concrete behavior in a group of normal aged subjects. J. Geront., 1956, 11, 404–9.

573. TOOL, R. Reliability (internal consistency) of Wechsler Memory Scale and correlation with Wechsler Bellevue Intelligence Scale. J. consult. Psychol., 1957, 21, 131–35.

574. WECHSLER, D. Die Messung der Intelligenz Erwachsener. Trans. by A. Hardesty and H. Lauber. Bern: Hans Huber, 1956.

575. WECHSLER, D. La mesure de l'intélligence de l'adulte. Trans. by M. Commandre. Paris: Presse Universitaire, 1956.

576. WECHSLER, D. Scala d'intelligenza Wechsler-Bellevue, Forma I (manuale). Trans. by O. Roser. Firenze: Organizzazione Speciali, 1956.

577. WECHSLER, D. Scala d'intelligenza Wechsler-Bellevue, Forma II (manuale). Trans. by G. Tompieri. Firenze: Organizzazione Speciali, 1956.

Author Index*

Aborn, M. (135)
Abt, L. E. (71)
Acklesberg, S. B. (1)
Adcock, C., 123, (2)
Aeppli-Tanner, L. (3)
Aita, J. A. (4)
Alderdice, E. T. (5)
Alessi, S. L. (258)
Alexander, R. S. (6)
Alexander, W. P., 13, 14, (7)
Alimena, B. (8)
Allen, R. M. (9–15)
Altman, L., 221, (400a)
Altus, W. D. (3)
Anastasi, A. (19)
Andersen, A. L., 221, (20, 21)
Anderson, E. E., 105, (22)
Ansbacher, H. L. (23)
Armitage, S. G. (4, 24)
Armstrong, C. P. (25)
Armstrong, R. G. (26)
Aronov, B. (28)
Arthur, G. (29)
Atkey, R. R. (30)

Babcock, H. (32)
Baggett, M. (112a)
Baldwin, J. M., 3, 182, (33)
Balinsky, B., 124, 230, 231, (34–36), (56a),
  (527, 528)
Barbeau, G. L. (37)
Barnett, I. (38)
Barry, J. R. (553)
Bassett, M. (268)
Batcheldor, K. J. (571)
Battersby, W. S., 19, (39–40), (489)
Bauer, R. W., 219, (41)
Bay, M. (41a)
Bayley, N., 135, 137, 157, (42–44)
Becka, D. M., 219, (41)
Becker, G. J. (45)
Bell, E. G. (547)
Belmont, L. (259)
Bender, L. (46)

Bender, M., 19, (39, 40), (489)
Bensberg, B. (499a)
Bensberg, G. J. (47)
Benson, S. (62)
Benton, A. L. (48, 49), (554)
Berkowitz, B. (51)
Bernstein, R. (50)
Bijou, S. W. (52)
Bilodeau, I. (296)
Binet, A., 3, 9, 16, (53, 54)
Birren, J. E., 124, (55), (60, 61), (164–
  166)
Blackburn, H. L. (554)
Blake, R. (56)
Blauvelt, J. (49)
Blum, M. J. (56a)
Blumberg, E. S. (286)
Boehm, A. E. (57)
Boshes, B. (551)
Botwinick, J. (58–61)
Bradway, K. (62)
Brecher, S. (63)
Brieger, B., 184, (64, 65)
Brody, A. B. (66)
Brody, M. B. (68, 497)
Brooks, L. E. (69)
Brower, D. (70, 71)
Brown, C. C. (138, 138a)
Brown, J. F. (75, 78)
Brown, M. N. (72, 74, 79)
Brown, R. R. (77, 78)
Bryan, E. (73, 74)
Bryan G. C. (79)
Burgmeister, B. B. (552)
Burik, T. E. (81, 82)
Burnham, C. A. (82)
Buros, O. K. (83–85)
Burt, C., 29, 30, (86, 87)
Burton, A. (88)
Butler, A. J. (5, 89)

Caldwell, M. B. (555)
Cameron, D. E. (156)
Canepa, G. (90)

* Numbers in parentheses ( ) refer to reference numbers in Bibliography (pp.
256–284); those not in parentheses to pages in text.

Sands, H. (441)
Sappenfeld, B. R. (442)
Sarason, S. B. (57, 443)
Sartain, A. Q. (444)
Schafer, R., 162, 173, (357, 420), (427, 445, 446)
Schillo, R. J. (447)
Schlosser, J. R. (448)
Schmidt, D. G. (449)
Schnadt, R. (450)
Schneider, B. (240)
Schofield, W. (451)
Schwartz, N. G. (361)
Seaquist, M. R. (553)
Segal, S. (129)
Semmes, J. (452, 453)
Senti, M. M. (212)
Shannon, C. E., 21, (54)
Shaw, H. W., 230, 231, (36)
Sheerer, N., 80, 221, (200)
Shipley, W. C. (454a)
Shoben, E. J. (455)
Shock, N., 135, (455a)
Siegman, A. W., 71, (456, 457)
Silliman, L. R. (549)
Silverman, H. (129)
Simon, L. M., 226, 227, (458)
Simon, T. (54)
Simpson, M. (345)
Singer, J. L., 214, 215, (288)
Sloan, W. (47, 125, 459–461, 499a)
Smykal, A. (462)
Snider, H. L. (212)
Soddy, K. (495, 495a)
Soglow, O., 74
Somer, R. (571)
Somerset, H. (2)
Sorsby, F. D. (463)
Soslow, G. (354)
Spache, G. (464)
Spaner, F. E. (465)
Spearman, C., 3, 4, 9, 11, 12, 13, 14, 21, (466, 466a)
Spitz, J. C. (467)
Springer, N. (468)
Stacey, C. L. (469–471)
Stanley, J. C. (472)
Stanton, J. M. (473)
Stefic, E. C. (474)
Steilsel, I. M. (105, 475, 476)
Stengen, C. A. (15)

Stern, A. W., 22, 124, (478)
Stoessiger, B., 200, 201, (435)
Strange, R. B. (478a)
Strauss, A. A. (487b)
Strauss, H., 221, (400a)
Strother, C. R. (379)
Super, D. (480)
Sunukjian, H. (161)

Tagiuri, R. (481)
Talkoff, A. (258)
Tamarin, S. (324)
Tamminen, A. W. (482, 483)
Tatom, M. H. (484)
Taylor, G. J. (151)
Taylor, J. (253)
Taylor, J. A., 127
Tendler, A. D., 81, (486)
Teicher, M. I. (485)
Terman, L. M., 30, 31, 39, 40, 41, 73, 74, (487, 488)
Teuber, H. L., 17, 19, 222, (39), (452, 453, 489, 490, 533)
Thaler, M. (149, 572)
Thomson, G., 123, (490a)
Thorndike, E. L., 8
Thornton, T. E. (15)
Thurstone, L. L., 9, 11, 15, 34, (491–493)
Thurstone, T. G. (493)
Tillman, C. G. (75, 76)
Tool, R. (573)
Toops, H. A., 165, (494)
Tredgold, A. F., 50, 51, 52, (495–495a)
Trist, E. L. (496, 497)
Turing, A. M. (498)
Tyler, L. E. (498a)

Ulett, G. A. (354)
Umberger, J. (296)

Vanderhost, L. (499a)
Vane, J., 161, (499)
Vistica, N. J. (500)
von Neumann, J., 21, (501)

Waldfolgel, S. (501a)
Walker, H. (502)
Wallace, W., 140, 255, (147, 148)
Warner, S. (503)
Warren, 15, (503a)
Watson, R. I. (504)

Subject Index

Abbreviated scales, 112–114

Ability, definition of, 15; relation of to intelligence, 15

Abstract intelligence, 8

ACE tests, 105

Adaptive capacity, as related to ability to abstract, 183

Adolescent psychopaths, 173

Age, as factor in calculating IQ's, 25–28; as factor in mental decline, 200–203; as factor in standardization, 86–88; in relation to decline in the various abilities, 203–205; in relation to brain weight, 206; of maximum mental ability, 30–31; negative correlation with intelligence, 139–140; regression equation for, 242

Age curves, for WAIS, 96, 140, 202, 203; W–B I, 31, 201, 204, 205; of compared test scores with brain weights, 206; of compared W–B I and WAIS standardization data, 140

Age scales, suitability of, 61

AGCT, 63, 105

Alcoholism, effect of, on intelligence test scores, 222–224

Altitude score, 158

Analogue computers, 21

Animal intelligence, 6

Analogies Test, 65

Anxiety, disruptive effect of, 175

Anxiety States, test characteristics of, 172; clinical features of, 175

Aphasia, in cerebrovascular accidents, 219–222; test performance of patient with, 220

Arithmetic reasoning test, changes with age, 203; correlations with Full Scale and subtests, 70; description and historical background, 69; factorial composition of, 130; timed vs. untimed performance in old age, 137; sex differences on, 147

Army Alpha test, 34, 63, 65, 67, 68, 93

Army Beta test, 34, 82

Army Performance Scale, 74, 82

Assets, need of emphasis of, in test reports, 186–187

Automaton computers, 20

Binet Scale, 10, 16, 25, 29, 70

Biologic intelligence, 19

Bizarre responses, examples of, 180–182

Block Design, as measure of abstract ability, 80; correlations with Full Scale and subtests, 80; factorial analysis of, 133; description and historical background of, 79–80; how different from Koh's Block design, 79; influence of color factor, 79; timed vs. untimed performance in old age, 137

Brain, as organ of the mind, 17; role of, in intelligence, 17–20

Brain Damage, effect of on intellectual functioning, general, 214–225; after hemispherectomy, 216; after psychosurgery, 214–215; in cerebrovascular accidents, 219–220; in chronic alcoholism, 220–224; in missile wounds, 214; in space occupying lesions, 219

Brain Weight, changes in, with age, 205, 206; variations in, as compared with intelligence test scores, 206

C. A., as a test score, 28

Cartoons, international character of, 75

CAVD, 105

Cerebral hemispheres, effect of removal of, on intelligence, 216; function of, 17

Cerebral palsy, effect of, on intelligence, 54; incidence of, 54; symptoms of, 53

Cerebral vascular accidents, effect on intelligence test score, 219–222; illustrative cases of, 220

Changes in test scores with age, 94–97

Chess, memory factor in, 131

Childhood schizophrenics, test patterns of, 167

Chronic alcoholics, test performance of, 222–224

Clinical intelligence, definition of, 19